SAP PRESS e-books

Print or e-book, Kindle or iPad, workplace or airplane: Choose where and how to read your SAP PRESS books! You can now get all our titles as e-books, too:

▸ By download and online access
▸ For all popular devices
▸ And, of course, DRM-free

Convinced? Then go to **www.sap-press.com** and get your e-book today.

Implementing SAP® Global Trade Services

SAP PRESS is a joint initiative of SAP and Galileo Press. The know-how offered by SAP specialists combined with the expertise of the Galileo Press publishing house offers the reader expert books in the field. SAP PRESS features first-hand information and expert advice, and provides useful skills for professional decision-making.

SAP PRESS offers a variety of books on technical and business-related topics for the SAP user. For further information, please visit our website: *www.sap-press.com*.

Lauterbach et al.
Transportation Management with SAP TM
2014, 1079 pp., hardcover
ISBN 978-1-59229-904-1

Christian, Iyer, Sudhalkar
Implementing SAP Governance, Risk, and Compliance
2014, 712 pp., hardcover
ISBN 978-1-59229-881-5

Bryša et al.
SAP Treasury and Risk Management (2nd Edition)
2013, 1114 pp., hardcover
ISBN 978-1-59229-433-6

Martin Murray
Discover Logistics with SAP (2nd Edition)
2014, 412 pp., paperback
ISBN 978-1-59229-926-3

Yannick Jacques, Nick Moris, Chris Halloran, Pablo Lecour

Implementing SAP® Global Trade Services

Galileo Press

Bonn • Boston

Galileo Press is named after the Italian physicist, mathematician, and philosopher Galileo Galilei (1564—1642). He is known as one of the founders of modern science and an advocate of our contemporary, heliocentric worldview. His words *Eppur si muove* (And yet it moves) have become legendary. The Galileo Press logo depicts Jupiter orbited by the four Galilean moons, which were discovered by Galileo in 1610.

Editor Emily Nicholls
Copyeditor Miranda Martin
Cover Design Graham Geary
Photo Credit iStockphoto.com/22263284/© Danil Melekhin
Layout Design Vera Brauner
Production Graham Geary
Typesetting SatzPro, Krefeld (Germany)
Printed and bound in the United States of America, on paper from sustainable sources

ISBN 978-1-59229-975-1
© 2014 by Galileo Press Inc., Boston (MA)
1st edition 2014

Library of Congress Cataloging-in-Publication Data
Yannick, Jacques.
Implementing SAP Global Trade Services / Jacques Yannick, Nick Moris, Chris Halloran, Pablo Lecour. -- 1 Edition.
pages cm
Includes index.
ISBN 1-59229-975-X (print : alk. paper) -- ISBN 978-1-59229-976-8 (ebook) -- ISBN 978-1-59229-977-5 (print and ebook)
1. International trade. 2. Exports--Management--Computer programs. 3. Imports--Management--Computer programs.
4. SAP GTS. 5. SAP Business information warehouse. I. Title.
HF1379.Y3626 2014
382--dc23
2014028643

Contents at a Glance

Dear Reader,

Innovative technology is simultaneously expanding geographic horizons and closing virtual gaps for international business, so it seems fitting that this book about SAP Global Trade Services was written, edited, typeset, and printed across two different continents (with delivery available to the rest!).

Deloitte GTS practice leads Yannick Jacques, Nick Moris, Chris Halloran, and Pablo Lecour and a team of industry experts lent their considerable SAP know-how to this project, and the resulting product is truly global in nature. In it you'll follow the business and system processes of electronic device retailer Alpha, aerospace and defense giant Beta, and leather shoe manufacturer Gamma as they manage customs hurdles, compliance concerns, and potential risks around the world. By the end of the book, you'll have logged as many virtual miles as this manuscript did during its editorial and production processes.

So tell us what you think! We at SAP PRESS would be interested to hear your opinion of *Implementing SAP Global Trade Services*. Were the examples helpful? How could it be improved? Your comments and suggestions are the most useful tools to help us make our books the best they can be, so we encourage you to share your feedback.

But most important, we thank you for purchasing a book from SAP PRESS! It's been a pleasure doing international business with you.

Emily Nicholls
Editor, SAP PRESS

Galileo Press
Boston, MA

emily.nicholls@galileo-press.com
www.sap-press.com

Contents

4　Master Data 57

5　Classification 79

Contents

Foreword

Global trade has determined the fate of nations, regions, and pan-regional economies. Since the time of the first recorded civilization, trade—as much as industry, technology, and other building blocks of civilization—has defined and directed many aspects of nation-building, empire-building, and even the everyday life of the common person. In fact, historians theorize that agriculture, and hence, civilization, itself, spread through the transfer of knowledge and technology brought on by those same trading practices. All civilizations, great and small, flourished, expanded, and are remembered for what they brought to the commonweal of the world through trade.

Global trade is also a highly complex, technical, and constantly evolving topic. Trade regulations are proliferating rapidly as countries, regions, trading blocs and global organizations like the WTO strive to strike a healthy balance between protection of local economies' "customs" and encouraging global growth and prosperity. Countries and regions seeking competitive advantages form numerous and ever-expanding trading blocs, complete with their own regulations, preferences, and customs. Developed economies seek growth primarily through trade with developing economies like "BRICS" (that is, Brazil, Russia, India, China, and South Africa)—only to find some of the most complex trade accounting and law practices wrought by the diverse legal and political systems in developing countries.

Just as the Sumerians first developed writing as a means of accounting for goods and trade—and just as every epoch of civilization thereafter evolved and extended the technology of trade, so too have the computer age and the information age evolved technology to cope with complexity in pursuit of economic growth.

SAP Global Trade Services—the world's leading global trade management system—is SAP's globally recognized manifestation of this evolution. Simply put, SAP GTS' singular purpose is to open the broadest footprint of world markets to trading enterprises, expanding their business opportunities, enriching their businesses, the economies they participate in, and providing a better life for those economies' constituents. SAP GTS is built with a commitment to be the geographically broadest, most functionally complete, easiest to use, globally scalable trade management solution available. It is our sincerest hope this book will help students, trade practitioners, information technology professionals, and all those wishing to learn about trade better understand SAP GTS' ability to unleash the goodwill and wealth-building power of global trade.

Therefore, it is with great gratitude I thank Yannick Jacques, Nick Moris, Chris Halloran, and Pablo Lecour of Deloitte for their contribution to the body of trade knowledge with this publication.

Kevin McCollom
SAP Labs LLC
Group Vice President
General Manager of Governance, Risk, and Compliance Solution

Acknowledgments

This publication came together through contributions from a broad collection of skilled SAP GTS resources. These individuals have dedicated significant portions of their careers to this dynamic and exciting arena and this acknowledgment, a testament to unyielding dedication and continued personal development, goes out to the entire global Deloitte SAP GTS Center of Excellence. This has truly been a broad team effort and, without the time and expertise each of you provided, this initiative would not have been possible.

Recognitions for this achievement and a commitment to making this endeavor a success are as follows:

- Li Yu
- Filip Cooreman
- Dries Bertrand
- Giovanni Gijsels
- Robert Olson
- Maren Mintjens
- Luc Scheiff
- Liesje Robben

- Valentijn Van Driessen
- Nick Robyn
- Yannick Schroeyen
- Jeroen De Cuyper
- Caroline Boeckx
- Virginia D'hondt
- Simon Zutterman

We also want to thank the following colleagues for their support throughout this journey and its ultimate success:

- Grégory Albert
- Federico Balbo
- Anthony Clarke
- Xavi Just Serrano
- Prashanth Kaja
- Frank Verstappen
- Sheila Malhotra

- Riya Rajan
- Wouter Demuynck
- Gregory Menu
- Ben Lallemand
- Emilie Lens
- Assen Lozanov
- Gertjan De Boever

- Stefaan De Wael
- Eveline Meiresone
- Julien Ocula

- Raoul Schweicher
- Yin Lei Zhang

Next, we extend a special thanks to Kai Seela, SAP SE, Senior Director of Solution Management for SAP Global Trade Services, for his detailed contribution on the SAP GTS future outlook and to Kevin McCollom, SAP Labs LLC, Group Vice President, General Manager Governance, Risks & Compliance Solution & Platform Sales Team for the inspiring foreword.

Finally, our sincere thanks go to everyone at Galileo Press, and especially to Emily Nicholls for her immense support and dedication throughout the entire effort.

1   Introduction

Global trade continues to evolve as one of the most complex and crucial aspects of supply chain management. As goods cross international borders or customs territories, a transaction is completed, meaning that you must declare a number of transactional, global trade, and supply chain-based data elements at the time of export and import. Additionally, you must execute numerous compliance checks, qualifications, and critical cost-savings opportunities before proceeding with exports and imports.

In light of the constant mix of national security, foreign policy, revenue collection, and consumer protection objectives, the need for technology-based solutions across this data-intensive field with broad legal ramifications is imperative. Architecting the right solution and blending it across business processes requires a well-formulated approach and sound execution.

SAP Global Trade Services (GTS) is an enterprise trade management platform aimed at centralizing, managing, and automating these collective requirements. Companies deploy SAP GTS to meet numerous objectives, including reducing costs, minimizing delays, boosting productivity, maximizing compliance, and increasing customer satisfaction. SAP GTS includes three major components set forth to meet these objectives: Compliance Management, Customs Management, and Risk Management.

SAP GTS Compliance Management focuses on a mix of export controls (e.g., automating export authorization determinations and screening against restricted parties and sanctioned/embargoed countries) and streamlining the associated data management. As the regulatory landscape continues to shift, having a centralized management platform to comply with country- and jurisdiction-specific requirements is critical. The alternative approach is entrenched in fractured manual processes that are inherently risky and inefficient.

Customs Management in SAP GTS focuses on a broad array of requirements, including trade documentation; integration with customs authorities, brokers, and forwarders; and complex customs valuation and duty minimization strategies.

Risk Management functionality addresses free trade and preference programs that continue to be set forth at an unprecedented rate. Letter of Credit Processing and other trade-based reporting requirements are also part of the SAP GTS capabilities.

Collectively, this suite of functionalities offers a comprehensive approach to the complexities of global trade and supply chain operations management.

Over the past decade, Deloitte[1] has developed a market-leading service offering for implementing SAP GTS. This unique service offering combines a mix of global trade regulatory specialists and technical resources that have dedicated their careers to architecting and deploying SAP GTS. The result is a global, groundbreaking offering across the exciting and ever-evolving world of global trade.

Since the inception of SAP GTS over ten years ago, Deloitte has worked alongside SAP in pioneering the implementation of this solution around the world. This global, multi-year effort presented the opportunity for the Deloitte team to develop deep experience with the intricacies of architecting SAP GTS across all functional capabilities, including Compliance Management, Customs Management, and Risk Management. We have worked alongside the SAP GTS team in Walldorf with the joint goal of improving, developing, and maturing the SAP GTS solution and related implementation services.

Just over two years ago, the Deloitte GTS Global Competence Center initiated a journey that works across the maze of global trade regulatory requirements and technology solutions to manage increasingly complex supply chains in order to share this breadth of experience with the broad international community. The result is an SAP PRESS resource on this outstanding business tool that encompasses a mix of technical, functional, and regulatory content.

We hope that the information included in this publication will help companies, global trade professionals, and SAP GTS practitioners further their knowledge and understanding across the complex intersection of global trade regulatory

---

1 As used in this document, "Deloitte" means Deloitte & Touche LLP, Deloitte Tax LLP, Deloitte Consulting LLP, and Deloitte Financial Advisory Services LLP, which are separate subsidiaries of Deloitte LLP. Please see *www.deloitte.com/us/about* for a detailed description of the legal structure of Deloitte LLP and its subsidiaries.

requirements and this enterprise technology solution. The intent of this publication is to provide a resource to all, regardless of whether you are considering a first-time SAP GTS deployment, refining existing functionality, or deploying the solution in new regions globally. With various configuration options noted in detail, this unique publication should have something for everyone. The detailed material we'll discuss covers all the required steps to configure SAP GTS, including the Customizing settings with a focus on key decision points and related options.

As you'll see, the main chapters of this book are structured using the same sequential approach, starting with an overview of the different functionality and outlining the distinction between the business processes and the system processes. The business process overview describes the steps and events a company generally undertakes to manage a specific compliance and business requirement, while the system processes link the business process steps and events to the activities performed in SAP GTS to support the applicable process. Additionally, in the Compliance Management, Customs Management, and Risk Management chapters, we'll illustrate the compliance and customs business processes using applicable business case scenarios.

The structure is as follows:

- **Chapter 2** explains the connection between SAP GTS and feeder systems, including integration between SAP GTS and SAP ERP 6.0 or other SAP solutions, such as SAP TM or SAP CRM. It also covers basic SAP GTS navigation and authorization concepts.

- **Chapter 3** sets forth the SAP GTS functionality-specific activities to be executed across all modules. Basic Customizing settings, such as the plug-in (e.g., standard SAP GTS/SAP ERP 6.0 interface), organizational structure, partner structure, document type, and item category mapping are provided in detail. This chapter also introduces the important concept of legal regulations.

- **Chapter 4** provides an overview of all master data objects used in SAP GTS, including details on the source system and concepts of the initial master data transfer and change pointers.

- **Chapter 5** explains the different classification codes and their underlying business and system processes, including classification code uploads, individual classification, classification using the worklist, and re-classification.

▶ **Chapter 6** covers the different SAP GTS Compliance Management functionalities. The focus is on Sanctioned Party List Screening, Embargo, and Legal Control.

▶ **Chapter 7** covers not only the basic import and export customs processes, but also the more advanced procedures for special customs regimes, such as bonded warehouse functionality, inward and outward processing relief, and processing under customs control. This chapter also addresses requirements on filing import and export customs declarations directly with the authorities or via a customs broker and freight forwarder model. Finally, this chapter addresses the European Union's Excise Movement Control System and US reconciliation management.

▶ **Chapter 8** covers Risk Management functionality; it is divided into three sections, one each for Trade Preference Management (such as free trade agreements), Restitution Management, and Letter of Credit Processing functionality.

▶ **Chapter 9** focuses first on the standard and readily available SAP GTS reporting, and then on SAP Business Warehouse reporting capabilities.

▶ **Chapter 10** details options within the SAP ERP 6.0 plug-in for how master data and transactional data are transferred from the feeder system to SAP GTS, as well as filtering and the potential use of enhancements. The chapter also offers an overview of available BAdIs within SAP GTS.

▶ **Chapter 11** offers an outlook on the planned functionality for future SAP GTS releases. It was written by contributor Kai Seela, Senior Director of Solution Management for SAP Global Trade Services at SAP SE.

We hope this publication will be a source of inspiration for the SAP GTS community, raising the application to new levels of excellence and encouraging us all to continuously improve this outstanding business tool.

Before SAP GTS is operational, you have to interface it with a feeder sys-
tem and configure user authorizations appropriately. This chapter will
provide more details on both essential activities, as well as the basic navi-
gation in SAP GTS.

2   SAP GTS Basics: Setup, Authorizations, and Navigation

The objective of this chapter is to begin the SAP GTS conversation by setting up an operational SAP GTS system.

Because SAP GTS is not a standalone system, it always requires a working connection with a transactional system, or *feeder system*, to "feed" it with all necessary master data and transactions. This chapter will cover the most common way to connect an SAP ERP 6.0 system to SAP GTS: using the plug-in.

However, you can also use other feeder systems, such as SAP Transportation Management (TM), SAP Customer Relationship Management (CRM), or even non-SAP systems. In this case, you'll have to apply different interface techniques. We'll use SAP TM as an example to illustrate these different integration techniques and how you can apply them to set up a working connection with SAP GTS.

Next, this chapter teaches how to navigate through the different SAP GTS menus. In SAP GTS, a dedicated transaction has been made available to navigate in a user-friendly way to all functionalities, so we cover how to find your way in SAP GTS.

Finally, you'll learn how to control access to the SAP GTS application and its data by defining and assigning appropriate user authorizations. The last section of this chapter will introduce the basics of the SAP GTS authorization concept.

2.1   Connecting SAP ERP to SAP GTS using the Plug-In

SAP ERP 6.0 is by far the most common feeder system for SAP GTS. SAP GTS is fed with both master data (e.g., customers, vendors, materials, etc.) and transactional data (e.g., sales documents, purchase orders, or deliveries). We'll examine the necessary settings to interface an SAP ERP 6.0 system to SAP GTS.

2.1.1   System Architecture

SAP GTS (technical name: SLL-LEG) is an add-on system that uses a feeder system to provide logistics data for executing SAP GTS functionalities. Figure 2.1 shows the general exchange of data between SAP ERP 6.0 and SAP GTS.

It is possible to connect SAP ERP systems to SAP GTS using standard interfaces. To do so, you have to install an additional component—the plug-in (technical name: SLL_PI)—in your SAP ERP environment. This additional component will include all required functionality to integrate your SAP ERP 6.0 processes with SAP GTS. The plug-in is available for specific versions of SAP ERP. Because the plug-in contains only SAP GTS-related functions and does not affect other SAP modules, plug-in upgrades are considerably easier.

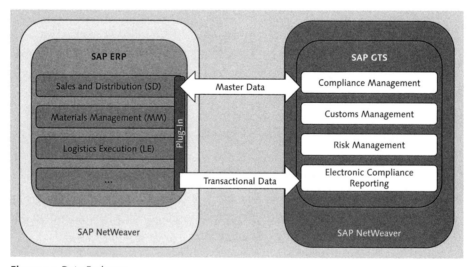

Figure 2.1 Data Exchange

When connecting SAP GTS and an SAP ERP system, two different scenarios are possible:

▶ All functionality is available in all clients of the physical system. In this scenario, customized settings determine the particular roles allocated to each system.

▶ The feeder system and SAP GTS are physically separated.

Note

For performance reasons, it's often favorable for the feeder system and SAP GTS to be physically separated. This is especially relevant to customers who intend to implement the services of the Compliance Management module in SAP GTS.

The plug-in makes extensively use of *remote function calls* (RFCs). An RFC makes a call to another SAP functional module and allows you to set up connections between different SAP modules or between an SAP system and a third-party system.

2.1.2 System Connection Configuration

The process of configuring the plug-in in SAP ERP 6.0 is similar to the customization of SAP GTS, so we'll address these settings concurrently. If the SAP GTS client is located in a different physical system—that is, on a separate platform—the first step is to replicate the system connection in both systems.

Logical Systems in SAP ERP and SAP GTS

Before data exchange can happen between SAP ERP 6.0 and SAP GTS, you must set up both the SAP ERP 6.0 system and SAP GTS as logical systems. You can do this in the plug-in menu within SAP ERP 6.0 via Transaction /SAPSLL/MENU_LEGALR3 by selecting the BASIC SETTINGS tab page. In SAP GTS, you can find this menu in Customizing for the SAP GTS system connection.

To reduce the burden of data maintenance on the user, you may want to group logical systems in SAP GTS into a single logical system group when more than one feeder system is activated. You can define a logical system group in SAP GTS Customizing and assign the logical system name(s) of the SAP ERP 6.0 feeder system(s) to it.

> **Note**
>
> All SAP GTS-relevant master data (business partners, products, and so on) has to be synchronized among all feeder systems in the same logical system group. If you assign several feeder systems to a single logical system group, the master record in SAP GTS is always created on the logical system-group level (e.g., one product master per system group).

The logical system creates a unique identifier for each client of an SAP system or non-SAP system in the system landscape.

To ensure that the logical system name is unique and the environment is simplified, SAP recommends using the naming convention *<System name>CLNT<Client key>*. However, it may be useful, in specific cases, to depart from the recommended naming convention.

Once the logical systems for SAP GTS and the feeder systems connected to SAP GTS are defined, you must then assign them to respective clients.

RFC Destinations in SAP ERP and SAP GTS

Once all relevant systems have been uniquely defined within the system landscape, you must establish a bi-directional connection to provide each system with a target host and logon details.

Because communication among the different systems occurs via RFCs, you have to set up an RFC destination in both SAP ERP 6.0 and SAP GTS. You can create new RFC destinations or change existing destinations via Transaction SM59 (Configuration of RFC Connections).

> **Note**
>
> You can also find this transaction in SAP ERP. Choose MAINTAIN RFC DESTINATIONS FOR RFC CALLS in the BASIC SETTINGS tab page of the SAP GTS area menu within the feeder system. Alternatively, choose the SYSTEM ADMINISTRATION AREA • MAINTAIN TARGET SYSTEM FOR RFC CALLS in the SAP GTS menu. You can also define RFC destinations in Customizing for SAP NetWeaver.

You must assign RFCs to a logical system and enable communication before the application program can call on a targeted logical system.

In the RFC destination, you need to specify a target host and an IP address. If applicable, also specify the system number, user data, and logon data to allow for remote logon to the target system. The RFC destination contains all technical information the requesting system needs to call the partner from within the network.

For SAP GTS, you do not need to give the RFC destination the same name as the logical target system.

Although SAP GTS is not based on ALE, it uses the ALE distribution model to help the SAP ERP 6.0 feeder system identify its SAP GTS partner systems. When a user in the SAP ERP feeder system carries out a transaction that involves SAP GTS functions—for example, creating a sales order that needs to be checked by SAP GTS Compliance Management)—the application program (ALE) determines where the call is received by querying the distribution model.

2.1.3 Connecting SAP GTS to Customs Authorities

For customs purposes, it is possible to transfer relevant data from SAP GTS directly to the customs authorities by using a third-party conversion provider such as Seeburger. The provider manages the communication between SAP GTS and the country-specific customs procedures for e-filing. The provider services include converting IDoc to XML, EDIFACT, and other formats. You can see the interaction among SAP GTS, a conversion provider, and customs authorities in Figure 2.2.

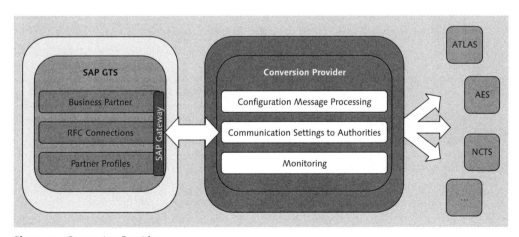

Figure 2.2 Conversion Provider

2.2 Connecting using Different Interfacing Techniques (SAP TM)

Now that you know how to use the plug-in to integrate SAP ERP 6.0 and SAP GTS, we'll go into detail on how to set up a connection with SAP GTS using different interface techniques. These techniques can be used to connect a different SAP product, such as SAP CRM or SAP TM, to SAP GTS, or to connect non-SAP systems to SAP GTS. We'll illustrate this connection using the integration with SAP TM as an example.

SAP Transportation Management (TM) is a separate module used to optimize the transportation processes. SAP TM can be used in two scenarios:

▶ In the scenario of the shipper, transactional data (sales orders and outbound deliveries) are transferred from SAP ERP 6.0 to the SAP TM system. This results in SAP TM transportation requirement documents (order transportation requirements and delivery transportation requirements).

▶ Logistic service providers (LSPs) can create forwarding orders in the SAP TM system immediately, based on the transportation requests received from their customers.

You can also use SAP TM to assign and tender shipments to carriers. Once you book the shipment via a specific carrier, the specific booking information can be housed in SAP TM. You can use this information, received from the carrier, as a base to create export declarations in SAP GTS to minimize manual data entry.

The integration between SAP GTS and SAP TM focuses on two functionalities: Compliance Management and Customs Management.

2.2.1 Integration with SAP TM from a Technical Perspective

The integration between SAP TM and SAP GTS is based on service-oriented architecture (SOA) web services. There are two possibilities to connect the systems: via a point-to-point connection or via SAP Process Integration (PI).

There are 12 web services (six in SAP GTS and six in SAP TM) in total to support the compliance and customs functionalities. In each system, there are three types of web services for the compliance functionality and three for customs functionality:

► Request web service to trigger the compliance screening/customs declaration from SAP TM to SAP GTS

► Confirmation web service to transfer back the result of the screening/export declaration

► Cancellation request web service to cancel the compliance/customs document in SAP GTS

Table 2.1 lists the compliance web services you need to implement.

SAP GTS (namespace http://sap.com/xi/GTS/Global2)	SAP TM (namespace http://sap.com/xi/TMS/Global)
TradeComplianceCheckSUITERequest_In	TradeComplianceCheckSUITERequest_Out
TradeComplianceCheckSUITECancellation-Request_Out	TradeComplianceCheckSUITECancellation-Request_Out
ExportDeclarationSUITEConfirmation_Out	TradeComplianceCheckSUITEConfirmation_In

Table 2.1 Compliance Web Services

Table 2.2 lists the customs web services you need to implement.

SAP GTS (namespace http://sap.com/xi/GTS/Global2)	SAP TM (namespace http://sap.com/xi/TMS/Global)
ExportDeclarationSUITERequest_In	ExportDeclarationSUITERequest_Out
ExportDeclarationSUITECancellation-Request_Out	ExportDeclarationSUITECancellation-Request_Out
ExportDeclarationSUITEConfirmation_Out	ExportDeclarationSUITEConfirmation_In

Table 2.2 Customs Web Services

Please note that, in a typical setup, SAP GTS is still connected to the SAP ERP system via the standard plugin (SLL_PI) to accommodate the transfer of master data (material master, customer master, and vendor master) and transactional documents. Data originating from SAP ERP 6.0 is transferred to SAP GTS and SAP TM simultaneously, as seen in Figure 2.3.

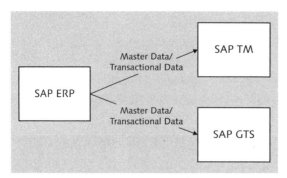

Figure 2.3 Master Data and Transactional Data Transfer from SAP ERP 6.0 to GTS and SAP TM

2.2.2 Compliance Screening

The compliance integration between SAP TM and SAP GTS is similar to the integration with any other feeder system (e.g., SAP ERP 6.0). A document, originating in SAP TM, is replicated in SAP GTS, and a compliance screening—that is, sanctioned party list (SPL) screening and embargo screening—is performed in SAP GTS on the document. The result of the screening (blocked/not blocked) is transferred back to SAP TM. Based on the result of the screening, you can block the document in SAP TM and prevent further processing.

The SAP TM interface to SAP GTS is triggered only after a document is saved in SAP TM. The compliance status of the SAP TM document is changed to Compliant/Not Compliant, depending on the outcome of the screening performed in SAP GTS. You can define the blocking effect of a specific status (for example, whether planning is allowed if the status is still Compliance Check Required) in SAP TM Customizing. When you perform a recheck of a document in SAP GTS, SAP GTS transfers the compliance status back to SAP TM.

You can perform both embargo screening and SPL screening on SAP TM documents. Legal Control is not possible because the product number is not part of the interface. The required screenings are determined based on the SAP GTS document type, which is mapped against the SAP TM document.

For SPL screening, SAP GTS checks address data that is derived from business partner master data, but not data derived from locations. In addition, it does not check addresses that a user enters in the printing address field on the business partner tab page in the forwarding order. For the embargo check, SAP GTS checks the countries in the transportation route.

Both freight orders (used in the shipper scenario) and forwarding orders (used in the logistics service provider scenario, as for a forwarder) can undergo a compliance screening. You can see this in Figure 2.4, where the shipper scenario is represented by light gray boxes and the LSP scenario by white boxes. The necessary Customizing step on the SAP TM side is to flag the ENABLE COMPLIANCE CHECK checkbox when defining the freight order/forwarding order.

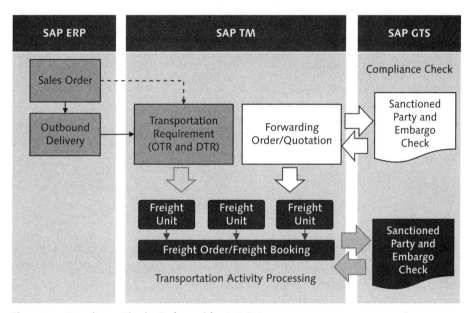

Figure 2.4 Compliance Checks Performed for SAP TM

On the SAP GTS side, the necessary Customizing is similar to the integration with SAP ERP 6.0 as feeder system. We'll explain SAP GTS Customizing required for SAP ERP 6.0 as a feeder system in later chapters of the book; for now, let's look at the differences between Customizing for SAP TM and SAP ERP 6.0 as feeder system:

▶ **Organizational structure mapping**
The sales/purchasing organization from SAP TM corresponds with the foreign trade organization (FTO) in SAP GTS. You need to map the business partner number to the respective FTO.

Please note that the legal unit mapping is not required for the compliance screening functionality. However, the mapping is required for the export declaration functionality.

▶ **Partner function mapping**

You need to map the partner functions used in the TM document to the corresponding SAP GTS partner functions. The following partner functions are transferred:

- ▶ TM Role "1": Sold-to party
- ▶ TM Role "10": Bill-to party
- ▶ TM Role "12": Carrier party
- ▶ TM Role "5": Ship-to party
- ▶ TM Role "8": Payer party

▶ **Document type mapping**

You need to map the two SAP TM predefined document types (transportation order for a freight order/booking and transportation request for a forwarding order) to SAP GTS-specific document types. No distinction can be made between different SAP TM document types (e.g., different transportation order document types).

2.2.3 Export Declaration

The customs integration between SAP TM and SAP GTS is similar to the billing document transfer from the SAP ERP 6.0 feeder system to SAP GTS. The freight order in SAP TM is blocked until the export declaration is completed in SAP GTS. The export declaration confirmation number (e.g., ITN for US AES), received from customs, is transferred back to SAP TM. This transfer allows you to print the number on the necessary paperwork (e.g., bill of lading).

The CUSTOMS tab of the freight order/freight booking consists of three important parts:

- ▶ The part on top contains all the global trade-relevant information (e.g., mode of transport, customs office of departure, etc.).
- ▶ The second part contains all the relevant customs activities (e.g., export).
- ▶ The last part is called *item groups*. The information from the TM freight order is split up in several item groups, as defined by the grouping strategy.

You can create a freight order based on multiple sales orders with a different ship-to party (i.e., consignee). A standard grouping strategy creates an item group per ship-to party. This ensures that one export declaration is created per ship-to party.

On SAP TM, several Customizing steps are necessary via Transaction SPRO • SAP TRANSPORTATION MANAGEMENT • TRANSPORTATION MANAGEMENT • BASIC FUNCTIONS • GLOBAL TRADE. There are a few main Customizing activities to execute:

▶ Activate the customs process for a specific SAP TM document by assigning a customs profile to the SAP TM freight order/freight booking via the Customizing task Define Freight Order Types.

▶ Define a customs relevance check for a specific SAP TM document per activity via the Customizing task Define Customs Relevant Check.

▶ Define several customs statuses and cumulated statuses via the Customizing task Define Cumulation of Customs Statuses. The customs status is shown on the transactional document in SAP TM, while the cumulated status defines the potential block reason.

▶ Define a customs activity via Customizing task Define Customs Activities and Profiles.

▶ Define the grouping strategy to indicate how the SAP TM document will be split up into several item groups. Configure the grouping strategy via Transaction SPRO • SAP TRANSPORTATION MANAGEMENT • SCM BASICS • PROCESS CONTROLLER.

▶ Assign the customs activity and customs profile to each other via the Customizing task Define Customs Activities and Profiles.

On the SAP GTS side, the necessary Customizing is similar to that of Compliance Management. However, please note the following differences:

▶ Organizational structure mapping—legal unit: The shipper partner function from SAP TM corresponds with the legal unit in GTS.

▶ Document type and item category mapping is not necessary. The SAP GTS system automatically determines the relevant document type based on the activity sequence.

Let's turn our attention to the basic navigation in SAP GTS and the structure of its components.

2.3 Navigating SAP GTS

SAP GTS has a general menu (often referred to as the cockpit, and shown in Figure 2.5) from which you can access different components. To access the menu, execute Transaction /SAPSLL/MENU_LEGAL.

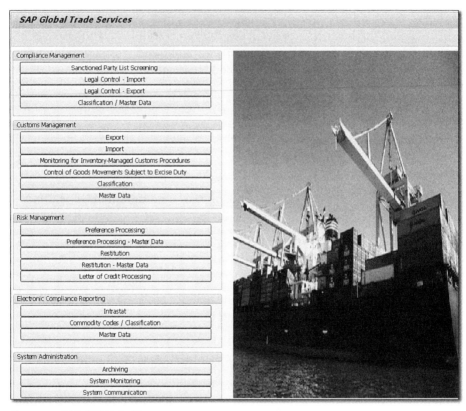

Figure 2.5 SAP GTS Main Menu

SAP GTS consists of five main modules:

- Compliance Management
- Customs Management
- Risk Management
- Electronic Compliance Reporting
- System Administration

The first three modules are the main functional areas of SAP GTS. These functional areas will be discussed in detail throughout this book.

2.3.1   Compliance Management

Within the Compliance Management module of SAP GTS, a company can monitor all business partners (or a selected group) via the SPL screening functionality. Depending on the business partner type, you can screen through the LOGISTICS, HUMAN RESOURCES, or FINANCIAL ACCOUNTING tabs. The cross-area monitoring provides an extended audit trail. You can maintain all master data related to SPL screening in the MASTER DATA tab.

The Legal Control Import or Export functionality in Compliance Management lets you monitor all blocked or technically incomplete documents and recheck them when needed. You can also manage import and export embargo checks on business partners.

The CLASSIFICATION/MASTER DATA section groups all activities relating to the classification of products and maintenance of master data (such as the upload of export control classification lists).

2.3.2   Customs Management

SAP GTS manages all inbound and outbound processes in the IMPORT and EXPORT areas of Customs Management. Both the IMPORT and EXPORT tabs contain an operative cockpit that you use to process ongoing documents. You can track previously processed documents in the MONITORING tab.

Aside from these main business flows, SAP GTS also lets you track transit movements that are legally relevant for a company. Here, you can create and monitor supplementary customs declarations, or periodic declarations. The IMPORT tab contains some additional functionality: pre-declaration (only in the United States) and presentation (including safekeeping).

Special customs procedures and activities are grouped in the MONITORING FOR INVENTORY-MANAGED CUSTOMS PROCEDURES section.

If a company qualifies to ship goods under excise suspension, you can manage these activities via CONTROL OF GOODS MOVEMENTS SUBJECT TO EXCISE DUTY.

You can maintain tariff and commodity codes and classify products for a specific country within the generic CLASSIFICATION area of Customs Management.

Within MASTER DATA you can maintain products and business partners in SAP GTS, define and monitor authorizations and securities related to Customs Management, maintain geographical information, and apply default data settings. In the OTHER tab, you can maintain exchange rates.

2.3.3 Risk Management

The Risk Management module is divided into three main functional subcomponents:

▶ Trade Preference Management
▶ Restitution Management
▶ Letter of Credit Processing

In Trade Preference Processing, you can determine the preference status and manage vendor-based declarations and vendor declarations for customers.

You can maintain products and display preference-related information on these products (such as duties, prices, and bills of product) in the MASTER DATA tab. Information on specific and applicable agreements, in addition to extensive transfer logs, is available in the same tab.

The Restitution Management subcomponent contains a monitoring area where customs documents relevant to the restitution process are displayed. You can actively manage both the CAP licenses and the securities here, as well as simulate a restitution calculation or calculate the valid restitution amount per customs declaration.

The Letter of Credit Processing subcomponent is structured in a different way. Other than the IMPORT and EXPORT tabs, you can access master data directly via the main Letter of Credit Processing subcomponent rather than a separate path.

Both the export and import tabs contain a monitoring and control data section. In the MONITORING section, you can display all relevant documents for the letter of credit procedure.

In the CONTROL DATA section, you can maintain the determination strategy for processing the letter of credit (L/C) as applicable for both import and export transactions. To create, maintain, or display an L/C, navigate to the MASTER DATA tab.

2.3.4 Additional Menus

The ELECTRONIC COMPLIANCE REPORTING menu is divided into three different components:

▶ INTRASTAT: For managing the Intrastat declarations in SAP GTS.

▶ COMMODITY CODES/CLASSIFICATION: Includes the maintenance and upload of product classification and commodity codes. Additionally, you can assign and display number sets here.

▶ MASTER DATA: Maintain information providers.

In SYSTEM ADMINISTRATION, the following activities can be performed:

▶ ARCHIVING: In this tab, select specific types of customs declarations and worklists, SPL screening results, or trade preference-related documents to be archived.

▶ SYSTEM MONITORING: This feature enables a number of settings, divided into six tabs.

  ▶ The LOGS tab provides more details on the documents transfer from the feeder system to SAP GTS.

  ▶ In FALLBACK PROCEDURE, you can activate the fallback procedure for Customs Management.

  ▶ BACKGROUND PROCESSING provides an overview of all processes that can run in the background of SAP GTS.

  ▶ The tab MESSAGE PROCESSING can be used to retrieve the output of active messages.

  ▶ The SYNCHRONIZATION tab contains information on master data transfer and customs documents from SAP GTS to the feeder system.

  ▶ Finally, TECHNICAL CHECKS allows you to check data consistency across the system.

▶ SYSTEM COMMUNICATION: This allows you to monitor batch jobs and spool requests. If EDI communication is set up, it groups sets of activities to manage this communication.

Now that we've covered basic navigation in SAP GTS and its menus, let's elaborate on authorizations in SAP GTS.

2.4   Using Authorizations

The SAP GTS authorization concept is part of the foundation that will protect the data within the system to maintain confidentiality, availability, and integrity. Proper user authorizations are required to protect transactions, programs, and services in SAP systems from unauthorized access. Since the same authorization concept is used as in SAP ERP, you can apply similar techniques to set up the necessary user authorizations. This section will introduce the authorization concept and give some basic information on how to define the necessary user authorizations.

To work with SAP GTS, all users are required to log on to the system using a unique user ID. For each user, user master data that contains the password and other relevant details, needs to be created. SAP programs utilize authorization checks to protect the system from unauthorized access. Profiles in the form of roles are assigned as authorizations to the user master record.

Different business flows are typically a group of activities performed by users, and these activities are included in a role.

The profile generator, used to create the roles, is divided into three main parts:

▶ Role menu, which consists of all available transactions
▶ Authorizations, which are the access rights given to different business functions and data
▶ User, which contains a list of all the user IDs that can have access to this role

The first step in creating roles in SAP GTS is to create the *business process master list* (BPML). A BPML is a document that primarily groups the transactions in a logical order to facilitate the creation of roles. It is worthwhile to create a large number of smaller groups so that authorizations can be assigned to the users more flexibly.

You can create SAP roles as single or derived roles. Further, you can combine these single or derived roles to form composite roles, as well. When you use the profile generator, the authorization objects of all the transactions are automatically determined, and when you generate the role, the authorizations are created. Typically, a role is created using the profile generator. You can use pre-defined roles provided by SAP as a basis for creating customer-specific roles.

Let's walk through creating a role, including the assignment to the user:

1. To call the profile generator, choose the following menu path: Tools • Administration • User Maintenance • Roles. The transactions that need to be included are added to the Menu tab. The authorization objects linked to the transactions are automatically populated in the Authorizations tab.

2. You can automate the values in the objects by using Transaction SU24; you can also modify them within the role. You can define organizational levels within this tab to restrict users to a few organizational units, rather than all of them.

3. Once you create/modify all the authorization objects as needed, the role is generated. You can now assign users to the roles in the User tab and assign a validity period.

4. Once you save the role, the procedure is complete, and the user can perform only those functions listed in the Menu tab (unless any other role is assigned).

2.5   Summary

SAP GTS requires a connection with a transactional or feeder system in order to perform the different SAP GTS functionalities. SAP ERP 6.0 is the most commonly used feeder system for SAP GTS, but you can use other feeder systems, like SAP Transportation Management or a non-SAP system, as well.

Besides connecting SAP GTS to a feeder system, we also explained the basic navigation in SAP GTS and gave an overview of the different modules and functionalities.

Finally, we dedicated a section to the user authorizations available in SAP GTS and how to set them up.

In the next chapter, we'll discuss the baseline settings of SAP GTS. These baseline settings are general, cross-modular settings that have to be configured at the start of any SAP GTS project.

The baseline settings discussed in this chapter are the activities that need to be carried out at a generic cross-module level and that apply to all SAP GTS functionalities and modules.

3   Baseline Settings

Baseline settings are activities related to master data and IMG Customizing that SAP GTS consultants must perform based on a company's business requirements.

As in SAP ERP 6.0, the baseline settings in SAP GTS cover areas such as the organizational structure, partner roles, document types, and so on, as well as some specific global trade concepts, such as the legal regulation. A specific aspect of the configuration in SAP GTS is that the baseline settings require extensive mapping activities that connect SAP ERP 6.0 and SAP GTS entities and objects.

These activities are performed at the start of the configuration phase of an implementation project and require a thorough understanding of the business and system processes and future needs of the implementation. This chapter will first talk about the settings for the organizational structure in SAP GTS (Section 3.1), followed by the plug-in settings (Section 3.2), the general settings in SAP GTS (Section 3.3), and SAP Case Management (Section 3.4).

3.1   Organizational Structure in SAP GTS

Just as in SAP ERP 6.0, a company's organizational structure must be set up in SAP GTS. The correct setup of the organizational structure is crucial because it will drive the tax ID number determination for relevant transactions, applicable export licenses, or customs authorizations, among other functions.

Organizational structure, like in the SAP ERP 6.0 system, is the backbone of every implementation. It is a necessary step to ensure communication between SAP GTS and backend feeder systems. Once this communication is established, organizational structure follows immediately. This section will cover how the

organizational elements in SAP GTS will be mapped to the organizational structure of the feeder system, walk through Customizing steps, and offer best practices related to setting up the organizational structure.

Let's first look at organizational elements.

3.1.1 Foreign Trade Organization

The foreign trade organization (FTO) within SAP GTS represents the legal entity
of the company. Within SAP GTS, the FTO acts as the authorization owner and
applicant for import/export licenses. Logistics processes from the feeder system
are integrated with foreign trade processes in SAP GTS, with the FTO acting as the
independent legal entity within the feeder system.

You define the FTO in business partner maintenance by creating a new business
partner and assigning the business partner role SLLFTO. Each FTO has its own
address, which represents the official address of the legal entity. Therefore, only
one country assignment per FTO is feasible. This country will determine the legal
regulation for customs processing.

The FTO corresponds to the company code in SAP ERP 6.0. In SAP GTS, each
company code can be assigned to only one FTO, but one FTO can be assigned several company codes (including company codes from different systems). Do note,
however, that it is a best practice to assign no more than *one* SAP ERP 6.0 company code per FTO in SAP GTS, although there can be some exceptions.

3.1.2 Legal Unit

Legal units (LUs) correspond and are linked to the plants in SAP ERP 6.0. As with
the company code, each LU can be assigned to only one FTO, but the same FTO
can have more than one LU assigned to it.

There are many different options to map LUs with plants in the feeder system(s).
Several plants can be assigned to the same LU, but each plant can be assigned to
only one LU. SAP ERP storage locations can also be assigned to an LU, even if the
physical location of the storage locations are different. This is because the legal
unit determines the legal regulation for compliance.

Figure 3.1 maps the company codes, FTOs, plant, storage locations, and legal units.

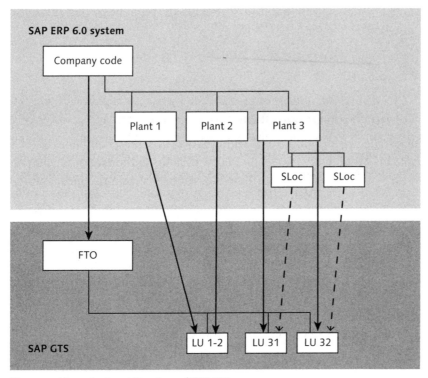

Figure 3.1 Organizational Structure of SAP GTS

Note

SAP GTS has the following restriction when you define the organizational structure: The user can assign LUs to FTOs only within the same country. If there is an LU in one specific country but the actual FTO resides in another country, then additional enhancements are necessary.

3.1.3 Administrative Unit

Administrative units (AUs) are located in the Risk Management module of SAP GTS, which we'll cover more thoroughly in Chapter 8. They are used to set up the organizational structure for trade preference determination. AUs are used to group all the enterprise entities (such as plants or plant groups) needed to request and dun, or issue and revoke, vendor declarations. They are set up as business partners with a business partner role SLLMGR.

You can assign any organizational structure business partner (that is, FTO or LU) with the additional role of AU.

3.1.4 Customs ID

A *customs ID* is a unique combination of plant and storage location that represents the physical location where special customs procedures can take place. Special customs procedures, like bonded/customs warehouses (BWH), inward processing relief (IPR), or outward processing relief (OPR), will be further explained in Chapter 7 on Customs Management. Customs IDs represent an authorized reporting unit for special customs procedures. This means that one administration can be retained per customs ID for reporting purposes. Since a customs ID consists of a combination of plant and storage location, this combination needs to be set up in the Customizing of the feeder system and SAP GTS.

3.1.5 Customizing

You need to set up these organizational structures in SAP GTS using Customizing steps, or via Transaction SPRO • GLOBAL TRADE SERVICES • GENERAL SETTINGS.

First, define the FTO as a business partner and assign the business partner role SLLFTO via Transaction BP. Figure 3.2 shows the creation of an FTO in Transaction BP.

Figure 3.2 Creating an FTO in Transaction BP

Next, assign the newly created FTO to a company code in the feeder system or a group of logical systems or group of feeder systems, as shown in Figure 3.3. Then, you can repeat the same process for the creation and assignment of LUs, which you can assign to a single feeder system or a group of feeder systems. You can assign a combination of plant and storage location from the feeder system to the legal units.

Change View "Mapping: Feeder System Company Code to Organizational Uni

New Entries

Mapping: Feeder System Company Code to Organizational Unit

LogSystem	Name	FS Org.	FT Organ.	Name 1
IDECLNT901	ECC6 for GTS10.0 Client...	1000	FTO_1000	FTO1000
IDECLNT901	ECC6 for GTS10.0 Client...	1200	FTODEMO_KR	Demo FTO KR
IDECLNT901	ECC6 for GTS10.0 Client...	1800	FTO_18000	Demo FTO BWH
IDECLNT901	ECC6 for GTS10.0 Client...	2202	FTO_FR	Company France
IDECLNT901	ECC6 for GTS10.0 Client...	3000	FTO_IN	FTO IN
IDECLNT901	ECC6 for GTS10.0 Client...	5400	FTO_NL5400	FTO NL5400
IDECLNT901	ECC6 for GTS10.0 Client...	5901	FTODEMO_US	FTO Demo US
IDECLNT901	ECC6 for GTS10.0 Client...	5902	FTODEMO_BE	FTO GTS BE
IDECLNT901	ECC6 for GTS10.0 Client...	5903	FTODEMO_SE	Demo FTO SE
IDECLNT901	ECC6 for GTS10.0 Client...	5904	FTOGT1DE01	Company Germany FTO DE01

Figure 3.3 Link between FTO and Company Code

Once you've created the FTOs and LUs, the legal units are assigned to the relevant FTO. Figure 3.4 shows the assignment of LUs to the FTOs.

Change View "Organizational Structure in SAP GTS": Overview

New Entries

Organizational Structure in SAP GTS

Legal Unit	Name 1	Foreign Trade Org. Unit
LUDEMO_AU	Plant Australia	FTODEMO_AU
LUDEMO_BE	Demo LU BE	FTODEMO_BE
LUDEMO_KR	LU South Korea	DFTODEM_KR
LUDEMO_PL	LU GTS PL	FTODEMO_PL
LUDEMO_SE	Demo LU SE	FTODEMO_SE
LUDEMO_US	Legal Unit - Demo	FTODEMO_US
LUGT1DE01	Company Germany LU DE01	FTOGT1DE01
LU_1000	LU_1000	FTO_1000
LU_17000	Demo Legal Unit- Normal	FTO_18000
LU_1800	Demo LU	FTO_18000
LU_18000	Demo LU	FTO_18000
LU_BP_TP	TP	FTO_DEMO
LU_DEMO	Demo LU	FTO_DEMO
LU_FR	Company France	FTO_FR
LU_IN	Legal Unit India	FTO_IN

Figure 3.4 Mapping LUs to FTOs

If the Risk Management module is activated, you must also set up administrative units within the SAP GTS organizational structure. See Chapter 8 for more on this.

When special customs procedures are applicable, you'll need to determine customs IDs in both the feeder system and SAP GTS.

3.1.6 Best Practices

When you're setting up the organizational structures in SAP GTS, you should take some best practices and guidelines into consideration:

▶ Each FTO has a single tax ID number. This means that two company codes with two different tax ID numbers can't belong to a single FTO.

▶ The FTO is the legal entity in SAP GTS. If two company codes representing two different legal entities are mapped to one FTO, it is impossible to determine the appropriate legal entity.

▶ The system will look at the country assigned to the FTO to trigger the customs legal regulations. Therefore, two company codes, located in different countries, can't be mapped to one FTO because two separate customs legal regulations would need to be triggered.

▶ The system will look at the country assigned to the LU to trigger the compliance/trade preference legal regulations. Therefore, two plants located in different countries can't be mapped to one LU because two separate compliance/trade preference legal regulations would need to be triggered.

▶ Merging FTOs can add flexibility on reporting with no increased burden during master data setup.

3.2 Plug-in Settings in SAP ERP

The feeder system and SAP GTS are linked together via a plug-in system. This plug-in provides the communication between both systems.

The goal of this plug-in is to transfer master data and transactional documents from SAP ERP 6.0 to SAP GTS. You can transfer a transactional document from SAP ERP 6.0 to SAP GTS only if you've already created all required master data—that is, the materials and business partners (customers, vendors, etc.) used in the transactional document—in SAP GTS. If the master data is *not* available in SAP GTS, then the document gets a technical incomplete status in the Compliance Management module or does not generate a complete customs declaration in the Customs Management module.

Before you can transfer transactional documents from SAP ERP 6.0 to SAP GTS, you have to activate business add-ins, or BAdIs. A BAdI is an enhancement to the standard version of SAP. You can define BAdIs by application levels, which in turn identify transaction categories (namely inbound or outbound, purchase or sales order, etc). We can divide the existing BAdIs into the following application levels:

▸ MM0A—Receipt/Import: Purchasing Document (e.g., purchase orders)

▸ MM0B—Receipt/Import: Inbound Delivery Document (e.g., inbound deliveries)

▸ MM0C—Receipt/Import: Material Document (e.g., goods receipt material documents)

▸ SD0A—Dispatch/Export: Sales Document (e.g., sales orders)

▸ SD0B—Dispatch/Export: Outbound Delivery Document (e.g., outbound deliveries)

▸ SD0C—Dispatch/Export: Billing Document (e.g., pro-forma invoices)

Figure 3.5 shows the application levels, which are further used during the configuration of the document structure in SAP GTS.

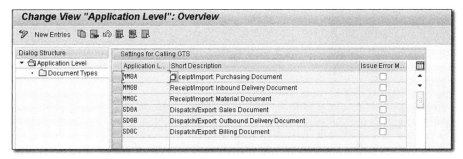

Figure 3.5 Application Levels

After you've activated the relevant BAdIs, you can specify transactional documents for each application level via Transaction SPRO (Configure Control Settings for Document Transfer). In this transaction, you choose which document types need to be transferred for every application level; for example, you might transfer the purchase orders with document type NB. In this scenario, an entry is added for application level MM0A with document type FNB. For document type FNB, F represents the document category (purchasing), and NB represents the purchase order document type.

As shown in Figure 3.6, you can further specify the services (e.g., compliance, customs, risk, etc.) for which the document must be transferred and whether an output dialog should be shown in the feeder system (e.g., stating that the document is blocked for compliance).

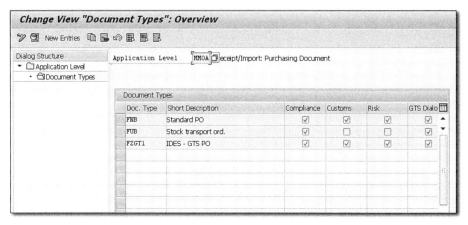

Figure 3.6 Application BAdI MM0A

In some cases, you may need to execute additional configuration. The available configuration settings depend on the applicable application level.

3.3 General Settings in SAP GTS

There are several settings in the SAP GTS system that apply to most of its modules. They are grouped in a dedicated section in the SAP GTS Customizing menu and, therefore, maintained centrally.

The settings also apply to all processes in SAP GTS, including defining and maintaining legal regulations, document types, and mapping to corresponding document types within the feeder system; defining business partner roles and mapping to the corresponding partner roles of the feeder system; and setting up number ranges. Let's examine each of these further.

3.3.1 Legal Regulation

Legal regulations are defined for the purposes of the transactional flows within SAP GTS. Legal regulations are largely used in the Compliance Management module for import/export control checks, including sanctioned party lists and embargo screening. The legal regulation is also referenced in Trade Preference Management flows as a representative of the free trade agreement and for customs processes.

The bottom of Figure 3.7 gives an overview of the general settings menu for legal regulations in Customizing.

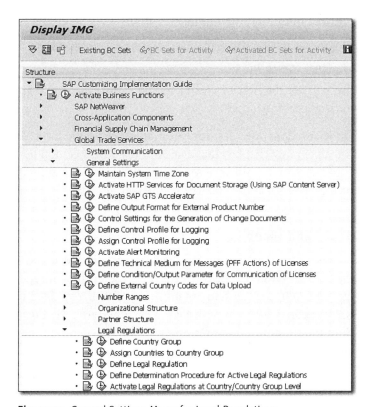

Figure 3.7 General Settings Menu for Legal Regulations

Legal regulations are assigned to a country and/or country group. As a result, it is necessary to first define the appropriate values for the countries and country groups and then define and assign the legal regulation to a specific process within SAP GTS, such as customs, foreign trade law (Compliance Management), or preference law (Trade Preference Management). The legal regulation could apply to only the import side, only the export side, or both. You set this within the definition of the legal regulation.

Next, assign the legal regulation a determination procedure that includes a determination strategy. This setting regulates at which country level the legal regulation determination is executed, or whether the determination is completed at the country or country-group level for both import and export functions. It is possible to define different determination strategies by partner group (a partner group is a grouping of business partners).

Two approaches are possible in setting a determination strategy:

▶ The determination executes all strategies in order to determine all the relevant legal regulations (i.e., legal control).

▶ The determination stops after the first successful strategy applies a legal regulation (i.e., trade preference or customs).

Subsequent settings for legal regulations are done at a module-specific level, so we'll explain them in the upcoming chapters that deal with the different modules. For example, refer to Chapter 6 on Compliance Management for the activation of the legal regulation for legal control at the country/country-group level.

3.3.2 Document Types and Mapping

You can transfer transactional documents from SAP ERP 6.0 (or other feeder systems via enhancements) to SAP GTS. Through this transfer, the document types and item categories used in the feeder system are also transferred. You need to map these SAP ERP 6.0 categories with those in SAP GTS; otherwise, the document has a technical incomplete status in the Compliance Management module, or the customs document is not created in the Customs Management module.

To set up the document structure in SAP GTS, perform the following steps, shown at the bottom of Figure 3.8:

▶ Define the SAP GTS-specific document type/item category.

▶ Activate the SAP GTS-specific document type/item category for the required functionalities.

▶ Map the SAP GTS-specific document type/item category to the corresponding SAP ERP 6.0-specific document type/item category.

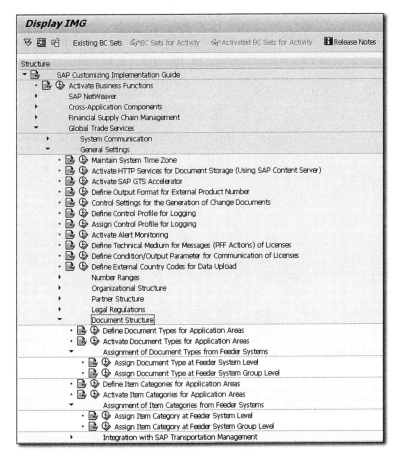

Figure 3.8 General Settings Menu for Document Structure

Let's pause and discuss the document type setup, and then turn our attention to the setup of item categories.

In SAP GTS, you can define SAP GTS-specific document types via Transaction SPRO • DOCUMENT STRUCTURE • DEFINE DOCUMENT TYPES FOR APPLICATION AREAS.

Each document type belongs to a specific document category. The document category defines the functionalities for which the document can be used; for example, the document types that are part of the customs documents category are used for the Compliance Management functionality.

SAP provides a number of standard document types that can be used for standard SAP GTS processes. However, sometimes you have to set up additional, specific document types, such as if your company creates a sales order for the sales of physical goods. For these physical goods movements, legal control checks are required. If the sales orders are also used for non-physical shipments, then they might not require legal control checks. To make this scenario feasible, you'd need to customize an additional document type for the sales flow that does not require legal control checks.

You can control each defined document via specific settings. Among these settings are the number range used and the transfer for SAP BusinessObjects BI/SAP BW reporting.

After you've defined SAP GTS-specific documents, you must activate them for the applicable functionalities via Transaction SPRO • DOCUMENT STRUCTURE • ACTIVATE DOCUMENT TYPES FOR APPLICATION AREAS. All functionalities are mentioned on the left-side menu, as shown in Figure 3.9. You must add an entry for a specific document type to activate the specific document type for that functionality.

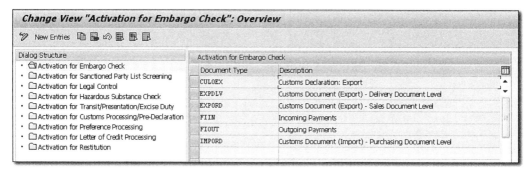

Figure 3.9 Activating Document Types for Appliction Areas: Functionalities

Finally, you need to map SAP ERP 6.0 document types to their corresponding SAP GTS document types in Transaction SPRO • DOCUMENT STRUCTURE • ASSIGN DOCUMENT TYPE AT FEEDER SYSTEM GROUP LEVEL. One best practice is to perform this mapping at the logical system-group level. If the mapping is done at the logical-system level (i.e., assigned to a specific system), then it must be re-done in case the configuration is transported across systems (e.g., from a development to a quality system). If the mapping is performed at the logical system-group level (i.e., logical system group SAP ERP 6.0), no additional Customizing is needed. The assignment of logical system to logical system group ensures that the existing Customizing entries are still correct (e.g., by changing the assigned logical system to the logical system group from the development system to the quality system).

Figure 3.10 shows document types mapped to a logical system at the group level.

Application Level	LS Group	Doc. Type Feed. Sys.	Document Type	
BEBD Billing Engine Billing... ▾	FDRTESTGRP	ZF8	CULOEX	▲
BEBD Billing Engine Billing... ▾	FDRTESTGRP	ZGT2	CULOEX	▾
MM0B Receipt/Import: Inboun... ▾	FDRTESTGRP	LR	DTAVI	
SD0A Dispatch/Export: Sales... ▾	FDRTESTGRP	ZOR	EXPORD	
SD0A Dispatch/Export: Sales... ▾	FDRTESTGRP	ZOR1	EXPORD	
SD0B Dispatch/Export: Outbo... ▾	FDRTESTGRP	ZGT1	EXPDLV	

Figure 3.10 Document Types Mapped to Logical Systems at the Group Level

You have to perform this mapping for each relevant application area. For example, the following would be a potential mapping for the previously mentioned purchase order NB:

▸ Application area: MM0A

▸ Logical system group: SAP ERP 6.0

After you've completed the mapping process, SAP GTS determines the appropriate functionality on the transferred purchase order NB.

Once you've set up the document types, you can configure item categories. The setup here is similar. First, set up SAP GTS-specific item categories and activate them for specific functionalities. Then map the corresponding item categories between SAP ERP 6.0 and SAP GTS, as shown in Figure 3.11.

Change View "Mapping: Feeder System Item Category to SAP GTS Item Cat.

New Entries

Mapping: Feeder System Item Category to SAP GTS Item Cat.

Application Level	LogSystem	Feed. Sys. Item Cat.	Item Category
FI0A FI Payment	IDECLNT901	FI0A	FI0A
MM0A Receipt/Import: Purcha...	IDECLNT901	0	IMORD1
MM0A Receipt/Import: Purcha...	IDECLNT901	7	IMORD1
MM0A Receipt/Import: Purcha...	IDECLNT901	FERT	IMORD1
MM0A Receipt/Import: Purcha...	IDECLNT901	IRAL	IMORD1
MM0A Receipt/Import: Purcha...	IDECLNT901	IRRE	IMORD1
MM0A Receipt/Import: Purcha...	IDECLNT901	IRRP	IMORD1
MM0A Receipt/Import: Purcha...	IDECLNT901	IRRS	IMORD1
MM0A Receipt/Import: Purcha...	IDECLNT901	REN	IMORD1
MM0A Receipt/Import: Purcha...	IDECLNT901	U	IMORD1
MM0B Receipt/Import: Inboun...	IDECLNT901	IRRE	IMPDLV
SD0A Dispatch/Export: Sales...	IDECLNT901	0	EXORD1

Figure 3.11 Mapping Item Categories

3.3.3 Partner Roles Mapping

Business partners are persons or organizations that perform a role within a company. These roles can include customers, vendors, FTOs, legal units, customs offices, data providers, and so on. It is necessary to link business partner roles of the feeder system to the partner roles in SAP GTS. Business partners are grouped in partner groups, which are relevant to several SAP GTS processes. For example, business partner groups assigned to a combination of legal regulation and document types determine which partner functions appear in a customs document.

You must create, group, and assign business partner functions according to the following steps:

1. Create the business partner functions (e.g., CUSEXP as exporter).
2. Define groups of partner functions. Partner groups provided by SAP group partner functions for specific modules (e.g., customs), specific transaction flows (e.g., import), and specific countries (e.g., Belgium).
3. The partner function groups allow you to define specific system behaviors for a specific group of partners (i.e., certain determination procedures by legal regulation).
4. Assign the partner function to a partner function in the feeder system. Then, set up a one-on-one link between the SAP GTS partner function and the feeder system partner function, as shown in Figure 3.12.

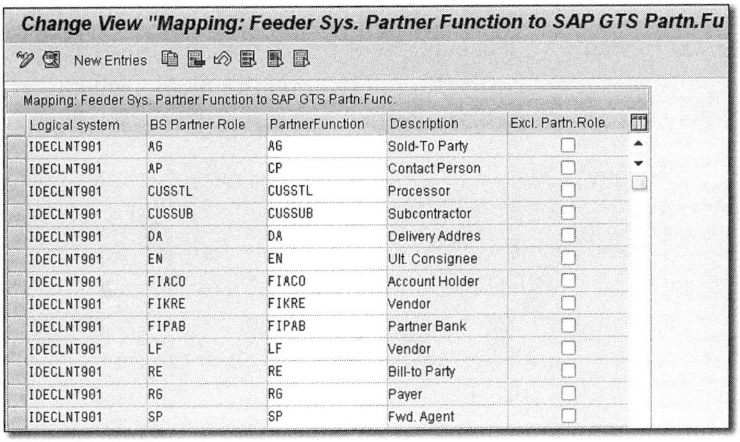

Logical system	BS Partner Role	PartnerFunction	Description	Excl. Partn.Role
IDECLNT901	AG	AG	Sold-To Party	☐
IDECLNT901	AP	CP	Contact Person	☐
IDECLNT901	CUSSTL	CUSSTL	Processor	☐
IDECLNT901	CUSSUB	CUSSUB	Subcontractor	☐
IDECLNT901	DA	DA	Delivery Addres	☐
IDECLNT901	EN	EN	Ult. Consignee	☐
IDECLNT901	FIACO	FIACO	Account Holder	☐
IDECLNT901	FIKRE	FIKRE	Vendor	☐
IDECLNT901	FIPAB	FIPAB	Partner Bank	☐
IDECLNT901	LF	LF	Vendor	☐
IDECLNT901	RE	RE	Bill-to Party	☐
IDECLNT901	RG	RG	Payer	☐
IDECLNT901	SP	SP	Fwd. Agent	☐

Figure 3.12 Mapping of Partner Functions

3.3.4 Number Ranges

Before you can execute any transactions in SAP GTS, you need to define some number ranges to determine how many numbers are used to uniquely define a document in SAP GTS. Number ranges can contain letters, numbers, and the validity year for which they have been set up. For example, consider the number ranges A to ZZZZZZZZZZ and 2014 0200000000 0299999999.

Some other examples are number ranges for business partners, customs products, licenses, vendor declarations, etc. You can perform the setup of these number ranges in Customizing by following this transaction path: Global Trade Services • General Settings • Number Ranges.

3.4 SAP Case Management

SAP Case Management is a component for processing problems, called *incidents*, that require a wide range of information, multiple processors, and/or lengthy resolution. SAP Case Management is a central collection point for information originating from multiples sources. A *case* is a folder that links all relevant information, objects, and parties.

SAP Case Management can be integrated with any SAP GTS Compliance Management block, such as SPL screening.

When a case is created, memoranda for individual activities can be entered, and decisions can be transferred to other employees or supervisors through a pre-defined process route. SAP Case Management allows you to store documents and background information that can support decision making.

Let's consider an example. Say that an analyst needs assistance to release a compliance block. She can create a case for the specific transaction in SAP Case Management. Relevant information and questions to assess the case are described in the case. The next analyst in the decision chain receives the case and can decide whether to release the block for further processing. As soon as a case exists for a process, it cannot be released until the supervisor involved in the case makes a decision. After assessment, the case can be resolved.

Figure 3.13 shows the case management setup in SAP GTS Customizing.

Figure 3.13 Setup of SAP Case Management in Customizing

In SAP Case Management, a defaulting mechanism is available to determine the process route model and respective case type automatically based on defined source fields. For example, when a case is created for the release of an SPL block, the system identifies the right person to handle the block and automatically forwards the case to him or her. Figure 3.14 shows the SAP Case Management defaulting data setup in SAP GTS Customizing.

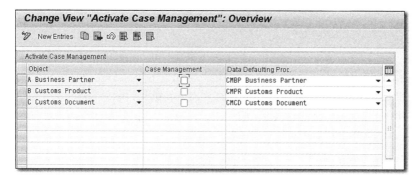

Figure 3.14 SAP Case Management Defaulting Data

Because SAP Case Management shows every step of an incident, such as the release of blocked documents or business partners, you can use it as a reliable tool for regulatory audits or as a decision tool for new business cases.

3.5   Summary

The baseline settings are the foundation of the SAP GTS implementation that allow the subsequent configuration of the SAP GTS functionalities. You need to have a detailed understanding of the global trade requirements and business flows in order to set up a stable and reliable baseline settings structure that can support all the processes of a company.

Now that these main settings have been set up, it's time to set up the relevant master data in SAP GTS, including master data transferred from SAP ERP 6.0 and master data specific to SAP GTS. These topics are discussed in the following chapter.

To identify the applicable rules or print the required legal documentation, you must maintain global trade-specific master data in SAP GTS. Sometimes the data must be transferred from the feeder system; other times master data will be native to SAP GTS. Let's dig deeper.

4   Master Data

Master data is the single source of basic business data that is used across multiple systems, applications, and/or processes. The common use of master data across systems increases efficiency. Therefore, you need to transfer any master data that is maintained in the feeder system to SAP GTS. Some master data is maintained in the feeder system and (partially) transferred to SAP GTS, and some is maintained wholly in SAP GTS. In this way, not all data needs to be transferred on a transactional basis, but can be used directly in SAP GTS for global trade purposes.

In this chapter, we'll first go into detail about the business processes that support the use of master data (Section 4.1), and then discuss the different uses of master data: business partner master data (Section 4.2), product master data (Section 4.3), bill of product master data (Section 4.4), and licenses and authorizations (Section 4.5). Some additional master data will be tackled as well (Section 4.6). The chapter ends with an elaboration on the Customizing steps (Section 4.7) and technical objects (Section 4.8) that need to be set up for master data maintenance in SAP GTS. These topics are relevant when transferring master data from a feeder system to SAP GTS.

4.1   Business Processes

Master data in SAP GTS represents all non-transactional data. It is the basic foundation for all processing in SAP GTS, so it plays an important role in various import and export processes supported by SAP GTS. Master data is information that is created once in a system and can be re-used in each transaction. The data is either transferred from the feeder system (e.g., business partners) or wholly maintained in SAP GTS (e.g., customs offices). The master data that is transferred from the feeder system can be further enhanced in SAP GTS. These enhancements consist of trade-specific data elements like tax ID numbers for business partners or commodity codes for products.

Two topics are relevant for discussion here: the source system of the master data and the initial transfer of the master data from the feeder system to SAP GTS.

4.1.1 Source System

The source or leading system for the master data can be either the feeder system or SAP GTS, as shown in Table 4.1. This means the master data can be set up and maintained in either the feeder system or SAP GTS. We recommend that you maintain master data like business partners and materials in the feeder system and transfer them to SAP GTS. For business partner exceptions and product exceptions, maintain these data in SAP GTS.

> **Note**
>
> A feeder system can be either SAP (ERP 6.0, SCM, SRM, or CRM) or non-SAP.

Source System of Master Data	Feeder System	SAP GTS
Business partners	×	
Business partner exceptions (e.g., customs offices)		×
Materials	×	
Materials exceptions (e.g., classification codes)		×

Table 4.1 Source System of Master Data

Even when the feeder system is the source system for data like business partners and materials, master data should be transfered to SAP GTS as well, so that not all data needs to be transferred on a transactional basis. For example, information that is not frequently updated can be directly copied into customs documents in SAP GTS. Next to this, the transfer of master data enables compliance checks like SPL screening or trade preference calculations for the Risk Management module.

Multiple feeder systems can be connected to one SAP GTS system. In this case, the best practice of maintaining business partners and materials in the feeder system as the source system remains the same.

4.1.2 Initial Transfer from the Feeder System to SAP GTS

In order to maintain the master data of the feeder system also in SAP GTS, you must perform an initial transfer of the master data. Master data of the feeder system is transferred asynchronously (i.e., on a non-transactional basis) to SAP GTS. In order to automate this transfer, data is transmitted via batch jobs. Business partners (such as customers and vendors) and material master records are usually transferred this way because they are data elements that are not frequently updated. However, you *can* set up change pointers in the feeder system to ensure that critical data elements (such as customer addresses) are automatically transferred to SAP GTS when changed.

Before you can transfer master data from the feeder system to SAP GTS, you must define the communication between the two systems. We already covered the technical setup of the communication between the feeder and SAP GTS system in Chapter 2.

Figure 4.1 shows how SAP ERP 6.0 and SAP GTS communicate by transferring data through the plug-in. Note that the figure distinguishes between master data and transactional data. Master data (double arrow) is transferred once to SAP GTS (with updates via change pointers), and only relevant data is retransferred to SAP ERP 6.0. Transactional data is transferred from SAP ERP 6.0 to SAP GTS in a one-way transfer (single arrow). This means that documents (e.g., billing documents) are transferred from SAP ERP 6.0 to SAP GTS on a transactional basis and not retransferred. SAP GTS transactional data, like SPL check results, are then wholly maintained in SAP GTS. They are only shown in SAP ERP 6.0 but not transferred back such that the results can be recalled in SAP ERP 6.0.

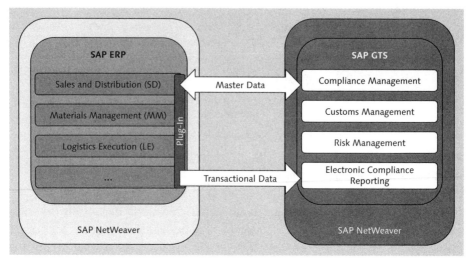

Figure 4.1 Communication between SAP ERP 6.0 and SAP GTS

You must execute the initial transfer of master data from the feeder system to SAP GTS before transactions can occur in SAP GTS. The data transfer from the feeder system to SAP GTS is foreseen by standard SAP. No additional Customizing settings or interfaces are required. Figure 4.2 shows the screen in SAP ERP 6.0 where the initial transfer of master data can be done via Transaction /SAPSLL/ MENU_LEGALR3.

The following initial transfers of master data can be launched via the plug-in:

▶ Transfer vendors

▶ Transfer customers

▶ Transfer contact persons

▶ Transfer applicants

▶ Transfer material masters

▶ Transfer BOMs

▶ Transfer banks

Master data is cross-area, so it can be used for the Compliance Management, Customs Management, and Risk Management modules.

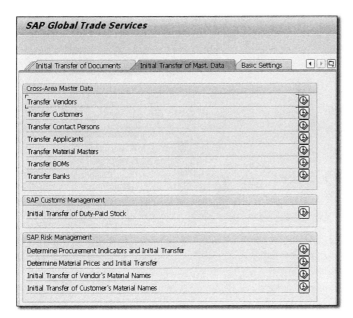

Figure 4.2 Initial Transfer of Master Data from SAPERP 6.0 to SAP GTS

There are also two area-specific transfers:

▶ Transfer of specific data for Risk Management, such as material prices

▶ Transfer of specific data for Customs Management, such as duty-paid stock when implementing a special customs procedure

After you've executed the initial transfer, you need to activate change pointers to ensure that the feeder system and SAP GTS are synched. Change pointers track the changes made to specific master data objects (e.g., material) and flag the new/changed entries. A batch job fetches all the changed entries and transfers all the information from the feeder system to SAP GTS. The change pointers are set up in the SAP GTS menu of SAP ERP 6.0 on the BASIC SETTINGS tab, which you can access via Transaction /SAPSLL/MENU_LEGALR3.

Several master data are maintained in SAP GTS. As you can see in Figure 4.3, a distinction is made among business partners, products, bills of products (BOPs), and licenses/authorizations. We'll look at these types of data next. Recall that some of this data uses SAP ERP 6.0 as the source system, and others use SAP GTS as the source system.

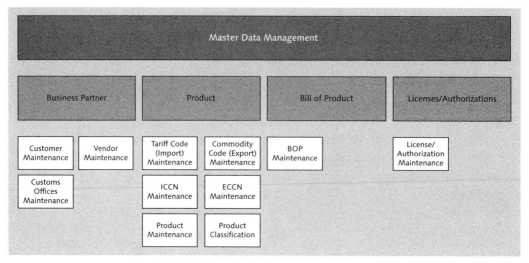

Figure 4.3 Master Data Types

4.2 Business Partner Master Data

The business partners that can be transferred from the feeder system are custom-ers, vendors, and contact persons. Customs offices are master data that are wholly maintained in SAP GTS.

When transferred from the feeder system to SAP GTS, business partners are not assigned to their corresponding account groups (e.g., ship-to party). As men-tioned in Chapter 3, this is done on a transactional basis and requires a prior map-ping between partner functions in the feeder system and the business partner roles in SAP GTS. Because a customer can exist in SAP GTS without a business partner function and the assignment is done on a transactional basis, a customer can, for example, be assigned to a ship-to partner function in one transaction and a payer partner function in another transaction.

When transferred to SAP GTS, business partners are created through different types: persons, organizations, or groups. Each type has different roles assigned to it. For example, a person can be given the role of contact person, and an organi-zation can be given the role of customer or vendor. This type represents the function that a business partner performs for a company. Within the different partner types, you can choose diverse roles. Table 4.2 lists available partner roles in SAP GTS.

Person	Organization	Group
▶ 000000 Business Partner (Gen)	▶ 000000 Business Partner (Gen)	▶ 000000 Business Partner (Gen)
▶ BUP001 Contact Person	▶ BUP002 Prospect	▶ BUP002 Prospect
▶ BUP002 Prospect	▶ BUP004 Organization Unit	▶ FS0000 Financial Services BP
▶ BUP003 Employee	▶ FS0000 Financial Services BP	
▶ BUP005 Internet User	▶ SLLAUT Government Agency	
▶ BUP008 Respons. for Preference	▶ SLLBNK Bank	
▶ FS0000 Financial Services BP	▶ SLLCOF Customs Office	
	▶ SLLCPC Customs Bus. Partner (Cus)	
	▶ SLLCPS Customs Bus. Partner (Ven)	
	▶ SLLDAP Data Provider	
	▶ SLLFTO Foreign Trade Org.	
	▶ SLLFTX FTO for Re-export	
	▶ SLLMGR Admin. Unit of Vend. Decl.	
	▶ SLLSIT Legal Unit	

Table 4.2 Business Partner Types and Roles in SAP GTS

Note

Before you can transfer any business partners to SAP GTS, you must complete the following Customizing activities:

▶ Define number ranges for business partners.

▶ Create and assign partner functions.

▶ Activate business partners for the respective SAP GTS areas.

For more information regarding these steps, refer to the respective chapters within this book.

4.2.1 Customer Maintenance

Data on customers, such as customer name, customer number, customer address, incoterms, shipping conditions, and partner functions, is managed in the customer master record in SAP ERP 6.0. In order to maintain the master data of customers in SAP GTS, you must transfer the following relevant master data from the feeder system to SAP GTS:

▶ Name

▶ Address

▶ VAT number (if relevant)

When customers are transferred from SAP ERP 6.0 to SAP GTS, they are not assigned to a partner function or account group. This means that a customer is set up as a customer and not as a sold-to or ship-to partner. All customer account groups in SAP ERP (e.g., sold-to, ship-to, bill-to, etc.) are mapped to one single business partner role in SAP GTS (e.g., customer).

This is because, in SAP GTS, different partner functions are not distinguished as master data. Mapping of the different partner functions is done on a transactional basis via sales order documents, billing documents, etc. This enables one customer to be a sold-to party in one transaction and a ship-to party in another transaction. In order to be able to assign these different partner functions, prior mapping in SAP ERP 6.0 and SAP GTS needs to be set up.

After the transfer of the customer master data, additional tabs are created in SAP GTS, which can be seen as global trade-specific enrichments of data. An example of such enrichment is the SPL screening status. Whenever a business partner is screened, the result is maintained in the master data of SAP GTS. The status can be blocked or non-blocked and is represented by a flag.

Note that customers do not use the feeder system numbering, but instead receive an internal number within SAP GTS. This is an automated process to ensure the connection of different feeder systems to one single SAP GTS client without incurring overlapping business partners. Both numbers can be displayed in the business partner master records and used as a search term when searching for business partners. Both numbers are displayed in Figure 4.4; here, BUSINESS PARTNER refers to the internal SAP GTS number, and EXTERNAL BP NUMBER refers to the external feeder system business partner number. Before transferring customers, you need to set up number ranges in SAP GTS in order to enable this number assignment.

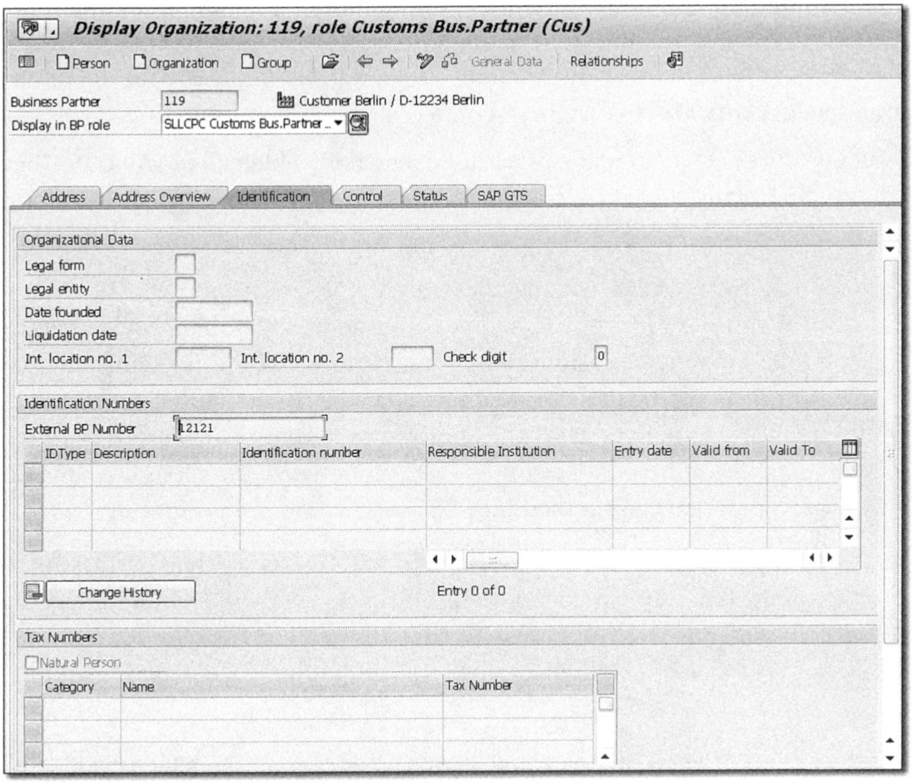

Figure 4.4 Customer Master Data in SAP GTS

4.2.2 Vendor Maintenance

Just like customers, vendors' master data, such as vendor number, name, address, currency used, terms of payment, and tax information, can be maintained in SAP GTS, as well. This data is managed in SAP ERP 6.0 and transferred from the feeder system to SAP GTS. When you transfer this data to SAP GTS, only global trade-relevant information is adopted, including the following:

- Name
- Address
- VAT number (if relevant)

As for customers, vendors are enriched with additional information and given their own internal numbering in SAP GTS after the initial transfer from the feeder system. This enables a company to connect multiple feeder systems to one SAP GTS client.

4.2.3 Customs Offices Maintenance

Customs offices are an example of master data wholly obtained in SAP GTS. They are customs management-specific and, therefore, maintained in the Customs Management module of SAP GTS.

Customs offices are where customs-relevant activities are monitored. The following types of customs offices exist, and you need to mention them when creating a customs declaration: the customs office of departure, exit, destination, and transit. The office of departure, for example, represents the customs authorities where you declare your goods when exporting goods out of the European Union (EU), whereas the office of exit represents the office where the goods leave the EU when you export goods from the EU.

Master data for customs offices are created in SAP GTS as separate business partners. Then, the different types of customs offices are set up in SAP GTS. Mapping between the two happens on a transactional basis so that a customs office can fulfill the role of office of exit in one transaction and office of departure in another transaction.

You can create customs offices manually or upload them using a file provided by government agencies. To create the customs offices manually (via Transaction BP), first create the customs offices as business partners in SAP GTS; then, assign these business partners to the official *customs office numbers* (OFN), each of which represents an external identification number provided by the relevant customs agency. This way, each customs office can be identified in a unique way. For uploading the customs offices, select CUSTOMS MANAGEMENT • MASTER DATA • PARTNERS. Figure 4.5 shows the screen where customs offices are maintained in SAP GTS from the PARTNERS tab.

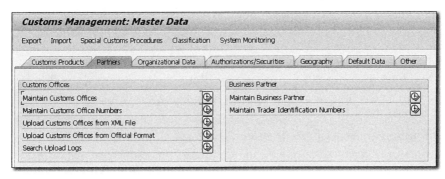

Figure 4.5 Customs Office Maintenance

4.3 Product Master Data

Products are also maintained in SAP GTS; their data consist of tariff and commodity codes, ICCN and ECCN codes, products, and product classification. In order to create customs documents, you need to transfer the data to or obtain it in SAP GTS. Calculations for trade preference or compliance checks are also enabled in this way.

4.3.1 Tariff and Commodity Codes

Tariff and commodity codes are used to place goods into different product categories. *Tariff codes* are used specifically for import processing, whereas *commodity codes* are used for export processing. You'd use these codes when applying the appropriate duties and/or import/export taxes, tracking trade flows, handling quota restrictions, and so on.

The process of assigning a specific code to a product is called *classification*. In this process, you have two options:

▶ **Use SAP GTS as the leading system**
Products are classified in SAP GTS and, after classification, the commodity codes are retransferred to the feeder system when necessary.

▶ **Use the feeder system as the leading system**
Products are classified in the feeder system, and commodity codes are transferred to SAP GTS on a transactional basis. Note that SAP ERP 6.0 has foreseen only one field to store the commodity and/or tariff code.

The best practice is to classify the products in SAP GTS and retransfer the product classifications (commodity codes) to the feeder system, when applicable.

4.3.2   ICCNs and ECCNs

Import control classification numbers (ICCNs) and *export control classification numbers* (ECCNs) represent legal codes that are assigned to different products. ICCN and ECCN codes are used to check products against import and export license control. The classification numbers determine products' license requirements, reporting requirements, record-keeping requirements, and so on. They are commonly used for military products, for example.

You perform the classification via COMPLIANCE MANAGEMENT • CLASSIFICATION/ MASTER DATA. First, manually maintain the classification numbers or upload them from an XML file from a content provider. Then classify the products.

4.3.3   Products

Products are set up and maintained in SAP ERP 6.0. The feeder system can therefore be seen as the leading or source system for product information. Even though SAP ERP 6.0 is the source system, you still need to maintain some information in SAP GTS in order to minimalize the transactional data that needs to be transferred each transaction. Moreover, some additional product master data can be managed in SAP GTS.

Unlike business partners, products keep their feeder system numbering. In combination with the feeder system, a product number uniquely defines a product in SAP GTS, meaning that multiple systems can use the same SAP GTS system. You can then easily display a product by entering the combination of feeder system number and external product number.

Only relevant product master data, as follows, is transferred from the feeder system to SAP GTS and copied into the GENERAL BASIC DATA tab:

▶ Product number

▶ Description and language

▶ Base unit of measurement

- Alternative unit of measure
- Gross weight
- Net weight

After you transfer the product from the feeder system to SAP GTS, additional views are created in SAP GTS. The following tabs host extended product master data, and are shown in Figure 4.6:

- CUSTOMS COMMERCIAL DESCRIPTION: Maintain the commercial description of the product, including in several languages, when necessary for a global trade purpose.
- CLASSIFICATION: Define the assignment of commodity and tariff codes (also see the next chapter on classification).
- LEGAL CONTROL: Define specific product master settings related to specific legal regulations, such as re-export for the US (also see Chapter 6 on Compliance Management). You maintain ICCN/ECCN codes in this tab, as well.
- PREFERENCE: Define settings that support the Trade Preference Management functionality (see Chapter 8 on Risk Management). This screen also shows the result of the trade preference calculations performed for a specific product.
- SPECIAL CUSTOMS PROCEDURES: Define the relevance for use of specific customs procedures, such as bonded warehouse (BWH), inward processing relief (IPR), and outward processing relief (OPR); also see Chapter 7 on Customs Management. Relevance for special customs procedures is a typical example of information that needs to be transferred back from SAP GTS to the feeder system.
- TAX CLASSIFICATION: Define the tax liability of materials used in SAP GTS and find information for calculating import turnover tax.
- AUTHORITIES: Maintain two key details:
  - Product-specific documents and evidence that the system will reuse for customs shipments and customs declarations
  - Codes or rules based on other government agency (OGA) regulations, which are checked during customs processing
- BILL OF PRODUCT: Maintain data concerning bill of products (BOPs), which we'll elaborate on shortly.

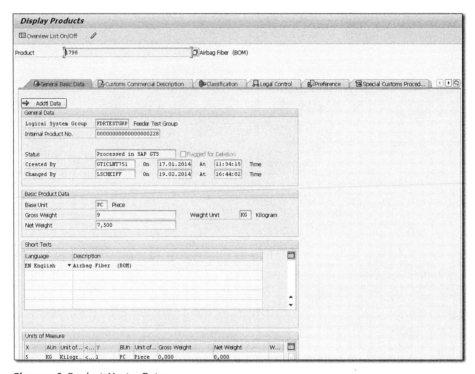

Figure 4.6 Product Master Data

> **Note**
>
> Country of origin is not part of the SAP GTS product master. The country of origin data is retrieved from each transaction (outbound delivery, material document, and invoice) in the feeder system and transferred to SAP GTS on a transactional basis.

4.3.4 Product Classifications

Product classification is the process of assigning a customs code to a product. In order to be able to perform this assignment, you first have to set up the different classification numbers in SAP GTS. For this, two options are available:

▶ Upload the tariff, commodity, and ICCN and ECCN codes using an external data provider (XML file format). The external data provider must be defined as an external business partner.

▶ Maintain the codes manually in the SAP GTS system.

Before you can upload or create the codes, you must first define a numbering scheme in SAP GTS that represents the official structure to follow when creating official customs codes. SAP has pre-defined templates for some countries (e.g., Germany).

For the assignment of the classification code to a product, you can use two different methods:

▶ **Individual classification**
Classify products individually. In this way, you can view all different classifications of a product.

▶ **Classification based on a worklist**
Classify products for one numbering scheme, such as for compliance export classification or customs management HTS numbers. Worklists let you select products that are due for classification based on the various selection options available (e.g., newly transferred to GTS, created by, etc.).

In Figure 4.7, notice the top sections of the screen, where you can manually maintain the ICCN and ECCN codes or upload them via an XML file. The bottom half of the screen distinguishes between classifying a product manually and classifying multiple products at once via a worklist.

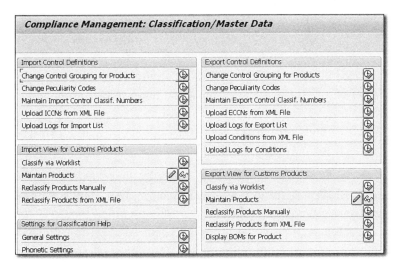

Figure 4.7 Classification of Products in SAP GTS

We'll spend more time on the classification process in the next chapter.

4.4   Bill of Product Master Data

Bills of products contain the components (e.g., raw materials) and quantities of components needed to manufacture a finished product. Bill of product (BOP) is the naming convention given within SAP GTS. In SAP ERP 6.0, that naming convention is BOM. The leading system of the BOMs is SAP ERP 6.0 or any other feeder system that collaborates with SAP GTS.

The BOMs in SAP ERP 6.0 are retained at the plant level. For some global trade purposes, you might be required to transfer the BOMs from the feeder system to SAP GTS.

BOPs are used throughout different SAP GTS functionalities. They are used differently in the Compliance Management, Customs Management, and Risk Management modules. In this section, we'll distinguish between BOPs that are manually maintained in SAP GTS and those that are transferred from the feeder system to SAP GTS.

4.4.1   BOPs Manually Maintained in SAP GTS

You can manually maintain BOPs in SAP GTS for two modules: Compliance Management and Customs Management. The processes for which they are used are ITAR, IPR, and OPR. Though the creation and maintenance of the BOPs is the same for both modules, using them in these modules differs from one to the other. Since not all components of the BOM in SAP ERP 6.0 are relevant for the processes now described in SAP GTS (i.e., ITAR, IPR, and OPR), it doesn't make sense to transfer the entire BOM. Therefore, maintaining the BOP manually in SAP GTS and adding only relevant components, as seen in Figure 4.8, has its benefits. The BOP with ID number 1233452 has two components (nylon and dyed nylon) that are relevant for Compliance Management or Customs Management. Other components are not maintained in SAP GTS.

BOPs in the Compliance Management module are used for ITAR purposes. (ITAR is a regulation for military products!) When products are classified for ITAR, you have to be able to present a license when they are exported. Any time an ITAR component is integrated into a finished product, that finished product also becomes ITAR controlled. For this reason, in SAP GTS, companies can maintain a BOP for the finished product that contains all ITAR-classified components in order to have an overview of which ITAR licenses are required.

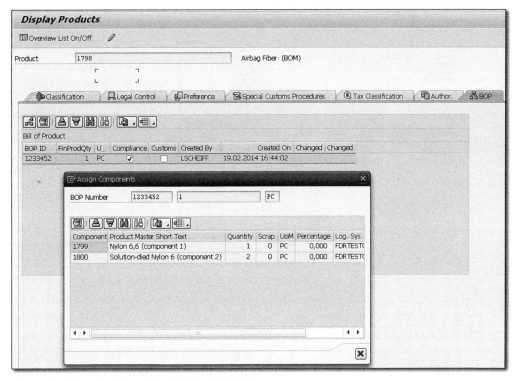

Figure 4.8 Manually Maintaining BOPs in SAP GTS

BOPs in the Customs Management module are used for IPR and OPR. These two special customs procedures will be further explained in Chapter 7. The BOP is used for calculating the (relief of) duties regarding these procedures; because only relevant duty-suspended components are retained, you must manually maintain the BOP in SAP GTS.

4.4.2 BOPs Transferred from SAP ERP 6.0 to SAP GTS

These BOPs are transferred from SAP ERP 6.0 to SAP GTS and are used for Compliance Management and Risk Management processing. Since the complete production BOM of SAP ERP 6.0 is relevant for these SAP GTS calculations, the entire BOM (including all components) is transferred.

Figure 4.9 gives an example of a BOP that was wholly transferred from the feeder system. The product (an almond chocolate bar) and all components (almond powder, liquid chocolate, etc.) are displayed.

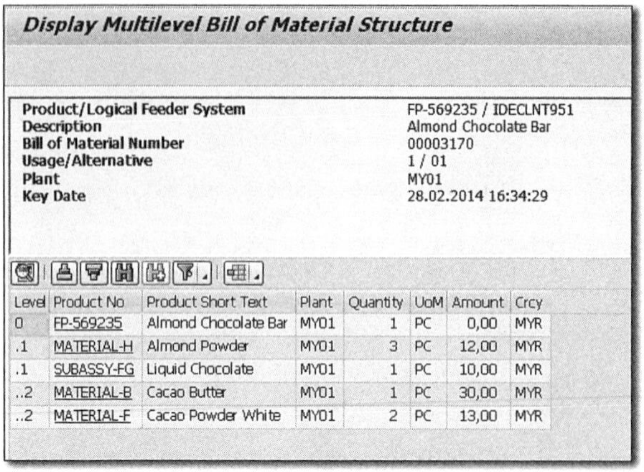

Figure 4.9 Transferred BOP from the Feeder System to SAP GTS

The BOPs that are transferred as a whole from the feeder system to SAP GTS and used for Compliance Management are the BOPs to execute de minimis calculations. These calculations are done to check whether a product consists of US components and needs a license for export. Several rules for this calculation are set up in SAP GTS. In order for you to execute the calculations, all components of a BOP need to be available in SAP GTS and, therefore, the whole BOP is transferred from the feeder system to SAP GTS. More information on de minimis can be found in the Compliance Management chapter.

Bills of products are also used for trade preference calculation in the Risk Management module, which we'll get into later. The trade preference calculation is used to analyze which products can obtain a preferential origin status when a product complies with the preferential rules of origin, foreseen in a free trade agreement. All components of a finished product are thus needed in this calculation, so the complete BOP is transferred from the feeder system to SAP GTS.

4.5 Licenses and Authorizations Master Data

You'll need to maintain different licenses and authorizations in SAP GTS for its three main modules:

▶ For Compliance Management, you may have to maintain licenses for import and export control (e.g., when exporting military products, as shown in Figure 4.10).

▶ For Customs Management, you may need authorizations when operating under a special customs procedure. For example, when a customs warehouse is set up for a company, you need an authorization in order to process these activities.

▶ For Risk Management, you may need a license for restitution. Such a license would allow companies in the European agricultural sector to claim refunds.

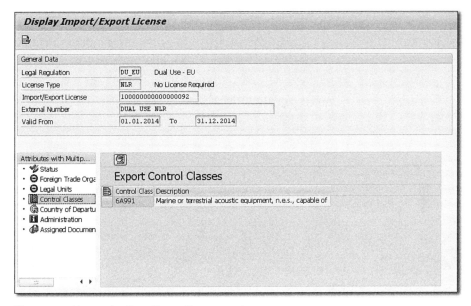

Figure 4.10 License for Compliance Management

4.6   Additional Master Data

Besides business partner master data, products, BOP master data, and licenses/authorizations master data, some additional master data is maintained in SAP GTS. Some of this data can be seen as genuine master data, while some of it can be seen as configurations of settings for global trade transactions.

Let's first consider an example of the first master data group: sanctioned party lists (SPLs). SPLs are maintained manually or uploaded to SAP GTS via an XML file obtained by a content provider in order to screen business partners. Whenever adjustments are made to the list, updated versions can be uploaded, and business partners can be rechecked.

You can see an example of master data set up as configurations in default data for customs purposes and determination strategies for compliance purposes. Default data consist of fields that can be populated automatically in customs declarations according to a predefined logic (defaulting rule), automatic e-mail notifications, and outputs that need to be created each time for a specific country of destination. Define them in SAP GTS in order to facilitate the completion and process automation of customs documents. In this way, for example, goods are always exported by plane by default when the destination is China.

Another example of master data as configuration is maintaining a determination strategy for the licenses that were uploaded and maintained in SAP GTS. Different types of licenses are set up; in order to determine which license type is applicable for which transaction, define a determination strategy. You can maintain this strategy manually or upload it via an XML file.

4.7 Customizing

Customizing for master data is limited because the transfer of master data from the feeder system to SAP GTS is part of the standard functionality offered by SAP. Let's look at a few cases where it may be necessary:

▸ When you are transferring business partners from the feeder system to SAP GTS, it is necessary that the country and postal codes of the feeder system exist in SAP GTS as well. So, the country Customizing must be aligned between SAP ERP 6.0 and SAP GTS for the transfer of master data to be feasible.

▸ When transferring products to SAP GTS, the units of measurement of the feeder system must already exist in SAP GTS and be mapped correctly.

These Customizing steps enable the transfer of master data from the feeder system to SAP GTS. Besides this, you need to establish a mapping between partner functions in the feeder system and those in SAP GTS to enable the mapping of customer-partner functions (e.g., when transactional data like sales documents are transferred to SAP GTS).

4.8   Technical Objects

All master data of the feeder system are transferred to SAP GTS. However, you can define specific criteria to filter or enrich the dataset when transferring to SAP GTS. User exits, which are maintained in the plug-in and are further explained in the chapter about technical objects, enable these filters or enrichments.

For example, when filtering business partners, you decide that only business partners from one specific sales organization may be transferred to SAP GTS, you'd determine user exits in the Customizing settings via Transaction SPRO • Sales and Distribution • Foreign Trade/Customs • SAP Global Trade Services — Plug-In • User Exits for SAP Global Trade Services.

4.9   Summary

This chapter covered how master data—or the single source of basic business data that are used across multiple systems, applications, and/or processes—is handled in SAP GTS. To improve efficiency, it is thus set up in the feeder system and SAP GTS; some of it is maintained in the feeder system and (partially) transferred to SAP GTS, while some of it is wholly maintained in SAP GTS.

We first discussed the business processes that are in place when you are dealing with master data and then explored business partner master data, product master data, BOP master data, licenses and authorizations master data, and additional master data. To end the chapter, we explained Customizing steps and technical objects.

In upcoming chapters, we'll discuss the business processes for Compliance Management (Chapter 6), Customs Management (Chapter 7), and Risk Management (Chapter 8) in detail using specific business scenarios to illustrate the applicable flows or processes. First, though, let's explore further details about classification in Chapter 5.

Classification is the assignment of specific legal codes to products. This chapter explains the different classification codes and the underlying business and system processes.

5   Classification

Classification is a key driver in the different processes within SAP GTS and represents the link between the product master data and the importing and exporting requirements. Classification itself will be the assignment of specific legal codes to products. These codes, among other factors, make a few important determinations:

► Applicable duties when importing goods into a specific country (e.g., the calculation of duties to import pharmaceutical products into the European Union [EU], done in Customs Management)

► Potential permits required to import or export goods into or out of a specific country (e.g., the export of pharmaceutical/military products or ITAR-restricted products from the US, done in Compliance Management)

► Applicable rules for determining the preferential origin of exported goods (e.g., identifying which specific rules need to be applied in the Mercosur agreement to determine whether a product may be exported under a preferential status, done in Risk Management)

Commodity codes follow an internationally recognized standard of names and numbers known as the Harmonized Tariff Code (or Harmonized Tariff Schedule). All 170 member countries adhere to this system, developed and maintained by the World Customs Organization (WCO). The member countries use universal headings and nomenclature for products, yet can independently determine the country-specific rates of duty. Harmonized codes are broadest at the four- and six-digit levels, with country-specific descriptions from the eight-digit level.

Classifications are generally country specific, depending on the importing and exporting country requirements. Classification codes are sometimes determined on a regional basis (e.g., the commodity codes for the EU Member States).

This chapter will discuss in more detail the purpose of product classification and how it is set up in SAP GTS. We first explain the business and system processes of classification in Section 5.1, including uploading classification codes, classification in both Compliance Management and Customs Management, and reclassification. We then consider system setup based on the most important Customizing steps related to product classification.

5.1 Business and System Processes

Every product must be specified with the official customs codes when you submit customs documentation to the authorities.

SAP GTS facilitates this classification process. Before you can assign a classification code to products, you must maintain the master data linked to those classification numbers within SAP GTS. The entire process requires that you maintain the classification numbers before performing the actual SAP GTS classification, as shown in Figure 5.1.

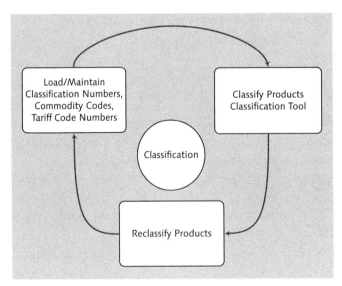

Figure 5.1 Classification Process

Specific transactions will allow users to automatically or manually reclassify products if existing sets of code require updates. The classification codes themselves can be either manually maintained or uploaded based on information from a content provider. You can manually maintain import and export classification numbers via the respective transactions in the COMPLIANCE MANAGEMENT or CUSTOMS MANAGEMENT menus.

5.1.1   Uploading Classification Codes

You can upload all classification numbers and codes through files provided by a third-party content provider in XML format. For this option, you don't need to manually maintain classification codes, meaning that part of the classification process is automated.

Uploading Import/Export Control Classification Numbers

The CLASSIFICATION/MASTER DATA section of the SAP GTS COMPLIANCE MANAGEMENT menu includes two transactions to upload both the import and export control classification numbers (ICCNs and ECCNs) from XML files. Other transactions display summary logs of all codes previously uploaded, as well as detailed information about a specific upload. Before you can upload classification codes, you must define the data provider as a business partner within SAP GTS and define and assign a numbering scheme. We'll go into more detail on the setup of the different prerequisites in Section 5.2.1.

Figure 5.2 shows the selection screen with the different selection parameters (the data provider and number scheme) within the upload transaction.

Certain data fields are mandatory before the upload of ECCNs can be run; you must fill the DATA PROVIDER and NUMBER SCHEME fields before you can activate the local path of the number file in the APPLICATION SERVER section. The path for the text file is optional.

SAP GTS 10.1 features an extra built-in functionality to select the language for the upload. This field allows you to select the language in which text is displayed and entered.

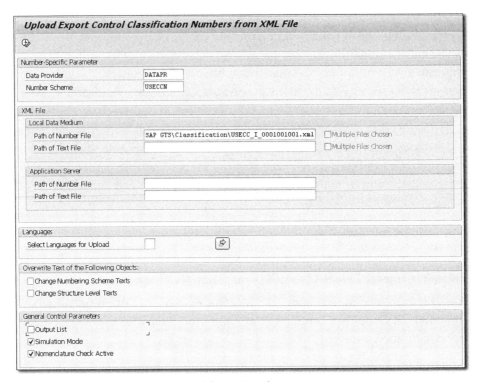

Figure 5.2 Classification Number Upload from XML Files

The OVERWRITE TEXT OF THE FOLLOWING OBJECT section lets you update the text linked to the numbering scheme being updated. If you don't select the CHANGE TEXTS OF NUMBERING SCHEME and CHANGE TEXTS OF STRUCTURE LEVEL options, SAP GTS updates only the actual ECCN numbers provided in the XML file. If you check the first option, the text assigned to each number is updated, as well. The second option overwrites the existing structure elements in the respective numbering scheme.

Once you run the upload, the GENERAL CONTROL PARAMETERS section provides additional functionalities. The OUTPUT LIST flag generates a list of the classification codes included in the XML files prior to performing the actual upload. The list gives an overview of all codes that were uploaded and whether they were successful uploads. The SIMULATION MODE checkbox lets you simulate the upload before actually loading the numbers into SAP GTS. This simulation mode also provides an overview of the upload success. The last functionality, NOMENCLATURE CHECK

ACTIVE, enables checks on the actual name of the file. When you set this indicator, SAP GTS executes version checks and determines whether a file is uploaded in the right sequence, whether it has been fully imported, and so on.

Maintain Import/Export Control Classification Numbers

Beyond uploading classification numbers via XML files, SAP GTS 10.1 enables you to manually maintain and display all classification numbers. You can manually enter or change classification codes per numbering scheme, including relevant categories and classes. SAP GTS does not foresee a change mode to manually created classification numbers, and once you assign it to one or multiple products, you cannot delete it from the numbering scheme, either.

You should not use the Uploading Import/Export Control Classification Numbers transaction together with the manual maintenance of classification numbers within the same numbering scheme. You could disable the ability for future uploads of XML files by adding classification numbers manually.

The same functionality is enabled within the SAP GTS CUSTOMS MANAGEMENT menu for tariff code numbers and commodity codes.

Figure 5.3 represents an overview of the structure after manual maintenance within a given numbering scheme. Category 0 represents all nuclear materials, facilities, and equipment within the EAR legal regulation (enabled by numbering scheme USECC). Within this category, several classes and actual export control classification numbers (ECCNs) apply to further distinguish the export control requirements between different product groups.

Uploading Tariff Code Numbers and Commodity Codes

Uploading tariff code numbers and commodity codes requires the same setup as uploading the import/export control classification numbers. Since these codes are linked to the customs processes, you can find the transaction path in the CUSTOMS MANAGEMENT section of SAP GTS. The two transactions to upload the codes are displayed within the CLASSIFICATION menu in the CLASSIFICATION MASTER DATA tab.

You also have to maintain all the data fields described in the upload transaction within Customs Management in order to upload the customs classification numbers.

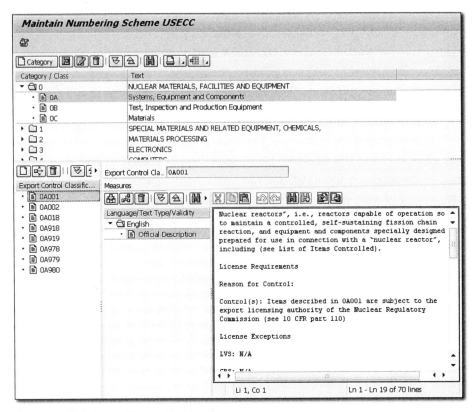

Figure 5.3 Maintaining Classification Numbers

A correct upload of classification master data depends heavily on the information provided by the content provider. The files allow for the addition of footnotes, notes, and keywords to the uploaded codes and numbers. If no files are provided, you can still manually maintain the classification codes and numbers.

5.1.2 Classifying for Compliance Management

You are legally required to report import and export control classification numbers to the authorities when importing or exporting any goods. Classification numbers determine whether a company is eligible to import or export specific products and whether a license is required. After uploading the respective codes, you must assign these codes to the relevant products in the SAP GTS PRODUCT MASTER section.

SAP GTS offers two options for product classification: classifying individual products and generating a to-do worklist to facilitate the classification process. The classification menu in SAP GTS Compliance Management has designated sections for the IMPORT and EXPORT VIEW FOR CUSTOMS PRODUCTS. These sections are subdivided further into the different classification processes, as shown in Figure 5.4.

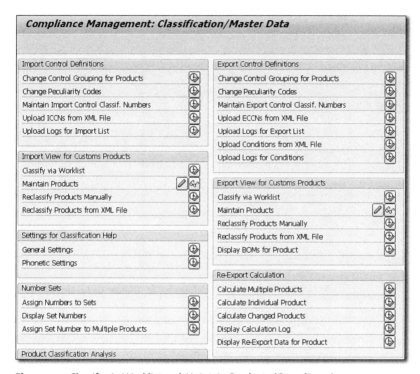

Figure 5.4 Classify via Worklist and Maintain Products (Compliance)

Individual Product Classification

To classify products individually, access the MAINTAIN PRODUCTS transaction in that same section. The transaction lets you search for products based on different filtering criteria (e.g., product number, created on/by, etc.). You can add extra data in the LEGAL CONTROL part of the transaction, where you can also specify the applicable legal regulation along with grouping details, peculiarity code, and so on, as shown in Figure 5.5.

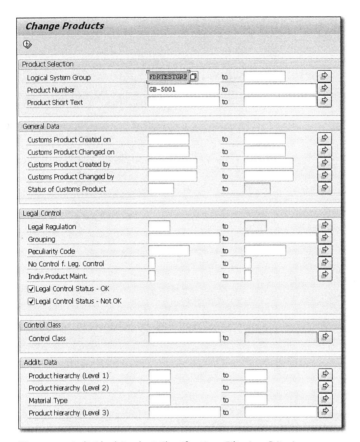

Figure 5.5 Individual Product Classification: Filtering Criteria

You can access a product's master data by selecting that product to be classified. In the LEGAL CONTROL tab of the product master (Figure 5.6), select the desired legal regulation and classify it by using the "Find" functionality (binoculars icon). A list of classification numbers is generated based on the upload or manual maintenance, as described earlier, allowing you to browse through all numbers in the system and select the desired ones. After you save the product master, the product adopts the classification number for the specific legal regulation.

If you don't need a classification, you can set the NO CONTROL flag to indicate that the product-legal regulation match does not require a specific classification code, and a search for further details during the screening process is ignored.

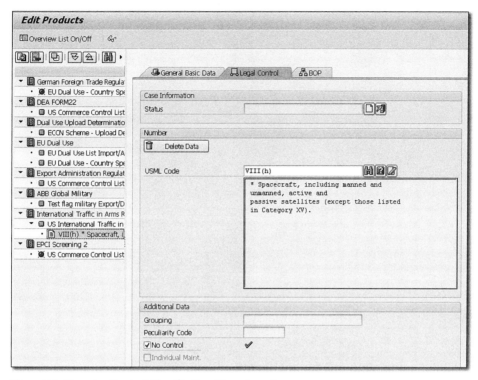

Figure 5.6 Changing Product Classification (Compliance)

Classification Using the Worklist

Classifying via worklist facilitates the creation of a list with all products that still have to be classified for a legal regulation within SAP GTS. You can specify general criteria, such as import/export and the legal regulation, as well as product-specific criteria, shown in the first two sections of Figure 5.7.

After you generate the worklist (displayed in Figure 5.8), there are two options for further classifying the remaining products in SAP GTS:

▶ Select the products and classify each one individually in each product master.

▶ Select the CLASSIFY MULTIPLE PRODUCTS option, and all selected products are classified for a single selected classification code within the same legal regulation. This last option is called the *mass classification process*.

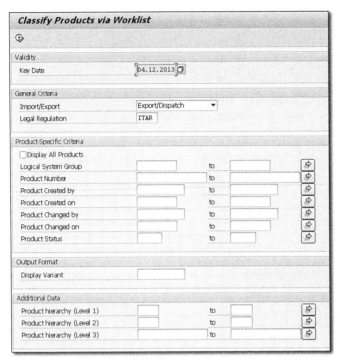

Figure 5.7 Worklist Classification: Filtering Criteria

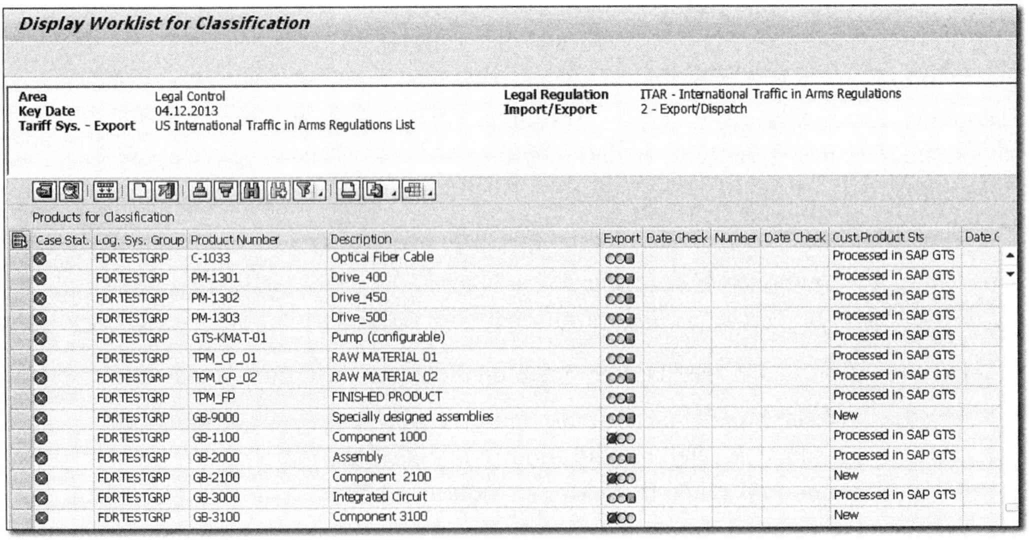

Figure 5.8 Displaying Products for Classification

5.1.3   Classifying for Customs Management

Specific legal requirements, trade security measures, and duty tariffs apply to products as they cross borders. Legal implications and duty applications are supported by a coding system that controls import and export processes. Products are linked to classification codes for customs purposes, such as statistical reporting, customs declarations, duty calculations, preferential treatment, and others.

Just as in Compliance Management, SAP GTS offers two options for classifying products from the CLASSIFICATION menu within Customs Management in Figure 5.9: individual or mass classification via worklist.

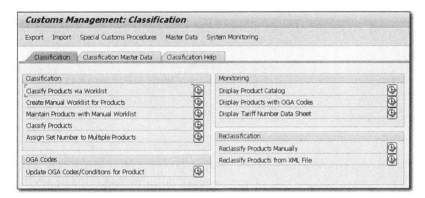

Figure 5.9 Classify Products via Worklist and Classify Products (Customs)

Individual Product Classification

You can classify products on an individual basis, similarly to the classification process described in the Compliance Management section. By accessing the Classify Products transaction, you can again select specific products before classifying them. Detailed classification is possible by specifying the legal regulation for which the product must be classified. Within the product master, you can specify the numbering scheme for which the product must be classified.

Classification using the Worklist

The classification process via a worklist is identical to the classification process described in the Compliance Management section of this chapter. The same functionalities, such as mass classification, are available in SAP GTS in the Customs Management module.

5.1.4 Reclassifying Products

You can re-classify products for the following reasons:

▶ Incorrect classification of a product

▶ Periodic reclassifications due to regulatory changes

Product reclassification is an additional tool to help you address classification numbers already maintained in SAP GTS that are subject to change. A few reclassification transactions in SAP GTS are available for these classification numbers or codes:

▶ In the Compliance Management module:
  ▪ Import control classification number
  ▪ Export control classification number
▶ In the Customs Management module:
  ▪ Tariff code numbers
  ▪ Commodity codes

Whenever a reclassification transaction is triggered for one of these, SAP GTS updates all product classifications linked to the changed numbers/codes within the respective number scheme. Content providers often provide updated XML files whenever the authorities make a regulatory change. A similar transaction exists to manually reclassify products.

One advantage of SAP GTS is that historical classification data is kept for a user-specified validity period.

5.2 Customizing

Before you can upload import and export classification numbers or classify products within any legal regulation, you need to set up a few system configurations. This allows different numbering schemes uploaded by content providers to function within SAP GTS. You can optionally set control procedures for text to enable classification.

5.2.1 Setting up Numbering Schemes

Different numbering schemes define the structure of the numbers and codes provided. You can set up numbering schemes for all classification-related master data: import/export control classification numbers, commodity codes, and tariff code numbers.

The setup for these numbering schemes is located in the GLOBAL TRADE SERVICES node of the IMG of SAP GTS, which is where you'll find the required transactions under GENERAL SETTINGS • NUMBERING SCHEMES.

The setup process is always twofold. First, you define the numbering schemes for the codes or numbers in question. After assigning numbering schemes to the legal regulations, you define the control setting for classification help. In SAP GTS 10.1, the assignment steps are bundled into one transaction in which all numbering schemes are configured.

Since most numbering schemes (aside from some sub-settings) are defined similarly, we'll offer only a tariff code number example here. This is usually the most complex numbering scheme to set up.

Defining Numbering Scheme (for Tariff Code Numbers)

In this IMG activity, you choose the numbering scheme and structure for tariff code numbers. For each numbering scheme related to tariff codes, you must determine the structure of the export/import list, unit of measurement systems, measure types, coding schemes, maintenance of customs products, and end use. These are shown in the list on the left of Figure 5.10.

In the STRUCTURE OF TARIFF CODE NUMBERS section, you determine the length of the different levels in the numbering scheme. This length is determined based on the legal regulation for which the structure is set up. A numbering scheme in SAP GTS must consist of at least two levels. This structure determines the format of the XML files for uploading classification numbers or the format for manually maintaining the same set of classification numbers. Figure 5.10 shows an example of a numbering scheme structure from chapter through HTS code.

In the UNIT OF MEASUREMENT SYSTEM section, you can assign the unit of measurement system defined. Through this definition, along with the assignment, you determine which units of measurement to communicate to the customs authorities.

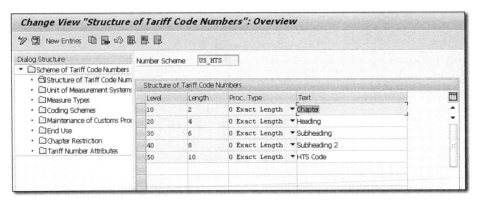

Figure 5.10 Numbering Scheme Structure

In the CODING SCHEMES section, assign any additional codes that are usually provided by national authorities or other governmental agencies. Indicate where these were defined earlier by the reference type.

In the MAINTENANCE OF CUSTOMS PRODUCT section, indicate whether there is a date dependency for a specific classification. This way, you can make the validity time-dependent, configuring different numbering schemes for different lengths of time. Set the validity start date to activate the data in a numbering scheme starting at a specific time, which lets you change the data provider, among other things.

Another option is to add end uses to numbering schemes for tariff code numbers. When end uses are maintained, you can classify a product in one numbering scheme for different codes depending on the end use of that specific product. Before you can assign the end use to a numbering scheme, you first need to define the END USES FOR NUMBERING SCHEMES FOR TARIFF CODE NUMBERS.

Assigning Numbering Schemes to Legal Regulations of the Application Areas

You must link a numbering scheme to the relevant legal regulation to define which set of classification codes can be used per given regulation or country. In the example in Figure 5.11, tariff codes are assigned to the legal regulation created for CUSTOMS PROCESSING.

Change View "Assign Scheme for Tariff Code Numbers": Overview

New Entries

Dialog Structure
- ☐ Assign Scheme for ICCNs
- ☐ Assign Scheme for ECCNs
- ☐ Assign Scheme for Numbers in Legal Control
- ☐ Assign Scheme for Commodity Codes
- ☐ Assign Scheme for Tariff Code Numbers
- ☐ Assign Scheme for FDA Classification
- ☐ Assign Scheme for Excise Duty Codes
- ☐ Assign Scheme for Numbers in CAP License
- ☐ Assign Scheme for Restitution

Assign Scheme for Tariff Code Numbers

Legal Regulation		Valid from	Scheme for Import	
ACE Customs Processing - US Automated Customs E…	▼	01.10.2007	US_HTS1 Harmonized Tarif	▼
ATLAS Customs Processing - Germany (ATLAS)	▼	01.10.2007	DEEZT Electronic Custo…	▼
CUSAT Customs Processing - Austria (eZoll)	▼	01.10.2007	EU_TARIC Integrated Ta…	▼
CUSAU Customs Processing - Australia	▼	09.07.2013	MY_HTS10 Malaysia - Ha…	▼
CUSBE Customs Processing - Belgium	▼	01.10.2007	EU_TARIC Integrated Ta…	▼
CUSCH Customs Processing - Switzerland	▼	01.01.2008	CH_IMP Swiss Import Co…	▼
CUSCN Customs Processing - China	▼	09.07.2013	CN_HTS Chinese - Harmo…	▼
CUSDK Customs Processing - Denmark	▼	01.10.2007	EU_TARIC Integrated Ta…	▼
CUSFR Customs Processing - France	▼	01.10.2007	EU_TARIC1 Integrated T…	▼
CUSGB Customs Processing - Great Britain	▼	01.10.2007	EU_TARIC Integrated Ta…	▼
CUSIN Customs Processing - India	▼	09.07.2013	MY_HTS10 Malaysia - Ha…	▼
CUSJP Customs Processing - Japan	▼	09.07.2013	MY_HTS10 Malaysia - Ha…	▼
CUSKR Customs Processing - Korea	▼	09.07.2013	MY_HTS10 Malaysia - Ha…	▼
CUSMY Customs Processing - Malaysia	▼	09.07.2013	MY_HTS Malaysia - Harm…	▼
CUSNL Customs Processing - Netherlands	▼	01.10.2007	EU_TARIC Integrated Ta…	▼
CUSNZ Customs Processing - New Zealand	▼	01.01.2008	NZ_WTON Tariff Code - …	▼
USISF US Pre-Declarations (ISF)	▼	01.01.2007	US_HTS Harmonized Tari…	▼

Figure 5.11 Assigning Numbering Schemes for Tariff Code Numbers to Relevant Legal Regulations

Defining Numbering Scheme and Structure of Number Set

This IMG activity allows you to use one number set for different existing numbering schemes. You can classify products for a specified number set, meaning the products can be classified for multiple countries at once or multiple application areas at once (e.g., for both the compliance and customs modules within SAP GTS). You must define both the numbering scheme for this number set and the number set must be defined. Further details are managed by assigning existing numbering schemes to the defined number sets.

Assigning Numbering Schemes to Set Schema for Classification

This subsequent IMG activity is needed to complete the use of number sets. You can choose to which numbering schemes the defined number sets should be linked and which of the assigned schemes serve as the reference numbering scheme. The reference scheme is determined by applying the 01 – TRANSFER OF NUMBER TO SET label. The reference numbering scheme must have the same structure as the number set.

5.2.2 Setting Up Classification Help

Setting up Classification Help allows you to classify products easily and correctly. Classification Help is based on text comparison and assigns customs codes to products depending on the text in the description of a specific product. You must set up this text comparison in the relevant IMG activities, and you can enable it for both import and export control numbers, as well as tariff and commodity codes.

SAP GTS 10.1 offers a standard setup of the following text comparison procedures:

▸ DEALT: Control Procedure Product Classification Help—Export List Numbers DE

▸ DEEZT: Control Procedure Product Classification Help—Import List Numbers DE

▸ DESTA: Control Procedure Product Classification Help—Commodity Codes DE

▸ NLSTA: Control Procedure for Commodity Code Classification Help NL

▸ USECT: Control Procedure Product Classification Help—Export Control Class Numbers US

Defining Control Procedures for Text Comparison

After you set the control procedures, you can enable text comparison by entering a control procedure name and description, then linking a specific language for which SAP GTS should compare against. You can also add a phonetic search option as necessary.

Assigning Control Procedures for Text Comparison to Import/Export Lists

After you've created the comparison procedures, you must assign the different procedures to the correct numbering schemes before Classification Help is activated. You can assign different comparison procedures to numbering schemes based on the language of the text.

The standard configuration is as follows:

Comp. proc. DEALT is assigned to numbering scheme DEALN
Comp. proc. DEALT is assigned to numbering scheme USECC

Assigning Control Procedures for Text Comparison to Commodity Codes/ Tariff Numbers

The setup in this IMG activity relates to the text comparison for commodity codes/tariff numbers.

Standard configuration for both commodity codes as tariff codes numbers is established as follows: *Comp. proc DEEZT is assigned to numbering scheme DEEZT.*

5.3 Summary

This chapter focused on classification, or the task of assigning specific legal codes to products. Products must be classified so that customs documentation can include whether any duties apply to imported goods, any permits are required for import or export, and any rules apply that will determine preferential origin of exported goods.

SAP GTS accommodates these legal requirements by enabling you to upload classification codes and set them up in the system, classify them in both Compliance Management and Customs Management, and, finally, reclassify them as necessary. This chapter also documented Customizing steps for configuring the classification settings within SAP GTS.

The following chapters cover the three main modules of SAP GTS. All of these modules are strongly impacted by the topics explained in Chapter 4 on master data and Chapter 5 on classification:

▸ SAP GTS Compliance Management: Transactions relevant for import and export control will be screened by SAP GTS by the master data and classification tied to it.

▸ SAP GTS Customs Management: Import and export declarations in SAP GTS are constructed out of all master data and classification elements required to correctly declare transactions.

▸ SAP GTS Risk Management: The calculation of preferential eligibility relies on the classification of the finished product and its components.

Let's begin with Compliance Management!

Companies face increased pressure from export and import control regulations, and violating these regulations can result in major fines and penalties. The SAP GTS Compliance Management module helps companies remain compliant when trading under complex and continuously evolving international trade regulations.

6 Compliance Management

In today's global environment, the significance of distance trade barriers has diminished. More and more organizations maintain a global supply and sourcing strategy by shipping and procuring products and services to and from numerous customers and vendors.

As a result of the increased activities in global trade, international regulations evolve. One of the major trends in international trade is the increase of rules and export controls imposed by governments to control and monitor movements and transfers of certain goods, software and technology. These export controls prevent exporting and importing goods without the proper authorizations or to prohibited destinations. By implementing these controls, governments may protect their countries' interests, prevent the unwanted use of sensitive goods, and more.

Throughout this chapter, we'll elaborate on the different functionalities of SAP GTS Compliance Management (Sanctioned Party List Screening, Embargo, and Legal Control). For each functionality, we'll make a distinction between the business process and the system process. First, the business process explains the steps and events a company generally goes through in the applicable compliance process; then, the system process links the steps and events from the business case to the activities performed in SAP GTS to support the process. We'll explain both processes using an applied business case scenario. Finally, we'll cover the relevant master data and Customizing steps required in each compliance functionality.

Figure 6.1 displays the SAP GTS cockpit, from which the Compliance Management functionalities may be accessed. This chapter offers a high-level overview of the functionality of each of these main processes.

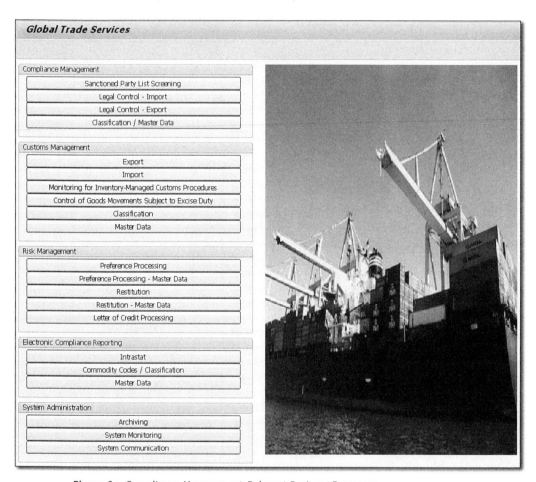

Figure 6.1 Compliance Management-Relevant Business Processes

▶ **Sanctioned party list (SPL) screening (Section 6.2)**
You can manage the screening of business partners against government-sanctioned parties using this functionality. The screening process covers customers, logistics partners, employees, and financial institutions. Processing options, such as the blocking and releasing of business partners, are available, as well as detailed information to analyze the reasons of a block or release.

▶ **Embargo (Section 6.3)**

The embargo functionalities are embedded within the LEGAL CONTROL–IMPORT and LEGAL CONTROL–EXPORT buttons in Figure 6.1. From this functionality, you can monitor, release, and analyze shipments to business partners situated in embargoed countries.

▶ **Legal control (Section 6.4)**

The legal control aspects applicable to inbound and outbound processes may be managed in LEGAL CONTROL–IMPORT and LEGAL CONTROL–EXPORT, which include all transactions to manage and automate the required license assignments.

Additionally, the legal control outbound process includes US re-export. To track and manage licenses for US-controlled products, a product's US content needs to be calculated and, if applicable, foreseen of an appropriate license.

Further, SAP GTS provides menu options for classification and master data, which is where components may be classified for both import and export purposes. Every material that is relevant for Legal Control processes needs to be classified. Master data relevant for SPL screening is included in a designated tab accessed via COMPLIANCE MANAGEMENT • SANCTIONED PARTY LIST SCREENING • MASTER DATA.

Note

We won't elaborate extensively on classification and master data for Compliance Management in this chapter. For a more detailed overview, refer to Chapter 5.

Beta's Global Trade Requirements

Using a fictitious company, Beta, this chapter on Compliance Management will take you through the main business processes that are supported by SAP GTS Compliance Management. This chapter demonstrates how the relevant government authorities control imports and exports of certain sensitive items in most jurisdictions.

Beta, a company in the aerospace and defense industry, is an independent subsidiary of an international manufacturing company. Beta produces various turbine engines used in multiple aircrafts and tanks. The significant content provider for several aircrafts has its European headquarters in Belgium, where various production activities take place.

Figure 6.2 illustrates the business case. The business case, which is the backbone of this chapter, captures the following import/export transactions, which are discussed further in Section 6.4:

1. The Belgian subsidiary temporarily exports aerospace military products (aircraft engine parts) and gas turbine engine components to a US vendor (Vendor A) and re-imports them in order to perform manufacturing operations on them. The business process in Section 6.4.1 approaches the legal control checks from the US vendor's point of view (import into United States).

2. Subsequently, both products are incorporated in the manufacturing process, and an aircraft engine is produced in Belgium. This engine is exported to Customer W in Qatar. Section 6.4.2 explains the export business process from Belgium to Qatar.

3. Assemblies and integrated circuits (with US content) are similarly exported to Customer X in Brazil, addressed in Section 6.4.3.

Furthermore, Beta receives an order for one of its products from Customer Y based in Malaysia. This flow illustrates a restriction on a specific organization in Malaysia, imposed by the national government (Section 6.2) because the screening of the Malaysian business partner against sanctioned party lists results in a block imposed on that customer.

When attempting to sell products to Customer Z in Syria, the sales representative in Belgium encounters an embargo hit (Section 6.3). This section illustrates a destination restriction on Syria.

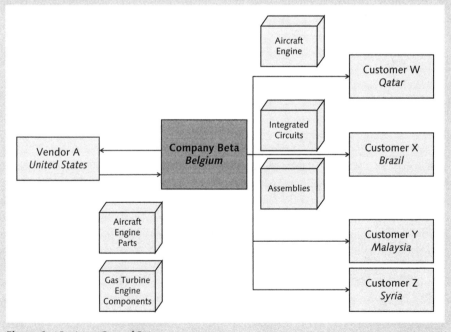

Figure 6.2 Business Case of Beta

6.1 Customs Documents

Upon creation of certain feeder system documents, mirror documents called *customs documents* are created in SAP GTS. SAP GTS checks are immediately performed upon creation and transfer of the feeder system document to SAP GTS.

Depending on the feeder system document, a distinction between inbound and outbound documents may be made. The SAP GTS customs documents for inbound processes (e.g., purchase orders) are created within LEGAL CONTROL–IMPORT. On the other hand, customs documents corresponding to an outbound process (e.g., sales orders) are created within LEGAL CONTROL–EXPORT.

Customs documents in SAP GTS contain information at the header and item levels, as displayed in Figure 6.3. The header level applies to the entire document, including the organizational data, business partners, values, etc. Information regarding the specific items in the document is found on the item level. This includes general data, classification information, and item values.

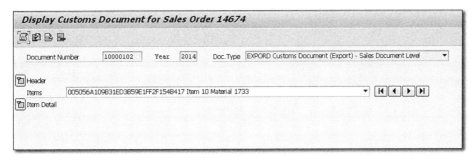

Figure 6.3 SAP GTS Customs Document

The SAP GTS customs document contains an overall processing status, as well as an individual status of each screening process for which the document may be blocked. Figure 6.4 displays the customs document STATUS tab on the header level. A status check is available for the following Compliance Management processes:

- SPL screening
- Embargo
- Legal control
- Hazardous substance check

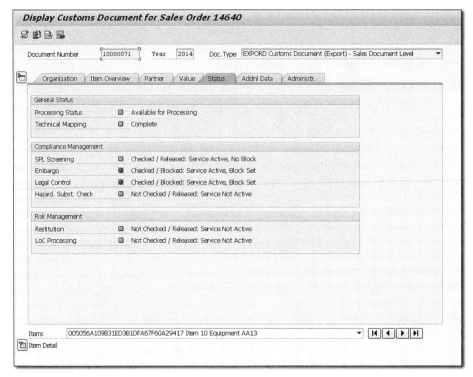

Figure 6.4 Customs Document Status Overview

In order to reflect the latest information, the customs document is updated instantly each time the corresponding SAP feeder system document undergoes a change and is saved. In this way, an automatic recheck of the SAP GTS functionalities is performed.

In the next three sections, we'll elaborate on each SAP GTS Compliance Management functionality. Section 6.2 covers the SPL screening functionality, preventing companies from dealing with unlawful business partners.

6.2   Sanctioned Party List Screening

In today's global environment, it takes just a few clicks to create sales orders and fulfill shipments crossing international borders. As a result, the risk of dealing with parties and entities named on government agency or country-specific denied party lists has increased steadily over the last decade.

The sanctioned party list screening functionality in SAP GTS screens parties involved in a company's export, import, domestic, and payment transactions in order to minimize compliance risks with the regulatory requirements across applicable jurisdictions.

There may be strict prohibitions or export authorization requirements when engaging with prospective transactions and entities on a restricted or denied party list, which requires additional due diligence. For example, the United Nations and supranational government agencies issue denied party lists (or boycott lists). These lists are generally provided by, and may be procured from, external content service providers.

Similarly, national governments may restrict persons, organizations, groups, and entities by designating them as sanctioned or restricted parties. Such denials or restrictions can be imposed if it is established that a specific party has violated national export control regulations or is involved in weapons proliferation or activities that threaten national security and/or foreign policy concerns.

Before engaging in any business, the company must establish whether the potential recipients of items, including any intermediaries involved in the transaction, are included in any SPL under the applicable country-specific regulatory requirements.

Some nations may publish specific lists of denied parties, restricted entities, or other similar persons to whom transactions are denied or restricted, but many nations do not. In either case, it is the responsibility of the company or other applicable legal entity to verify whether the ultimate consignee (e.g., customer or end user), freight forwarder, banks issuing letters of credit or financing transactions, or any other entity involved in a potential transaction, appear on any denied- or restricted parties lists. If so, it may be necessary to refuse shipment of items or the transfer of technology to that person or entity. This process is hereafter referred to as *sanctioned party list (SPL) screening*.

SPL functionality in SAP GTS can achieve the following:

- ▶ Automate SPL checks in international or domestic trade, eliminating manual efforts
- ▶ Increase transparency of supply chain transactions and associated parties to prospective transactions for audit purposes
- ▶ Minimize compliance risks with international trade regulations
- ▶ Potentially serve as a mitigating factor in penalty scenarios

Let's apply SPL screening to our business case.

6.2.1 Business Process

Belgian company Beta receives an order for one of its products from a customer, Freelance Aviation Corporation, based in Malaysia. At the time of order placement, Beta is obligated to screen all parties involved in the transaction against the applicable jurisdictions' denied party lists.

Figure 6.5 indicates what Beta's export process looks like. Multiple business partners are involved, including Freelance Aviation Corporation, the carrier who will transport the shipment overseas, and a forwarding agent who will ship the products from the port to the end customer. All partners involved in the transaction must be screened. Furthermore, if any of the partners change (e.g., there is a change of carrier), the new partner needs to be checked, as well.

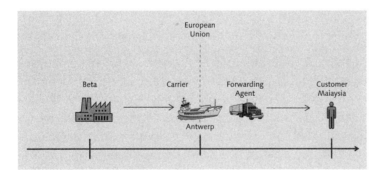

Figure 6.5 Export Screening Business Process

Beta can either perform the screening process themselves or outsource the screening process to a third party—but if it chooses the latter, it still remains ultimately responsible not to be involved in trading with denied parties.

Because manually screening business partners would be a highly time-consuming task that is also prone to errors, Beta decides to use SAP GTS to automate this screening process.

6.2.2 System Process

From a system process perspective, SPL screening in SAP GTS can occur at several different points:

▸ Creation of a business partner (e.g., vendor, customer, bank)

▸ Changes to a business partner

▸ Changes to government agency-specific lists when changes are uploaded (delta files)

▸ Transactions (e.g., sales orders, purchase orders, quotes, or deliveries)

All relevant business partner types are subjected to SPL screening in SAP GTS to ensure that they are eligible for prospective business transactions. Domestic business transactions can be included in or excluded from SPL screening.

Business partners are screened either synchronously when they are created or transferred from the feeder system to SAP GTS or asynchronously via a manual trigger or batch job. Names and addresses of business partners in documents are screened only if they have been manually modified. Otherwise, the result of the previous screening for each business partner (status check) is used to determine whether a document should be blocked.

Figure 6.6 links the SPL screening business to the system process applied in SAP GTS. Beta chose to screen all business partners named in the feeder system document at all times, including at quotation creation, sales order, outbound delivery, and billing document.

Note, however, that the screening may take place for import scenarios, as well (e.g., against partners in a purchase order).

SAP GTS performs an automatic check of all the business partners in the feeder system document. The system screens the business partners one by one against the SPL list entries present in SAP GTS, as displayed in Figure 6.7. You can upload these lists as master data, and this upload is addressed in Section 6.2.4.

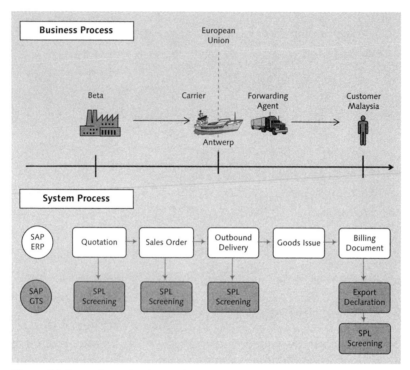

Figure 6.6 Export Screening System Process

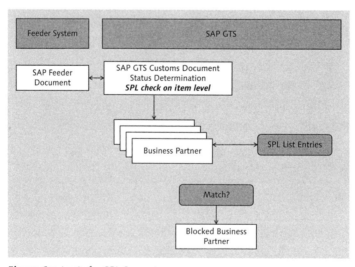

Figure 6.7 Logic for SPL Screening

If a match is detected, meaning that the business partner appears on a denied list, the system blocks the business partner. You can configure the system to block the feeder system document and prevent any further transactions until action is taken in SAP GTS.

Prior to the actual screening, the business partner master data could be transferred from the feeder system to SAP GTS and screened. An SPL status is assigned to every SAP GTS business partner, and the partners maintained in a document undergo only new screening (versus a status check) if the address is changed within the document.

As soon as the sales order is created in Beta's feeder system, it is transferred to SAP GTS. Then the sales order is checked against the legal regulations for SPL screening. In this instance, Freelance Aviation Corporation results in a hit in the EU sanctioned party lists, and the pop-up window in Figure 6.8 appears.

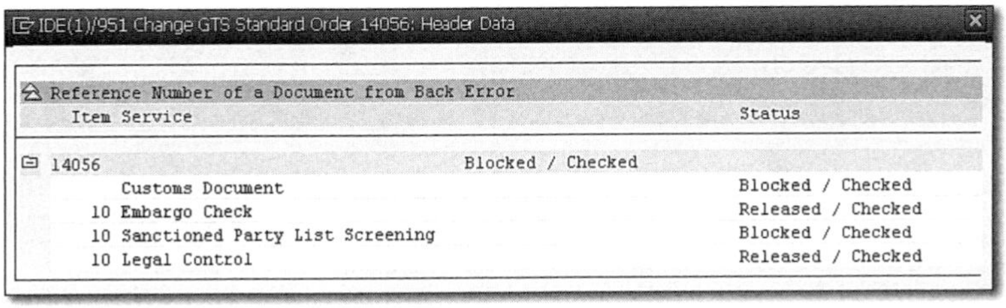

```
IDE(1)/951 Change GTS Standard Order 14056: Header Data                    X

  Reference Number of a Document from Back Error
      Item Service                                            Status

  14056                               Blocked / Checked
          Customs Document                          Blocked / Checked
       10 Embargo Check                             Released / Checked
       10 Sanctioned Party List Screening           Blocked / Checked
       10 Legal Control                             Released / Checked
```

Figure 6.8 SPL Block in the Feeder System

As a result, the order cannot be processed due to an SPL compliance check, and a block is placed on the ongoing activities (e.g., creating the outbound delivery). The shipping operator attempting to create the outbound delivery receives an error message stating that the order cannot be delivered due to an SAP GTS block.

The responsible person within Beta monitors the status of the blocked business partner and relevant blocked documents in SAP GTS. Trade compliance personnel may display the SAP GTS log and process (i.e., analyze, release, and confirm) the block in SAP GTS.

Figure 6.9 displays the log for the sales order created by Beta. Each partner function (e.g., sold-to, ship-to, payer, etc.) is screened against sanctioned party lists. Since Freelance Aviation Corporation (business partner number 353 in this example) has been identified as an entry on these lists, the customs document is blocked for further processing.

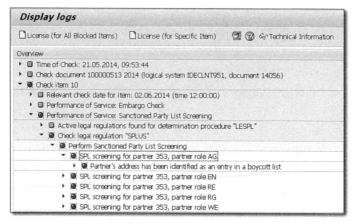

Figure 6.9 Customs Document Log

With SAP GTS, you can configure the system to notify the responsible department via automatic e-mail when an SPL block occurs. In the BLOCKED BUSINESS PARTNER and BLOCKED DOCUMENT MONITORING sections in SAP GTS, several options are available to process the screening outcome.

Figure 6.10 displays the blocked Malaysian business partner as a result of the SPL screening, accessed via COMPLIANCE MANAGEMENT • SANCTIONED PARTY LIST SCREENING • DISPLAY BLOCKED BUSINESS PARTNER.

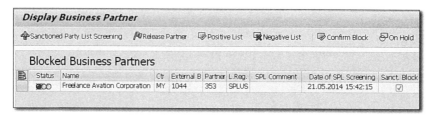

Figure 6.10 Business Partners Blocked for SPL Screening

The top section lists the different options available to process the screening outcome:

▶ **Sanctioned party list screening**
Re-screening the business partner or document gives insight into the actual match rate between the generated SPL terms and address terms.

▶ **Release partner**
When a business partner is released, SAP GTS will not block this partner again

in future transactions unless there is a change to the business partner or a relevant change of the SPL list triggers a new block on the business partner.

► **Positive/negative list**

A business partner can be put on a positive or negative list. These partners are excluded from further checks and will keep that same status until a re-screening of that list is performed. The positive list indicates that the business partner is always released; the negative list indicates that the business partner is always blocked.

► **Confirm block**

This option may be used if a hit can be confirmed or identified as a true SPL match. Further processing of the document in the feeder system is not possible.

► **On hold**

If the person handling the release needs more time or further details to decide whether to release or confirm the block status, the business partner may be temporarily be put on hold.

To further analyze the actual SPL block, click the aforementioned Sanctioned Party List Screening button. Figure 6.11 displays the entry on the government's SPL list that Freelance Aviation Corporation was identified against.

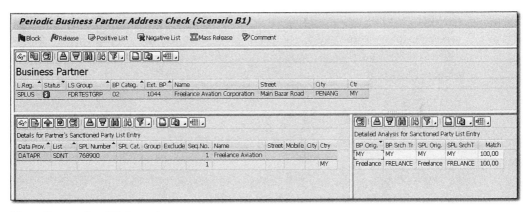

Figure 6.11 Analyze SPL Screening

Additional processing options, such as adding comments in order to detail the analysis results or pass on information to the group handling the worklist of a blocked business partner, are available.

Further processing options may be available for the customs document, as well. Beta may view its blocked documents, and release a particular document, while postponing the decision about the blocked business partner by selecting COMPLIANCE MANAGEMENT • SANCTIONED PARTY LIST SCREENING • MANUALLY RELEASE BLOCKED DOCUMENTS.

The release procedure can be managed in different ways. The business can detail a workflow and define specific release reasons (pre-defined or free text fields).

Within the different business areas, SAP GTS provides functionalities to conduct asynchronous or periodic screenings and simulate screenings, along with different monitoring options for business partners and documents.

The transfer of the relevant master data to SAP GTS takes place via change pointers. Each time the user creates or changes a business partner address in the feeder system, a change pointer is updated, and a report selects the relevant partner address. The address is then sent to SAP GTS via the RFC connection. Depending on the SPL setup, you can perform one of two kinds of screening:

▸ **Asynchronous**
If you select asynchronous screening, you need to schedule batch jobs in order to trigger the screening; otherwise, the screening is performed manually. The screening does not happen at the same time as the data change.

▸ **Synchronous**
The system automatically triggers synchronous screening each time a business partner is created or changed in SAP GTS via the feeder system change pointer mechanism.

You may select the type of the SPL block when using asynchronous screening. There are two options: either the process is automatically blocked until the partner is screened in SAP GTS, or the process continues until the user explicitly sets a block.

SAP GTS integrates SPL screening into the business process as follows:

▸ Master data screening: Check business partners transferred from a feeder system to SAP GTS (after creation or modification)

▸ Transactional screening: Transactional document screening (e.g., sales orders, deliveries, purchase orders, or payments)

▸ Simulate screening: Check new business partners prior to creation in feeder system environment

Furthermore, the SPL screening functionality provides the following additional advantages:

▸ Provides flexible audit and monitoring mechanisms

▸ Screens against changes to government agency-specific lists when delta files are uploaded

In this chapter, the term *business partner* represents all business area partners (e.g., vendors, account holders, and employees), and the term *document* represents the relevant business area documents (e.g., sales orders, purchase orders, deliveries, and payment documents).

▸ **Business partner or master data screening**
The business partner or master data screening displayed in Figure 6.12 is triggered on newly created or changed partners. The screening result is saved in the SAP GTS SPL status information and subsequently retrieved for comparison in transactional screening.

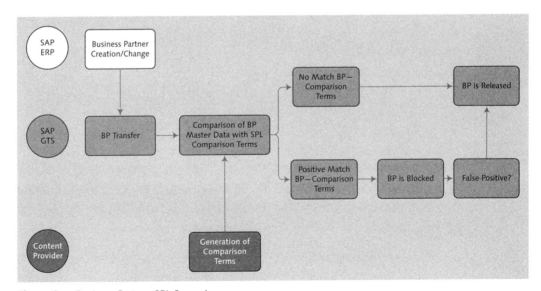

Figure 6.12 Business Partner SPL Screening

▶ **Document or transactional screening**

In transactional screening, document partner addresses are compared with SPL entries. If the address has not been manually changed, a status is retrieved based on the latest master data screening result. If the address *was* manually changed since the last screening performed, a new screening takes place to determine whether the address matches an entity on an SPL list. The SAP GTS process for this scenario is displayed in Figure 6.13.

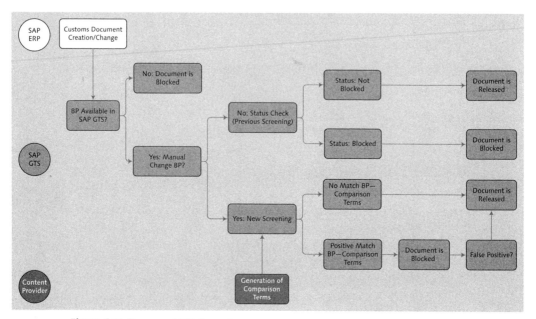

Figure 6.13 Document SPL Screening

SPL Screening Areas

SPL screening can be used in five main business areas. You can find the different SPL functionalities over the various tabs of the SPL menu displayed in Figure 6.14:

▶ **Business areas**

  ▷ Logistics: Integration with SAP SD and MM, Logistics Processes

  ▷ Human resources: Integration with SAP ERP HCM, employees, and applicants

  ▷ Financial accounting: Integration with SAP FI-CA, payments

► **Cross-business areas**

  ► Cross-area monitoring: Internal and external audit

  ► Master data: Sanctioned party lists, business partners, and comparison terms

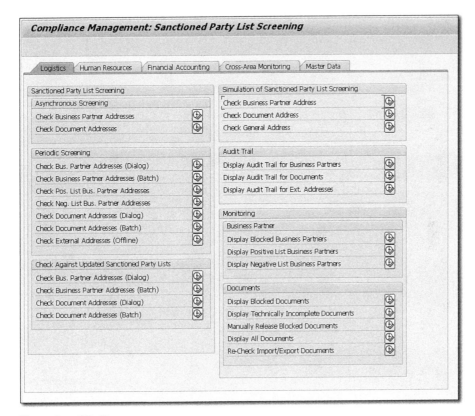

Figure 6.14 SPL Menu

Let's zoom in on these five SPL tabs, focusing in particular on SPL integration with logistics processes.

SPL Integration in Logistics

SPL is integrated in the logistics flow in a few scenarios:

► Screening of partners and documents (master data and transactional)

► Screening simulation

- Audit trail
- Monitoring of business partners and documents that have already undergone screening

The compliance manager in our Belgian-Malaysian (Beta-Freelance Aviation Corporation) SPL entity scenario monitors the process from this area.

The type of scenario is based on two parameters:

- Screening of business partner address and/or document partner address
- Synchronous and/or asynchronous screening

Table 6.1 lists SAP GTS predefined scenarios. Understanding these scenarios is crucial for performing a correct screening of partners.

Scenario	Name	Data to be screened
A1	Business Partner Address Check	New/changed addresses in business partner master data
A2	Document Partner Address Check	New/changed addresses in document partner
B1	Periodic BP Address Check	Unchanged and already-screened business partner
B1(P), B1(N)	Positive/Negative BP Address Check	Business partners placed on positive/negative list
B2	Periodic Document Partner Check	Unchanged and already-screened documents
C1	SPL Data Basis Change—Partner	Unchanged and already-screened partner (against new SPL list entries—delta files)
C2	SPL Data Basis Change—Document	Unchanged and already-screened documents (against new SPL list entries—delta files)
O3	Offline, External SPL Check	External XML file containing address data
S1	Simulation BP Master Data	One business partner master data

Table 6.1 SAP GTS Predefined Scenarios

Scenario	Name	Data to be screened
S2	Simulation Document Check	One document partner address
S3	Simulation Independent Address	Free address input

Table 6.1 SAP GTS Predefined Scenarios (Cont.)

It is considered a leading practice to use asynchronous screening for the initial transfer of master data (or other volume transfer) and to set it on synchronous screening for the regular transfer. Next, let's look at every SAP GTS scenario in more detail.

▶ **A1/A2**

Scenarios A1 and A2 are used in the initial transfer and changes of business partner master data. If a new business partner is created or changed, or an address of a business partner in the document is created or changed, these two scenarios are triggered, and the data is compared to the complete SPL list. Partners that have been placed on positive or negative lists are not considered in these screening scenarios.

If you choose synchronous screening, this scenario is started in the background during transfer, and you don't have to set up batch jobs to initiate the screening. In case of asynchronous screenings, you have to trigger the screening scenarios via a batch job or manually trigger them.

▶ **B1/B2**

The periodic SPL check allows you to re-screen all business partners and documents against the entire SPL database at regular intervals (e.g., on a quarterly basis). The business partners that have already been screened and released are excluded from the screening if there is no change in partner or SPL master data. The partners you've put on a positive/negative list are only considered in the specific B1 scenarios foreseen for these partners.

▶ **C1/C2**

Business partners and documents are checked against the SPL delta files (i.e., only against changed or new SPL records). Existing blocked business partners or those placed on a positive or negative list are not taken into account.

▶ **O3**

Offline screening allows you to screen external master data files (in XML format) against the SPL lists. The purpose of this scenario is to validate business partners from an external system. The result is a target file with the status of the business partner; there is no status change in the system.

▶ **S1/S2**

The simulation functionality allows screening against only one business partner master data or one document. You can use this scenario for testing purposes to check whether the address will be blocked in a real screening scenario.

▶ **S3**

In this scenario, you can screen a manually entered address (without master data) against the SPL database.

The overall screening process should follow a specific sequence you can partially run using batch jobs. Consider the following sequence:

1. Initial upload of volume master data (technical go-live before business go-live), which includes the following steps:

   ▶ Master data transfer, no document transfer: Documents are not screened on transactional basis yet. Only the business partner master data itself will be screened against the SPL lists in the SAP GTS environment (preparation activity during technical go-live).

   ▶ Asynchronous screening: The master data are screened all together (not at business partner creation or change).

   ▶ Manual execution of Scenario A1.

   The action to take after these items have been executed is to evaluate the results and to release the relevant BPs, to confirm the SPL blocks, or to put the BP on positive/negative list (different results of the evaluation).

2. Transactional screening (business go-live), which includes the following steps:

   ▶ Activate document transfer: At this point in time, the relevant documents are transferred from the feeder system to SAP GTS.

   ▶ Synchronous screening: Via the change pointer mechanism and RFC calls, automatic screening is performed on master data changes and document addresses.

   ▶ Regular delta file upload: The upload of the changes in SPL lists need to occur directly into the SAP GTS environment.

▶ Generation of SPL comparison terms in the SPL master data cockpit: As explained in the Customizing settings, the search-term origin is a critical setting that defines the leading object for the origin of the search term or comparison term.

▶ Aggregate SPL comparison terms: This step needs to be executed after the generation of the SPL comparison terms.

▶ If applicable, transfer SPL comparison terms to TREX. As further explained in Section 6.2.3, TREX, short for Text Retrieval and Information Extraction, is a search and classification tool.

▶ Generation of business partner comparison terms for all addresses or for changed partner addresses only.

As soon as these preparation steps are completed, the following scenarios can be executed in order to make the environment ready for further processing:

▶ Scenario C1: Business Partner Delta Screening

▶ Scenario C2: Document Delta Screening

When you're following this sequence, the screening should be in line with the latest published SPL. In addition, a periodic screening process may be performed against all SPL entries.

SPL Integration in HR

The scenario logic in the SPL screening HR tab (HUMAN RESOURCES, second tab in the SAP GTS cockpit) is similar to the one used in the LOGISTICS tab (first tab in the SAP GTS cockpit). For example, a company may want to screen job applicants or employees against denied party lists. Documents are not screened in the HR module.

From a legal perspective, the screening of applicants or employees is a complex scenario. You must consult the applicable legal regulations per country before setting up such screenings.

SPL Integration in Financial Accounting

The integration with FI allows you to screen business partners in payment transactions (incoming or outgoing payments), as well as partners such as the account holder, customer, payer, and partner bank and notes to payee.

In order to activate the SPL integration for FI, you must activate the functionality in the Financial Accounting Customizing settings in SAP ERP 6.0. The respective

BAdIs are found under the menu path FINANCIAL ACCOUNTING (NEW) • FINANCIAL ACCOUNTING GLOBAL SETTINGS (NEW) • CHECK IN SAP GTS FOR FI.

The screening scenarios are structured similarly to the scenarios in the Logistics module.

Cross-Area Monitoring

The cross-area audit functionality provides a complete set of audit reports that covers all internal and external audit requirements concerning SPL transactions. *Cross-area* refers to logistics, HR, and financials screening scenarios. If you are only using Logistics, cross-area monitoring isn't required.

Two audit reports are available: Audit Trail for Partners and Documents, and Audit of Release Reasons.

6.2.3 Customizing

In this section, we'll cover the Customizing settings for SPL screening. Note that you must correctly set up all general settings discussed earlier (document transfer and legal regulations) before you can customize. The following transactions are within Transaction SPRO • GLOBAL TRADE SERVICES • SANCTIONED PARTY LIST SCREENING.

Activate Business Partner at the Business-Partner Function Level

Through this transaction, you can define which business partner types will be screened, the timing and sequence of screening, the block type to be triggered, and the business area (i.e., logistics, finance) for which the screening takes place.

You must define the application object (e.g., BUPA—SAP business partner or FICO—Financial conditions) and the business partner role (e.g., SLLBNK—Bank or SLLCPC—Customer) to be screened.

The timing of screening is a crucial decision point. The choice between the following two settings defines the time at which SPL screening is performed if a new address is created or an address has been changed:

▶ **0 Asynchronous: By calling the function/service**
You must schedule batch jobs to run the SPL screening or manually trigger the screening using scenario A1 (business partner address) and/or A2 (document

address). The system sends the new or changed address data to SAP GTS and assigns a status, depending on the block type selection: please refer to Table 6.2.

▶ **1 Synchronous: At update**
The system sends the address information to SAP GTS and screens it at runtime. This means the status is updated directly and available in the feeder system for further processing.

The block type is relevant only if the user selects asynchronous screening. This determines whether you want a system block in the feeder system until screening is performed. From a compliance point of view, option 1 (process is interrupted; service removes block) is the option that minimizes compliance risk most because it ensures that the order processing is blocked if the partner has not undergone SPL screening.

The block type has a direct effect on the SPL status assigned to the business partners, shown in Table 6.2.

⬤⬤⬤	Status Not Blocked—Positive SPL screening result
⬤◯⬤	Status Soft Block—Not processed yet (relevant only in case of asynchronous screening)
⬤⬤⬤	Status Hard Block—Negative SPL screening result

Table 6.2 Statuses of SPL Screening Results

Another option in the Customizing settings is to restrict (or permit) review of screenings by the organizational structure level (e.g., FTO).

Assign Determination Procedure for Active Legal Regulations

You must configure a determination procedure for the determination of active legal regulations in SPL screening. But first, the user has to define a determination procedure for active legal regulations under general settings. LESPL is the standard SPL determination procedure, pre-defined by SAP. This determination procedure is based on the country level. Depending on this setting, the legal regulation used for SPL screening uses the country of the legal unit and the business partner.

Activate Legal Regulation

Table 6.3 shows options for the import and export site to activate the SPL legal regulations for multiple countries or country groups.

SPL Import Active	SPL Export Active
1—Check: Receipt (Exclusively)	1—Check: Dispatch (Exclusively)
2—Check: Import (Exclusively)	2—Check: Export (Exclusively)
3—Check: Receipt/Import (excluding domestic)	3—Check: Dispatch/Export (excluding domestic)
4—Check: Receipt/Import (including domestic)	4—Check: Dispatch/Export (including domestic)
Check: Not Activated	Check: Not Activated

Table 6.3 Activation Options for SPL Screening

Since SPL screening is largely intended for all transactions, option 4 is often deployed because it checks all import and export scenarios and domestic transactions. This ensures that all inbound and outbound flows for a specified country or country group are subject to SPL screening.

Define Control Procedure for Address Comparison

Within this step, you can customize and define the data compared under SPL screening. The comparison terms are built based on these settings, and the direction of screening is determined.

First, you must define the overall screening structure before defining the screening logic details. The setup is defined on three levels (control structure, detail control, and assign address fields).

Control Structure for Address Comparison

The control structure, or the schema for address/string comparison, is a central element of SPL screening, and you must define several elements within it. A comparison procedure is first defined and then later mapped to a legal regulation. Choosing one comparison procedure scheme per legal regulation (e.g., comparison procedure SPLUS for legal regulation SPLUS) allows flexibility in case regulations or country- or region-specific approaches change.

You must also determine the language in which text is displayed or entered and printouts are created. You may choose to store more than one version of an address (various character sets) at the same time. If it has been determined, the SPL screening will check against the central SAP international address versions used in the feeder system (e.g., Arabic, Hebrew, Chinese, International, or Cyrillic).

Search-term origin is a critical setting that defines the leading object for the origin of the search term (comparison terms). Using three options, the basis for comparison can be one of the following:

▸ Exclusively from SPL

▸ A string from partner addresses

▸ Parallel from SPL/address

If the user selects the first option, the string generated from partner addresses is the basis for the string comparison percentage match calculation between SPL master data and business partner master data, whereas the second option takes into account the highest percentage of either result. For the third option, the system uses the SPL entry as a basis for determining the percentage value.

To illustrate this setting, let's use an example with the following parameters:

▸ SPL List Comparison Term (e.g., Name): Mickelson (9 letters)

▸ Business Partner Comparison Term (e.g., Name): Mikaelsond (10 letters)

▸ Field MINIMUM MATCHES–SEARCH TERM is set to 85%

Here are our three options:

▸ **Using exclusively SPL entry as a basis**
Eight (Mikaelsond) out of nine (Mickelson) letters match between the business partner and SPL entry, so the system calculates a match rate of 89% (8/9 = 0.888). If the minimum hit rate for screening is set to 85%, this screening results in a match.

▸ **Basis for comparison from partner address**
Eight (Mickelson) out of 10 letters (Mikaelsond) match, so a match rate of 80% is calculated. If the match threshold is set to 85%, no hit is returned.

▸ **Basis for comparison parallel from SPL/address**
The system first calculates 89% with SPL data as the basis, then 80% with BP data as the basis, and then returns a hit because one of the two calculated outcomes lies above the minimum match rate.

Another setting allows the conditional elimination of duplicate characters and the inclusion of initials during the screening. Note that the use of initials may increase the number of search terms, runtime, and number of false-positive hits.

Text Retrieval and Information Extraction (TREX), a search and classification tool, is part of the SAP Search Integration capabilities and allows searches of unstructured and structured data. It is an optional search utility you can use along with SAP GTS (beginning with version 8.0), but you must install it separately. TREX provides two very important services that cannot be customized in the standard SPL settings:

▶ Removes the "word within word" constraint that prevents very similar terms from matching unless one of them is completely present in the other. Misspelled words can be recognized up to a certain level, such as transposed or additional letters (e.g., *preference* and *perference*).

▶ Prevents matches between terms of completely different lengths. Without TREX, words with a short character string can result in a hit against words with longer character strings because they are found within the longer term.

That being said, the search utility, integrated alongside strong SPL settings logic, can raise the quality of positive hits without substantially raising the quantity of false-positive matches.

The scope of the check allows you to use a logic for phonetic replacement. Within the SPL master data setup, you can enter character substrings or combinations of letters that would be replaced by a target string.

Detail Control
Figure 6.15 provides the standard settings of the detailed control search terms.

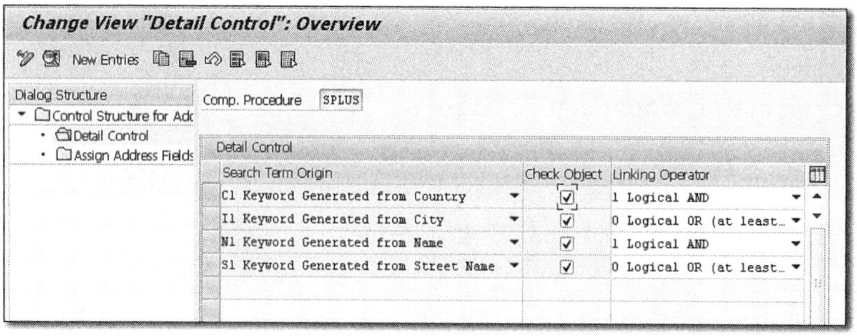

Figure 6.15 SPL Standard Control Search Settings

Figure 6.15 can be read as shown in Table 6.4.

C1—Country	Must always match
I1—City	Must match if Street does not match
N1—Name	Must always match
S1—Street	Must match if City does not match

Table 6.4 Settings for Detailed Control Search Terms

The elements of the address that should be screened against SPL entries are defined in the search-term origin. The following standard generated keywords allow a flexible setup of personalized SPL screening logic:

▶ A1—ID/Passport Number
▶ B2—PO Box
▶ C1—Country
▶ C2—Country of PO Box
▶ C3—Country of ID Card
▶ H1—House Number
▶ H2—Building and Room Number
▶ I1—City
▶ I2—City for PO Box
▶ I3—City of Residence
▶ K1—Telephone Number
▶ K2—Fax Number
▶ N1—Name
▶ P1—Postal Code of City
▶ P2—Postal Code of PO Box
▶ P3—Company Postal Code
▶ R1—Region
▶ R2—Region of PO Box
▶ S1—Street Name
▶ T1—General Text

For each search-term origin, the screening details must be defined. Flagging the CHECK OBJECT checkbox activates this business partner attribute for SPL screening. The linking operator is one of the most important settings within your screening logic, controlling the combination in which address parts must match to result in a hit. Use of *AND* means that this part of an address *must* match in the SPL check. Use of *OR* means that *at least one* of the terms marked with an *OR* must match in the check.

Of course, companies may choose a different approach and apply an adapted screening logic instead of using the SAP standard approach.

In addition to specifying these indicators, you must determine the details displayed in Figure 6.16 for every single search-term origin intended for use in the screening logic. These settings are crucial for the overall performance of the SPL logic in use, so you should heavily test them to refine and optimize the settings.

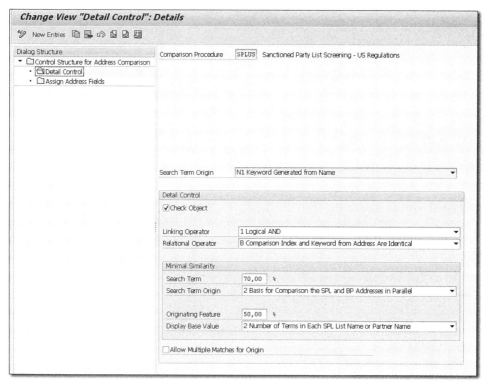

Figure 6.16 SPL Screening Detail Control

The relational operator controls whether the search terms in a partner address are considered one word or separate terms. Generally, you should view the search terms as separate terms.

The minimum match percentage per search term determines the minimum match rate between two terms in order to produce a hit. The system recognizes to what extent the same letters of the comparison terms match each other, regardless of the sequence of appearance.

Consider the following example parameters:

▶ Original term from address: Watson (number of letters = 6)
▶ Original search term from comparison index: Wadzon
▶ Number of matches = 4

The calculated percentage would be 66% (4/6), and depending on the defined percentage rate, the comparison would or would not result in a hit (e.g., whether the defined rate is, respectively, 65% or 70%).

The search-term origin setting has been detailed already at the SPL-procedure level in the control structure for address comparison, but it can be further detailed per origin term. The options are the same as for the control structure.

The originating feature definition allows you to specify the minimum match percentage among all search terms within an address and all search terms from the originating address.

Consider the following example parameters:

▶ Content address: Luke Donald Simpson
▶ Originating comparison index: Luke, Tiger Simpsan

Let us assume the system determines two hits out of three words, based on the other settings, resulting in a calculated result of 66.67%.

The percentage defined in the originating feature (e.g., if the percentage match is set to 65% or 70%) determines whether the screening results in a hit. All percentage rates in the SPL screening process represent minimum requirements and read as "greater or equal to." If you define a 70% match rate, and the calculated outcome is exactly 70%, a hit occurs.

The base value of number of found terms is required to calculate the number of instances (referenced as a percentage) where the terms and screened addresses match. As part of this calculation, the percentage match is checked against the minimum threshold value defined earlier. You can choose among three standard options:

▸ Only number of terms in each SPL name

▸ Number of terms in each SPL list name AND partner name

▸ Number of terms in each SPL list name OR partner name

Consider the following example:

▸ Number of terms in BP name (e.g., Peter Lafleur) = base value 2

▸ Number of terms in SPL list (e.g., Peter Lafleur Parker) = base value 3

Based on the setting, there are three different outcomes:

▸ Selecting only the number of terms in each SPL name would take only base value 3 into account. Therefore, the calculated percentage would be 2/3 = 66.67%.

▸ Option 1 ("Number of terms in each SPL List Name AND Partner Name") takes both base values (2/3=66.67% and 2/2 = 100%) into account. Both values must lie above the defined threshold to result in a hit.

▸ Option 2 ("Number of terms in each SPL List Name OR Partner Name") takes both base values (66.67% and 100%) into account again; however, only one of the values has to lie above the threshold to generate a match hit.

Allowing multiple matches for origin includes identical matches in percentage match determination.

Consider the following example parameters:

▸ Address content: Felipe Luca Enzo Felipe

▸ Comparison index: Marcos Felipe Luca (number of search terms = 3)

The setting influences the calculation in the following way:

▸ If set, the number of matches found (3 = Felipe & Felipe & Luca) constitute a percentage match = 100% (3/3)

▸ If not set, the number of matches found (2 = Felipe & Luca) constitute a percentage match = 66.67% (2/3)

Based on the defined percentage match threshold, the results would or would not generate a hit.

Assign Address Fields

When changes in specific address fields of a business partner or document partner address are made, SPL checks are performed.

The standard solution provides many options for address fields and offers a great deal of flexibility to meet industry-specific or company-specific screening requirements for addresses:

- Address Group
- Box City
- Box Region
- City
- Country Key
- District
- Extension
- Fax
- House Number
- House Number Range
- Name
- Name 2
- Name 3
- Personal Address
- PO Box
- PO Box Postal Code
- Region
- Search Term 2
- Street
- Street 2
- Street 3
- Street 4

▸ Supplement

▸ Telephone

Defining Identity Card Types for Ad Hoc Sanctioned Party List

This setting defines the types of identity documents within a scheme. You can define these documents as optional or mandatory information during a simulated screening of general addresses (scenario S3). You must activate the ID entries within the control settings of SPL screening. You can define a scheme for the ID card types and then assign the desired types to use in that scheme. Thereby, the ID types are grouped for a specific legal regulation.

Control Settings for Sanctioned Party List Screening

This Customizing activity sets forth the control settings for the legal regulations intended for use in SPL screening.

Control Settings

You must assign a control procedure and partner groups for each legal regulation used in SPL screening, for both import and export activities.

You can consider the validity periods for SPL master data during screening. If the validity period has expired, you can flag the corresponding SPL entry for deletion. You also have the options to include flagged SPL entries in the generated comparison index and consider the address validity for screening.

The cross-check indicator has a significant influence on the overall performance of the SPL functionality. If it is active, address elements are compared with one another regardless of the address section (e.g., comparing street data in an SPL entry with name entry in a BP address). If TREX is used within the comparison procedure, the flag is not relevant.

Considering past SPL screening results may improve the performance of your SPL configuration. The setting defines whether the SPL screening is re-run with similar circumstances or if the results from the last screening run are used.

All criteria for the business partner master data and the SPL must be the same as the pre-existing screening parameters; otherwise, new checks will be performed.

You may screen business partners with several address types in the BP master data via the multiple address check setting. You must define the address activation level at which the address should be checked in the SPL screening.

The check logic for documents provides two options:

▶ Status check of unchanged partner addresses (partner address)
▶ New check of a changed address

If you choose the first option, a manual change of the document partner address will trigger a block in SAP GTS SPL screening, stating that the "Partner's address was manually changed". The system performs checks of the business partner master data via a status query for unchanged document addresses of the business partner. The second option, new check of changed addresses, screens the document address synchronously in case a change from the master business partner is detected.

The setting you choose influences the logic behind the check and the resulting block of the screening types as follows:

▶ Status query of business partner screening causes a block.
▶ Changed document address causes a block.

The search strategy provides two options:

▶ SPL entry searches in address entry and vice versa
▶ SPL entry searches in address entry

The setting in the control procedure Customizing steps provides a choice of logic to compare addresses. The search strategy setting provides a solution to the constraint that the target word must be longer than the source word.

If you select the first option, the constraint is removed, and it is no longer important if one word is longer or shorter than the other. This setting is adjusted in the first screen, DEFINE CONTROL PROCEDURE FOR ADDRESS COMPARISON, where it determines which terms are matched and in which direction. Note that if you use TREX, you can ignore this setting.

The employee check base is relevant only if you integrate the human resource module within SAP GTS SPL screening. The employee or applicant who is subject to the screening is checked only against persons master data records within the SPL list or all denied party list entries.

SPL screening is performance intensive; dividing the data into packages can improve the following performance parameters:

▶ Minimize runtime for screening and update

▶ Optimize use of buffer mechanisms

▶ Optimize use of the queue server

▶ Prevent memory overflows

SPL screening is performed for each package, and the result is updated in the database. Due to buffering mechanisms, the more partners included in one package, the shorter the runtime for each object. Other processes may be affected due to locking partners and documents, so there's an increased risk of memory overflow with the package size. The default setting is 1,000, but the system and master data properties determine and affect which value should be applied.

The audit trail is an important function within SPL screening for both external and internal audit/reporting purposes. Checking this setting ensures that the audit trail is updated during SPL screening for business partners and documents.

The WRITE AUDIT FOR SIMULATION setting ensures that an entry is logged or business partners are screened in simulation modes (S1 or S2). You can also log an entry in the audit trail for an ad hoc screening simulation of general address data (S3) or through a screening performed on external addresses from an XML file (O3).

You can improve SPL check runtimes by storing the comparison index in the application server buffer. This way, when you run an SPL check, you can read the SPL comparison index quickly in the application server rather than from the database. Frequently run SPL checks can significantly improve response times. Note that response times may be slow if the application server buffer is not large enough.

Another way to improve the performance of SPL checks is to store the SPL comparison index in summarized form in a cluster table. The system can access this cluster table more quickly than a traditional transparent database table.

The TIME INITIALIZED setting defines when the generated comparison terms are initialized—i.e., when they are reset to allow new comparison words to be created. You must do this if the SPL logic changes or new terms are generated.

The Notification Parameter setting activates the email notification workflow. The system automatically sends an email if a business partner or document obtains a blocked status during an SPL check.

There are two available options:

▸ Send mail when document is blocked

▸ Send mail when business partner is blocked

You can configure the email settings within the communication settings of SAP GTS and further define user groups emailed per FTO and legal regulation.

Based on the release reasons defined in Define Reasons for Releasing Blocked Documents and Business Partners section in the overall Compliance Management Module setting, you can activate a release reason determination procedure for SPL screening.

The incompleteness check for transit and customs processing is linked to the customs module in SAP GTS. When the replicated feeder system document is blocked after a compliance check in SAP GTS (in this case, an SPL block), a message is categorized in the incompleteness log of the customs declaration. If the message is added to the customs module incompleteness check as an error message, you cannot send the customs declaration to the customs authorities until the underlying document is released in Compliance Management.

Finally, you can define different text types to use for the license types maintained in Compliance Management. You can also activate ID identifications, specified in an earlier step. The ID identifications for SPL ad hoc screening are optional, mandatory, or inactive.

List Type

This setting defines the list types (e.g., specially designated nationals, or SDN) relevant for a company's legal requirements. Certain list types are pre-delivered within the standard legal regulation SPLUS, but other legal regulations would be defined here, as well. For every list type you must define whether the SPL content is uploaded via an XML file or via manual maintenance.

For each list type, you must define several parameters that influence the comparison term generation. Defining the license type description and assigning a government agency (defined as a specific business partner type within SAP GTS, such as SLLAUT Government Agency) is optional.

The MAXIMUM NUMBER OF INDEX ENTRIES PER OBJECT setting defines how many terms are generated for each name/address of a master data entry. Though the quality of SPL screening results improve with the number of search terms generated, the increased load on the system can present performance issues. Both the quality of screening and system load pressure depend on the master data in use and the system sizing, so you should perform several test runs to identify the optimal settings.

You can also add the legal regulation behind the SPL list and comments. These fields do not influence the SPL screening logic and are only informational in nature.

Reference Type
You can define reference types for each legal regulation and each name in an SPL master data record as a reference name. To use this functionality, define the reference types in the master data (e.g., "also known as" becomes "AKA" and "formerly known as" becomes "FKA").

Assign Time Zone to Deadline Type
Time zones are defined per legal regulation and allow a time zone adaptation per country or region. Time zones affect validity periods and inclusion dates for compliance functions.

Address Activation
You can maintain possible usage types for addresses. When maintaining business partners, you can use the function address usage to assign business partner addresses to address types (e.g., correspondence address and delivery address). The address types differ from the address versions in that the address version is connected to the language setting, and the type is connected to the type of address.

Configure Technical Controls for Web Dynpro Applications

It is possible to monitor the SPL functionality via a Web Dynpro application. The technical parameters necessary for this include data formatting entries, which define whether the results of the initial or final screening are displayed. Within the SPL Web Dynpro application, you can identify specific queries for

SPL information retrieval. You can monitor detailed analysis of the business partner and release documents and business partners online.

6.2.4 Master Data

SPL-related master data is maintained in a dedicated tab, displayed in Figure 6.17 and accessed via COMPLIANCE MANAGEMENT • SANCTIONED PARTY LIST SCREENING • MASTER DATA. It allows following operations:

▶ Upload and maintenance of SPL master data

▶ Maintenance of business partner master data and mapping to organizational units

▶ Monitoring of SPL master data

▶ Settings, generation, evaluation, and aggregation of SPL and business partner comparison terms

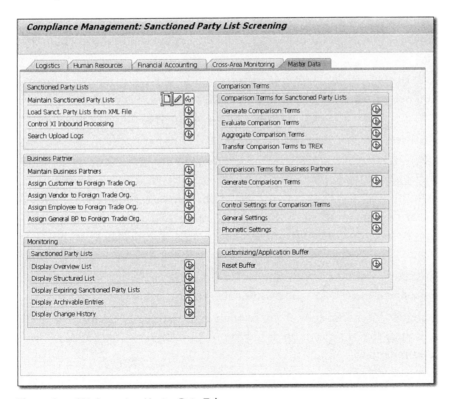

Figure 6.17 SPL Screening Master Data Tab

In order to effectively use the SPL logic defined in Customizing, you still have to define master data entries within the SPL menu. Let's look at two subsections of this screen—the SPL lists upload functionality and control settings for comparison term generation.

▶ **Sanctioned party lists**
Typically, content providers publish a master file with all the SPL entries that exist at that point in time. You may then update the master data file using delta files, which include only new and changed entries. You can automate or manually upload the purchased XML lists, and can create your own internally generated restricted party lists by defining a specific list type for the relevant legal regulation.

It is important to note that, when uploading an SPL list, you cannot manually add or update entries in the lists that are uploaded. You have to maintain a separate list for these entries in which the address and name details to screen against can be manually added. The master data purchased from various content providers is uploaded via XML files. Most of the data providers provide specific user guides on how to handle the initial upload and subsequent update files.

To load the SPL lists via SAP Process Integration (SAP PI), you must define the specific settings in this area. In order to verify that uploads were correctly performed and no errors occurred, you can search the different monitor logs.

▶ **Control settings for comparison terms**
The general settings include different details you may want to define per comparison procedure.

  ▷ Delimiter: With delimiters, you can define characters and/or numbers to be used as separators in the SPL screening logic. If a separator is used, the algorithm splits the name into separate words, and matches can be recognized.

  Most companies start with standard delimiters, such as (,_:;/\()"[]{}?.-), that are adapted to each specific master data requirement.

  Example: Mother-in-law. If the hyphen (-) is defined as a separator in the delimiter, the algorithm splits the word into three words for SPL match determination.

▶ Excluded texts: Excluded texts are ignored during the SPL check. The words used depend on the master data of each company and depend on the industry sector and business partners you are dealing with. Some examples of possible exclusion words are AG, AVE, GROUP, LLP, ORG, RD, AND, INC, LT, THE, LP, AB, ON, BANK, OF, MBH, PTE, CORP, ASSOCIATION, FOR, INDUSTRIES, PLC, PT, and STREET.

▶ Alias terms: SAP GTS allows the replacement of terms to defined aliases before performing SPL screening. The alias basis defined in this setup is replaced by the term defined in the alias field in the SPL screening (e.g., *Dan* for *Daniel* and *Ted* for *Theodore*).

Depending on the language used, you might want to replace letters or strings of letters with other letters or combinations. In Germany, for example, the letter *ö* could be replaced with *oe*. The same applies for French words, where *é* and *è* could be replaced with *e*.

6.2.5 SPL Mobile Solution

As of SAP GTS version 10.0, SPL screening became available as a mobile application for mobile devices running on iOS. The solution is available on the Apple App Store.

Let's briefly consider mobile SPL functionality. In the setup, additional hardware and software requirements need to be fulfilled.

Within the application, there is functionality to view the blocked business partners and documents (in line with the data of your SAP GTS interface), displayed in Figure 6.18.

Blocked partners or documents can be processed via the mobile device. Figure 6.19 displays the various processing options, which are similar to the ones in SAP GTS. You may confirm, put on hold, or release the block on business partners or documents.

Section 6.2 has covered the process of screening the business partners involved in trade transactions against government agency or country-specific sanctioned party lists. SAP GTS helps companies automate this process by screening documents and the involved business partners against sanctioned party lists uploaded in the system.

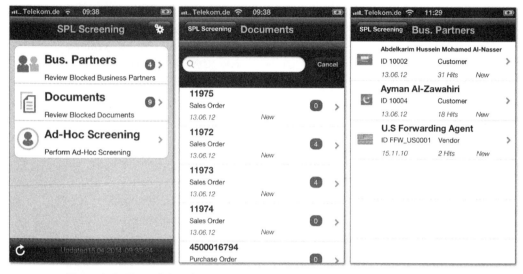

Figure 6.18 SPL Mobile Solution

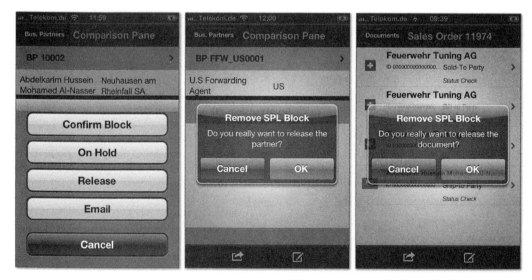

Figure 6.19 Mobile SPL Processing Options

Let's turn our attention to the embargo functionality of SAP GTS Compliance Management, which ensures that companies avoid trading with business partners situated in embargoed countries.

6.3   Embargo

Destination restrictions, such as embargoes and sanctions, refer to restrictions on trade with certain countries ranging from a comprehensive embargo, to a targeted financial sanction, to a more limited arms (i.e., weapons) embargo. Government agencies administer and enforce comprehensive embargoes and sanctions, such as UN Security Council (UNSC) resolutions against certain countries. Because they are imposed to address a specific political situation or foreign policy objective, each embargo or sanction program can vary extensively.

Embargo and sanction programs may cover imports, exports, and/or financial transactions. They may block assets or target specific individuals, entities, or commodities. They may apply to foreign countries, as well as nationals and legal entities from those countries, and may extend to imports or exports of services. They may prohibit or restrict export and re-exports, financial transactions, and travel to certain countries.

The terms *embargo* and *sanction* technically have different meanings, but they are often used interchangeably to refer to controls prohibiting trade and transactions with certain countries. A comprehensive embargo prohibits the export of *all* goods and services to certain countries with a few limited exceptions, such as trade in certain eligible medical or agricultural goods to certain end users. A sanction (or partial embargo) is narrower in scope than an embargo and restricts the sale of specific materials and services to particular countries or parties within a country.

Embargoes and sanctions can take on a variety of forms, although the most common forms include the following, ordered from least to most restrictive:

▶ **Prohibitions on financial transactions**
Prohibitions may be put in place for transactions with certain persons related to certain countries, including restrictions on investment, payments, or capital movements; the freezing of assets and economic resources; or the withdrawal of tariff preferences that are designed to target specific persons, groups, or entities by freezing their funds and economic resources.

▶ **Arms embargoes**
Arms embargoes are applied to keep arms and military equipment from reaching conflict areas or authoritarian regimes that are likely to use them for internal

repression or aggression against a foreign country. Arms embargoes normally involve the prohibition of two things:

- ▸ Selling, supplying, transferring, or exporting arms or related material of all types, including weapons and ammunition, military vehicles or equipment, paramilitary equipment, or specific spare parts
- ▸ Providing financing or financial assistance, technical assistance, brokering services, or other services related to military activities, or the provision, manufacture, maintenance, or use of arms or related material of all types

- ▸ **Restrictions**
  Restrictions on the export of strategic goods may be applicable, including prohibitions or restrictions on the export of controlled items to sensitive countries.

- ▸ **Comprehensive trade embargoes**
  Finally, trade embargoes may include the prohibition of all exports to and specific imports from a particular foreign country.

As we did with SPL, let's walk through the business and system processes for embargoes.

6.3.1 Business Process

Belgian company Beta receives an order for one of its products from a new customer based in Syria. At the time of the order, the sales representative in Belgium faces an immediate issue: Syria is part of the embargoed-countries list.

Figure 6.20 indicates what Beta's export process looks like. In this scenario, the export shipment cannot occur because Beta is not allowed to export products to any customer in Syria.

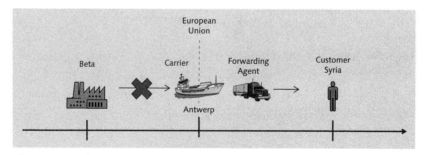

Figure 6.20 Embargo Export Business Process

6.3.2 System Process

Embargo checking within SAP GTS is used to ensure that the system blocks all documents that contain business partners from embargoed countries.

Embargo screening therefore works on the basis that the check is performed in relation to the business partner's country/location and in relation to the relevant prospective transaction. As such, the embargo functionality in SAP GTS only considers the country/location of the customer or supplier, and not the material being transacted. For embargo screening that includes product information, the license determination functionality can be used within SAP GTS. This functionality will be described in Section 6.3.

Figure 6.21 shows the feeder system documents and SAP GTS checks performed for an outbound process flow. Similar checks are applicable on the inbound process flow. Because Beta is trying to sell a product to a Syrian customer, SAP GTS sets an embargo block.

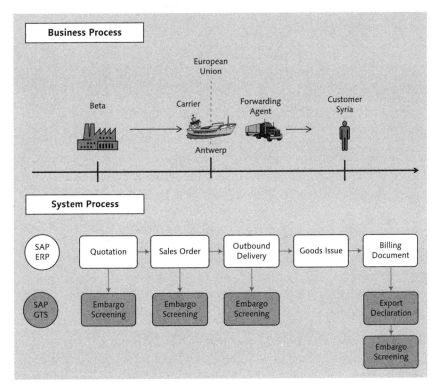

Figure 6.21 Embargo Export System Process

When quotations, sales orders, outbound deliveries, and so on are created in the feeder system, they are transferred to SAP GTS, and the embargo check is executed. This process includes the screening of the relevant business partners' country, which is maintained in the system (master data). If a business partner's location is on the embargo list in SAP GTS, SAP GTS blocks the feeder system document, which also prevents the creation of any subsequent documents in the feeder system document flow.

Let's return to our case study. A sales employee at Beta is trying to sell a non-export–controlled kit to a customer in Syria. The employee gets a pop-up within the sales document identifying the block. The message in Figure 6.22 notifies the feeder system user that the document is blocked by SAP GTS. Unless a trade compliance officer approves the sale by releasing the document in SAP GTS, it is not possible to create the outbound delivery in the feeder system and ship the non-export–controlled kit to Syria.

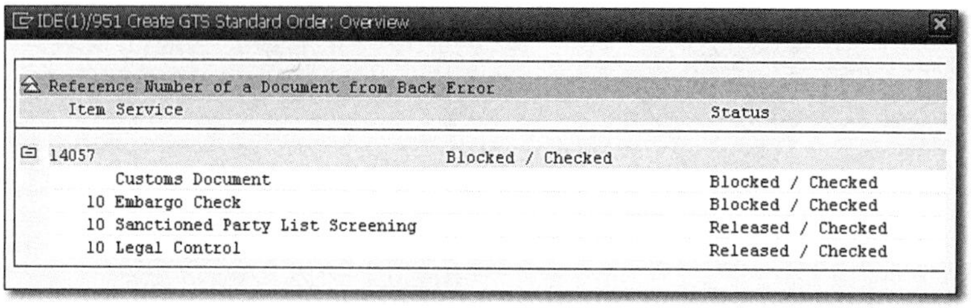

Figure 6.22 Embargo Block in the Feeder System

As soon as one of the business partners used in a feeder system document (e.g., the customer, payer, freight forwarder, etc.) is identified as located in an embargoed country, that identification causes a block on the customs document.

This section explains in detail how the status for embargo for all items in the SAP GTS document is determined based on the business partners used in the document and the existing master data settings for embargo in SAP GTS. As with SPL screening, you may not perform further processing steps if documents are blocked for embargo reasons, but you can take steps to analyze and possibly release the block imposed on the document.

You can access a worklist of blocked documents via COMPLIANCE MANAGEMENT • LEGAL CONTROL—EXPORT • DISPLAY BLOCKED DOCUMENTS. Note that the selection screen for this transaction in Figure 6.23 is used across the various Compliance

Management functionalities; you can apply filters on documents blocked for SPL, embargo, or legal control reasons.

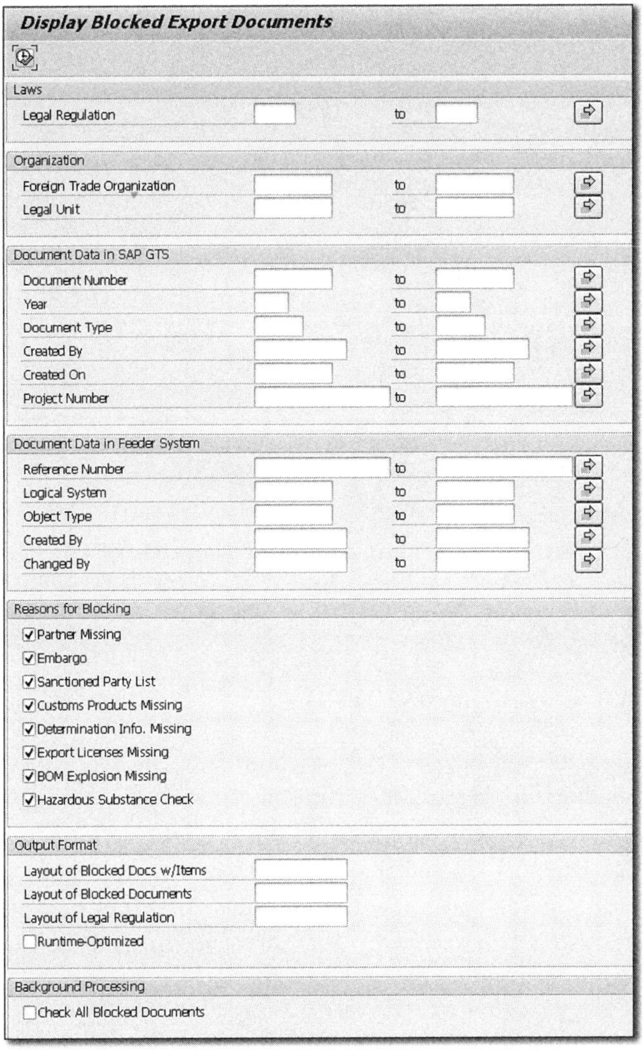

Display Blocked Export Documents

Laws

Legal Regulation		to		⇨

Organization

Foreign Trade Organization		to		⇨
Legal Unit		to		⇨

Document Data in SAP GTS

Document Number		to		⇨
Year		to		⇨
Document Type		to		⇨
Created By		to		⇨
Created On		to		⇨
Project Number		to		⇨

Document Data in Feeder System

Reference Number		to		⇨
Logical System		to		⇨
Object Type		to		⇨
Created By		to		⇨
Changed By		to		⇨

Reasons for Blocking

- ☑ Partner Missing
- ☑ Embargo
- ☑ Sanctioned Party List
- ☑ Customs Products Missing
- ☑ Determination Info. Missing
- ☑ Export Licenses Missing
- ☑ BOM Explosion Missing
- ☑ Hazardous Substance Check

Output Format

Layout of Blocked Docs w/Items	
Layout of Blocked Documents	
Layout of Legal Regulation	
☐ Runtime-Optimized	

Background Processing

☐ Check All Blocked Documents

Figure 6.23 Selection Screen for Displaying Blocked Export Documents

For example, using the feeder system's document reference number as a search criteria in the selection screen, Beta can easily retrieve the blocked document. Figure 6.24 shows the result of executing the transaction and depicts how the sales order is cleared for all but the embargo check.

Figure 6.24 Customs Document Blocked for Embargo Reasons

You can access the document's log to further analyze the reason of the imposed block. Figure 6.25 shows the corresponding log for Beta's sales order.

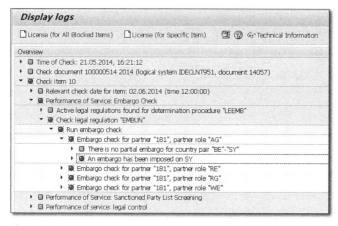

Figure 6.25 SAP GTS Customs Document Log Describing the Embargo Block

You may release blocked documents in specific circumstances, such as when governmental authorities approve shipment to the customer, via COMPLIANCE MANAGEMENT • LEGAL CONTROL—EXPORT • RELEASE BLOCKED DOCUMENTS. A dropdown list and/or text field is available for you to specify why the document may be released; these options correspond to acceptable reasons of release outlined in Customizing.

As soon as the document is released, it is on the list of released documents and included in the Analyze Reasons for Release transaction for audit purposes.

6.3.3 Customizing

Once you've taken the baseline Customizing steps and identified the general settings within SAP GTS Compliance Management (including defining the applicable legal regulations for embargo purposes), you may apply the three settings within GLOBAL TRADE SERVICES • COMPLIANCE MANAGEMENT • EMBARGO CHECK:

▶ Assigning determination procedure for active legal regulations

▶ Activating legal regulations

▶ Controlling settings for "embargo check" service

This assumes that the relevant document types have also been flagged for compliance in the feeder system plug-in. Let's look at each of these settings.

Assign Determination Procedure for Active Legal Regulation

In this activity, you specify which determination procedure to use to determine the active legal regulations for embargoes. The relevant legal regulations are determined based on the destination and/or departure country.

Standard SAP GTS defines the default determination procedure as "LEEMB," which consists of the following determination strategies:

▶ Determine legal regulation at the country level

▶ Determine legal regulation at the country-group level

Depending on the rule option you select, the system runs both determination strategies or stops after the first strategy resulting in a successful legal regulation.

Within standard SAP GTS, the DETERMINATION USING FIRST SUCCESSFUL STRATEGY option is selected, which means that when a legal regulation can be found using the country level, the country-group level is not triggered.

Activate Legal Regulation

Activating legal regulations for embargo purposes is analogous to the corresponding Customizing step for SPL screening, described in Section 6.2.3. In this step, it is defined whether the legal regulation is active for the various combinations of directions, based on the countries or country groups you have defined in the baseline settings.

By adding countries to this table, you can specify whether the selected legal regulation is active on the country or country-group level. Depending on those settings, the legal regulation is triggered for both import and export and both from and to the specified countries or country groups.

Control Settings for Embargo Check

Once the embargo regulations for which a check should be performed have been defined, you define the business partners to be checked by assigning partner groups to the legal regulation(s) used in import and export transactions, as noted in Figure 6.26.

SAP GTS has pre-defined default partner groups that can be changed based on specialized business requirements. For more details on how to define partner groups, please refer to Chapter 2 on baseline settings.

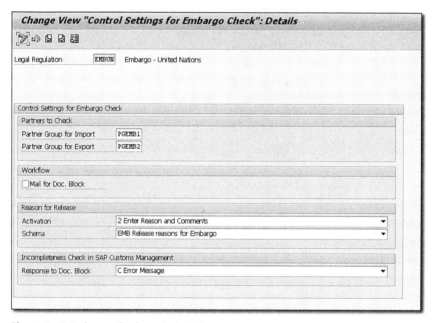

Figure 6.26 Embargo Check Control Settings

Within this step, you can define whether to receive an email notification when a document is blocked; this is the MAIL FOR DOC BLOCK flag. The Customizing step to activate the reason for release includes multiple options that can apply when releasing a blocked document. This setting determines if the user must select a predefined release reason and/or if the user has the ability to enter a comment. The schema that can be selected contains predefined reason codes that should be defined in the Customizing step Define Reasons for Releasing Blocked Documents and Business Partners.

6.3.4 Master Data

The master data related to embargo checks is limited to the combinations of countries and legal regulations for which an embargo block must be imposed.

There are three possibilities for entering master data in order to impose embargoes, and you can access all three of them via COMPLIANCE MANAGEMENT • LEGAL CONTROL—EXPORT • EMBARGO. Note that the following three transactions and their entries are identical to the corresponding transactions in COMPLIANCE MANAGEMENT • LEGAL CONTROL—IMPORT • EMBARGO.

▶ **Embargo on country level**
Set an embargo on a particular country, valid for all possible cases. This implies that transactions to or from this country are blocked, regardless of the departure or destination location of the business process flow. Note that you can set the embargo flag for a certain validity period, e.g., for one year. Enter this master data via COMPLIANCE MANAGEMENT • LEGAL CONTROL—EXPORT • EMBARGO • MAINTAIN COUNTRY-SPECIFIC INFORMATION.

▶ **Embargo on legal regulation and country of destination level**
Set an embargo on a country that is valid for only a particular legal regulation. You can specify different embargoed countries per legal regulation. Standard SAP GTS setup includes one legal regulation for embargo, but various business requirements may dictate otherwise. Enter this master data via COMPLIANCE MANAGEMENT • LEGAL CONTROL—EXPORT • EMBARGO • LEGAL REGULATION/COUNTRY OF DEPARTURE.

▶ **Embargo on legal regulation and country of departure/destination**
Set an embargo on a country that is valid for only a legal regulation and a country of departure and/or destination. This option allows for the most flexibility because it defines embargoed countries at the greatest level of detail. Enter this master data via COMPLIANCE MANAGEMENT • LEGAL CONTROL—EXPORT • EMBARGO • LEGAL REG./COUNTRY OF DEPARTURE/DESTIN.

Figure 6.27 gives an example of the third scenario. The entry implies, for example, that a shipment from Belgium (BE) to Syria (SY) includes an embargo block if the legal regulation EMBUN is triggered.

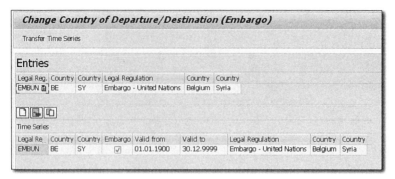

Figure 6.27 Embargoes Set by Legal Regulation and Countries

6.4 Legal Control

Importing and exporting certain sensitive items is controlled, in most jurisdictions, by the relevant government authorities. The export classification of such items, their end use, the intended end user, destination/departure country, combination of the items, or technology determine whether an import or export authorization is required.

Licenses and similar authorizations are not required for all exports, but only for controlled items and technology or restricted end uses, for example. Licenses or other authorizations are granted on a case-by-case basis and can cover a single transaction or multiple transactions. Authorization and license determinations require an understanding of all the facts related to a prospective transaction, including an item's technical characteristics.

Prior to exporting, or in certain cases importing, items and technology, the exporter or importer of record must establish whether a license or other applicable authorization is required for the prospective shipment or technology transfer to be made in accordance with national import and export control legislation. The following five elements should be examined to establish whether an export license is required:

▶ **What is the item being exported?**
Before an item can be exported or re-exported to a permissible end user, the item must have assigned to it a proper *export control number* (ECN), which identifies what the item is and determines the related controls.

▸ **Where is the item going?**
The country of ultimate destination, along with transshipment locations, for an export or re-export is an important factor in determining export licensing and authorization requirements; exports to some countries are more restricted than exports to other countries.

▸ **Who will receive the item?**
The ultimate end user of the exported item cannot be a restricted or prohibited end user (in some cases a specific authorization can be obtained depending on the citation-specific requirements).

▸ **What will the end user do with the item?**
The ultimate end use of the exported item cannot be a restricted end use.

▸ **What other activities is the end user involved in?**
Activities such as contracting, financing, and freight-forwarding in support of a proliferation project, for example, may prevent the exporter from engaging with a given party.

The inbound and outbound license determination process in SAP GTS is the compliance process of checking the existence of the appropriate authorizations, when an import or export transaction is initiated.

The license determination process validates whether the required authorization is available for the specified product. You have numerous options for configuring SAP GTS to determine and assign the applicable authorization to the product in question. One option is to automatically assign products to the appropriate authorization when available. Alternatively, you can configure SAP GTS such that you have to manually assign the appropriate authorization to a blocked line item on an order or delivery.

The determination is performed when the applicable feeder document type, such as a sales order, purchase order, outbound and inbound delivery, is created and transferred to SAP GTS. If a line item on a sales order or purchase order is blocked for a missing license or authorization, you can set up SAP GTS to block the subsequent creation of a delivery or the next document in the feeder system document flow. For example, when you create a sales order with two line items, one with the authorization in place and one without, you can create a delivery note for only the approved line item.

Given the broad number of configuration settings available in SAP GTS, you can architect nearly any rule set to authorize or block prospective goods movements. For example, some country-specific encryption controls require an authorization or license when sending encryption items to government end users. You can also configure SAP GTS to address end-use controls and determine export authorizations and license requirements for entities that may be involved in restricted military- or weapons-based programs.

Many companies also use SAP GTS to determine permit requirements related to drug precursors or government agency requirements related to medical agency and food and drug agency authorizations. Thus, when beginning an automated process to manage a specific regulatory requirement that depends on specific permits, authorizations, licenses, and other related requirements, review SAP GTS across all its capabilities and architect it accordingly.

With the onset of global terrorism and increased risk of nuclear proliferation, securing the supply chain has become a priority for many countries and global companies. Legal control functionality is a key component of a leading practice to vet prospective transactions and minimize compliance risks across dynamic and complex international supply chain management.

This section presents the multiple benefits of the SAP GTS Legal Control functionality, which is designed to help companies manage licenses or other authorizations required for import and export shipments. In addition, SAP GTS reduces the manual work effort via automated system checks, increases the security of the inbound and outbound flows, and provides users with the necessary reporting capabilities.

Again, let's begin with an overview of the business and system process flows for the standard licensing functionality, including the automatic BOM explosion. We'll then look at re-export functionality.

6.4.1 Import Licensing

Although many transactions fall outside the scope of legal control authorization or license requirements, importers and exporters must make this determination and report the relevant data as required by the country-specific regulatory authorities at time of export and import as applicable. A license or other authorization requirement may at any time be triggered due to product or technology-specific controls, its end use, end user, and/or final destination.

Business Process

In this business process scenario, company Beta exports defense articles to a US vendor and re-imports them after necessary modifications have taken place. The import licenses discussed in this section are the import licenses the US vendor needs to import the products shipped by Beta. This implies that the US vendor also uses SAP GTS to manage its import process. This process is depicted in Figure 6.28.

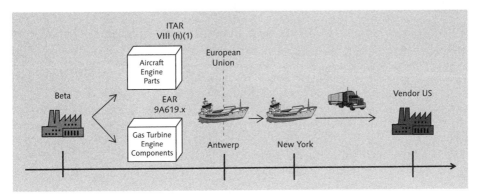

Figure 6.28 Import Business Process of Defense Articles into the United States

The imported articles include aircraft engine parts and specially designed gas turbine engine components. Because the aircraft engine parts are considered for military applications, they are subject to the jurisdiction of the US Department of State International Traffic in Arms Regulation (ITAR).

A United States Munitions List (USML) is assigned to the ITAR legal regulation, containing all restricted military products that are heavily monitored and subject to license requirements. More specifically, the aircraft engine part are classified within the USML list as VIII(h)(1) products.

Furthermore, the gas turbine engine components temporarily exported by Beta are not considered military products, but they are considered dual-use products, implying they *could* be applied for military applications. Because they are a US product, this falls under the Export Administration Regulations (EAR), which covers products with both commercial and military applications. To classify products within the EAR regulation, products are assigned a specific export control classification number (ECCN). The gas turbine engine components are classified with ECCN 9A619.x.

When you import goods from third countries, a customs broker needs to create a customs import declaration. Please refer to Chapter 7 on Customs Management for further information on customs processes. However, this import declaration alone is not sufficient to import the goods in this case, given that an import of defense articles is subject to the ITAR regulation.

Because the aircraft engine parts are subject to ITAR, a license or other authorization is required to import the parts from Belgium to the US. Vendor A decides to apply for a DSP61 license, which covers importing the US military products.

Once the US vendor has received the applicable license authorizing the import of the aircraft engine parts, it notifies company Beta to continue with the export process. This ensures that the goods do not leave the Belgian premises until the necessary documentation is in place to import the goods.

System Process

The vendor in the United States temporarily imports two types of products from company Beta in Belgium: aircraft engine parts and specially designed gas turbine engine components. The SAP GTS system process for handling this scenario is displayed in Figure 6.29.

When you create the inbound delivery at the US vendor, you get the pop-up notification shown in Figure 6.30 about the SAP GTS block stating that item 10—that is, the aircraft engine parts, ITAR part classified as VIII(h)(1)—requires a license. The import of item 20—the gas turbine engine components, EAR part classified as 9A619.x—does not result in a legal control block.

The inbound license determination takes place based on the Customizing setup, determination strategy, product classification, and departure and destination countries.

In this process flow, a license is required to import the aircraft engine parts because they are classified as defense articles subject to ITAR. A legal control check is also performed on the second item, but it is immediately released because it does not require an import authorization.

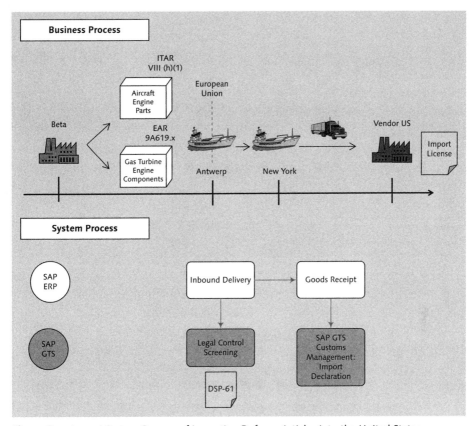

Figure 6.29 Import System Process of Importing Defense Articles into the United States

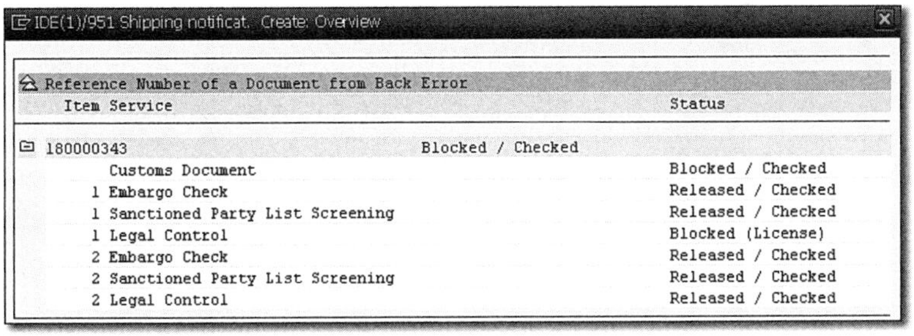

```
IDE(1)/951 Shipping notificat. Create: Overview                           [x]

 Reference Number of a Document from Back Error
   Item Service                                      Status

 180000343                          Blocked / Checked
        Customs Document                             Blocked / Checked
      1 Embargo Check                                Released / Checked
      1 Sanctioned Party List Screening              Released / Checked
      1 Legal Control                                Blocked (License)
      2 Embargo Check                                Released / Checked
      2 Sanctioned Party List Screening              Released / Checked
      2 Legal Control                                Released / Checked
```

Figure 6.30 Legal Control Block in the Feeder System

To analyze the block, you can display the blocked document in SAP GTS, accessed via COMPLIANCE MANAGEMENT • LEGAL CONTROL—IMPORT • DISPLAY BLOCKED DOCU-MENTS, using the inbound delivery number as the reference number. Note that this is the same transaction used to display the documents blocked for embargo reasons.

Figure 6.31 displays the blocked document in SAP GTS. The US vendor's inbound delivery is blocked for legal control, specifically for the aircraft engine parts (product number GB-1005).

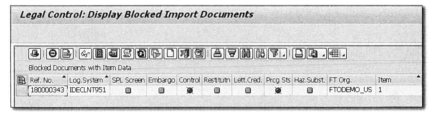

Figure 6.31 Import Document Blocked Due to Legal Control Check

If you don't know why the document is blocked, check the SAP GTS log, as shown in Figure 6.32. The log contains the two items included in the inbound delivery and provides information on the checks performed on that document.

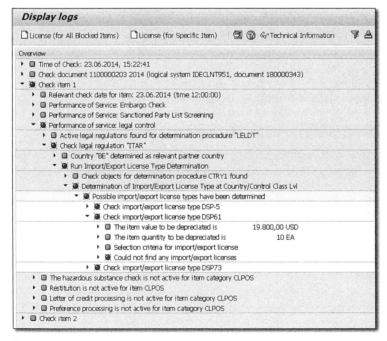

Figure 6.32 SAP GTS Log for the Blocked Import Document

A license is required to import these parts into the United States from Belgium because aircraft engine parts (material GB-1005) are subject to ITAR. The US vendor does not yet possess an applicable license to cover the import of that product, cueing a block for the ITAR regulation. Furthermore, product GB-2000 is not an EAR-classified material and does not require an import EAR license ("No License Required"), so it is cleared for the legal control check.

The US vendor decides to apply for a DSP61 license, which is specifically designed for the temporary import of military items. As soon as it has received the license, the license master is maintained in SAP GTS, displayed in Figure 6.33. All attributes (objects to be checked) are maintained based on the paper copy received from the US Directorate of Defense Trade Controls.

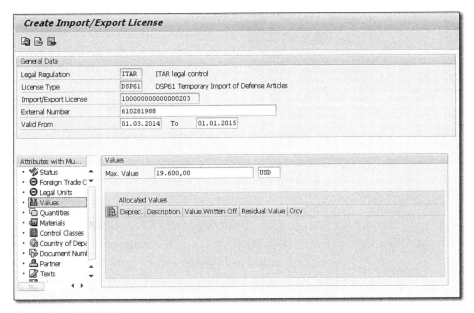

Figure 6.33 DSP61 License

One of the attributes in the left-hand list is DOCUMENT NUMBER, so the US vendor has to assign the inbound delivery number to the license in order to release the inbound delivery. As noted in the log in Figure 6.34, the open value of the DSP61 license is not sufficient to receive all parts: the total value of the aircraft engine parts is $19,800. In this case, the log recognizes the open license with external number 610281988 but it notifies that the open value is not sufficient to cover the shipment.

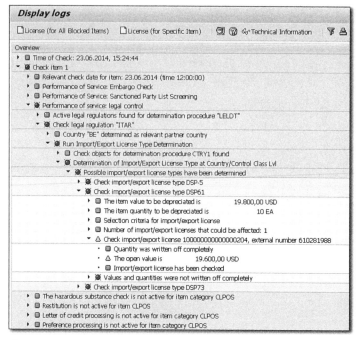

Figure 6.34 Log Displaying Insufficient License Open Value

If the inbound delivery item line contains a value of less than or equal to $19,600, you can assign the license to the inbound delivery item line (on the condition that all other attributes match).

Once you take the necessary action (decreasing the value or quantity in the inbound delivery or applying for another import authorization) and the customs document is rechecked, the DSP61 license is assigned to the inbound delivery.

You can use different reporting tools. For example, when displaying assigned documents (Figure 6.35), the US supplier can search for all inbound delivery assigned to the DSP61 license.

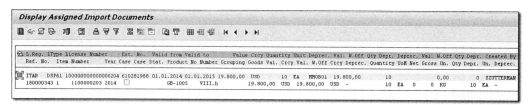

Figure 6.35 Assigned Import Documents

Within the license, the value is written off for the depreciation group on the inbound delivery level, as shown in Figure 6.36.

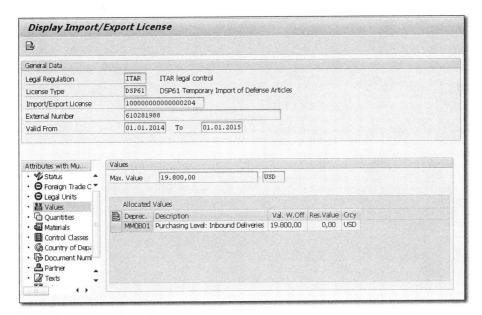

Figure 6.36 DSP61 License Depreciation

Let's explore the most important elements within the SAP GTS Legal Control functionality. Before going into the import and export system process flows, you should have basic knowledge about the elements that form the backbone for the Legal Control functionality.

Legal Control Backbone

In order to determine whether an import or export license or authorization is required for a material (hence, for an item in an SAP feeder system document), SAP GTS performs an automatic validity check of the license or authorization criteria upon creation of the mirror document (i.e., the SAP GTS customs document). However, before the actual license check is made in the customs document, SAP GTS determines the legal regulations that apply to the document. Then, within each legal regulation, open licenses in SAP GTS are assigned when applicable.

The backbone of the SAP GTS Legal Control functionality is shown in Figure 6.37 and serves as a foundation for the following sections.

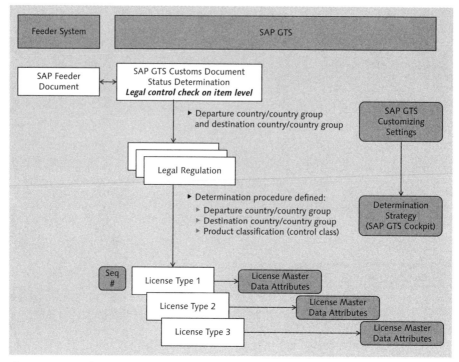

Figure 6.37 Legal Control Structure

The rest of the chapter explains in detail how the status for legal control for all items in the SAP GTS document is determined, based on the business transaction (business partner countries), product classification of the items included in the shipments, determination strategy setup, and existing license master data in SAP GTS.

The import and export legal regulations used in the Beta business case that support the business process flows in the Legal Control section of this chapter are the following:

▶ Export Administration Regulations (EAR) and US Re-export (USREX)

▶ International Traffic in Arms Regulations (ITAR)

▶ EU Dual-Use (EUDU)

▶ Belgian regulatory framework for military licenses (BEML)

Recall that the SAP GTS customs document determines the legal control status on the item level. In order to determine the status for legal control, SAP GTS first determines the applicable legal regulations to be checked based on the country/country-group activation. The country/country-group activation is performed in Customizing settings, discussed in Section 6.4.4.

For example, in order to import aircraft engine parts and gas turbine engine components (import business process flow), the SAP GTS customs document retrieves all active legal regulations in the Customizing "from" Belgium "to" the United States. On the other hand, for the SAP GTS check on the sales order to export the aircraft engine (export business flow) to a customer located in Qatar, SAP GTS processes all applicable legal regulations active "from" Belgium "to" Qatar. This means that, for each item in the SAP GTS customs document, multiple legal regulations can be applicable.

Determination Strategy

Regulatory requirements ultimately architected in SAP GTS are set forth by the applicable authorities. Specific import or export transactions require explicit approval. Likewise, within the above business process flows, Beta's US vendor is receiving (importing)—and later Beta will be shipping (exporting)—materials for which a license is required.

Beta needs to apply to the applicable regulatory authorities for the required licenses and authorizations, and you can maintain the license approvals as master data in SAP GTS. Apply the relevant licenses to the customs document representing the feeder system document. In order for this to be done, SAP GTS customs document system logic goes through two additional steps:

▶ Identifying the license or other authorization types (e.g., exceptions or exemptions) that could be applicable for this transaction, based on the regulatory jurisdiction, product classification, and business transaction

▶ Identifying whether a license is already set up in the SAP GTS master data for which all attributes match (see next section)

The purpose of the determination strategy is to obtain a list of applicable license and authorization types to be checked in SAP GTS based on the import and export governmental regulations. Thus, as soon as the legal regulations are identified on an item level of the customs document, the determination strategy is triggered. You need key regulatory knowledge to maintain this critical and foundational information to set up this determination strategy.

In addition to the necessary Customizing steps, define the determination strategy as master data in the SAP GTS cockpit for legal control. You can create the table manually (via LEGAL CONTROL–IMPORT • MAINTAIN DETERMINATION STRATEGY) or upload it via an XML file.

You may interpret the determination strategy as a table used in order to define the applicable license or authorization types for each item in a customs document. Typically, these can include the departure country or country group, the destination country or country group, and a classification number. This classification number should be part of the classification codes loaded for the numbering scheme assigned to that legal regulation within the import/export control definitions section.

Figure 6.38 displays the determination strategy applicable to the Beta business case.

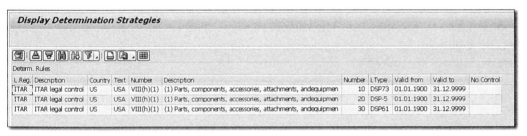

Figure 6.38 Determination Strategy

A specific entry in the table is valid only if the customs document check is done between eligible VALID FROM and VALID TO dates.

Referring to the business import scenario, the US supplier is planning to import aircraft engine parts from Belgium, so SAP GTS tries to determine a license with license type DSP61 for import of a material classified as VIII(h)(1). Within the log of the customs document for the inbound delivery (Figure 6.32), SAP GTS first checks all license masters with potentially applicable license types set forth in the ITAR legal regulation. If SAP GTS cannot identify a license master with license type DSP61 that is applicable for this flow, it goes and searches for a license master with another potentially applicable license or authorization type. The sequence number within the determination strategy defines which license types are being checked first.

To summarize, within each legal regulation, the determination strategy determines the applicable import/export license type(s) for the item in the customs document. There is only one exception: when the material master of the item is flagged as "No Control" for the specific legal regulation. In this case, the item is not subject to the specific regulatory jurisdiction requirement (e.g., ITAR), so the product is not subject to the specific legal regulation as architected in SAP GTS.

Licenses

Because Beta is receiving and shipping materials for which various country- and jurisdiction-specific licenses are required, the automatic determination of the applicable legal regulations for the shipment item lines, as well as the automatic guidance toward the applicable license types via the determination strategy, enable it to comply with the country and jurisdiction regulatory and import/export control requirements (including the ITAR extraterritorial reach) for all process flows transacted in the feeder system.

The prerequisite to using this functionality is that Beta (or any other company, e.g., the US supplier) maintain the import and export license approvals it receives from the applicable country-specific governmental agencies as master data in SAP GTS.

You may create import and export licenses in SAP GTS as master data via, respectively, LEGAL CONTROL – IMPORT • MAINTAIN IMPORT LICENSES and LEGAL CONTROL – EXPORT • MAINTAIN EXPORT LICENSES.

One of the main advantages of using SAP GTS is the automatic comparison of the data within the customs document item and the data within the license attributes of all license and authorization master data set up for each license type in SAP GTS. The criteria for license and other authorization assignments are automatically checked based on the license or authorization type attributes, as illustrated in Figure 6.39.

The rest of this section sets forth the concepts of license types, license type attributes, and license assignment in SAP GTS in general.

We've already shown how the system determines the potentially applicable license types via the determination strategy. By design, it is because of this backbone framework that every license master in SAP GTS can be set up for only one legal regulation and one license type: when you create a license master, you need to specify the legal regulation and license type as part of the initial setup.

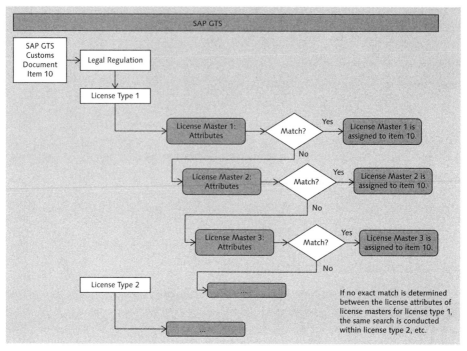

The diagram contains the following labels:

SAP GTS

SAP GTS Customs Document Item 10

Legal Regulation

License Type 1

License Master 1: Attributes → Match? — Yes → License Master 1 is assigned to item 10.

No

License Master 2: Attributes → Match? — Yes → License Master 2 is assigned to item 10.

No

License Master 3: Attributes → Match? — Yes → License Master 3 is assigned to item 10.

No

License Type 2

...

...

If no exact match is determined between the license attributes of license masters for license type 1, the same search is conducted within license type 2, etc.

Figure 6.39 SAP GTS License Assignment Structure

You must set up the different license types in Customizing. Then, the license type determines which license attributes you need to maintain to enable the automatic license determination for a customs document, as displayed in Figure 6.40.

The purpose of setting up multiple license types is to accommodate the different types of licenses and authorizations issued by the applicable governmental authorities. Many export authorizations include a total approved value and a total approved quantity over a specified validity period, but other export license exceptions or exemptions do not specify a maximum value or quantity.

As soon as the license is created, you should maintain the data for all attributes in the license based on the license received from the applicable government authorities. Because the license type setup predefines which attributes you should maintain, you have a clear indication when the license master creation is complete. The license-type attributes are key objects to ensure automatic license assignment to the customs document item line.

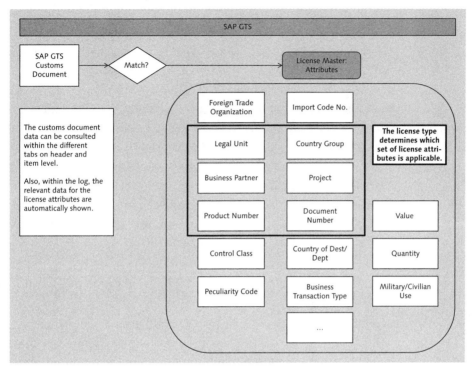

Figure 6.40 License Attributes

The most important license attributes in SAP GTS are the following:

▶ Organizational structure attributes FTO and LU: Specifies whether the license is valid for only one or multiple FTOs, which are mapped to the company code(s) in the feeder system, and whether the license is valid for only specific legal units, which are mapped to the plant(s) in the feeder system. Some licenses might be issued to company Beta for all entities across Europe, and others might be specific to the one plant in Belgium.

▶ Control class attribute: Determines whether the license is valid for only specific export control classifications, e.g., ECCN code. During license assignment, the system compares the classification code of the product with the codes maintained in the license.

▶ Country of destination/departure: Captures whether the license is valid only for shipments to and from business partners in specific countries. All the countries for which the license is valid must be captured in this attribute. The system takes the country from the first existing business partner function maintained in the partner group, which is assigned to the legal regulation and can contain various business partner functions like ship-to party, end user, and sold-to party. Flagging the MULT. PART. COUNTRIES setting ensures that the countries from all the business partners in the group assigned to the legal regulation are checked (see Customizing settings).

▸ Product number: If license is valid only for specific products, you should maintain the product numbers.

▸ Value and quantity of the products in the licenses (with possible definition of tolerances): Different settings in Customizing determine whether you should specify the values and quantities on the license level or product level. For example, a DSP5 issued by the US Directorate of Defense Trade Controls usually contains the maximum value and maximum quantity allowed per product. However, Beta might deal with many other licenses for which no maximum value is specified.

▸ Business partner: Controls whether license is valid for only a specific business partner or multiple business partners.

▸ Partner function: When this object is flagged, you also need to maintain a partner group. The system can check whether all the partner functions maintained in the partner group are also maintained in the corresponding document (e.g., sales order). This option allows you to force the end user to be filled in as an ultimate consignee.

▸ Document number: Enabling this object forces the compliance users to fill in every relevant document for which the license is valid. When a sales order is created, the order is blocked because the system requires the sales order number to be maintained in the license. The same happens for the delivery and subsequent documents. Thus, this setting sets forth a manual license assignment. You can architect SAP GTS to assign export authorizations manually or using an automated process. These are key decisions to be made as part of the blueprint. If you're using the automated export authorization setup, consider export authorizations with potentially overlapping attributes (e.g., a DSP5 could overlap with a DSP73 and have the same part numbers, export control classifications, legal entities, and destination countries). Thus, you need to include specific configuration to prevent inadvertent assignment to the incorrect import or export control authorization.

- CHECK FIRST.DOC IN DOCUMENT FLOW flag: Enables some automation as the compliance user manually adds the license to the first document in the feeder system document flow (e.g., sales order), and the same license is then automatically assigned to the subsequent documents (e.g., outbound delivery) if all other attributes match.

- Value and quantity update: Activate automatic decrementing of the license. Several options exist to adjust the specifics of the functionality. You can specify whether the maximum value is valid for all products or for specific products, or whether the maximum value can be exceeded, among others.

Summarized, it is via the setup of the specific license types in Customizing that the global trade regulations are also set forth within SAP GTS: depending on the license, certain attributes might or might not be applicable.

To ensure that the license determination functionality performs effectively, be sure to properly set up the legal regulations and specific master data, namely the license determination strategy and the license master data.

As soon as the system finds a match with a specific license or authorization type, SAP GTS assigns the license or authorization (including license exceptions or exemptions, as applicable) to the customs document, and the status for legal control is positive for that item. Furthermore, SAP GTS notifies the user if a *nearly* identical match is identified, but where not all attributes match. An example of this is illustrated in the import system process flow in Figure 6.29, where the system notified the SAP GTS user that a DSP61 license could be applicable, but the open value was not sufficient.

6.4.2 Export Licensing

Let's turn our attention from import licensing to export licensing.

Business Process

As soon as the US vendor performs the necessary operations on the aircraft engine parts and gas turbine engine components, both products are re-exported from the United States to Beta in Belgium using the same DSP61 license (for the aircraft engine parts) and an individual validated license (IVL) 748QV export license (to cover the gas turbine engine components).

Beta manufactures the aircraft engine following the technical routing sheets (usually not set up in the feeder system). As part of the production process, numerous items, including the defense articles subject to ITAR, are assembled. The ITAR aircraft engine parts are included in an aircraft engine for final export to an end user in Qatar. This export transaction is the basis for this sequence, as shown in Figure 6.41.

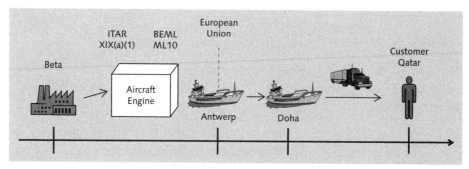

Figure 6.41 Business Process of Exporting Regulated Articles

The regulatory and business requirement is to perform a license determination on the ITAR components embedded in the engine. Additionally, the shipment of the engine is also subject to the Belgian regulatory framework for defense articles. To comply with the imposed regulations, Beta must apply for licenses to cover the export of a product with an ITAR component, as well as a Belgian military license.

System Process

Beta wishes to export regulated materials to its customer in Qatar. But besides analyzing the finished product to determine the required licenses, Beta also needs to analyze the finished product's components.

Chapter 7 about Customs Management explains that Beta—or a customs broker or freight forwarder—needs to create a customs export declaration in order to proceed with the shipment and export the engine from the European Union (EU) via the port of Antwerp. Within SAP GTS, the necessary licenses assigned at the shipment within the Legal Control functionality are automatically included in the customs export declaration on an item level. Therefore, they can be contained within the electronic declaration, and the license information can be printed on the customs shipping documentation generated in SAP GTS.

Figure 6.42 displays the SAP GTS system process for Beta's business case, in which the company determines the required licenses for both the finished product and its components by analyzing the finished product's bill of material (BOM).

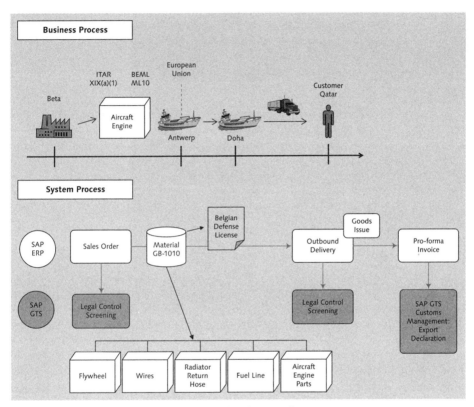

Figure 6.42 System Process of Exporting Regulated Materials

Beta manufactures the aircraft engine following the technical routing sheets. During production, the flywheel, wires, radiator return hose, two fuel lines, and imported aircraft engine parts are assembled—but you should note that the BOM is composed for illustration purposes only. As a prerequisite to perform automatic BOM explosion on the export transactions using SAP GTS, the BOM should be transfererd to SAP GTS as a master data element. Alternertively, BOMs can be created in the SAP GTS product master directly, as illustrated in Figure 6.43.

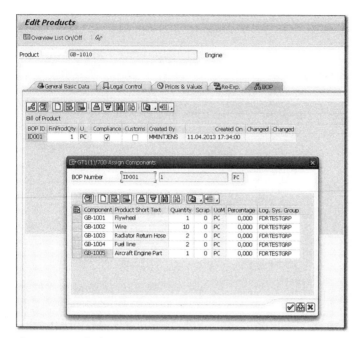

Figure 6.43 Bill of Material of the Aircraft Engine

First, the regulatory requirement (and thus also the business requirement) is to perform a license determination on the ITAR components embedded in the engine. Second, the export of the engine is also subject to the Belgian military regulations.

Beta creates a sales order for the sale of the engine (material GB-1010). Using SAP GTS, the customs document recognizes that a BOM is embedded in the material master GB-1010. Initially, the customs document contains only one item line, representing the final product. However, as soon as the bill of product is exploded in SAP GTS, the customs document also contains all components of the final product. In Figure 6.44, the legal control status for each component for the final product is provided (item numbers on the left, starting with B00001).

When recognizing that Beta's finished product contains an ITAR-classified component, SAP GTS proposes using a DSP5 license (alongside other possible licenses). Beta is notified of this license requirement upon saving the sales order in the feeder system (the parties to this prospective transaction and other item-specific details are defined for the sale of the aircraft engine to the customer in Qatar).

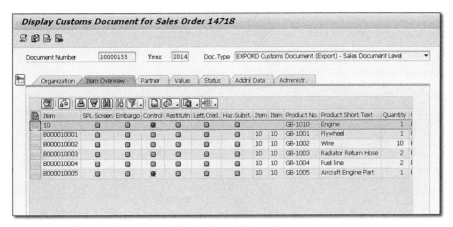

Figure 6.44 Customs Document of Beta's Export Sales Order

The BOM explosion proposes using a DSP5 license for the aircraft engine, which is classified in SAP GTS with USML classification XIX(a)(1). As soon as the sales order number is added to the DSP5 license, the legal control status for this item is cleared because Beta has already requested and set up the DSP5 license up front in SAP GTS. A recheck of the sales order customs document to confirm that all attributes match is required before the status of the document changes.

Additionally, the shipment of the engine is also subject to the Belgian regulatory framework for defense articles. Within the system process flow, the customs document also recognized the legal regulation BEML for the shipment from Belgium to Qatar. Beta has classified the aircraft engine as ML10 for the Belgian Military list. Hence, you must also maintain the determination strategy for the Belgian Military Legal Regulation for classification code ML10 for shipments "from" Belgium "to" Qatar in SAP GTS in order to assign the Belgian Military license in legal regulation BEML. Because the sales order remains blocked and the shipment cannot occur, Beta decides to apply for the Belgian defense license via the official request form issued by the Belgian government. In this form, Beta indicates all details about the customer in Qatar, including the classification and description of the products to be sent, among other details, and attaches the necessary export control authorization details.

As soon as authorities receive the license, the license master is set up in SAP GTS, the sales order is rechecked, and the outbound delivery can be created, as long as all attributes of the Belgian license master are in line with the characteristics of the customs document representing the sales order.

Agreements

Agreements in SAP GTS allow the company to define and manage export control authorizations that can be linked with licenses as applicable or serve as the sole export authorization. This functionality is primarily set forth to meet applicable ITAR requirements, but other export control jurisdictions have related requirements. The functionality also allows the grouping of several export authorizations within one agreement, making use of the "nested" license concept.

Agreements can depend on value, quantity, or both, as determined during Customizing for which method is used for depreciation.

This paragraph illustrates the use of agreements, separate from the business case import/export transactions introduced in Section 6.1.

In this example, Beta has set up an agreement in SAP GTS to represent the Technical Assistance Agreement (TAA). The total quantity of the agreement is 100 PC for a specific aircraft engine part. The total value allowed to be transacted against is $50,000. Furthermore, all additional agreement attributes are maintained (similar to license attributes), as shown in Figure 6.45.

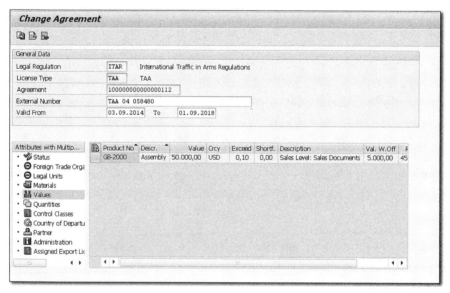

Figure 6.45 Agreement

The process in SAP GTS in order to clear the blocked document can be split into two steps:

1. Agreement-license assignment: Once the DSP5 license is assigned to the agreement, the open quantity of 100 in the agreement is decremented by 20, which is the maximum quantity specified in the corresponding DSP5 license (see Figure 6.46).

2. License-document assignment: After the sales order assignment to the DSP5 license, the license itself has a remaining open quantity of 4 because the feeder system document contains 16 pieces. If the feeder system document contains 35 parts of the material, this license is not sufficient; an additional DSP5 license or other export control authorization needs to be obtained. The amounts can be depreciated on the sales document level and outbound delivery level, depending on the Customizing settings for depreciation groups.

You can consult both the total and remaining quantity of the agreement, as the total and remaining quantity of the license, in the QUANTITIES attribute of the license shown on the left in Figure 6.46.

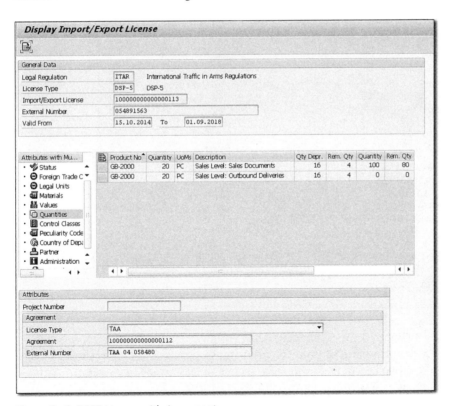

Figure 6.46 DSP5 License with Agreement

SAP GTS Cockpit for Legal Control

The transactions for Legal Control import and export are similar, as is the handling of outbound and/or inbound documents, licenses, and agreements. Let's look at various transactions within the SAP GTS Legal Control menu based on the layout of the SAP Compliance Management Legal Control—Export cockpit in Figure 6.47.

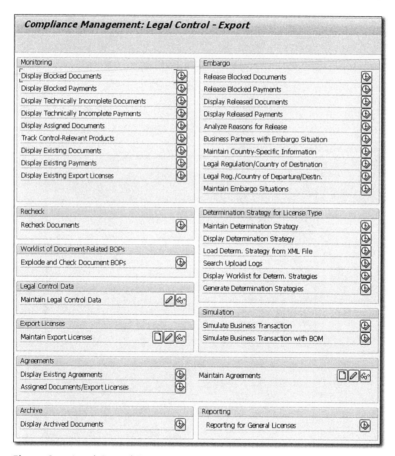

Figure 6.47 Legal Control Export Menu

▶ **Monitoring**

The monitoring functions in the licensing service of SAP Compliance Management enable Beta to maintain an overview of all business transactions. You can see which documents the system has blocked for further business transactions and react accordingly, for example, by assigning the appropriate licenses for import or export transactions.

Within Monitoring, you can use the DISPLAY BLOCKED DOCUMENTS worklist for tracking and reviewing transactions. You can set several selection criteria to work effectively. For archiving purposes, all trade compliance information is captured in the SAP GTS customs document for each transactional document in the SAP feeder system. You go into the document itself (header/item) or the log to view available information as applicable.

The overall status of a document determines whether you can execute follow-on activities. If a document is technically incomplete, the log of the document is not available. You can investigate why the document is technically incomplete in the specific transactions.

In the example in Figure 6.48, the company code 2700 was not yet mapped to an FTO in SAP GTS and the system could not identify a legal unit mapped to plant 2730. However, the feeder system document was transferred and thus technically incomplete. Furthermore, you need to transfer the customer and product to SAP GTS before the legal control checks can be performed. After making the necessary corrections, you can manually retransfer the document to SAP GTS.

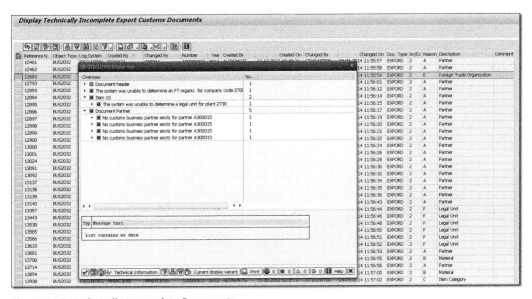

Figure 6.48 Technically Incomplete Documents

When Beta reports a license assignment that occurred in the past, SAP GTS reporting functionality offers to search in both directions: from document to license and from license to document. First of all, you can use the DISPLAY ASSIGNED DOCUMENTS transaction to search by document number and display which licenses have been assigned to each individual item. You can use the DISPLAY EXISTING EXPORT LICENSES transaction to report all created, active, and expired licenses in SAP GTS by legal regulation, license type, FTO, and many more. When going into the license master, the assigned documents report is available in the ASSIGNED DOCUMENTS attribute.

▶ **Recheck**
The recheck of the customs documents is necessary to determine the latest status of a document when updates have been made in SAP GTS (e.g., a license creation/change). You can execute the recheck within the specific dedicated transaction or with the REFRESH button at the display blocked documents itself.

This function enables you to recheck all documents in the feeder system regardless of their processing status.

▶ **Legal control data**
The MAINTAIN LEGAL CONTROL DATA transaction allows you to manually change the license assignment to a specific document from the SAP feeder system.

▶ **Agreements**
Similarly to the DISPLAY EXISTING EXPORT LICENSES, you can use the report DISPLAY EXISTING AGREEMENTS as an overview of all ITAR agreements or other related export-control jurisdiction requirements in the system. The second transaction provides an overview of the assigned licenses to the existing agreements, similarly to the DISPLAY ASSIGNED DOCUMENTS transaction, but one level higher in the structure. This assignment is shown in Figure 6.49.

Figure 6.49 License—Agreement Assignment

▶ **Simulations**
Beta can also use the simulation functionality within SAP GTS. You can simulate the compliance check for customs documents in Legal Control. As a result,

you can immediately identify whether an export control authorization is required for a potential business transaction. Furthermore, you can also simulate the check of document-related BOMs in Legal Control for exports.

6.4.3 US Re-Export

When goods which are subject to US controls are re-exported to another nation, special legal requirements apply. This section explores these legal requirements by demonstrating the SAP GTS de minimis functionality. In short, by calculating the de minimis value, a US civil license might need to be assigned to the transaction in case this value exceeds the threshold.

Business Process

As part of outgoing shipments from Belgium, Beta provides specially designed assemblies and integrated circuits to an end user in Brazil. Because the assemblies contain parts that were previously imported and contain US content, they are also subject to the EAR controls mentioned earlier in this section.

You have to perform a de minimis calculation to determine whether the re-exported materials require an additional US license. If the US content in the exported materials exceeds a given threshold determined by the country of destination and classification of the US components, such a license is required.

Beta's business process for exporting materials containing US content is displayed in Figure 6.50.

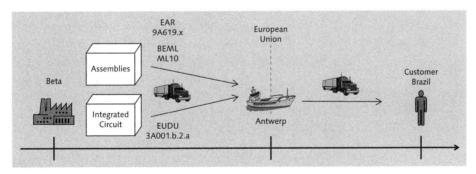

Figure 6.50 Business Process of Exporting Materials with US Content

On top of US re-export legal regulations, the assemblies are also subject to a Belgian military license (analogous to the aircraft engine of Section 6.4.2).

System Process

Figure 6.51 illustrates Beta's system process for exporting materials containing US content to a customer in Brazil. SAP GTS picks up the BOM of both products when creating the sales order in the feeder system and determines the US content of both materials. This amount of US content is then compared against a set threshold percentage, which determines whether a US license is required.

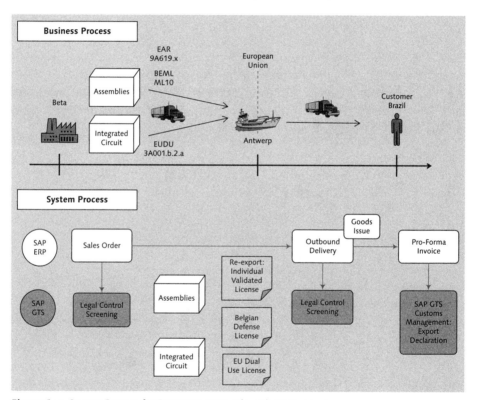

Figure 6.51 System Process for Exporting Materials with US Content

At the level of product master data in SAP GTS (for the finished product), more specifically on the RE-EXPORT tab in Figure 6.52, you can give a product a certain re-export control relevance. This re-export control relevance and its related threshold value are the result of the de minimis calculation performed in SAP

GTS. You have to maintain this control relevance for each applicable country (e.g., the "critical" threshold of 10% for EAR Country Group E:1 and the "uncritical" country group of 25%).

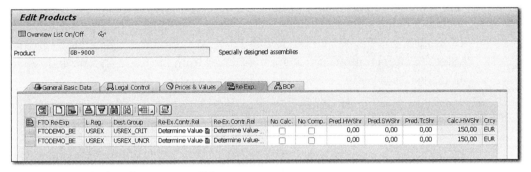

Figure 6.52 Finished Product Re-Export Tab

This data has to be entered for each FTO making use of this product (given recent regulatory changes as part of the US Export Control Reform, a 0% de minimis tolerance applies to specific items classified under EAR 600 series to applicable destination countries). In this example, notice that two lines have been added to the product master: one for the critical and one for the uncritical country group. Both values have been set to €150.00 (value for the US controlled component). Figure 6.54 shows how SAP GTS has determined the finished good exists of a total value for the US re-export share of €150.00, based on the US re-export shares of the components in the BOM.

Three different statuses apply; the setting determines the system behavior regarding de minimis for these products:

▶ CHECK/CONTROL: The product is always relevant for US re-export.

▶ DO NOT CHECK/CONTROL: The product is never relevant for US re-export.

▶ DETERMINE VALUE-DEPENDENT CONTROL RELEVANCE: A US re-export value is determined for this product.

Before calculation in SAP GTS can take place, it must be indicated which components in the finished product's BOM are subject to the EAR regulation. This can be done via classification of the SAP GTS products for legal regulation EAR (the assignment of ECCN code to the individual product masters). Recall from Chapter 5 that this can be achieved via various transactions, including the Maintain Products transaction (COMPLIANCE MANAGEMENT • CLASSIFICATION / MASTER DATA).

Furthermore, the same re-export control relevance discussed at the product level also has to be maintained at component level. For all the relevant components, you have to maintain a value of the US content. For components that are not EAR controlled, you don't have to enter a value. SAP GTS makes it possible to use the values per legal unit/plant that are transferred from the feeder system and stored in the PRICES & VALUES section of the product master.

In our example, Beta is shipping the specially designed assemblies and integrated circuits on one shipment to its customer in Brazil.

▶ The integrated circuits are built with only components produced in house, and the value of US content is equal to zero.

▶ The specially designed assemblies (product GB-9000) have a BOM with three components: one main US-controlled part classified with ECCN 9A619.x and two parts of Belgian origin. The value for the US-controlled component (GB-10001) is €150, while the value for the Belgian item not subject to EAR is €0. Consecutively, SAP GTS calculates the total US re-export share for the specially designed assemblies based on the BOM.

You can find several calculation transactions in the RE-EXPORT CALCULATION section on the right side of Figure 6.53, accessed via COMPLIANCE MANAGEMENT • LEGAL CONTROL — EXPORT.

With these transactions, you have the options to perform the calculation for a range of products (option 1), one individual product (2), or the products for which the BOM changed in a certain period (3).

If SAP GTS is unable to retrieve the US value for a component (e.g., if it is not maintained in its product master), it determines that the finished product is control required, meaning that an EAR authorization is required independently of the price of the product. Thus, you can configure SAP GTS in a way that, when no US value is maintained, the component has an infinite US value. This is a worst-case approach, and SAP GTS does not consider the final selling price of the finished product because the US re-export share is always higher and, therefore, the threshold is exceeded, making the finished good subject to the EAR in any follow-on scenario.

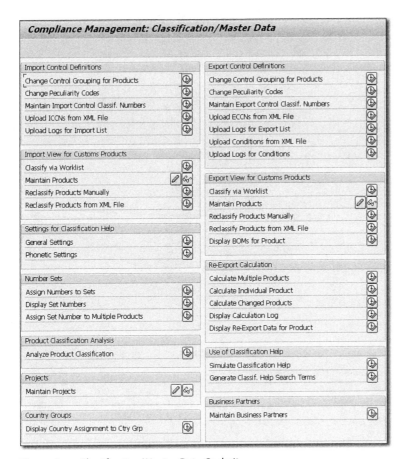

Figure 6.53 Classification/Master Data Cockpit

If you maintain the product master correctly, including transferring the value and bill of product from the feeder system, SAP GTS calculates the actual US re-export share for the applicable assemblies. Figure 6.54 shows where the transaction was executed for one individual product (option 2)—the specially designed assemblies GB-9000.

SAP GTS determines that the finished good has a total value for the US re-export share of €150. As previously discussed, you extract this value from the component's PRICES & VALUES tab in Figure 6.55.

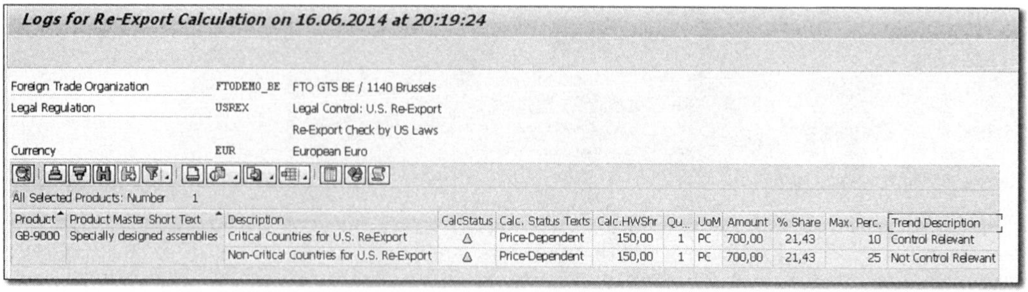

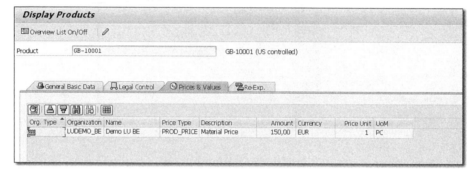

Figure 6.54 Calculation of US Re-Export Share

Figure 6.55 Prices & Values Tab on Component Material

When comparing this with the price of the product as maintained in its material master, the system determines that the 25% threshold is not surpassed (while the 10% is). It is always possible, however, that the transactional net value of the product is higher or lower than the price of the product. This result, however, can already be seen as an indicator.

After the calculation is executed with this transaction, the value is stored in the product master of the finished product (the CALC.HWSHR column in Figure 6.52). You can overwrite this value with a manually added value: this can be used as a security measure to make sure that the value of the US content of the finished product is never lower than a specific amount, even if the sum of values of the components is lower (see the PRED.HWSHR column in Figure 6.52).

De Minimis Calculation

At the transaction level, SAP GTS picks up this US re-export share from the product master of the items that are shipped and compares it with the actual sales price in the document. The log per document in SAP GTS displays the threshold percentage, item value, and re-export share percentage. If the re-export share percentage exceeds the threshold percentage, the finished product is subject to the EAR legal regulation.

In Figure 6.56, we see the SAP GTS log for the shipment for Beta going to the customer in Brazil; the specially designed assemblies exceed the 25% de minimis threshold for the "uncritical" country group (which includes Brazil) within the USREX legal regulation because the selling price varies from the price indicated in the calculation (27.27% versus 21.43%).

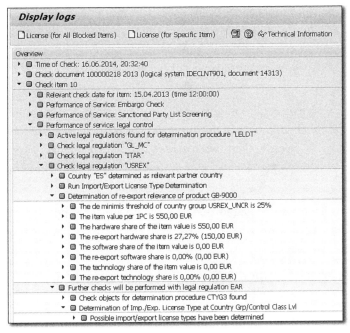

Figure 6.56 Re-Export Relevance Determination

An IVL license is proposed for the specially designed assemblies (item 10 in Figure 6.56), classified as 9A619.x. This license type is proposed within the EAR legal regulation, triggered via USREX as the threshold is reached. The legal control check is still red because, now, the necessary Belgian military license has yet to be assigned; the product is classified as ML10 within the Belgian military framework. (The BEML legal regulation is triggered separately.)

The integrated circuits (item 20) do not require a license assignment because they are not subject to the EAR. Because the integrated circuits do not contain US components, the de minimis calculation does not apply for item 20.

After the assignment of the licenses for the European export controls, as well as the relevant licenses covering the re-export of products subject to US export control requirements, the transaction SAP GTS releases the product, and further processing becomes available. All legal control checks have now been executed.

6.4.4 Customizing

Setting up the general settings of legal control is similar to the general settings of embargo. As soon as you maintain the baseline Customizing steps, including the definition of a legal regulation based on the applicable regulatory requirements, you can continue with the following settings within the Compliance Management Legal Control functionality.

Note that you must set a legal regulation per legal requirement. If, for example, the requirements are to check whether the product is an ITAR product *or* whether the product requires an EAR license, then two legal regulations are needed. However, it is possible to assign different license types (e.g., DSP5 and DSP73) to one single legal regulation.

This assumes that you have also activated the relevant document types for the Legal Control functionality in SAP GTS and assigned the legal regulation to a numbering scheme.

Let's look at the Customizing activities.

Assign Determination Procedure for Active Legal Regulation

This IMG activity is the same as the one explained in the embargo section.

As part of the standard configuration settings, the determination procedure defined is "LELDT," which consists of the following determination strategies:

▶ Determine legal regulation at country group level

▶ Determine legal regulation at country/country-group level

▶ Determine legal regulation at country-group/country-group level

- ▸ Determine legal regulation at country-group/country-level
- ▸ Determine legal regulation at country level

Furthermore, depending on the rule option selected, the system runs through all four determination strategies, or stops after the first strategy that results in a hit (i.e., one or more legal regulations). Within standard SAP GTS, the DETERMINATION USING FIRST SUCCESSFUL STRATEGY option is selected, which means that when you can find a legal regulation using the country level, the country-group level is not triggered.

In the next step, we will define whether the legal regulation for those countries and/or country groups is active for the different directions (import/export).

Activate Legal Regulation

This IMG activity is, again, similar to the Activate Legal Regulation topic in the embargo section.

In this IMG activity, you have to select one or several legal regulations for the Legal Control service. In this menu, you can activate your legal regulation for the countries you have nominated in GENERAL SETTINGS • LEGAL REGULATIONS • ACTIVATE LEGAL REGULATIONS AT COUNTRY/COUNTRY GROUP LEVEL.

Note that, for Legal Control purposes, regulations are set up with legal code 00 (FOREIGN TRADE LAW — SAP COMPLIANCE MANAGEMENT services) when defining the regulations.

In the menu, choose the legal regulation you would like to activate for the Legal Control service. Depending on the determination procedure you choose, you should activate the legal regulation on different levels.

If your determination procedure runs at only the country level, it is sufficient to select the COUNTRY folder from the left menu and activate the legal regulation for all the relevant departure countries. This is displayed in Figure 6.57. However, if your legal regulation is running on the country/country level, you first have to select the departure country by clicking on the COUNTRY folder on the left and selecting the departure country on the right. Then, you can select the destination country by clicking on the COUNTRY/COUNTRY sub-item of the country folder.

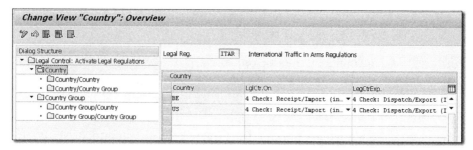

Figure 6.57 Activating Legal Regulation in Customizing

Define Determination Procedure to Automatically Determine License Types

In this Customizing activity, Beta can define a determination procedure that can be used to automatically determine a license type. A license type (e.g., DSP73 for ITAR) consists of several attributes.

You need to create a determination procedure and assign a determination strategy. The determination strategy can be built by using one or more of the following levels:

▶ Country/control grouping level

▶ Country/control class level

▶ Country group/control grouping level

▶ Country group/control class level

▶ Country level

▶ Country group level

▶ Control grouping level

▶ Control class level

▶ Legal regulation level

▶ Country/control class/control grouping level

▶ Country group/control class/control grouping level

▶ Control class/control grouping level

▶ Control class/measure/country group level

▶ Control class/measure/country level

▶ Country group/country group/control class level

- Country group/country group/control class/control grouping level

- Region/region/control class level

- Region/region/control grouping level

A determination procedure such as the one in Figure 6.58 can be made up of different strategies that consist of a hierarchy based on a *sequence number*. The system cycles through the different determination strategies based on the sequence number. The leading practice is to start with a specific determination strategy with an overflow to a more general strategy. When you use this procedure, the system first tries to pick the specific license (linked to the specific determination strategy) and, if no authorization is identified, the more general licenses are assigned.

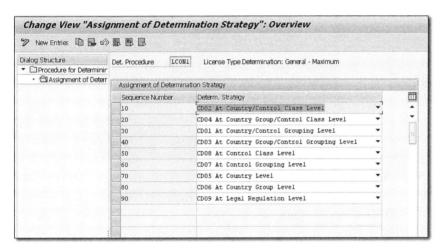

Figure 6.58 Determination Strategy Assignment to Determination Procedure

Standard determination strategies that can be used are set up in the system. You can also define your own determination strategies.

The determination procedure defined in this Customizing activity is linked to the legal regulation in the CONTROL SETTINGS FOR LEGAL CONTROL activity.

Control Settings for Legal Control

You can specify several configuration settings per legal regulation in this Customizing activity. You can find most of the settings by selecting the legal regulation and then clicking on the binocular icon. We'll only describe the most important settings—that is, the setup of partner groups.

For example, for company Beta, the partner group in Customizing is set up as in Table 6.5.

Sequence Number	Partner Group
10	Sold to
20	Ship to

Table 6.5 Assignment of Partner Functions to Partner Grouping

The sequence number determines the legal regulations being selected.

▶ If there is a shipment from Beta in Belgium with "Sold to" the United States and "Ship to" the United Kingdom, the system triggers all the licenses needed to ship to the United States. If no "Sold to" partner function is maintained in the document, the system triggers the regulations needed to ship to the United Kingdom.

▶ If there is a shipment from Beta in Belgium with "Sold to" the United Kingdom and "Ship to" the United States, the system triggers all the licenses needed to ship to the United Kingdom. If this is not the requirement, Beta should consider changing the sequence numbers in the partner group (e.g., 10 END USER; 20 SHIP TO; 30 SOLD TO). This would mean that only the country of the "Sold to" party determines the selection of legal regulations if there is no end user or ship-to party maintained in the SAP feeder system document.

When the MAIL DISPATCH flag is active, the system sends an e-mail if a transactional document is blocked because of this legal regulation. This option, however, requires additional configuration.

The MANUAL ASSIGNMENT DEFAULT setting determines how the assignment of the license to the document takes place. You need to decide whether the license assignment is done automatically, manually, or a combination of both. The CHECK EXTERNAL LICENSE NUMBER setting enables you to check whether a specific external license number is already being used by another license master. BOP (BILL OF PRODUCT) CHECK determines whether the legal regulation must also be activated for BOP items (the components when a finished product is exploded). You need to flag this checkbox for ITAR.

Configure Country Group of Legal Regulation for Re-Export

In this Customizing activity, you maintain the re-export settings per country group. Two standard country groups are maintained in Customizing (critical countries and uncritical countries). You can set up the maximum percentage of relevant US content, as well as the calculation rule. This calculation rule defines where the fair market value of the US component is coming from (manually maintained or transferred from the feeder system on the legal-unit level) and how the system should respond when no value is maintained.

Finally, it is possible to filter out components with specific export control classification numbers (e.g., EAR99). You can use this functionality to limit manual deselection of different components.

Define Control Procedures for Address Comparison for License Types

When you update or amend the address information of a business partner in the feeder system, you need to reevaluate the licenses or authorizations that include the specified business partner(s) to confirm validity.

You can update the applicable fields using this functionality.

Define Types of Agreements

You can set up agreements and see them as a broader framework in which you can create applicable licenses in furtherance of an agreement or with a reference to an agreement. Relevant information is copied over from the agreement to the license, and the quantity and value of the agreement is decremented automatically based on the quantity and value set forth in the license. An agreement is created in the same way as a specific license type.

Define Depreciation Groups (in Documents and Agreements)

You can depreciate a license in different groups (e.g., on the sales-order level or the delivery level). You can specify a maximum amount or quantity to be written off in every deprecation group. The different depreciation groups also allow you to trace the items (e.g., a sale has already been made, but the goods have not been delivered yet).

You need to map item categories to specific depreciation groups. You can also define whether the item group needs to add to, deduct from, or neither add to nor deduct from the remaining quantity/value.

Define License Types

You can maintain different license types per legal regulation. You need to map the paper version of the license to attributes, which you can maintain in the system. Per attribute, you can define how many values of the attribute can be maintained (one or multiple) and whether the system needs to compare the value of the attribute with the variables in the sales order. If there is a complete match, that license is taken (in case of automatic license assignment).

Return to Section 6.4.1 for more details on the most important attributes.

6.4.5   Master Data

Chapter 4 and Chapter 5 already covered the master data elements for Compliance Management in SAP GTS, but let's review them:

▶ Numbering schemes: You can load ICCN and ECCN classification codes (content provider) or maintain them manually in SAP GTS. Please refer to Section 4.3.2 and Section 5.3.1 for more information.

▶ Product classification: As soon as the classification codes exist, you can classify products in SAP GTS with the existing ICCNs/ECCNs as explained in Section 4.3.3, Section 4.3.4, and Section 5.2.2.

▶ Bill of product: Bills of product are required in SAP GTS in order to perform the de minimis calculation. For more information on the setup of BOMs in SAP GTS, please refer to Section 4.4.

▶ Licenses and agreements: Licenses have the same structure for import and export, and you can customize their having different attributes (Section 4.5. and Section 6.4.1). You can create licenses in reference to an agreement.

▶ Determination strategy: You set up the determination strategy as master data.

6.5   Summary

As we have discussed in this chapter, you perform SAP GTS export control checks at specific times in the order lifecycle. We have outlined and discussed in this chapter the specific checks related to compliance for import and export flows.

Once you have performed compliance checks, the next step is to ensure that the correct customs declarations are created and filed with the appropriate customs authorities. Which declaration needs to be filed with whom and at what time depends on the applicable customs procedure and legal regulations. Customs authorities are focusing more and more on tightening the integration between export control requirements and customs filing.

SAP GTS allows you to take over assigned classification or license information directly into the customs document. Hence, there's a direct link between the compliance functionality and customs; considering the number of companies performing direct customs e-filing with the authorities, that link will become increasingly important.

The following chapter deals with Customs Management and elaborates on how SAP GTS supports companies in declaring the import or export of goods to the customs authorities.

In an international trade environment where goods are crossing borders, information regarding these goods, the applicable duties and taxes, and safety and security data are essential. This chapter will explain the relevant business and system processes and the underlying Customizing for Customs Management.

7   Customs Management

Your company is purchasing and selling on an international level. Every time goods cross the international borders, the local authorities need to be informed. Depending on the local rules and regulations, a set of documentation needs to be submitted to the customs authorities. Submitting this data to the customs authorities can be done via a customs declaration, which can be transmitted either on paper or through electronic data exchange. Most authorities prefer electronic data exchange.

One of the major developments in the area of customs and global trade over the past decade is the increasing implementation of electronic customs declaration processes in many countries, whereby the imports and exports of goods are declared to the local customs authorities using electronic data interchange (EDI) processes.

The significant increase in trade volumes owing to globalization necessitates an automated environment that enables customs authorities to better monitor cross-border movements. In addition, pre-arrival or pre-departure information becomes necessary for the customs authorities to be able to perform risk analysis up front, based on safety- and security-related data.

Warehousing and manufacturing also play a vital role in the supply chain. Governments encourage a landscape of inward investments for warehousing and manufacturing to remain competitive and create a positive cycle of prosperity by providing tax efficient structures and incentives. In this respect, various customs authorities across the globe authorize special customs procedures, allowing the economic operator to apply for duty exemption schemes based on the applicable conditions. In this chapter, we'll describe the economic customs procedures applicable in the European Union (bonded warehouse, inward processing relief, outward processing relief and processing under customs control), taking into account the principles used by various authorities implementing their special customs procedures.

Throughout this chapter, we'll make a distinction between the business and system processes, as we did in Chapter 6. In the business process, the steps and events a company typically goes through will be described. The system process only describes activities a user has to go through in the system. Some of the steps in both the system and business process can run simultaneously.

Figure 7.1 shows the SAP GTS cockpit, displaying the four main processes of Customs Management (import, export, special customs procedures, and EMCS); we'll cover all of them in this chapter and then include some more information on the classification of products and master data. For a more detailed view on product classification, refer to Chapter 5.

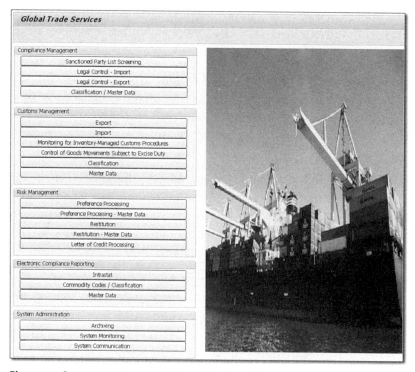

Figure 7.1 Customs Management-Relevant Business Processes

Before we begin, let's get a high-level overview of the functionality of each of these main processes:

- **Importing (Section 7.2.1)**
  The general inbound processes, inbound transit activities, and periodic declarations can be managed in the Import function. Information related to the presentation of goods to the customs authorities, a pre-declaration, and the tax statement is also available.

- **Exporting (Section 7.2.2)**
  The Export function manages all outbound movements in which the goods are leaving the country of the foreign trade organization (FTO)—or in the case of EU countries, leaving the customs union. In addition, you can monitor outbound transit activities here (where transit declarations are applicable).

  SAP GTS also provides menu options for classification and master data. Within master data, there are several tabs for all four business processes: CUSTOMS PRODUCTS, PARTNERS, ORGANIZATIONAL DATA, and AUTHORIZATIONS. You need to classify every material that is relevant for Customs Management processes. This classification is also relevant for Compliance and Risk Management.

- **Special customs procedures (Section 7.3)**
  Within Customs Management, SAP GTS supports the special customs procedures, such as bonded warehouse, inward processing relief, outward processing relief, and processing under customs control. You manage and monitor these procedures using the MONITORING FOR INVENTORY-MANAGED CUSTOMS PROCEDURES or SPECIAL CUSTOMS PROCEDURES menu options.

- **Excise duty monitoring (Section 7.4)**
  In addition, excise duties may be applicable on some goods, depending on their nature (e.g., beer, oil, tobacco, etc.). SAP GTS does not support keeping excise inventory for trading such goods; specific industry solutions can be used for such purposes. Nonetheless, for the movement of excise goods under excise duty suspension (called the EMCS process in the EU), SAP GTS offers the CONTROL OF GOODS MOVEMENTS SUBJECT TO EXCISE DUTY function to manage the related processes.

This chapter also includes coverage of the US reconciliation process (Section 7.5). Reconciliation is a program that allows an importer to file entry summaries with the applicable government authorities.

Section 7.6 on electronic communication elaborates on what SAP GTS offers for setting up an interface between your company and the customs authorities or an external party, and which transactions are useful when monitoring these electronic messages that are sent back and forth.

We'll conclude this Customs Management chapter with an overview of the countries that are supported by SAP GTS (Section 7.7).

Using our fictitious company, Alpha, this chapter on Customs Management will take you through the main business processes supported by SAP GTS Customs Management. Figure 7.2 gives a visual representation of the business case.

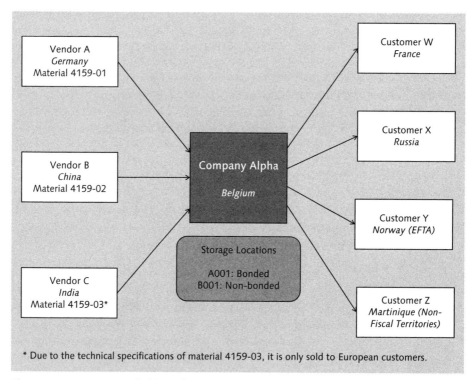

Figure 7.2 Business Case of Alpha

Alpha's Global Trade Requirements

Alpha, a company selling electronic devices (phones, mobile devices, and digital radios) on the B2C market, has a growing volume of export sales. Alpha is an independent subsidiary of an international company. The European headquarters is located in Belgium.

All EMEA orders are shipped from the European Distribution Centre (EDC), which is also located in Belgium.

No production activities take place in Belgium. Alpha buys goods from a foreign vendor in Asia and an affiliated company in Germany.

Alpha sells a limited number of finished products:

▶ Material 4159-01: This product is procured exclusively from a vendor located in Germany (Vendor A). This product is designated for both the domestic market and export to Russia (Customer X).

▶ Material 4159-02: This product is procured from a vendor in China (Vendor B), and after importation, it is stored in a BWH. The product can be exported to Russia (Customer X) or sold in the French domestic market (Customer W).

▶ Material 4159-03: This product is imported from a vendor in India (Vendor C) and is mainly sold in the European market (Customer W). The products are imported and will be stored in a non-bonded (free) warehouse, and duties are paid.

7.1 Customs Documents

This section will cover the SAP GTS cockpit, which is the daily worklist for customs declarations, the fields that can be maintained within these customs declarations, and how to communicate with customs authorities.

7.1.1 Operative Cockpit in Customs Management

SAP GTS is equipped with the operative cockpit, where all documents that require the user's attention can be accessed and are grouped into activities. You can set up the structure of the cockpit depending on the business needs of a company. SAP GTS is set up such that separate import, export, inbound, and outbound transit cockpits are available.

Split business processes let you clearly distinguish different business processes and their corresponding tasks. Furthermore, separate tasks for each of these processes can be defined. The setup makes it easy for companies with a large trade compliance team to divide the workload based on these processes. In this way, team members can work on a specific shipment, on their domain, without interfering with their colleagues.

Figure 7.3 shows the GTS cockpit, where you can access the more specific customs options under CUSTOMS MANAGEMENT.

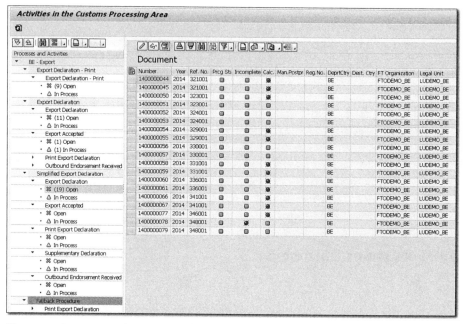

Figure 7.3 Operative Cockpit in SAP GTS—Export

From a business point of view, each main process can be divided into multiple sub-processes. In SAP GTS, each sub-process is called an *activity*. You must perform one or more tasks in each activity in order to complete it and move to the next activity.

The cockpit displays all the documents and their statuses in the corresponding activity so that you can identify the pending actions for each document, depending on the progress made until then. Once you've finished all tasks that are relevant for a certain activity, the document is automatically transferred to the next required activity.

Let's take a look at Alpha's operative cockpit. When designing the SAP GTS solution implemented at Alpha, the business identified the following activities that needed to be performed in order to provide a correct and complete export declaration. It is crucial that the sequence of these activities is respected:

1. Complete the export declaration to ensure that all legally required information is available.

2. Send the information from the declaration to the customs authorities.

3. Anticipate a technical response from the customs authorities, confirming the receipt of the information.

4. Anticipate the validation of the export declaration from the customs authorities. This message confirms the approval of the export declaration.

5. Print the export accompanying document (EAD) for the transporter and internal bookkeeping.

Alpha decided to create three sequential activities in SAP GTS:

1. **Export declaration**
   You complete the declaration and send the information to the customs authorities via an IDoc. You are not able to send out the IDoc if the document is not complete (concept of incompleteness check). Once the IDoc is sent out, the document moves to the next status.

2. **Export accepted**
   You need to wait for the two reply EDI messages from the customs authorities to return. The first EDI message informs you that the information is received by the customs authorities. It does not release the shipment for export. Only after the receipt of the second incoming EDI message is export of the goods approved. Once the second EDI message is received, the document moves to the next activity.

3. **Print export declaration**
   You aren't able to print the export declaration from the system until this point. In this way, the system guarantees that the correct information is printed onto the paper forms, which will accompany the goods during transportation. By not allowing you to print the document earlier in the process, Alpha is certain there is no difference between what is printed on the forms and what is declared to the customs authorities (via the EDI message).

   Depending on the legal regulation and the system version your company is operating in, there can be additional activities in the e-filing procedure.

Once all activities are completed, the document disappears from the cockpit. However, you can always display it via the monitoring functionality.

7.1.2 Monitoring

The monitoring functionality of SAP GTS gives you an alternative way of displaying an overview of the customs declarations.

In monitoring, all customs declarations are listed, independent of the activity they are in. This means you can also find back documents that are fully processed or cancelled, beyond open or ongoing documents. But because the documents are not grouped into activities, it's harder for you to determine which actions to take in order to get this declaration approved by the customs authorities and completed.

Figure 7.4 displays an example of the monitoring functionality. The lack of structure makes it more difficult for you to follow up on actions.

Display Existing Customs Export Declarations

Number	Year	Doc. Type	Ref. No.	Prcg Sts	Incomplete	Calc.	Man.Postpr	Reg.No.	DeprtCtry	Dest. Ctry	FT Org.	Legal Unit	Custs Sta.
1400000020	2014	CULOEX	90038638						BE	CN	FTODEMO_BE	LUDEMO_BE	
1400000028	2014	CULOEX	90038639						BE	CN	FTODEMO_BE	LUDEMO_BE	
1400000029	2014	CULOEX	307001						BE	RU	FTODEMO_BE	LUDEMO_BE	
1400000030	2014	CULOEX	307001						BE	RU	FTODEMO_BE	LUDEMO_BE	
1400000031	2014	CULOEX	308001						BE	RU	FTODEMO_BE	LUDEMO_BE	
1400000032	2014	CULOEX	308001						BE	RU	FTODEMO_BE	LUDEMO_BE	
1400000036	2014	CULOEX	90038644						BE	CN	FTODEMO_BE	LUDEMO_BE	
1400000040	2014	CULOEX	90038652						BE	CN	FTODEMO_BE	LUDEMO_BE	EX
1400000076	2014	CULOEX	90038654						BE	CN	FTODEMO_BE	LUDEMO_BE	EX
1400000093	2014	CULOEX	90038679						BE	CN	FTODEMO_BE	LUDEMO_BE	
1400000094	2014	CULOEX	90038680						BE	CN	FTODEMO_BE	LUDEMO_BE	
1400000095	2014	CULOEX	90038682						BE	CN	FTODEMO_BE	LUDEMO_BE	
1400000101	2014	CULOEX	90038692						BE	CN	FTODEMO_BE	LUDEMO_BE	

Figure 7.4 Monitoring—Export

7.1.3 Customs Declaration

SAP GTS can create a customs declaration for the movement of goods relevant for customs purposes. Each customs declaration created in SAP GTS is structured in the same way and looks similar. Regardless of whether the customs declaration is an import, export, transit, or EMCS declaration, all documents consist of a header level and an item level. Within SAP, information that is valid for the entire document is available at the header level, whereas item-specific information is available at the item level.

The customs declaration has several tabs at the header level:

▶ ITEM OVERVIEW: A general overview of all the items of the declaration.

▶ COMMUNICATION: A list of the relevant messages required to communicate with the customs authorities by electronic means or based on printed paper declaration.

▶ PARTNERS: The partners in the customs documents, transferred from the corresponding document in the feeder system. You can add additional partner roles and business partners in SAP GTS.

▶ GEOGRAPHY: The customs-relevant geographical information, such as the country of destination/departure, transportation route, place of loading/unloading, and customs offices.

▶ TRANSPORTATION: Foreign trade data, such as information regarding date and times, means of transport at the border, inland means of transport, and movement reference number (MRN).

▶ PACKAGING DATA: Information related to packaging, such as packaging data, transportation unit, container and seal information, and product weights.

▶ DOCUMENTS: The relevant supporting documentation and authorizations.

▶ LOGISTICS COSTS: Values required for customs duty calculation (according to the duty framework, additional header-level duty costs and values).

▶ INVOICE: Reference data for the invoice.

▶ STATUS: Customs declaration status.

▶ DOCUMENT FLOW: The document flow with reference to the SAP GTS documents.

▶ REFERENCES: The reference documents with document numbers from the feeder system.

▶ TEXTS: Additional texts that can be edited.

▶ ADMINISTRATION: Administrative data.

Figure 7.5 shows the ITEM OVERVIEW tab of an export declaration.

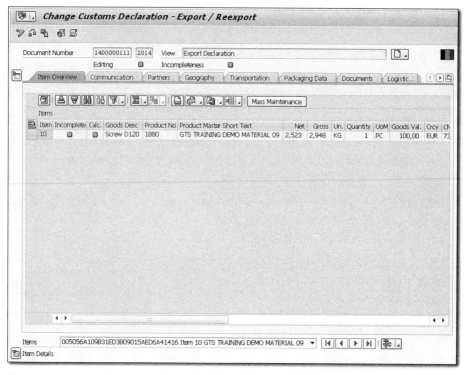

Figure 7.5 Customs Declaration Export Header

At the item level, the following tab pages are available:

- GENERAL DATA: Basic item data, such as customs product description, weights, country of origin, and commodity code.

- PLACEMENT: Invoice information, customs status placement (customs procedure), the customs ID in case of special customs procedures (customs authorization).

- PACKAGING DATA: Container number and packaging information for the individual item.

- DOCUMENTS: Additional documents that you must present to the customs authorities (e.g., invoice, certificate of origin, etc.).

- CUSTOMS VALUE: The structure for the calculation of the customs value is defined in a duty framework, which displays the invoice value, relevant deduction/addition elements, customs value, import duties, and sales taxes.

▶ STATUS: The status for the customs declaration, specified for the item.

▶ PREFERENCE (if TRADE PREFERENCE MANAGEMENT is activated): For each product of the customs declaration, it is indicated whether this product is eligible for trade preference.

▶ CLOSING PORTION: Closing portion specific to items relevant for special customs procedures.

▶ TEXTS: Additional texts that can be edited, specifically for this item.

▶ CONTROL: Legal regulation, license type and license numbers, and integration with Compliance Management.

▶ ADMINISTRATION: Additional data and administrative data for the item.

Figure 7.6 displays the GENERAL DATA tab at the item level.

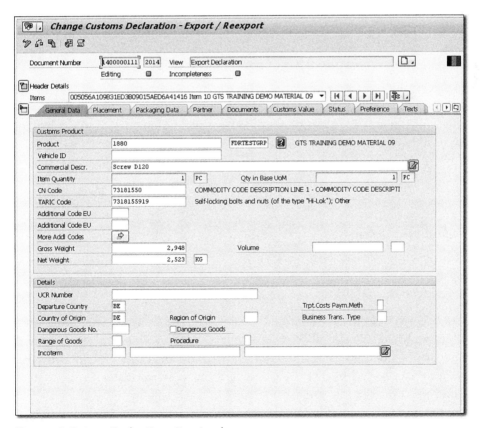

Figure 7.6 Customs Declaration—Item Level

In order to reduce your effort, you can transfer certain fields of this declaration from the feeder system to SAP GTS. In most cases, information regarding the shipping of the goods is available in the feeder system, and a standard interface transfers this data from the feeder system into SAP GTS. Automatic transferal of this information to SAP GTS significantly reduces your workload.

It is possible to change the information that is transferred from the feeder system, and SAP GTS allows you to complete the missing data manually after transfer.

You must enter some fields manually, whereas others can be filled by using defaulting rules in SAP GTS. Which fields are transferred over or defaulted depends on the type of data and company-specific requirements, among other factors.

For more information on defaulting data into a customs declaration, please refer to Section 7.2.3.

7.1.4 Communication with Customs Authorities

In theory, there are three ways to declare goods to the customs authorities. First, the declaration can be lodged verbally. The issue with verbal declarations is, of course, that none of the parties involved have any documentation to confirm the transaction. Therefore, in practice, this is not a workable solution.

In the international trade environment, both paper-based and electronic communication are accepted.

Paper-Based Declaration

The conventional way of declaring goods to the customs authorities is done using a paper-based declaration. The form that can be used for this type of declarations depends on the country's specific legal rules and regulations.

SAP GTS enables the use of a paper-based declaration because it can incorporate all information from the customs document into a form. This form can be printed directly from the SAP GTS customs document under the COMMUNICATION tab. For countries supported by SAP GTS, standard forms are available in the system. However, if the country you are operating in is not supported by SAP GTS, you can develop additional forms or broker instruction sheets.

Figure 7.7 displays a standard export accompanying document (or EAD) for a country in the EU. An exact copy is created in SAP GTS so that you can print a fully automated version of the form from the system.

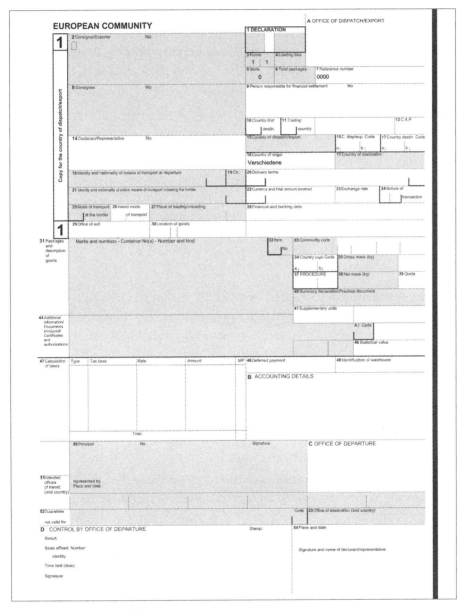

Figure 7.7 Printed Form EAD

Section 7.7 gives an overview of the countries that are supported by standard SAP GTS.

Electronic Communication (E-Filing)

In addition to paper-based declarations, you can communicate electronically with the customs authorities for the declaration of imports, exports, EMCS, and transits using SAP GTS. This electronic method of communicating with the customs authorities is known as *e-filing*.

E-filing is possible only if the country in which the company is located enables this procedure; the company must have an IT system that can handle the processing of electronic communication.

The major benefit of electronic communication is the reduction of processing time. In some countries, e-filing is compulsory, and paper-based declarations are not accepted (unless a temporary fallback procedure is active). Every country that enables e-filing has defined a framework of incoming and outgoing messages. In this framework, the customs authorities have defined a sequence in which they need to receive these messages.

In countries that are not supported by SAP GTS, e-filing can also be set up with a broker. You need to build an interface to support the electronic communication. If your business process allows it, it can be beneficial to use to the standard EDI structure to communicate with an external party. In this way, the amount of development required to support this communication is limited.

In the system, a decent design of the operative cockpit can encourage the correct application of sending and receiving these messages. Figure 7.8 shows an example of a simplified communication framework. You can use this example when declaring an export shipment.

Initially, the company declares the goods to the customs authorities, sending out the information in an IDoc called an *M-message* and in that way providing all the relevant information.

The COMMUNICATION tab in the customs declaration (Figure 7.9) displays this communication by showing which message can be executed by the system.

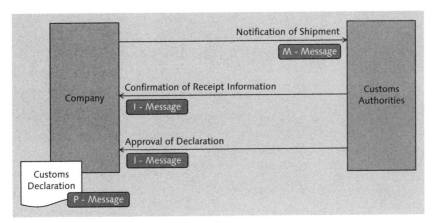

Figure 7.8 Communication Scheme for E-Filing

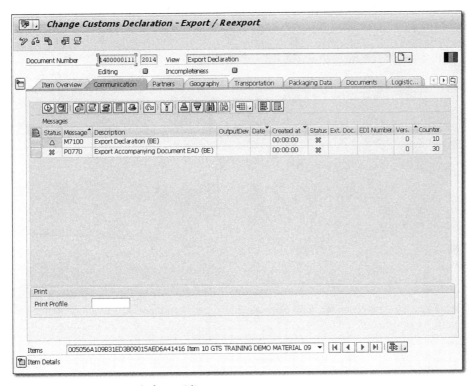

Figure 7.9 Initial Situation before e-Filing

As soon as the first message is sent out, the system freezes you from making changes to the declarations. Therefore, the document is automatically switched to display mode, which means the user can only display the document, but make not any edits.

The customs authorities first confirm that they have received the information properly. They confirm this receipt by sending a first message back; in SAP GTS, these are called *incoming* or *I-messages*. You can monitor I-messages from the COMMUNICATION tab of the customs declaration in Figure 7.10.

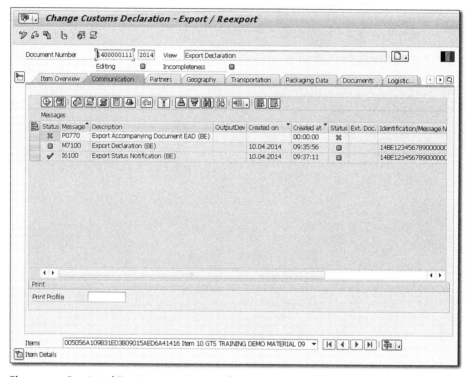

Figure 7.10 Receipt of First Incoming Message from Customs Authorities

The receipt of this message does not allow the company to start the export process; the customs authorities only confirm the receipt of the information, and do not grant the official approvals yet.

After the customs authorities validate the data, the declaration may be accepted or rejected. Communication regarding this confirmation from the customs authorities is again organized via IDocs—more specifically, using an I-message.

Figure 7.11 displays the receipt of the second incoming message, which informs the company of the approval of the export shipment.

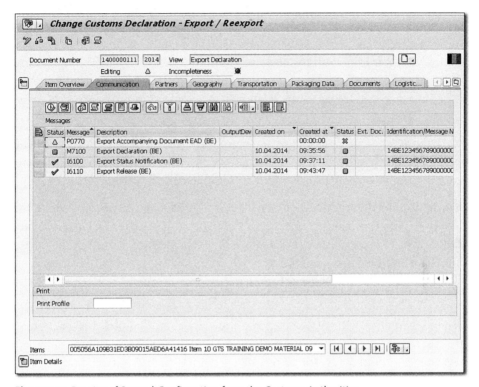

Figure 7.11 Receipt of Second Confirmation from the Customs Authorities

Once all approvals from the customs authorities are gathered in the system, supporting documents (such as documents accompanying the goods during transportation, certificates of origin, etc.) can be printed.

Communication (printed forms and/or electronic communication) with the customs authorities takes place in the customs document; all communication activities are grouped in the COMMUNICATION tab on the document header. The system is also able to receive standard error messages from the customs authorities, depending on how the communication platform of the customs authorities is set up.

Section 7.6 will offer a few useful standard transactions related to the EDI messages.

Fallback Procedure

The e-filing offered by SAP GTS makes the administrative tasks involving the customs authorities much easier and faster than the paper-based tasks. But there's a downside to e-filing: the customs authorities' IT system can face downtime caused by technical issues, updates, etc. During periods of downtime, no electronic communication with the customs authorities is possible, which might lead to delays in the shipping operations of a company. To prevent logistic interruption, the economic operator can request the customs authorities to apply a *fallback procedure*.

When the authorities grant a company-specific or general fallback procedure, you enable functionality in SAP GTS that allows the printing of export documents without prior electronic communication with the customs authorities.

In order to activate the fallback procedure, you must switch the process on in the SYSTEM MONITORING tab of SAP GTS. In the MANAGE NUMBERS FOR FALLBACK PROCEDURE activity, you must define a fallback number before activating the procedure. This number is an official number provided by the customs authorities. When the fallback number is set up, the ACTIVATE FALLBACK PROCEDURE activity allows the actual activation of the fallback procedure.

Depending on the country, the customs authority communicates a fallback number that has to be printed on the fallback declaration. The fallback procedure can be switched on separately for all possible activities, such as export, import, transit, EMCS, entry into a special customs procedure, and so on.

In some countries, customs authorities can require subsequent e-filing after the fallback procedure is terminated. This process is called buffering and is also supported by SAP GTS.

All documents created when the fallback procedure is enabled are assigned to a special activity within the operative cockpit. This special fallback activity is designed to replace the e-filing activities with a printed form. It is up to the consultant to design the activity according to the countries' legal regulations.

Supplementary Customs Declaration

Aside from the option of communicating a declaration to the customs authorities on a transactional basis (via e-filing or paper-based), there is an option for grouping all documents and declaring them on a periodic basis, such as weekly or monthly. This type of declaration is called the *supplementary customs declaration* (SCD).

SAP GTS enables this functionality, and when you switch it on for a specific process, the system automatically groups all the relevant shipments or customs declarations into a supplementary customs declaration. The system allows you to select and deselect certain shipments from this global declaration. Again, this declaration can be e-filed with the customs authorities, or a printed form can be generated. The requirements depend on the local authorities.

Please note that you need prior customs approval for an SCD. Before setting up an SCD, you must obtain a specific authorization from the local customs authorities (e.g., authorization for simplified procedures, periodic declaration).

Now that we've examined the customs documents related to Customs Management in SAP GTS, let's turn our attention to import and export processes.

7.2   Import and Export Processes

This section focuses on both the business and system process of import and export, the related Customizing, and the required master data for creating correct and complete declarations. Let's begin!

7.2.1   Import Processes

When goods are entering a country or customs union such as the EU from a foreign country, they are considered an import.

Normally—and some exceptions are listed in Section 7.3—import duties need to be paid when importing goods. The person responsible for paying these import duties is defined in the incoterm. Depending on the type of product (expressed in the classification it is given) and the country where the goods are coming from, these import duties can vary. It is possible that the relevant duty rate is zero percent; in this case, no duties need to be paid to the customs authorities. Besides these import duties, also known as third-country duties, there may be others, such as anti-dumping duties or pharmaceutical products duties.

Business Process

Alpha purchases finished product 4159-03 from a vendor in India. Because the goods are shipped by boat, it usually takes around 30 days for these goods to arrive in the port of Antwerp. Because material 4159-03 is sold exclusively to the European market, an import declaration is created by a customs broker in the port.

Figure 7.12 provides insight into the importing business process for Alpha.

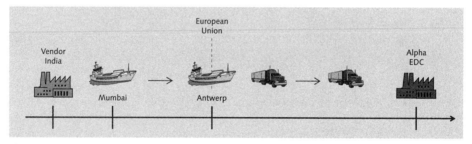

Figure 7.12 Business Process—Import

You can decide the timing of the creation of an import declaration based on the legal regulations of a country and/or a company's business requirements. There are two possibilities for when to create the import declaration.

Import Declaration after Goods Receipt

Alpha is located in Belgium and has chosen to create an import customs declaration after the goods are received in its warehouse. This implies that Alpha is able to receive the goods duty-suspended at their premises (inland) and do the customs clearance from its location.

The customs broker usually initiates an outbound transit procedure to ship the goods under suspension of duties to Alpha.

In the EU, two types of transit procedures exist: A *T1 procedure* applies to duty-unpaid goods, and a *T2 procedure* is for the shipment of duty-paid goods.

When the goods arrive at Alpha's premises, you discharge the transit procedure by communicating the arrival to the authorities or via e-filing or paper form.

Alpha then unloads the container and starts posting the receipts in its administration. After all the materials, their quantities, and so on are registered, Alpha can create an import declaration and send it to the customs authorities for approval. During the approval process, the customs authorities provide the receiving company with a unique reference number for the shipment. In the EU, this number is the MRN. In other countries, it is often referred to simply as the *registration number*.

Import Declaration before Goods Receipt

If a company in the United States or Asia needs to create an import declaration, it has to create it before the goods receipt, meaning that the import declaration is created before the goods are physically checked and stored in the warehouse.

It is important to note that quantity differences between the official declaration and what is physically received can occur and, depending on the legal requirements, you may potentially need to report them. These differences occur when the supplying party physically sends more or less goods than was ordered.

Because the import declaration is often created in the port of arrival, there is no need to start a transit procedure (if this procedure is even used or known in the importing country).

Import Duty Calculations

Because Alpha is importing goods from India into the EU without placing the goods under a special customs procedure, the company is obligated to pay import duties and any other applicable taxes for the goods brought into free circulation on the European market.

The concept of paying a duty and/or taxes can be generalized and is also valid in other countries when goods are imported. The applicable duty rates depend on the country in which the goods are being imported.

In order to calculate the import duties (or third-country duties) for a specific shipment, start the calculation from the transactional value of the shipment and add or deduct certain costs, such as insurance and freight, depending on the incoterm. This results in the *customs value*, which is the calculation base for determining the amount of duty that needs to be paid to the customs authorities. Additional duties like pharmaceutical duties and anti-dumping duties might apply on top of standard duties.

In the event that you need to pay some sort of VAT or sales tax, the base for applying this rate consists of the customs value and the duties relevant for that shipment. Hence, VAT and sales tax also need to be paid on duties.

Table 7.1 shows the duty framework for Alpha on the import side.

	Duty Type	Amount	Percentage
	Value of the Goods	€ 350.00	
+/−	Transportation Costs	€ 3.50	
+/−	Other Charges	€ 1.25	
=	Customs Value	€ 354.75	
	Third-Country Duty	€ 17.74	5%
+	Other Duties	0	0%
=	Total Duties	€ 17.74	
	Customs Value	€ 354.75	
+	Total Duties	€ 17.74	
=	Calculation Base for VAT or Sales Tax	€ 372.49	
	Calculation Base for VAT or Sales Tax	€ 372.49	
	VAT or Sales Tax	€ 78.22	21%

Table 7.1 Duty Framework for Import

System Process

In the import process, products entering the customs territory of a country/country group are assigned a desired customs procedure by lodging a customs declaration with the competent customs authorities (e.g., bringing goods into free circulation, placing goods under a BWH, placing goods under inward processing, and so on). Completion of the customs declaration differs depending on the specific customs procedure under which the products are placed—that is, different data elements to be mentioned on the declaration.

Customs Management in SAP GTS enables automated filings of the required import declarations/documents by integrating customs processing and logistics processes. Based on the legal requirement, you can create the import customs declaration in SAP GTS before or after the goods receipt (potentially requiring a transit declaration to ship goods to the premises under suspension of duties). Generally speaking, in the United States, import declarations are created before goods receipts, whereas in Europe, companies create their import declarations either before or after the goods receipt (depending on the need).

Although it's technically possible, don't mix both concepts for one foreign trade organization. In what follows, we'll discuss the systems trigger points and its behavior in further detail.

Import Declaration after Goods Receipt

In the feeder system, the inbound process starts when Alpha creates a purchase order with its Indian supplier.

When the supplier sends information about the shipment of the goods (shipping notification), an *inbound delivery* (ID) is created with reference to the purchase order. The creation of an inbound delivery is a prerequisite for the Customs Declaration after Goods Receipt process. The inbound delivery can be created at any time after the creation of the purchase order but before the goods arrive at the premises of the receiving company.

In the EU, for example, duty-suspended goods can be delivered from the border to an inland warehouse using the New Computerized Transit System (NCTS) procedure, whereby the goods remain under duty suspension.

Figure 7.13 displays the business and system process of the creation of an import declaration after the posting of the goods receipt.

The parameter that controls the creation of the inbound delivery is the *control confirmation key*. You can enter this key in the vendor master record or the purchasing info record (vendor/material combination) in order to default it in the purchase order.

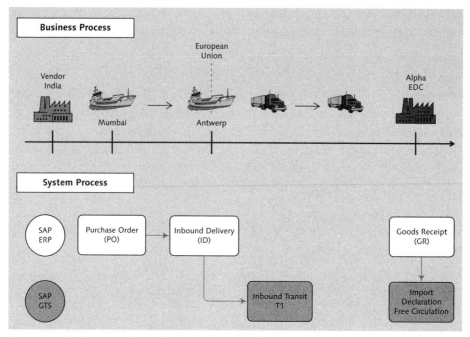

Figure 7.13 Business and System Process—Import Declaration after Goods Receipt

When the goods arrive at the border, a transit procedure is initiated. The supplier or broker communicates the MRN code to the company. You should enter this information in the inbound delivery. In the FOREIGN TRADE tab (header level) of the inbound delivery, a PRELIMINARY DOCUMENT checkbox is available for the customs status and reference number (e.g., T1 status and MRN). You must update this before the goods receipt. The type of preliminary document that should be used (T1 or T2) is set up by country in the configuration menu. Once you enter the MRN in the inbound delivery, this document is transferred to SAP GTS and triggers the automatic creation of the transit document in SAP GTS.

Once the goods arrive at the inland warehouse, an accompanying customs shipment document containing a unique number from the authorities (say, the MRN number that was communicated earlier), is presented. Then, the transit declaration in SAP GTS created with a reference to the inbound delivery closes the transit procedure and, you can proceed with assigning a customs destination to the concerned goods.

> **Note**
>
> The transit procedure is initiated at the port or border and allows non-Community products to be shipped under bond to the local and responsible customs office or directly to the premises of the consignee (simplification procedure).

Receipt of products at the consignee's premises triggers the import declaration process. At that moment in time, two options are available:

▸ The posting of the goods receipt (material document) in SAP ERP 6.0 automatically triggers the creation of an import declaration in SAP GTS.

▸ The posting of the goods receipt document (material document) is transferred to a worklist in SAP GTS, and the import declaration is created manually, allowing you to group several items/documents.

The transit and import declarations created in SAP GTS follow the standard layout of any other customs declaration in the system. For more information on the content of a customs declaration, consult Section 7.1.

The import declaration should have data coming from SAP ERP 6.0 from the goods receipt material document, data that could be defaulted in SAP GTS (if determination rules are defined), and data that has to be completed manually. An incompletion log ensures that all the data is entered before you are allowed to send information to the customs authorities.

Local customs regulations determine the declaration requirements and treatment of customs and other applicable taxes. Both paper-based and electronic declarations can be supported within the system, as well as generating broker instruction sheets that instruct a broker to file the actual customs declarations.

In Belgium, because approval can be obtained to file import declarations on a monthly basis, Alpha has decided to apply for this simplification of its import process. The processing time is reduced significantly, and the legal requirements are met. The simplification removes the burden of transactional communication (via either paper-based or electronic communication). Instead, a periodic declaration or SCD is created. As with the transactional communication, you still need to provide this information to the customs authorities.

Import Declaration before Goods Receipt

In the event that the company has decided to create the import declaration *before* goods receipt, again, a purchase order and an inbound delivery are created. Again, the inbound delivery can be created at any time prior to the arrival of the goods. Figure 7.14 shows this system process.

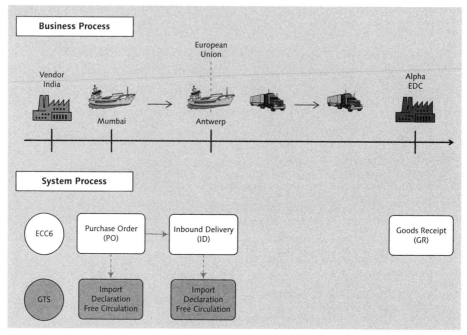

Figure 7.14 Business and System Process—Import Declaration before Goods Receipt

The information from both the purchase order and the inbound delivery are transferred to SAP GTS. It is possible to create an import declaration based on either of these two documents. Depending on the selection criteria, the system lists all the relevant feeder system documents. Figure 7.15 displays an example of what the selection screen of the worklist looks like.

Because the inbound delivery contains shipping and logistics information that is crucial in order to complete the import declaration, we use the inbound delivery as a reference document for the import declaration.

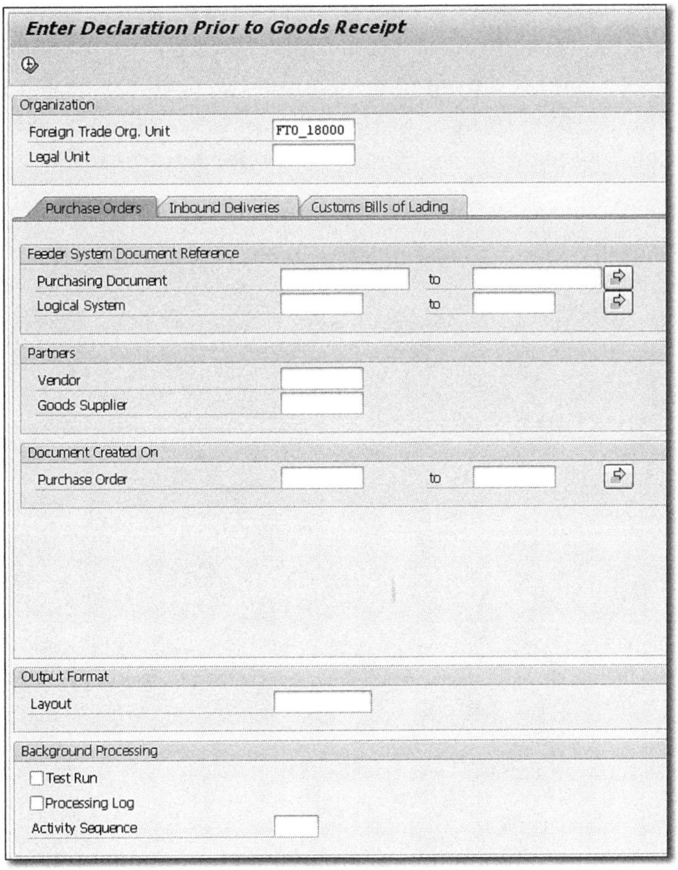

Figure 7.15 Selection Screen of Worklist to Create Import Declaration Prior To Goods Receipt

In case the bill of lading number is maintained in the standard SAP field of the inbound delivery, this information can also be displayed in the worklist. This allows you to easily select all inbound deliveries with the same bill of lading number and group them into one import declaration.

Note the CUSTOMS BILLS OF LADING tab in Figure 7.15. This concept is not referring to the bill of lading in the inbound delivery, but a separate document in SAP GTS. This additional document contains more or less the same shipping information that can be entered in the inbound delivery from the feeder system. Therefore, if a company is already using the inbound delivery with shipping and logistics information, it is not necessary to activate the customs bill of lading document in SAP GTS because it would be duplicate information.

Import Duty Framework

In order to calculate the import duties and other applicable taxes, the customs declaration in SAP GTS contains a duty framework. The framework is divided into Logistics Costs and Customs Value tabs. The first tab is at the header level, and the second is at the item level.

Figure 7.16 displays the Logistics Costs tab, which is available at the header level of an import declaration for Alpha.

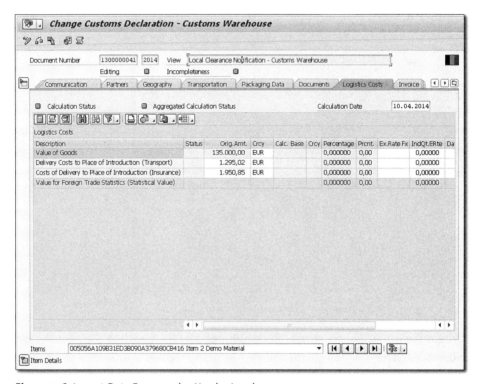

Figure 7.16 Import Duty Framework—Header Level

Figure 7.17 and Figure 7.18 display the Customs Value tab, which displays the relevant costs on the item level of an import declaration for Alpha. Figure 7.17 shows all relevant values for the first item of the declaration, while Figure 7.18 shows the details for the second and last item of the declaration.

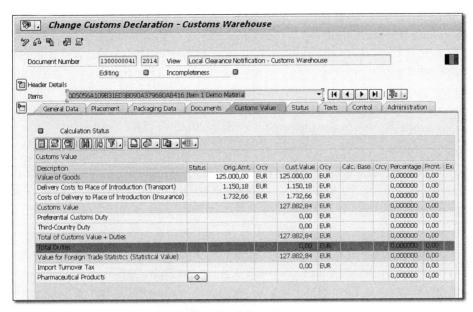

Figure 7.17 Import Duty Framework—Item Level: Item 1

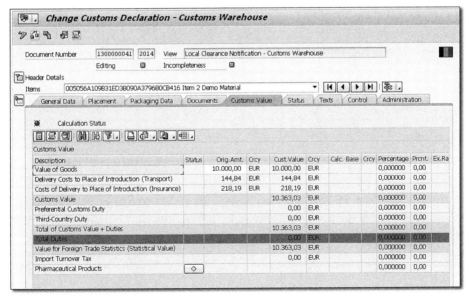

Figure 7.18 Import Duty Framework—Item Level: Item 2

The CUSTOMS VALUE tab shows all required elements for the duty calculation. The customs value calculation is based on the net price of the purchase order (value of the goods), which is transferred from the feeder system. Depending on the applicable sales conditions, certain elements can be added or deducted from the value of the goods (e.g., shipping and insurance costs). Elements such as the value of the goods and transportation costs can be transferred from the feeder system, while other data, such as duty rates, are maintained in SAP GTS.

SAP GTS provides this type of calculation at two levels; it is possible to have a specific cost at the header level (meaning that it applies for the entire document) and distributed among the items. You can do this based on the proportional value of each item or based on the weight. SAP GTS enables the automatic distribution of costs.

From the calculations in Figure 7.16, Figure 7.17, and Figure 7.18, we can see this concept put in place. The transportation cost for this entire shipment is €1,295.02. From the GENERAL DATA tab of each of the items, we learn that item 1 has a gross weight of 13,500 kg, while item two weighs only 1,700 kg. Table 7.2 gives an overview of the distribution of the transportation costs based on the weights.

	Weight (in kg)	Share (in %)	Distributed Transportation Cost (in Euros)
Item 1	13,500	88.82	1,150.18
Item 2	1,700	11.18	144.84
Total	15,200	100	1,295.02

Table 7.2 Distribution of Transportation Costs

The insurance costs related to this shipment can also be distributed. Because the decision about how to distribute the costs— via either weight or value—is made at the level of each duty type, it is possible to have different types of distribution in the duty framework.

For more information on the settings of this import duty framework, refer to Section 7.2.3.

7.2.2   Export Processes

Every time a company sells its products to a customer located abroad or, in the case of the EU, outside of this customs union, an *export process* takes place.

The administrative requirements are different depending on the local rules and regulations. Generally speaking, a company who wants to export its goods to a foreign country needs to file an export declaration with the customs authorities. The different options of getting the approval from the customs authorities are described in Section 7.1 and also apply here.

This export declaration accompanies the goods during transportation to its destination. Commercial invoices, packing lists, and other documents might be required, as well.

Business Process

Figure 7.19 shows Alpha's outbound process when it sells its finished products to a customer in Russia.

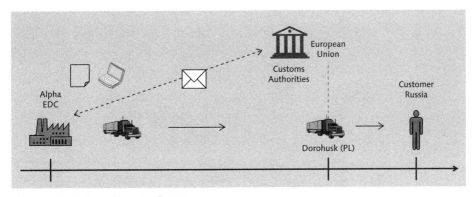

Figure 7.19 Business Process—Export

The outbound process starts when Alpha receives a request from its Russian customer in which the customer expresses his willingness to purchase the goods offered by Alpha.

Once the goods are ready to be sent to the Russian customer, Alpha needs to create an export declaration, which requires approval from the local customs authorities. Because the Belgian authorities allow e-filing, Alpha has made the decision to implement software that enables electronic communication with the customs authorities' platform. Return to Section 7.1 for an example of a simple communication scheme.

As soon as the approval from the authorities is received, the goods are allowed to leave the EU. Because the goods leave by truck, they take about three weeks to arrive in Russia. In the example described in Figure 7.19, the goods cross the border in Dorohusk, Poland.

At the moment the goods cross the border, a confirmation message is sent to the Belgian customs authorities by the customs office of exit in Dorohusk. They send a similar confirmation message to Alpha, which has now received the confirmation that the goods have left the customs union. This closes the export procedure for the European customs authorities.

System Process

From a system perspective, the export process starts when Alpha creates a sales order in the feeder system. This sales order already contains relevant information on the business partners, products, and quantities that are sold.

The outbound delivery can be created with reference to the sales order. After the goods are picked, packed, and loaded, they are ready to be declared for export. You can generate an export declaration by creating a billing document for this specific delivery.

In general, a *pro forma invoice*, which functions as the trigger to transfer information from the feeder system to SAP GTS, is created. An export declaration is created for relevant billing documents. This export declaration contains the relevant information from the feeder system but needs to be completed. In order to reduce the effort involved, you can apply the defaulting data rules in SAP GTS.

Figure 7.20 describes the system steps that need to be performed in order to create an export declaration in SAP GTS.

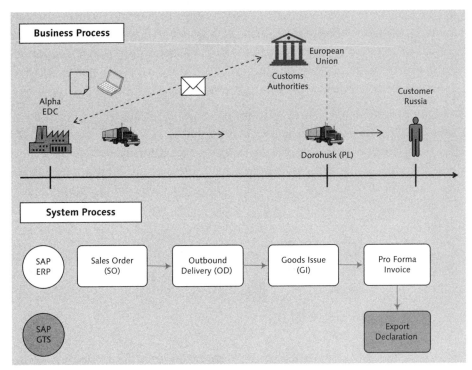

Figure 7.20 Business and System Process — Export Declaration

Once an export declaration is created and completed, the system allows you to check whether all required fields are populated in the customs declaration. This functionality is called the *incompleteness check*. SAP GTS has defined a number of standard incompleteness checks, which can be adapted or enhanced to suit the company's requirements. If e-filing is applicable, it is useful to add all mandatory fields to this check. In this manner, the system performs a first check on completeness of the data, which can save you time during the communication process.

Once the export declaration is completed, this information must be provided to the customs authorities. Alpha interacts with the customs authorities using the e-filing method. The customs declaration is sent to the customs authorities in the form of an IDoc. The authorities confirm the receipt of this message by sending back an approval message updating the export declaration with the MRN. The export accompanying document (EAD) is printed subsequently.

These printed forms accompany the goods during transportation. Once the goods have left the country (or the EU, in this case), an export confirmation needs to be entered in the system to close the export process; for tax purposes, it's important to prove that the goods have left the EU. Also, you can follow up these export confirmations within SAP GTS.

Depending on the applicable regulations of a ship-from country and the country of the ship-to party, an outbound transit document may be required. SAP GTS allows the creation of this transit document either at the same time the export declaration is created or when the export declaration is fully approved by the customs authorities. If relevant, an *outbound transit* or *open transit procedure* document is created. The structure of the transit document is similar to the export document.

Again, this transit declaration needs to be validated with the customs authorities via one of the different ways we've explained. SAP GTS is able to send and receive all the required information via e-filing or printing the required forms.

7.2.3 Customizing

Let's take a look at the most important Customizing steps for Customs Management. Note that prior to performing these steps, it is crucial to set up the correct legal regulations and document types. For a detailed explanation regarding these settings, please consult Chapter 3.

General Settings

SAP GTS offers a number of functionalities in order to reduce your manual effort. One of these features is the incompleteness check that confirms whether all the required information is available in the customs document. For each message that is available in the customs document, a separate check can be defined.

For e-filing, the system requires you to perform an incompleteness check before you are allowed to initiate the communication process with the customs authorities. In this manner, the system checks whether all data is available to make a correct declaration. This can save time significantly.

In the Customizing activity Control Incompleteness Checks for General Documents in Customs Management, you must define the incompleteness procedure that groups a set of fields that need to be checked. At a later stage, assign these incompleteness procedures to messages, meaning that for every message that is setup, you can define a new incompleteness procedure.

This Customizing activity needs to be performed on two levels. First, one must define an incompleteness procedure, as shown in Figure 7.21. It is possible to link a function module to this incompleteness procedure, but it is not required. For a simple incompleteness procedure, the function module is not used, but if there are dependencies in the logic, you need to use the function module because the standard functionality does not allow advance checks.

It is this incompleteness procedure that is assigned to one or more messages in Define Messages for Communication Process.

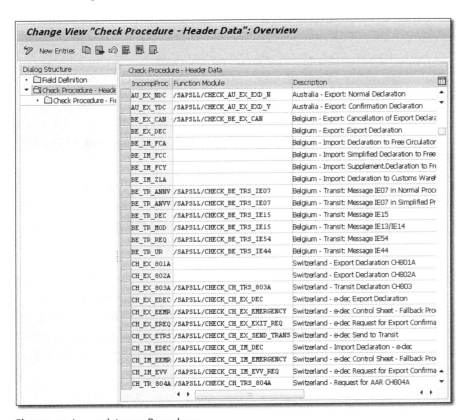

Figure 7.21 Incompleteness Procedures

Once the procedure is created, you can continue defining the fields that must be verified during every incompleteness check. SAP GTS provides a very long list of all the fields you can potentially add to the incompleteness check.

As shown in Figure 7.22, you can improve the quality of the check by adding information such as the field length, type, category, and so on.

Change View "Check Procedure - Field Assignment": Overview

New Entries

Dialog Structure
· ☐ Field Definition
▾ ☐ Check Procedure - Heade
· ☐ Check Procedure - Fi

Incompl. Proc. ID   BE_EX_DEC

Check Procedure - Field Assignment

Field Definition N...	Description	Fld Length	Field Type	Fld Catgy	Lgth Qual.	Zero Allowed	
HD_DCSTA	Header: Customs Status	4	C Letters	▾ A Requir...	▾ EQ Equal to	▾ Zero Is No... ▾	▲
HD_INCOLO	Header: Incoterm - Location		B Alphanumer...	▾ A Requir... ▾	▾	Zero Is No... ▾	▾
HD_INCOT	Header: Incoterm		C Letters	▾ A Requir... ▾	▾	Zero Is No... ▾	

Figure 7.22 Defining Fields per the Incompleteness Procedure

In the FIELD DEFINITION NAME column, define additional fields to be added to the incompleteness check. This is useful if certain data is mandatory for e-filing or for printing the form.

FIELD LENGTH allows you to specify the number of characters you need to use when completing a specific field, while FIELD TYPE indicates whether the field needs to be alphanumeric, numeric, or letters only.

If you indicate that a field is required in the FIELD CATEGORY column and it is not completed, the system does not allow you to execute a message in the COMMUNICATION tab. This results in a *hard block,* which is indicated by a red traffic light in the customs declaration. However, the FIELD CATEGORY can also be set to the status OPTIONAL ENTRY field. This leads to a warning (orange traffic light) when that information is missing in the customs declaration, but you are able to proceed with the business operations. This setting results in a *soft block* or warning message, which is useful when a particular field is required only in very specific scenarios. A hard block would not enable continuity of the process; therefore, the alternative is to always have a warning message to remind you to complete the field.

Please note that SAP GTS offers a predefined set of incompleteness checks for the countries that are supported by SAP GTS, based on the local legal requirements. However, this can be insufficient to meet the company's requirements, so additional checks may be added.

Communication Processes

The group of Customizing activities related to the communication processes and the setup of the structure of the operative cockpit is crucial in the implementation of Customs Management. Because most of these settings are interdependent, it is important to perform the Customizing activities in the correct sequence.

As with the standard Customizing for the incompleteness check, SAP GTS comes with predefined settings for the supported countries. A list of these countries can be found in Section 7.7.

Define Technical Medium for Messages (PPF Actions for General Documents)

The first step for setting up communication processes is to define the technical medium for messages. The Customizing needs to be set up at multiple levels.

First, as indicated in Figure 7.23, an action profile needs to be defined. An *action profile* is a group of actions that can be executed for a customs declaration.

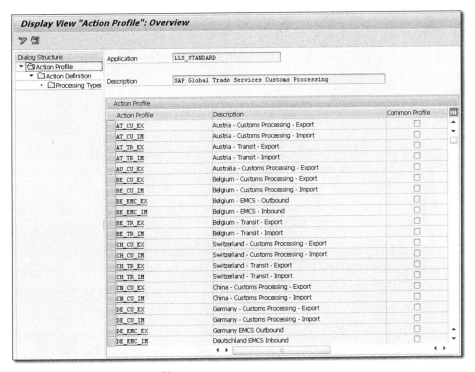

Figure 7.23 Defining Action Profiles

SAP GTS makes a distinction between imports and exports and, where relevant, between transit and EMCS. In the event that the country for which you want to set up the Customs Management module is not yet available, the best practice is to extend SAP's naming convention and logic.

As shown in Figure 7.24, you need to define at least one action per action profile and one action definition per message used in the customs declaration. For more information on messages, please see the upcoming subsection Define Messages for Communication Processes.

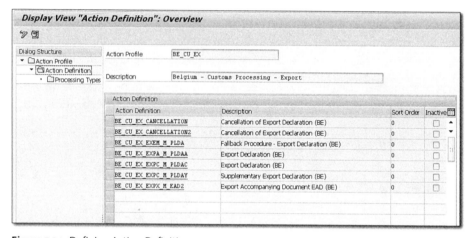

Figure 7.24 Defining Action Definitions

If a new printed form is defined as an additional message, you need to define a new action definition, which is linked to this message. The name of this action definition needs to start with ZGTS_xx (xx for your own naming convention). By using this naming convention, you can execute the message correctly from the COMMUNICATION tab of the customs authorities.

The final step of this Customizing activity is to define a processing type for each action definition (Figure 7.25). The commonly used processing types are external communication (for printed forms) and method call (for e-filing declarations in the form of IDocs).

In the lower section of the screen, you can link the form that has been created to the action definition. Furthermore, in the FORM TYPE field you need to indicate whether the form is created as a PDF form or smart form.

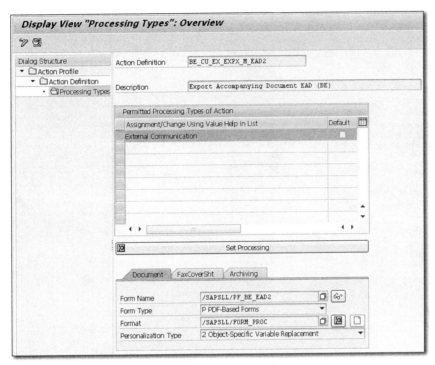

Figure 7.25 Defining a Processing Type for Each Action Definition

Define Conditions/Output Parameters for Communication of General Documents

This Customizing step specifies start conditions or printer specifications.

As shown in Figure 7.26, the screen for customizing output parameters consists of three parts. The upper left part displays all action profiles defined in the system. Only the action profiles defined in the previous activity are displayed here.

The upper right part displays the action definition of the selected action profile, and the lower part displays the details of a selected action definition.

Although it may appear that most of the information in this Customizing activity is already defined in the previous step, it is crucial to list all the active action definitions here, as well. Therefore, in case a new action definition is created in the previous step, make sure to add it in this right-hand box, as well.

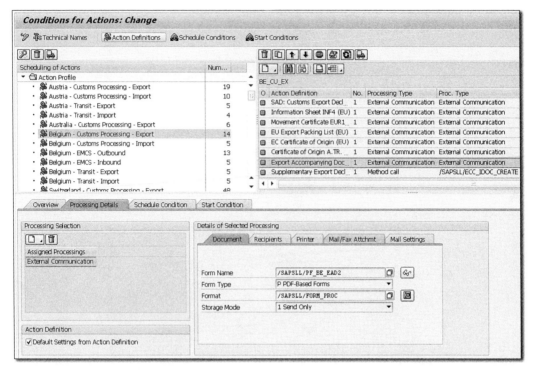

Figure 7.26 Defining Output Parameters for Action Definitions

Furthermore, in the lower box, you can select a few more details regarding the action definitions. For instance, under PROCESSING DETAILS—PRINTER, you can specify which printer needs to be used in order to print a specific form, the number of copies it needs to print, etc. You don't necessarily have to fill in this information because similar settings can be done in via the master data (see Section 7.2.4).

It can be useful to select the option TECHNICAL NAMES. This displays the technical names of the action profiles and action definitions as created in the previous Customizing step.

If the customs authorities require an SCD or period declaration (see Section 7.1), the following activities need to be performed, as well. Define Technical Medium for Messages (PPF Actions) for Supplementary Customs Declarations and Define Conditions/Output Parameters for Communication of General Documents are similar to the settings described earlier; they need to be completed with the same logic.

Define Technical Messages for a Message Schema

SAP GTS generates IDocs for its communication with customs. In SAP GTS, we can create multiple messages that can be sent to the customs authorities. However, the names that are given in SAP GTS are not recognized by the customs authorities. Therefore, each country uses its own set of so-called *technical messages*.

The purpose of this Customizing activity is to list the messages known by the customs authorities so they can be used in other Customizing transactions in which they are linked to messages known by SAP GTS.

As Figure 7.27 shows, SAP GTS starts with defining a message scheme.

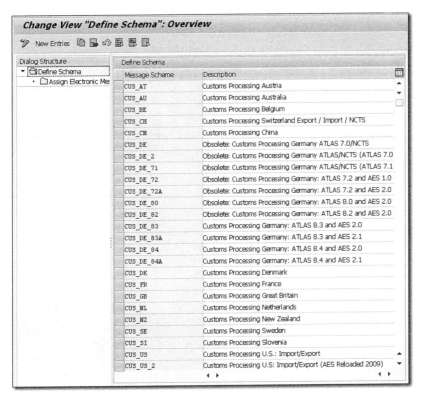

Figure 7.27 Defining Message Schema

This scheme contains all the technical messages for any specific country. Again, when creating a message scheme for a company located in a country that is not supported by SAP, you should follow this naming convention.

As displayed in Figure 7.28, when you select one of the message schemes, you can choose from a list of all the technical messages.

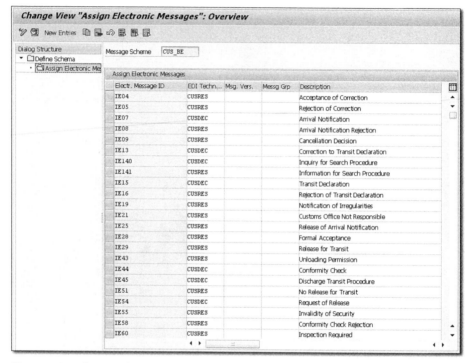

Figure 7.28 Defining Technical Message in Message Schema

The column ELECTR. MESSAGE ID refers to the technical message name known with the customs authorities. The DESCRIPTION column is related to this electronic message ID.

The EDI TECHNICAL NAME column refers to the type of IDoc recognized by SAP GTS. As you will read later, during the definition of a new SAP GTS message, you need to link this EDI technical name (also called *message ID*) to the newly created message.

Define Messages for Communication Processes

While the previous transaction is used to maintain all messages provided by the customs authorities, this transaction is used to maintain all internal SAP GTS messages.

In this Customizing activity, the message is linked to both a technical message, interpretable by the customs authorities, and an incompleteness check.

As indicated in Figure 7.29, for every message defined, you can add a description, message type (not required), message scheme (defined in previous step), message ID (see previous step), and an incompleteness procedure (see Section 7.2.3).

Change View "Messages for Activity": Overview

New Entries

Messages for Activity

Message	Description	Message Type	Scheme	Message ID	Ch...	Do...	Cl...	IncompProc
M2310	Import Declaration - Incomplete, Simplified (NL)	/SAPSLL/CUS_DEC	CUS_NL	SAGAIN	☐	☐	☐	NL_IMP_AIN
M2320	Import Declaration - Advance Declaration (NL)	/SAPSLL/CUS_DEC	CUS_NL	SAGAIN	☐	☐	☐	NL_IMP_AIN
M2330	Import Declaration - Subsequent Declaration (NL)	/SAPSLL/CUS_DEC	CUS_NL	SAGAIN	☐	☐	☐	NL_IMP_AIN
M2340	Import Declaration - Supplementary Declaration (NL)	/SAPSLL/CUS_CON	CUS_NL	SAGAVA	☐	☐	☐	NL_IMP_AVA
M4010	Customs Declaration U.S. ABI (EI)	/SAPSLL/CUS_ABI	CUS_US_2	ABIEI1	☐	☐		
M4060	Pre-Declaration U.S. ISF (SF)	/SAPSLL/CUS_ABI	CUS_US_2	ABISF	☐	☐	☐	US_IMP_ISF
M4070	Correction to Pre-Declaration U.S. ISF (SF) Before AMS	/SAPSLL/CUS_ABI	CUS_US_2	ABISF	☐	☐	☐	US_IMP_ISF
M4080	Correction to Pre-Declaration U.S. ISF (SF) After AMS	/SAPSLL/CUS_ABI	CUS_US_2	ABISF	☐	☐	☐	US_IMP_ISF
M4100	Reconciliation Summary ABI (RA)	/SAPSLL/CUS_ABI	CUS_US_2	RA	☐	☐	☐	US_RECON
M4200	U.S. ABI ACH Approval QN/PN	/SAPSLL/CUS_ABI	CUS_US_2	ABIQNPN	☐	☐	☐	US_STA_ACH
M5000	Export Declaration NON-Secure Export Scheme Partner (N...	/SAPSLL/CUS_EXP	CUS_NZ	NZ830	☐	☐	☐	NZ_EX_40
M5010	Export Declaration SECURE Export Scheme Partner (NZ)	/SAPSLL/CUS_EXP	CUS_NZ	NZ830	☐	☐	☐	NZ_EX_40SE
M7000	Export Declaration (AU)	/SAPSLL/CUS_EXP	CUS_AU	EXD	☐	☐	☐	AU_EX_NDC
M7010	Confirming Export Declaration (AU)	/SAPSLL/CUS_EXP	CUS_AU	EXD	☐	☐	☐	AU_EX_YDC
M7020	Confirmed Export Declaration (AU)	/SAPSLL/CUS_EXP	CUS_AU	EXD	☐	☐	☐	AU_EX_CDC
M7030	Status Request (AU)	/SAPSLL/CUS_STA	CUS_AU	STREQ	☐	☐	☐	
M7100	Export Declaration (BE)	/SAPSLL/CUS_EXP	CUS_BE	SADEXPORT	☐	☐	☐	BE_EX_DEC
M7110	Export Declaration (BE)	/SAPSLL/CUS_EXP	CUS_BE	SADEXPORT	☐	☐	☐	BE_EX_DEC
M7120	Supplementary Export Declaration (BE)	/SAPSLL/CUS_EXP	CUS_BE	SADEXPORT	☐	☐	☐	BE_EX_DEC
M7130	Export Declaration (BE)	/SAPSLL/CUS_EXP	CUS_BE	SADEXPORT	☐	☐	☐	BE_EX_DEC
M7140	Import Declaration (BE)	/SAPSLL/CUS_DEC	CUS_BE	SADIMPORT	☐	☐	☐	BE_IM_FCA
M7150	Simplified Import Declaration (BE)	/SAPSLL/CUS_DVZ	CUS_BE	SADIMPORT	☐	☐	☐	BE_IM_FCC
M7160	Supplementary Import Declaration (BE)	/SAPSLL/CUS_CON	CUS_BE	SADIMPORT	☐	☐	☐	BE_IM_FCY
M7170	Single Customs Declaration - Customs Warehouse (BE)	/SAPSLL/CUS_EZL	CUS_BE	SADIMPORT	☐	☐	☐	BE_IM_ZLA
M9000	Draft e-AD (DE IE815)	/SAPSLL/EMC_IE815	EMC_DE	N_AAD_SUB	☐	☐	☐	DE_IE815

Figure 7.29 Defining Messages for Communication Process

As shown in the MESSAGE column of the same figure, you can see that the messages defined by standard SAP follow this logic:

▶ M message: For outgoing messages to the customs authorities in an e-filing setup

▶ I message: For incoming messages from the customs authorities in an e-filing setup

▶ P message: For all printed forms, used for both e-filing and a paper-based setup

Define Control Settings for Communication Processes

The Define Control Settings for Communication Processes activity is where you set up the structure and process of the operative cockpit. But before you perform this crucial step, you have to complete all previous Customizing steps.

As displayed in Figure 7.30, this Customizing activity is set up in multiple levels. The highest level, on the left (PROCESS TEMPLATE), is creating a process template. This process template groups all the activities related to Customs Management for a specific country.

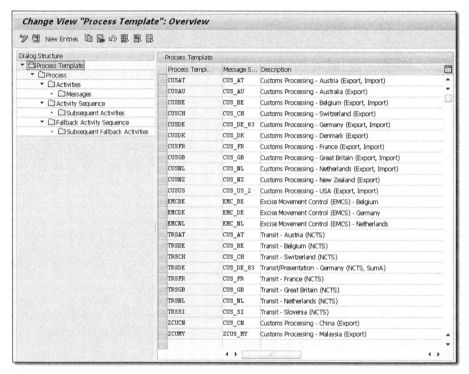

Figure 7.30 Defining Process Template

For each process template, several processes are defined, as displayed in the PRO-CESS pane in Figure 7.31.

Crucial in this step is indicating whether a process is related to either import/arrival or export/dispatch so that the system knows how the process needs to be handled and, subsequently, in which corresponding operative cockpit to display it.

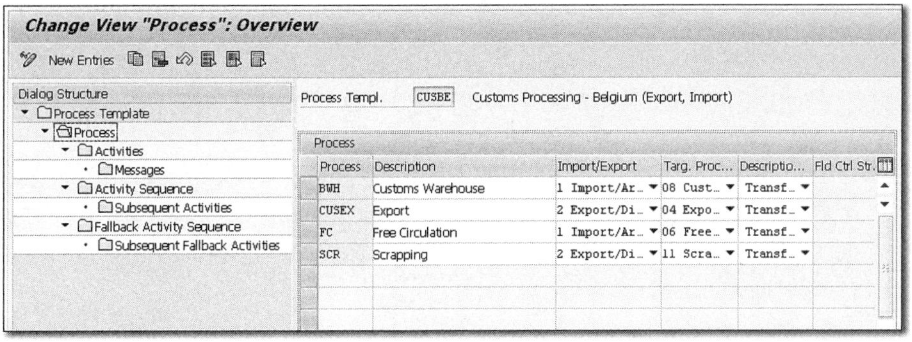

Figure 7.31 Defining Processes per Process Template

Furthermore, you need to indicate the *target procedure*—that is, what will happen with the goods. For example, when an import declaration needs to be created for a specific shipment, a process needs to exist for the creation of such an import declaration. Therefore, the process needs to be described as "Import/Arrival" with a target procedure set to "Free Circulation." In the case of Alpha, which operates in a BWH, it also needs to have an import process with target procedure Customs Warehouse.

At the next level (ACTIVITIES), the activities or process activities need to be defined. These are the different steps that should occur in a specific process. Each activity represents a specific status.

Recall from Section 7.1 that the operative cockpit helps you group ongoing declarations according to certain processing statuses. This results in a framework whereby each declaration needs to follow a predefined number of activities before the process is complete. Those activities, displayed in the operative cockpit, are the ones you need to define here.

As shown in Figure 7.32, for each of the process activities, you can indicate whether it takes place before presentation to the customs authorities (premature entry flag), the activity is part of a simplified procedure (only allowed after approval of the customs authorities), or a certain activity is optional. You can also indicate whether a license is required for the selected activity, and if so, which one.

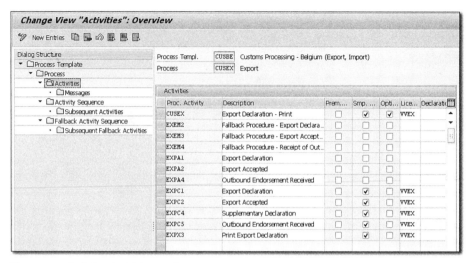

Figure 7.32 Defining Activities per Process

Optional activities need to be executed only in specific scenarios. The logic behind these scenarios is determined by the determination data logic of the message. If the logic of the defaulting data determines that the message needs to be displayed in the customs declaration, then the process needs to be complete before you can continue with the next activity. However, if the logic of the defaulting data does *not* trigger the message in the customs declaration, this activity is skipped. For more information on the defaulting data, consult Section 7.2.3.

At the lowest level of this Customizing activity (MESSAGES), you can list all the relevant messages for a process activity, as displayed in Figure 7.33.

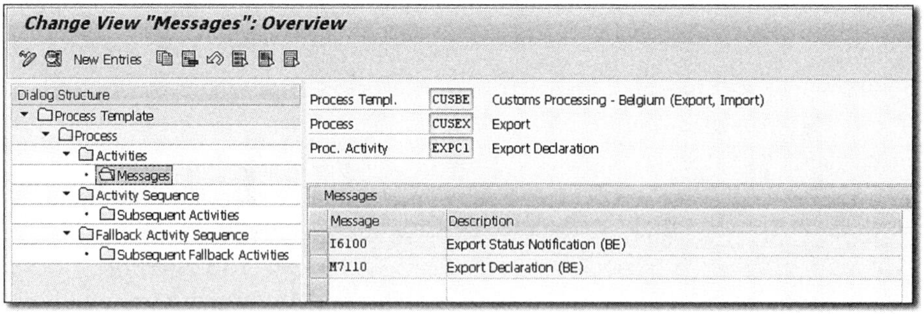

Figure 7.33 Defining Messages per Activity

It is important to include all the incoming, outgoing, and/or print messages that are expected in this activity. Executing or receiving messages that belong to a previous or later activity is not possible.

Once all activities are defined and linked to one or more messages, you need to define the sequence in which these activities must be performed and appear in the operative cockpit. Figure 7.34 shows that this process starts with defining an *activity sequence*.

Figure 7.34 Defining Activity Sequence

In the SUBSEQUENT ACTIVITIES pane, you can group the required activities that were created in the previous steps and assign a number to the activity in the ACTIVITY COUNTER column (Figure 7.35). The system considers the activity with the lowest number to be the first activity it needs to execute, and so on.

Change View "Subsequent Activities": Overview

New Entries

Dialog Structure
▾ ☐ Process Template
  ▾ ☐ Process
    ▾ ☐ Activities
      · ☐ Messages
    ▾ ☐ Activity Sequence
      · ☐ Subsequent Activities
    ▾ ☐ Fallback Activity Sequence
      · ☐ Subsequent Fallback Activities

Process Templ.	CUSBE	Customs Processing - Belgium (Export, Import)
Process	CUSEX	Export
Activity Seq.	EXPC	Simplified Export Declaration

Subsequent Activities

Activ. Counter	Proc. Activity	Description
10	EXPC1	Export Declaration
20	EXPC2	Export Accepted
30	EXPX3	Print Export Declaration
40	EXPC4	Supplementary Declaration
50	EXPC5	Outbound Endorsement Received

Figure 7.35 Assign Sequence in Subsequent Activities

It is important to note that you can identify a fallback procedure for each activity sequence (see Section 7.1), as shown at the bottom of Figure 7.36.

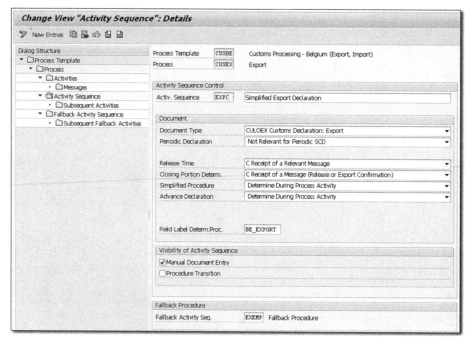

Figure 7.36 Defining and Assigning of Fallback Activity

By assigning a fallback activity to a normal activity, you allow the system to determine which actions it should perform if the system gets set to the fallback procedure. Especially for the activities with electronic communication to either the customs authorities or the broker, it is crucial to have this fallback procedure in place because sending and receiving message will temporarily not be possible.

In such a scenario, you should assign an activity with a printed output as a fallback activity instead of using an activity with electronic communication. In this case, the system prints a form instead of waiting for incoming and outgoing messages. With this form, the customs authorities will be notified of the outgoing or incoming shipment.

Define Determination for Activity Sequence

In Define Determination for Activity Sequence you define which activity sequence needs to be assigned to a specific legal regulation in all possible relevant target procedures.

By making use of the target procedure and, potentially, an authorization type, the system determines the activity sequence for which a customs declaration needs to be created.

Figure 7.37 shows how you can add a license type to these settings, as well. In such an event, the system confirms whether the required authorizations are available in the system and uses this information to determine the activity sequence.

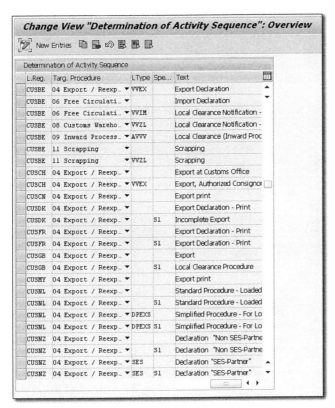

Figure 7.37 Defining Determination for Activity Sequence

In order for these settings to work as described, it is crucial that you assign a process template to the legal regulation. This action needs to be performed in the Customizing activity Control Settings for Application Areas by Legal Regulations of a Legal Code. The required settings are already performed for the countries supported by standard SAP GTS. For countries that are not supported, this mapping needs to be performed.

Classify Foreign Trade Documents

When a printed form is created in the system, it must be classified to indicate the type of customs document.

In Classify Foreign Trade Documents (see Figure 7.38), you can add an official document type to the newly created print message. The list of form types is defined by the system and is based on the legal regulation for different countries.

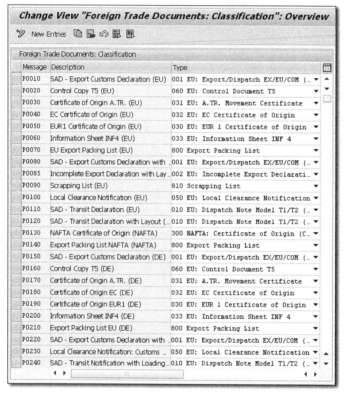

Figure 7.38 Customizing Activity for Classifying Foreign Trade Documents

Defaulting Data

Defaulting data, an important and very useful feature in the customs declaration of SAP GTS, can be used to automatically populate fields. All activities related to defaulting data are grouped in Procedures for Defaulting Data.

The purpose of defaulting data is to automatically populate these fields with the correct information based on rules that can be predefined. This reduces your workload for each customs declaration. In general, most data elements required for completing a customs declaration are being transferred from the feeder system. However, sometimes certain information is not stored in the feeder system, meaning that the corresponding fields in the customs declaration remain blank, as well.

The setup of defaulting data is performed at two levels. First, you need to define the logic or rules in the Customizing section of SAP GTS. Once these rules are defined, you can maintain the actual data that will be entered in the customs declaration in the master data.

Defaulting Alpha's Data (Part I)

Let's assume that the customs office of exit is one of the mandatory data elements of the export customs declaration. This is the customs office where the goods leave the country or customs union. Because this information is not available in the feeder system, the use of defaulting data rules could be beneficial.

Alpha knows that every shipment from its European Distribution Center in Belgium to a customer in Russia that is transported by truck passes through the same customs office in Poland. Therefore, the following rule can be set up:

If the country of destination is "Russia" and if the mode of transport is "truck" (expressed in a code), then enter "Customs Office Poland" in field Customs Office of Exit of the export declaration.

In SAP GTS Customizing, you need to define that the CUSTOMS OFFICE OF EXIT field can be populated based on the combination of country of destination and mode of transport.

In the master data of SAP GTS, you would populate the rule as shown in Table 7.3:

Country of Destination	Mode of Transport	Customs Office of Exit
RU (for Russia)	03 (for Truck)	Customs Office Poland

Table 7.3 Default Data Example

This rule results in the automatic population of the field CUSTOMS OFFICE OF EXIT, based on the information available in the fields COUNTRY OF DESTINATION and MODE OF TRANSPORT. More specifically, the customs office of Poland is defaulted in every export declaration to Russia where goods are moved via truck.

Furthermore, the system makes a distinction between date fields, partners, messages, email notifications, and normal data fields. For each of them, there is a separate transaction in SAP GTS Customizing.

Each of these types of defaulting data fields requires a default procedure. These procedures are assigned to a country-process combination. So for each country, you have at least one import and export defaulting procedure. The defaulting procedure groups all the default rules for that country-process combination.

In the event that no default procedure is predefined, because the country for which you want to set up SAP GTS is not supported by standard SAP, you need to define these default procedures first in the Customizing step Define Determination Procedure For Defaulting Data. Here, based on the legal regulation, the document type, and process, you can identify a default data procedure for dates, partners, general data fields, messages, and even email notifications.

Note that the defaulting possibilities for date fields and partners are less flexible than the defaulting of general fields and messages.

You can access the defaulting data of the general data fields and messages via menu option DEFINE DEFAULT DATA FOR DOCUMENT FIELDS, MESSAGES, AND DOCUMENT DATA.

This Customizing activity is built in several levels. At the highest level (DEFAULT PROCEDURE, as shown in Figure 7.39), you see the overview of all the defaulting data procedures. As we mentioned earlier, for each country-process combination, one procedure is in place. Furthermore, here, the distinction between document fields (or general data fields) and messages is made.

For each default procedure, a set of *target fields* or *rules* is defined. As Figure 7.40 shows, each of these target fields need to be set to status ACTIVE, and you need to identify a sequence. The sequence defined in this step determines the order of the default rule in the master data section.

At the top of the screen, the system indicates the procedure for which the rules are displayed. In this case, the rules for CDEBE (DOCUMENT FIELDS—EXPORT—BELGIUM) are displayed.

At the lowest level, you can define *accesses* for each of these target fields. These access determine which field or field combinations are used as input fields in the rule.

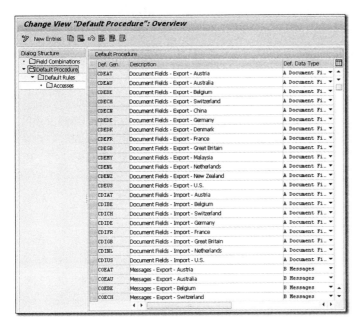

Figure 7.39 Default Data Procedure

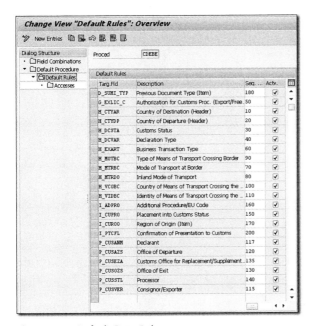

Figure 7.40 Default Data Rules

By assigning a number in this box, you determine the sequence in which the defaulting data program runs through the accesses. The field combination with the lowest number is considered first. If no determination can be performed, the system considers the subsequent accesses and uses them to determine the default value.

Figure 7.41 shows the access for field OFFICE OF EXIT (P_CUSOZS). In this example, the combinations of country of destination and mode of transport are accessed first. Only if no value can be populated in the customs declaration based on these accesses will the system continue its determination by considering the proceeding accesses.

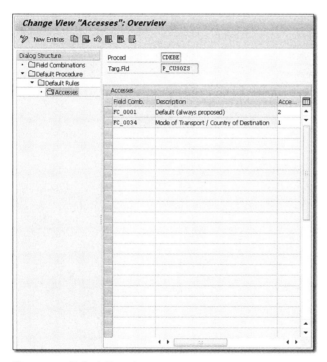

Figure 7.41 Default Data Accesses

As explained in our example, because the company knows how to identify the customs office of exit based on the mode of transport and country of destination, these fields need to be used as input.

SAP GTS comes with a variety of predefined field combinations. An important one is DEFAULT (ALWAYS PROPOSED), which implies that a certain target field is always populated in the same way without making use of (a combination of) input fields.

Defaulting Alpha's Data (Part II)

As an addition to the first, quite simple example in which goods from Belgium were shipped by truck through Poland to Russia, it is more likely that the defaulting rules are a combination of these simple rules.

Let's assume the same company also ships goods to Turkey often, and if these goods move by truck, they always leave the EU via a customs office in Bulgaria. The same defaulting rule can be applied, and in the Customizing activity of SAP GTS, nothing changes. In the master data section of defaulting data, a line is added that states that if the country of destination is "Turkey" and the mode of transport is "Truck," the system needs to default to "Customs Office Bulgaria," as shown in Table 7.4.

Rule Based on Country of Destination/Mode of Transport		
Country of Destination	**Mode of Transport**	**Customs Office of Exit**
RU (for Russia)	03 (for Truck)	Customs Office Poland
TR (for Turkey)	03 (for Truck)	Customs Office Bulgaria

Table 7.4 Default Data Extended Example

Besides these shipments by truck to Russia and Turkey, all other shipments of the company are shipped by sea. All of these sea shipments leave the territory via the port of Antwerp.

Now, you could add the code for sea shipments as the mode of transport in the first rule and add a new line in the master data for each country to which the company ships. However, it is also possible to make use of the DEFAULT (ALWAYS PROPOSED) rule; here, that means the system defaults Customs Office of Antwerp in every other case, as shown in Table 7.5.

Default (Always Proposed)

Customs Office Antwerp

Table 7.5 Default Data—Default (Always Proposed)

Here, it is important to note the access or sequence in which the defaulting data applies the rules. If the DEFAULT (ALWAYS PROPOSED) rule were applied first, then the truck shipments to Russia or Turkey would also have the Customs Office of Antwerp as their customs office of exit, which is, of course, incorrect.

Recall that standard SAP GTS has defined a number of rules or field combinations. But if the field combination you want to use is not yet defined, you can create this combination. In the same Customizing activity, in the column FIELD COMBINATION (see Figure 7.41) you can create a name and description for the field combination and add up to eight different fields to it.

Sometimes, a specific source or target field is not yet defined by SAP GTS. In this case, you can also create these fields in Customizing activity Extend Field List for Data Proposal. And if the defaulting logic is too complex and cannot be obtained via the standard SAP GTS Customizing, there is a specific BAdI available (see Chapter 10).

Customs Code Lists

SAP GTS uses the same document types (e.g., CULOEX for all export declarations, independent of the country) for the same processes. However, every country has specific data that is accepted by the customs authorities. For certain fields, SAP GTS provides a list of allowed values. These *customs code lists* are legal regulation specific, meaning that they're country specific. The following fields typically make use of customs codes lists, among others:

- CUSTOMS STATUS
- PLACEMENT INTO CUSTOMS STATUS
- PACKAGING MATERIAL
- TYPES OF SEALS
- MODE OF TRANSPORT
- TYPE OF PREVIOUS DOCUMENT

Using customs codes avoids incorrect values in a declaration and, therefore, avoids longer processing times. Since these code lists are aligned with the values used by the customs authorities, SAP GTS guarantees that you communicate "in the same language" as the eventual recipient.

All activities related to the customs code lists can be found under CUSTOMS CODE LISTS in the Customizing area of SAP GTS.

Before you can define the code lists, you need to define a procedure that applies for the country in which the FTO is located. The Customizing activity Define Procedures for Customs Code Lists allows the creation of these procedures for customs code lists. Separate procedures are created per country, but in special cases, it is useful to have additional customs code lists for different activities in a country: a standard procedure (triggered if there is an import or export declaration) and an additional one for transit activities. This last customs code list is valid only for transit declarations.

Figure 7.42 displays the overview of the different customs code list procedures available in standard SAP GTS.

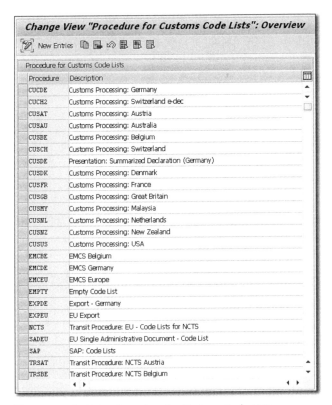

Figure 7.42 Defining Procedure for Customs Code Lists

Once you define the procedure, assign it to a legal regulation. In the activity Assign Customs Code Lists Procedure to Legal Regulation, a company can also identify which code list procedures it will use, as shown in Figure 7.43. Standard SAP GTS comes with a range of data objects. These data objects correspond to individual fields of the customs declaration. In order to maintain allowed customs values of a data object, you have to list that object here.

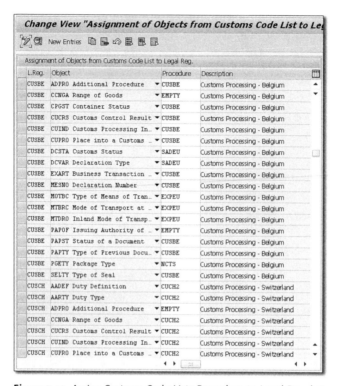

Figure 7.43 Assign Customs Code Lists Procedure to Legal Regulation

Finally, in the activity Maintain Customs Code Lists for Legal Regulation, you can create entries that will be available in the customs declaration. Figure 7.44 displays the entries that will be available in the MODE OF TRANSPORT AT BORDER field for customs declarations created for a Belgian company (legal regulation CUSBE). The system does not allow you to add any other values in the customs declaration than the ones maintained here.

There are a few more Customizing activities related to the Customs Code Lists; these additional transactions are related to the customs status and customs status placement. These fields (the first on the header level of the customs declaration and the second on the item level) inform the customs authorities of the origin and destination of the goods. The origin and destination of the goods are not from a geographical point of view, but from a customs procedure point of view. For instance, the customs status indicates that the goods are exported out of the country, while the customs status placement indicates that the goods were stored in a customs warehouse.

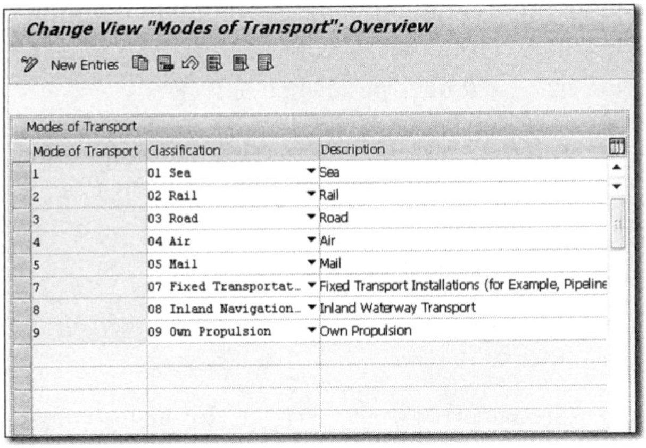

Figure 7.44 Maintain Customs Code Lists for Legal Regulation

Let's consider the example in Figure 7.45. In a customs declaration created for legal regulation CUSBE and in case of process CUSEX (export process), the customs status is maintained with the values CO, EU, or EX. In this way, you cannot select, for instance, IM for an export declaration because the code indicates that the customs declaration is an import. This limitation reduces the chance that incorrect information is communicated to the customs authorities.

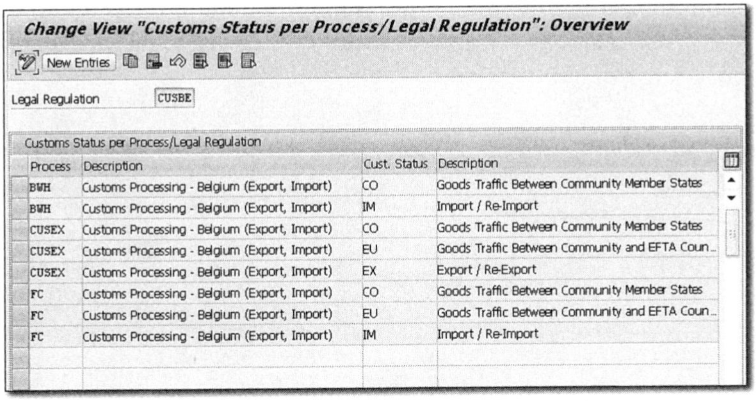

Figure 7.45 Assign Customs Status to a Process and Legal Regulation

Authorizations and Securities

Within the area of customs and global trade, an economic operator requires various types of authorizations for performing certain activities, such as simplified procedures for import/export/transit, periodic declaration processes, economic customs procedures, and so on. These authorizations need to be maintained in SAP GTS depending on the concerned activities performed (e.g., BWH).

In addition, an economic operator might need to foresee securities (e.g., simplified procedures, economic customs procedures, deferred duty payment schemes, etc.). Some securities can also be maintained in SAP GTS.

SAP GTS has identified several standard types of authorizations and securities. Additional types can be defined in Customizing if these predefined types do not meet the requirements of the company.

The section AUTHORIZATIONS AND SECURITIES of the SAP GTS Customizing consists of multiple transactions to specify the details of a specific authorization or security. In each of these transactions, you can indicate whether that selected authorization or security applies in a certain country (based on the legal regulation for which such an authorization or security is created). As indicated in Figure 7.46, besides specifying the relevant legal regulation, you need to choose the applicable license type. You have to specify a status for each of the authorizations or securities. These can be *Authorization Created*, *Authorization Active*, or *Authorization Expired*.

Once these settings are performed in the Customizing section of SAP GTS, you can create these specific authorizations or securities in the master data section of SAP GTS Customs Management.

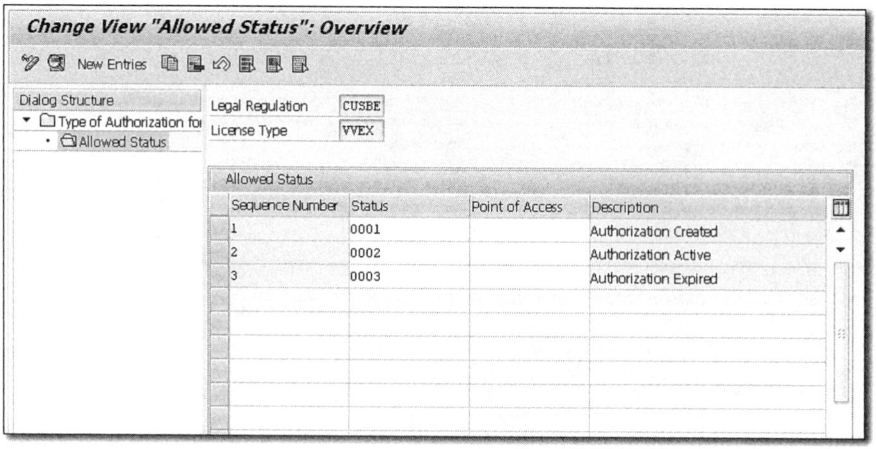

Figure 7.46 Allowed Statuses for Authorization

Duty Framework

The duty framework functionality in SAP GTS groups all the values and calculations that the customs authorities require you to report. Common required values are the value of the goods, shipment-specific insurance and freight costs, import duties and taxes, and so on.

By combining several of these values and creating subtotals, you create a *duty framework*.

Because the legal requirements for the declaration of certain values are country specific, the settings related to the duty framework are performed on the legal regulation level.

Recall from Section 7.2.1 that each customs declaration comes with a tab on the header level (LOGISTICS COSTS) and one on the item level (CUSTOMS VALUE). These tabs are available for import, export, and transit, and a framework for capturing values and calculating duties can be created.

SAP GTS allows you to fully design this framework yourself; however, it has to comply with the legal and business needs.

All Customizing settings for this duty framework can be found back in Calculation of Customs Duty. This group of Customizing activities contains several important transactions.

The duty framework is composed of duty types that can be configured into a framework. Therefore, the first step is to define these duty types in the Customizing activity Define Type of Customs Duty. SAP GTS comes with an extensive list of predefined duty types, but you can set up additional duty types as required. Figure 7.47 shows an overview of the existing duty types displayed from the Customizing activity.

During the definition of the duty type, you need to indicate the duty category that can be selected from a predefined list of categories; the duty category helps the system identify the nature of the duty types. As displayed in Figure 7.48, besides this duty category, other characteristics need to be defined, as well.

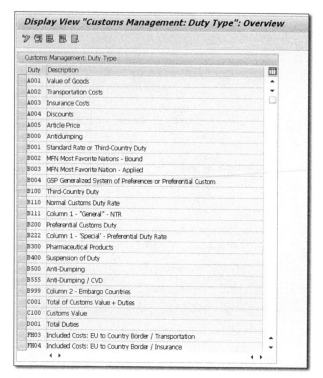

Figure 7.47 Standard Duty Types

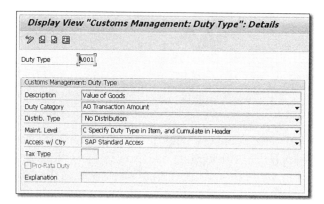

Figure 7.48 Duty Type Details

In the DISTRIBUTION TYPE field, select how the value on the header level gets distributed to the items (based on the weight or value). In such an event, the system calculates the proportional weight or value of each item compared to the total weight or value of the entire shipment. In this way, the costs at the header level are allocated to each of the items as a percentage of the total weight or value. In the MAINTENANCE LEVEL field, select whether the duty type needs to be included in the duty framework on the header level, item level, or both.

After you create these separate duty types, combine them into a framework in line with the legal and business requirements using the Customizing activity Define Calculation Procedure for Customs Duties. After selecting the correct legal regulation, you can create separate calculation procedure for import, transit, and export.

You need to list all duty types that need to be included in the framework and assign them a sequence number, as shown in Figure 7.49.

Display View "Calculation Procedure for Imports": Overview

Dialog Structure			
▾ Calculation Procedure for Imports	Legal Reg.	CUSBE	
• Assign Cost Components for Totaling			
▾ Calculation Procedure for Procedure Transitions	Calculation Procedure for Imports		
• Assignment of Cost Components	Seq.No. Duty Description	Value Type	Val.BAdI
▾ Calculation Procedure for Exports	10 A001 Value of Goods	001 Net Price / Invoice Value	▾ ☐
• Assign Cost Components for Totaling	200 H010 Delivery Costs to Place of Introduction (Transport)	Value not Shown Separately	▾ ☐
• Calculation Rules	210 H012 Costs of Delivery to Place of Introduction (Insurance)	Value not Shown Separately	▾ ☐
	500 C100 Customs Value	002 Customs Value	▾ ☐
	530 B200 Preferential Customs Duty	Value not Shown Separately	▾ ☐
	540 B100 Third-Country Duty	Value not Shown Separately	▾ ☐
	560 C001 Total of Customs Value + Duties	Value not Shown Separately	▾ ☐
	570 D001 Total Duties	Value not Shown Separately	▾ ☐
	580 W001 Value for Foreign Trade Statistics (Statistical Value)	003 Statistical Value	▾ ☐
	610 IVAT Import Turnover Tax	012 Import Turnover Tax	▾ ☐
	630 B300 Pharmaceutical Products	Value not Shown Separately	▾ ☐

Figure 7.49 Define Calculation Procedure for Customs Duties

As you'd expect, the duty type with the lowest sequence number appears first in the framework. For each of the duty types, you need to assign a value type; standard SAP GTS foresees a range of types, which allows the system to identify the duty type.

Besides adding duty types, the standard SAP GTS duty framework functionality allows the creation of (sub)totals of previous duty types. However, if you need to perform more complex calculations, you have to use a BAdI. In this particular case, select the checkbox in the column VALUATION BAdI for the duty types that require the complex calculation.

You can create a subtotal in the activity Assign Cost Components for Totaling by selecting the duty type from the CALCULATION PROCEDURE and drilling down to

ASSIGN COST COMPONENTS FOR TOTALING. Here, you need to add the elements that need to be summed up. Note that certain standard duty types, such as C100 Customs Value and D001 Total Duties, are set up as (sub)totaling duty categories. Therefore, in such cases, using the totaling functionality is not required.

Another important activity when setting up a duty framework is Define External Customs Duty Rate Types for Data Upload. When a company purchases duty rates from a content provider, it is required to link the duty types used in SAP GTS to the ones used by the content provider. Matching these duty types is done in this Customizing activity as displayed in Figure 7.50.

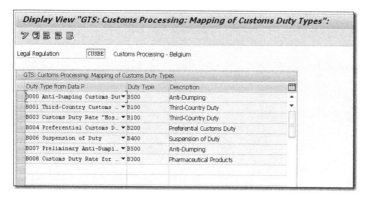

Figure 7.50 Mapping of Internal to External Duty Rate Types

In many of the Customizing activities, we have referred to corresponding settings in the master data that need to be created, as well. In the following section, we'll highlight the master data elements that are relevant for general Customs Management processes.

The master data for the special customs procedures and excise duty monitoring will be touched upon in Section 7.3.6 (for special customs procedures) and Section 7.4.4 (for EMCS).

7.2.4 Master Data

The following information is captured within the MASTER DATA tab:

- Customs products
- Partners
- Organizational data

Furthermore, the MASTER DATA section of Customs Management contains following tabs:

▶ Authorizations and securities

▶ Geography

▶ Default data

▶ Others

More information on this topic can be found in Chapter 4 on master data. Let's look at some of these more closely.

Partners

Besides the standard customers and vendors you transfer from a feeder system, SAP GTS Customs Management allows you to create, change, and display another type of business partner: the customs offices.

There are several roles a customs office can have: customs office of departure, destination, exit, transit, etc. It is usually mandatory to declare one of these types of customs offices to the customs authorities, meaning that they have to be specified in the customs declaration.

In order to create a new customs office, use the MAINTAIN CUSTOMS OFFICES transaction in the PARTNERS tab of the master data section of SAP GTS. This transaction works exactly like the transaction to create other business partners in SAP GTS. Note that, when creating a customs office, you need to select the correct business partner role (in the case of the customs office partner, SLLCOF Customs Office).

Authorizations and Securities

The layout and logic behind predefined authorizations and securities in SAP GTS is more or less the same.

As shown in Figure 7.51, the screen for license/authorization creation is divided into three sections. The upper box of the screen provides general information about the legal regulation, the authorization/security type, and so on. Besides an internal SAP GTS number, the official number of the authorization/security provided by the customs authorities needs to be maintained in the EXTERNAL NUMBER field.

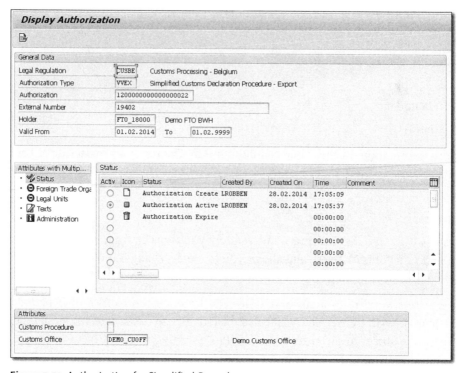

Figure 7.51 Authorization for Simplified Procedure

The attributes and their details are listed in the lower left section of the screen. Both authorizations and securities consist of multiple attributes that allow you to specify for which organizational unit they apply to and the status of this authorization. Although the setup is similar for authorizations and securities, the required attributes can differ.

Every authorization or security contains the STATUS attribute. Please note that creating an authorization/security is not sufficient. In order to use it, you need to set it to ACTIVE, and the validity period must not be in the past. The attributes FOREIGN TRADE ORGANIZATION and LEGAL UNIT contain the applicable organizational units.

Figure 7.51 shows the type of authorization that was specified in the Customizing. The legal regulation and authorization type were assigned in Customizing of SAP GTS, and the statuses were created. Here, you can see the AUTHORIZATION CREATED, AUTHORIZATION ACTIVE, and AUTHORIZATION EXPIRED statuses, as specified in Section 7.2.3.

Defaulting Data

Besides the information that is copied over from the feeder system, SAP GTS offers a set of rules to automatically complete certain information on the customs document. For instance, a sea/air shipment always leaves a country via the same harbor/airport, so one specific customs office is defined for sea transport, and another for defined for air transport.

These defaulting data rules are created in the Customizing, but the actual application of these rules with specific data is performed in master data.

Defaulting Alpha's Master Data

If we look back at the example of our company Alpha in Section 7.2.3, we can summarize that the following business logic is applicable:

▶ If the goods are transported by truck (Mode of Transport = 3) to Russia, then the customs office of exit is Customs Office Poland (CuO_Poland).

▶ If the goods are transported by truck (Mode of Transport = 3) to Turkey, then the customs office of exit is Customs Office Bulgaria (CuO_Bulgaria).

▶ In all other cases, the goods leave the customs union via the customs office in Antwerp (CuO_Antwerp).

Figure 7.52 and Figure 7.53 display how these rules need to be set up in the master data section of SAP GTS.

To access this activity, select DEFINE RULES FOR DEFAULT DOCUMENT DATA in the DEFAULT DATA tab. Before you can add any values, you need to select the default data procedure and legal regulation for which you want to define the default data.

The first two bullet points (goods trucked to Russia and Turkey) are based on the access MODE OF TRANSPORT/COUNTRY OF DESTINATION field.

The last bullet point can be obtained by using the DEFAULT (ALWAYS PROPOSED) access.

The data defaulting procedure and the legal regulation created during Customizing are shown at the top of the screen. By selecting these input parameters, you can influence the defaulting data of all export declarations for Belgium. The box on the left gives an overview of all the fields that can be defaulted (based on which fields are selected in the SAP GTS Customizing). If you drill down a certain field (or rule), you reach the accesses. In the box on the right, you can add or modify the default data logic applicable to the field that will be defaulted into the customs declaration.

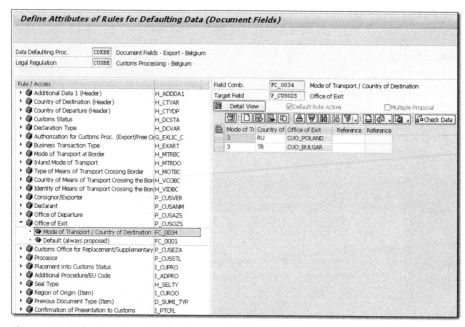

Figure 7.52 Defaulting Data Rule for Customs Office of Exit (1)

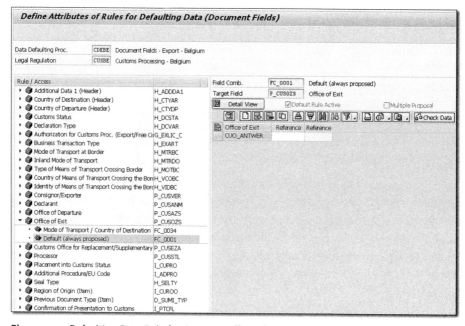

Figure 7.53 Defaulting Data Rule for Customs Office of Exit (2)

Remember from Section 7.2.3 that besides the document fields, you also have to default the correct messages into the customs declarations. In order to populate the rules for communication messages, select activity DEFINE RULES FOR OUTPUT DETERMINATION in the DEFAULT DATA tab. Figure 7.54 displays the outcome of this transaction.

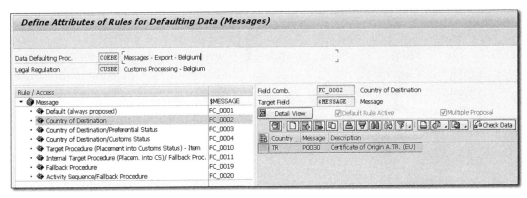

Figure 7.54 Defaulting Data Rule for Messages

Again, the legal regulation and data default procedure are shown at the top of the screen. The box on the left shows the only applicable rule in this activity (more specifically, MESSAGES and all the different accesses below). As with the defaulting of data fields, the DEFAULT (ALWAYS PROPOSED) can be a useful access. In the box on the right-hand side, the actual values are populated into the access.

From Figure 7.54, we learn that, if an export declaration is created that captures the information of a shipment between Belgium and Turkey (which is the country of destination), then a specific printed form (Certificate of Origin A.TR) is available in the COMMUNICATION tab of the Customs declaration for you to select and print.

By designing the defaulting functionality of the messages correctly, you can limit the risk of user error (or in this case, printing unnecessary forms).

Exchange Rates

All declared values in a customs declaration must be converted into the local customs currency. Of course, individual companies aren't allowed to decide which exchange rate they want to apply to their transactions; the customs authorities publish an exchange rate. This exchange rate must be maintained and updated in SAP GTS on a regular basis (often, monthly).

In Customizing (SAP NETWEAVER • GENERAL SETTINGS • CURRENCIES • ASSIGN EXCHANGE RATE TO WORKLIST), you can define which exchange rates to create. Once the exchange rates are defined, an exact rate can be maintained in the master data section of SAP GTS.

Because most customs authorities update the exchange rates on a periodic basis, the exchange rates need to be updated, as well. The updating can be done manually, in a worklist, or via the MAINTAIN EXCHANGE RATES transaction in the OTHERS tab. Figure 7.55 displays the worklist in SAP GTS.

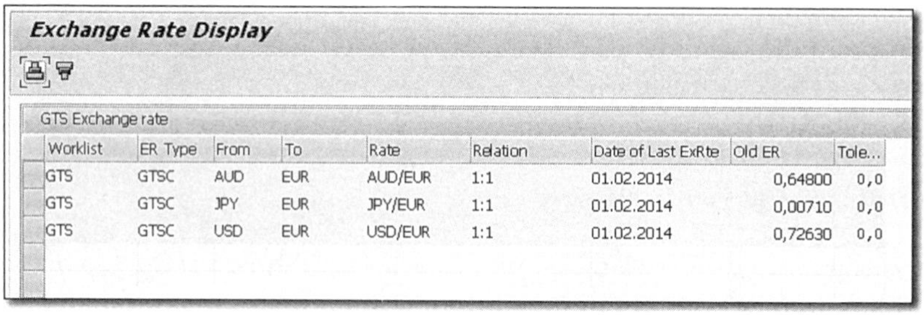

Exchange Rate Display

Worklist	ER Type	From	To	Rate	Relation	Date of Last ExRte	Old ER	Tole...
GTS	GTSC	AUD	EUR	AUD/EUR	1:1	01.02.2014	0,64800	0,0
GTS	GTSC	JPY	EUR	JPY/EUR	1:1	01.02.2014	0,00710	0,0
GTS	GTSC	USD	EUR	USD/EUR	1:1	01.02.2014	0,72630	0,0

Figure 7.55 Worklist for Maintaining Customs Exchange Rates

Manual maintenance of the exchange rates via the worklist is manageable if the amount of exchange rates is limited. However, SAP GTS also offers the possibility to upload these exchange rates when you buy them from a content provider. In this case, use the Upload Currency Exchange Rates transaction to upload the files.

If the system is using compensatory interest rates, these can also be maintained in the OTHERS tab.

7.3 Special Customs Procedures

Besides the standard import and export processes that are applicable to all international companies, some organizations also operate under a so-called *special customs procedure*. These procedures have the purpose of reducing import duties and, potentially, taxes.

Since duty drawback still impacts a company's working capital, operating under a special customs procedure suspends the payment of duties, meaning that no financial means need to be temporary invested.

In order for a requesting company to be allowed to operate under a special customs procedure, the local customs authorities need guarantee that the company is trustworthy. So, one of the requirements the customs authorities impose is an accurate bookkeeping of all goods that enter and leave that customs procedure.

If the customs authorities allow you to operate under such a procedure, a special authorization is granted. This authorization states what a company can and cannot do under the procedure. Among others, this is where using SAP GTS as a single Trade Compliance tool can make the difference for your company. The option of managing the customs procedures is seamlessly integrated with SAP ERP and SAP GTS Customs Management—and therefore also the other functionalities of SAP GTS.

Let's get a concise overview of the concept and functionality of a BWH (or customs warehouse), inward and outward processing relief (IPR and OPR), and processing under customs control (PUCC). We then highlight the most important specific master data related to these special customs procedures and the corresponding customizing.

7.3.1 Bonded Warehouse

A *bonded warehouse* (BWH), or customs warehouse, is the location where goods can be stored under suspension of duties and taxes. A BWH is different from other special customs procedures because of the type of activities that can take place under this procedure. In a BWH, manufacturing activities cannot be performed, but minor logistics activities such as repacking and regrouping materials and keeping them in good condition are allowed. The result of this arrangement is that a BWH is useful for a trading company or a company's distribution center, but not for performing manufacturing activities.

Before we start explaining the concept of a bonded warehouse in more depth, it is crucial to elaborate on the concept of duty-paid and duty-unpaid stock.

Stock in SAP GTS

As indicated by its name, in the case of a BWH (and also for the other special customs procedures), there are two types of stock, from a customs point of view.

For certain goods, a company has decided not to pay import duties and to store these goods as such in a customs warehouse (in this case, a BWH). These goods are referred to as *duty-unpaid goods*. The stock of this type of goods can be increased if a company buys its finished products from a supplier located outside the country or customs union or if goods are transferred in from another BWH. In this case (and more details will be provided in the business process), you have to create an inbound transit declaration; this is also known as a T1 declaration because it concerns duty-unpaid goods.

Of course, *duty-paid goods* are the opposite, and the stock can be increased by either paying import duties and taxes at the moment of importation or purchasing goods from a local supplier in the same country of customs union. In such an event, a system technical T2 declaration could be created in SAP GTS to indicate that the goods shipped are duty-paid goods.

Because the difference in stock types is not indicated in the stock keeping of the feeder system, it needs to be kept in SAP GTS. This implies that the sum of duty-paid and duty-unpaid stock in SAP GTS should always be in line with the total stock level in your feeder system.

Depending on the type of BWH that is applicable to the company, there may be a legal requirement to physically split the stock piles of duty-paid and duty-unpaid stock. In most cases in Europe, this is not required.

Now that we've clarified the concept of a BWH, we'll guide you through the high-level business and system processes. Please note that this is only a brief overview of the scope of a BWH; in practice, there is a range of specific flows, depending on the location of the warehouse and the country to which the goods are shipped.

Inbound Movements

Let's get back to Alpha. Whenever Alpha receives goods from its vendor in China, these goods are added to the BWH as duty-unpaid goods.

Figure 7.56 shows both the business and system process of the import process into the BWH.

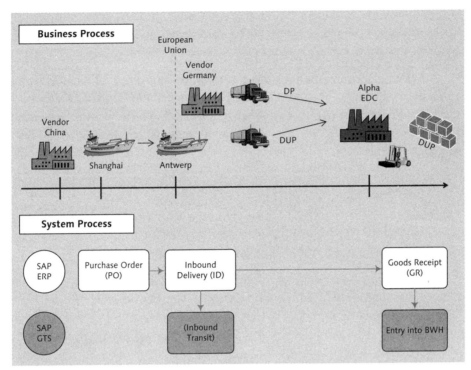

Figure 7.56 Bonded Warehouse—Import Process

The inbound process into the BWH starts when Alpha creates a purchase order in its feeder system with the Chinese vendor. An inbound delivery is created before the goods arrive at the plant.

When the goods arrive in the port of Antwerp, Alpha asks a customs broker to create an inbound transit declaration (T1 document) to bring the goods over under suspension of duties to the premises of Alpha. As soon as the goods arrive at Alpha's premises, Alpha has to notify the local customs authorities by clearing the transit declaration via a transit discharge declaration. The customs authorities, in turn, inform Alpha whether and when it is allowed to open the container. Since it involves duty-unpaid goods, the customs authorities may perform a physical check to make sure the shipment has been cleared correctly. This inbound transit is also represented by a declaration in SAP GTS.

When posting the goods receipt, a material document is created that triggers the creation of an entry into the BWH that will eventually increase the stock in SAP

GTS. Because nobody has paid the import duties yet, it is the duty-unpaid stock that is increased in the system. For BWH setups, you can only create import declarations after goods receipt.

The BWH entry document is a variant of an import declaration. In order to create such a document, it is sufficient to select the correct shipment in the ENTER DECLARATION AFTER GOODS RECEIPT worklist in SAP GTS. Every material document that is relevant for the BWH (meaning that the material is flagged as BWH-relevant, and the storage location is bonded) appears in this worklist. Refer to the customs ID section earlier in Chapter 2 for more information on whether a storage location is bonded.

In this BWH entry declaration, Alpha declares the exact quantity of the goods and the related value. The calculation of the values and corresponding duties is an important step and can be performed on two occasions:

▶ Calculation duties when the goods enter the BWH (can be legally required); at this point in time, the duties are not yet indebted, but the duty calculation in the import declaration is already performed.

▶ Calculation duties when the goods are released from the warehouse

For every BWH entry declaration created in SAP GTS, you can use the e-filing functionality as you would for any other standard import declaration. However, approval can be obtained by the customs authorities that these BWH entry declarations do not need to be declared on a transactional basis. In such an arrangement, an SCD can be created (see Section 7.1).

If Alpha purchases duty-paid goods from its German vendor, there is no need to create a BWH entry declaration. The posting of the goods receipt results in the creation of a material document in the feeder system. This material document does not generate any import declaration in SAP GTS, but it still increases the duty-paid stock in SAP GTS, as well. In this manner, the stocks in the feeder system and SAP GTS are in line.

Outbound Movements

Alpha's outbound process starts with the creation of a sales order, followed by an outbound delivery. As soon as the goods are picked and packed, the goods issue can be booked. However, before the goods are allowed to leave Alpha's premises, you need to create an export declaration. In order to create such a document in SAP GTS, create a *pro forma invoice* in the feeder system.

As with the standard export invoice, this pro forma invoice triggers SAP GTS to create an export declaration. Remember that it does not imply any financial bookings in the feeder system.

As with the standard export process, this export declaration can contain information from the feeder system, information that you entered manually, or information that is added automatically based on the defaulting data rules. Once the export declaration is complete, the same communication options are available: printed forms and electronic communication.

In this export declaration, a new tab is added to the item details. This tab contains information about the closing portion. We'll go into more detail about that tab shortly.

From a financial point of view, it is more beneficial for Alpha to send duty-unpaid goods to Russia, so the system automatically selects duty-unpaid goods when a shipment to Russia is initiated. This concept is called the *smart picking rule*.

Figure 7.57 shows both the system and business view of the outbound process.

SAP GTS supports the creation of an outbound transit document that can be relevant when you're sending goods to a specific country (EU-specific process). You can create this transit document simultaneously with the export document or postpone the creation of the transit document until the export declaration has been approved by the customs authorities.

When Alpha is selling its finished goods to a customer in France (domestic sales), there is no legal requirement to create an export declaration. In this case, the material document that is created when posting the goods issue decreases the stock. There is no need to create a pro forma invoice for this process. Because the customer in France does not want to be burdened with the administration of import duty payment, Alpha prefers to send duty-paid goods. Thanks to smart-picking, the system knows which type of stock is preferred, depending on the country of destination.

In short, a company prefers to sell duty-unpaid stock if its customer is located outside its country/customs union, and duty-paid stock if it is a domestic sale.

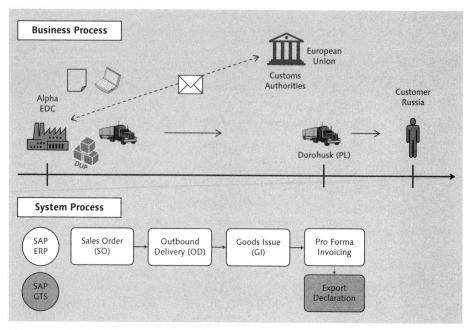

Figure 7.57 Bonded Warehouse—Export Process

As a result, two scenarios can occur:

▶ A customer in the same customs union wants a specific product, but only duty-unpaid stock is currently available in the BWH. In this event, the system automatically creates a *free-circulation declaration* (import declaration), and the required duties and applicable taxes are calculated and paid. This implies that the duty-unpaid stock decreases and, with this, the duty-paid stock increases. However, because this transaction is related to a sales flow, the duty-paid stock immediately decreases again.

▶ A customer outside the customs union wants to purchase a product, but at that moment, there is only duty-paid stock available. The company can choose to wait to send out the goods until it receives a shipment with duty-unpaid goods themselves. This is not always possible due to the promised delivery dates.

The alternative is to use the duty-paid stock, but in this event, the potential of the BWH is not used—that is, duties are paid in a scenario when it was not legally required. Therefore, which option a company chooses depends on its strategy.

Stock Overview

When a BWH is set up in SAP GTS, the stock is kept in both the feeder system and SAP GTS. The stock keeping in the feeder system does not change and always indicates a total number; in SAP GTS, the distinction between duty-paid and duty-unpaid goods is made.

To monitor the stock movements for a specific material, use the DISPLAY STOCK OVERVIEW transaction shown in Figure 7.58. Furthermore, the system also indicates the number of goods reserved for both stock types. Selecting the RECEIPT/ISSUE LIST option displays all individual movements.

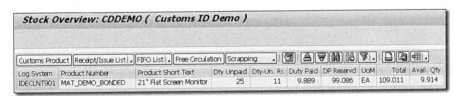

Figure 7.58 Stock Overview

> **Note**
>
> Refer to Chapter 9 on reporting for an overview of all other relevant stock transactions and reports.

Besides the stock overview per item, standard SAP GTS also provides a stock report that includes all materials that are relevant for BWH. To display the report, execute Transaction /SAPSLL/IVM_VIEWALL.

Closing Portion

As you know, the purpose of setting up a BWH is to suspend duties and taxes until further notice. At the moment that the goods arrive in the BWH, the destination of the goods might not yet be known. Once the destination of the goods is known and this destination calls for the payment of duties and taxes, the system calculate/retrieves the duty calculation performed at the entry of the goods.

In the case of Alpha, the system retrieves the duties calculated in the BWH entry document and reuses them in the declaration for bringing the goods into free circulation. This means that, for each outbound document, a link is made to one or more inbound documents. This concept is called *closing portion*.

Closing portion links the quantities of each material in an outbound document with the quantities of that same material in an inbound document using first-in, first-out (FIFO) logic. In this way, there is a clear link between the goods that entered the BWH and the ones that left it again. The open balance of all these inbound documents should represent the stock available in SAP GTS.

Closing Portion: Example

In order to see the full extent of this closing portion concept, let's go back to Alpha. In the last few weeks, Alpha has received incoming shipments with only duty-unpaid goods in Table 7.6.

Entry into Bonded Warehouse Declarations

Date	SAP GTS Document Number	Product	Quantity	Unit of Measure
01.05.2014	4000000293	Material A	40	PC
		Material B	10	PC
05.05.2014	4000000305	Material A	5	PC
		Material C	8	PC
14.05.2014	4000000349	Material B	90	PC

Table 7.6 Inbound Shipments

Now, a customer has placed an order with Alpha, and after the creation of the pro forma invoice, an export declaration is created in SAP GTS. The information displayed in Table 7.7 is deducted from the export declaration.

Export Declaration

Date	SAP GTS Document Number	Product	Quantity	Unit of Measure
06.05.2014	3000000321	Material A	42	PC
		Material B	17	PC
		Material C	6	PC

Table 7.7 Outbound Shipments

An additional tab on the item level is created in the export declaration stating the details in Table 7.8 for material A.

Document Number	Year	Item	Release Date	Quantity	Unit of Measure
4000000293	2014	1	01.05.2014	40	PC
4000000305	2014	1	05.05.2014	2	PC

Table 7.8 Reference on Additional Tab

After the determination of the closing portion, Table 7.9 displays the remaining open quantity per the BWH entry declaration.

Closing Portion		
Material	Document	Remaining Quantity of Document
Material A	4000000293	0
	4000000305	3
Material B	4000000293	0
	4000000349	83
Material C	4000000305	2

Table 7.9 Remaining Open Quantities

You can define the timing of the closing portion based on the business requirements. However, it is a best practice to delay the determination of the closing portion as long as possible because, once the closing portion is determined, the system does not allow a cancellation of the document anymore.

The determination of the closing portion can also be seen as writing off the import declaration. The stock is removed from the BWH and, therefore, from SAP GTS.

In the case of a domestic issue process, no export declaration is created, but an import (free circulation) declaration is. In this case, the import declaration determined by the closing portion indicates the applicable duty rate for the free circulation document.

Exceptional Procedures

Because stock movements are tracked both in the system and in the warehouse, it could happen that the stock level in the system is not synchronized with reality. Hence *stock correcting procedures* may be required in SAP GTS.

Scrapping is a process in which materials such as damaged goods are physically destroyed because they have lost their commercial value. Because the goods in a BWH are usually duty-unpaid goods, the customs authorities need to be informed of scrapping activities in advance. From a technical point of view, the scrapping procedure starts in SAP GTS, in the stock overview, where you indicate the material and quantity to be scrapped. This leads to the creation of a *scrapping document*. Then, it is necessary to perform the same scrapping activity in the feeder system by posting a confirmation of the scrapping movement. This movement of goods is transferred to SAP GTS, which books the stock off permanently.

On an annual basis, you need to compare the stock in the feeder system and the physical stock by doing a stock count. Because stock is kept in both the feeder system and SAP GTS, these stock difference also need to be captured in the stock levels of SAP GTS. Therefore, both positive and negative stock differences should be registered.

The inventory count process starts in the feeder system, but the posting of the inventory differences is transferred to SAP GTS. The material document created in the feeder system adjusts the stock levels in SAP GTS. Depending on the type of stock difference, a corresponding inbound or outbound declaration is created in order to justify the unaccounted stock changes in the warehouse. If the duty-unpaid stock decreases, the company is required to pay the import duties and taxes for these items.

Besides the stock correcting functionality and the scrapping process, a third important procedure is bringing the goods manually into free circulation without a reference to the feeder system. You can initiate this process from the stock overview. A free circulation document is generated for the quantity of goods selected. As a result, the payment of duties is required.

7.3.2 Inward Processing Relief

The inward processing relief (IPR) in SAP GTS allows companies to avoid paying import duties for components consumed in the production of finished goods that are re-exported later on.

In the context of our business scenario, displayed in Figure 7.59, the company Alpha can consider implementing IPR for its production facility in Belgium.

All the components used in the production of this plant that are sourced from vendors located *outside* the territory of the customs union can be received under the IPR procedure, allowing Alpha to avoid paying duties and taxes. The company has to apply for an IPR authorization from the customs authorities (in this case, in Belgium). Alpha has to present a list of materials (commodity codes) and could be requested to determine the maximum volume of materials that can be received under the IPR procedure.

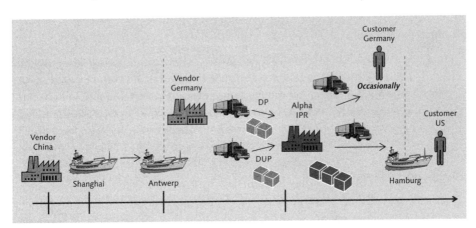

Figure 7.59 Business Process for Inward Processing Relief

The company has to identify precisely the bill of materials (BOMs) in which these components are used and list all the finished goods that contain IPR components. In the SAP GTS system, you have to create these specific IPR BOMs in the master data of the finished goods.

In an IPR procedure, you also keep track of the time of entry. Under an IPR procedure, the company has a limited time period to re-export the finished goods (defined in the authorization). Once the validity period passes, the import duties and taxes need to be paid, and a compensatory interest may be charged.

The *IPR settlement* report has to be executed on a regular basis to identify the IPR components that have expired—that is, are not yet re-exported—after the completion of the processing period. For these components (received by the IPR entry declaration), the duties have to be paid, and the declaration has to be made to the customs authorities.

Inbound Movements

The process that allows the receipt of the components under the IPR suspension procedure is similar to the process described for BWH. Similar to the BWH process, entry into IPR is not possible before the goods receipt in your feeder system. The goods receipt document triggers the option to create an IPR entry.

The customs value is calculated at the time of entering the procedure but, at that point, is not yet indebted.

Production Process

During the production of IPR finished goods, a percentage of waste could be allowed. These quantities have to be identified in the feeder system based on the production orders, and you can create a waste declaration manually in SAP GTS. You have to indicate the correct commodity code in order to avoid paying import duties for the waste quantities.

Outbound Movements

When the export flow is triggered in the feeder system for the finished product containing IPR components, it follows the usual sales document flow. Note that an export of an IPR component is not relevant for IPR processing and neither triggers an IPR export declaration nor reduces the IPR inventory. Only a finished product containing IPR components activates the IPR functionalities in SAP GTS. The creation of the pro-forma billing document in SAP ERP triggers the transfer of the information to SAP GTS and the creation of the export declaration. This newly created export declaration contains the reference to the required authorization.

The quantities of the components that are written off can be calculated in two different ways:

▶ **Static/theoretical approach**
Based on the bill of product (BOP) defined for the finished product, the corresponding quantity of the components is written off.

▶ **Dynamic approach based on real consumption**
There is a BAdI (/SAPSLL/BADI_CDOC_SCP_IPR) in the feeder system that, when transferring the pro forma billing document, allows you to calculate and transfer the real consumption of components based on the production orders in the feeder system. The prerequisite for using this function is to check the EXTERNAL BOP flag in the product master of the finished product in SAP GTS.

After the closing portion is determined for the IPR component in the export declaration, the stock posting in SAP GTS is done, the IPR inventory is reduced and cannot be reversed, and the document cannot be cancelled.

If an IPR component or a product containing IPR components is shipped to a domestic customer, the import duties and taxes have to be paid based on the components, and compensatory interests could be levied by the customs authorities.

7.3.3 Outward Processing Relief

Outward processing relief (OPR) allows a company to obtain a relief from import duties and/or VAT when re-importing finished goods that contain previously exported components (within a certain period of time). This procedure is used by companies who outsource the manufacturing or assembly of the finished products in a foreign country before re-importing the finished products. For instance, a company located in Italy manufactures high-quality fabrics but outsources its sewing activities to Vietnam. As soon as the fabrics are turned into wearable clothes, the Italian company re-imports these clothes to sale at the European market.

SAP GTS supports the added value method, whereby the value of the components is subtracted from the base product value of the finished product for the calculation of the customs value upon re-importation.

In our present business scenario, if the company exports components that are used for the manufacturing of a finished product to its vendor located in China (Vendor B), the OPR procedure can be applied. This is displayed in Figure 7.60.

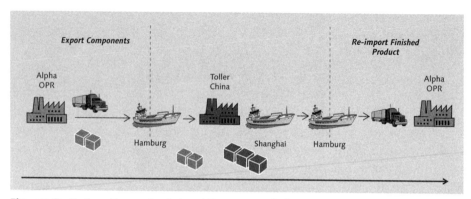

Figure 7.60 Business Process for Outward Processing Relief

The components are exported to China under OPR, the subsequent import of the finished goods produced with the OPR components is treated accordingly as OPR import, and the customs value is reduced by the value of the initially exported components. This reduces the amount of import duties to be paid. Similarly to the IPR procedure, the company needs to identify the commodity codes of the materials sent for manufacturing out of the customs union and apply for an OPR license for these components. The business partners who are processing the goods have to be included in the OPR license.

The OPR finished goods have to be identified, and the BOM has to be created manually in SAP GTS in the finished goods master data.

Outbound Movements

The outbound movements for OPR components follow the generic export flow in the feeder system. The difference from the standard export declaration is that you can decide to send the goods as either a normal export or an OPR export. There is an OPR release function in the export declaration.

If you choose the OPR functionality, it posts the stock of the OPR components to an SAP GTS-managed inventory for OPR components. This means that these components are sent out of the customs territory to a production facility and can be used to reduce the duties when a finished product containing them is re-imported. Furthermore, the OPR authorization and re-import period are calculated in the OPR declaration. The re-import period defined in the authorization indicates the period during which the finished product that contains the OPR components has to be re-imported.

Inbound Movements

The process of re-importing the finished goods is similar to the standard import process. In order to create an import declaration, you must use a specific OPR worklist. A pop-up with the list of components and default quantities appears, according to the pre-defined BOPs, which are consumed from the SAP GTS inventory. You can adjust the quantities and validate the screen.

7.3.4 Processing under Customs Control

The final special customs procedure covered in this chapter, processing under customs control (PUCC), allows organizations to produce goods under suspension of duties, eventually bring the finished products into free circulation, and pay duties on the latter. This procedure could be beneficial if the duty rates for a finished product are lower than the duty rates for the components from which the finished product is made; the duty rate for the finished product is used and not the one for the components. The system process is identical to the inbound process of IPR.

As displayed in Figure 7.61, goods can be sourced from both domestic and foreign suppliers. At the moment of importing these raw materials or components from the foreign vendor, no duties are calculated or indebted.

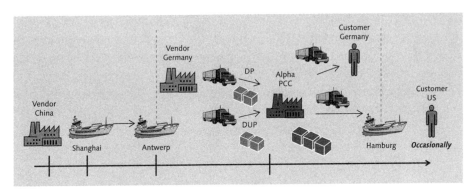

Figure 7.61 Business Process for Processing under Customs Control

The company, which has obtained the required authorization, is then allowed to manufacture the goods. In theory, these goods are used for the domestic market. It is only at the moment that these finished products are sold to a domestic customer that import duties need to be paid. These duties are calculated on the finished products and not on the raw materials or components, as with the OPR.

7.3.5 Customizing

There are a few Customizing steps that are specific to special customs procedures for both SAP ERP 6.0 and SAP GTS. We'll describe them next.

Customs ID in SAP GTS

In order to indicate in SAP GTS that a special customs procedure is applicable, you must add an additional organizational element, the customs ID (CUST. ID), to the organizational structure. Without this customs ID, you can't set up any of the special customs procedures.

You define customs IDs in DEFINE CUSTOMS ID FOR CUSTOMS PROCEDURES WITH ECONOMIC IMPACT (GLOBAL TRADE SERVICES • GENERAL SETTINGS • ORGANIZATIONAL STRUCTURE). You assign the newly created customs ID to both a logical system group and an FTO in ASSIGN CUSTOMS ID TO FOREIGN TRADE ORGANIZATION AND GROUP OF LOGICAL SYSTEMS activity (GLOBAL TRADE SERVICES • GENERAL SETTINGS • ORGANIZATIONAL STRUCTURE).

Communication Processes in SAP GTS

For each special customs procedure you set up, you need to create a new process template in order to capture additional processes. For instance, as displayed in Figure 7.31, in the case of a BWH, a process called customs warehouse needs to be added to capture the inbound process into the BWH. Although the contents of the settings are different, the logic to set up these new processes is identical to the Customizing described in the general Customs Management Customizing. Consult Section 7.2.3 for more information on this IMG activity.

Customizing in SAP ERP 6.0 (Plug-In)

In the SAP ERP 6.0 plug-in, you must define and assign the customs ID. You maintain the same customs ID you defined in SAP GTS. This can be done in the Customs: Customs Procedures with Economic Impact: Define Customs ID activity.

The next Customizing step is to complete the Customs: Assign Customs ID to Customs Procedures with Economic Impact activity. Please note that the system makes a distinction between BWH and IPR on the one hand and OPR on the other hand.

In this second activity, the system connects the customs ID to a combination of a plant and storage location. This means that the storage locations indicated here are special customs procedure-relevant storage locations.

7.3.6 Master Data

Besides the master data described in Section 7.2.4, we need to discuss a few special topics regarding the special customs procedures.

Customs Products

In order to indicate whether a material is relevant for one of the described special customs procedures, you need to flag the material. Flagging a material is very important for the correct handling of stock, so all activities need to be performed in the correct sequence.

The material master in SAP GTS contains a tab that is dedicated to the special customs procedures, as shown in Figure 7.62.

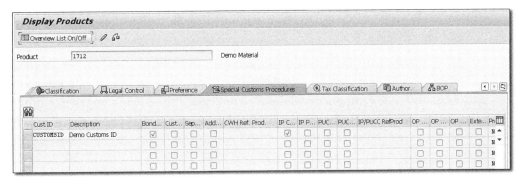

Figure 7.62 Material Master with Special Customs Procedures Flag

In this tab, you can define for which special customs procedure the material is relevant. Furthermore, for OPR, IPR, and PUCC, you must indicate whether the product is a component or finished good. You need to enter the customs ID and check the box for the procedure you want to activate.

Once all relevant materials are flagged for a special customs procedure, these flags need to be transferred back to the feeder system. This retransfer can be done either on an individual basis or for all materials by executing the Distribute Product Data to Feeder System for Special Customs Procedures transaction.

Now, in both systems, the materials are indicated as relevant for a special customs procedure. Once the materials are indicated as relevant for a special customs procedure, there is one last step that still needs to be performed. Most likely, there is already some stock physically available in the warehouse, and it is represented by the stock level in your feeder system. Because SAP GTS is also keeping stock, this initial stock needs to be transferred to SAP GTS, as well. This transfer of initial duty-paid stock is performed in the plug-in via the Initial Transfer of Duty-Paid Stock activity.

Please note that it is not possible to transfer initial stock for IPR. It requires special timing and preparation during the go-live period in case there is already stock available in the warehouse.

Bill of Product

For IPR, OPR, and PUCC, you must create the BOP at the level of the finished goods. Here, you link the IPR/OPR/PUCC components to the finished goods. In the BOP master data, a theoretical component usage is also entered. This component ratio is used when an inbound or outbound flow of the IPR, OPR, or PUCC process is initiated because the consumption of the component must be registered in SAP GTS.

The discussed BOP has to be created manually in SAP GTS, and it is not identical to the BOM in SAP ERP. This BOP in SAP GTS links the finished goods only to its IPR/OPR/PUCC components and does not contain the other components of the finished goods that are not relevant for the procedure. This BOM contains only the primary components that have been purchased (from a supplier outside the customs union for IPR/PUCC); it does not contain any semi-finished or interme-diate products that haven't been purchased initially. For OPR, it contains only the components exported to the warehouse of the external manufacturer. The components added in the manufacturer's premises are not taken into account.

Business Partners

In order for the OPR functionality to work as designed, you have to mark which OPR components are exported to and which business partners OPR finished products are imported from in the system.

Authorizations and Securities

Although the concept behind the different types of authorizations and securities is very similar, there are minor differences between authorizations and securities for the different special customs procedures. Mainly, the differences concern the attributes of the applicable authorization or security.

Bonded Warehouse

If a company decides to set up a BWH, it is legally required to apply for an autho-rization with the customs authorities. In SAP GTS, this authorization is called the *Authorization for Customs Warehousing Procedure*. In this authorization, you need to indicate the responsible customs office and type of BWH. This license is valid only for the legal unit specified in the attributes.

IPR/OPR/PUCC

The authorizations for IPR/OPR/PUCC have some specifics requirements:

► The products (components and finished goods) have to be listed.

► The number of the BOP has to be indicated for the finished goods.

► The processing period (IPR/PUCC) and re-import period (OPR) have to be spec-ified (this is the lifespan of OPR/IPR/PUCC product).

Another important indicator for IPR is the *closing portion determination* indicator, which regulates when the closing portion is created. There are two options: auto-matically at the creation of the export declaration or manually at later stage.

For the OPR process, all the relevant business partners have to be entered in the authorization, as well; these are the partners who receive components from the company and those who supply the finished goods back to the company.

7.4 Excise Duty Monitoring

Besides the standard import and export processes and the special customs procedures, some companies are obliged to have a process in place to monitor the transport of excise goods under excise duty suspension due to their business activities. In what follows, this process of Excise Duty Monitoring is discussed.

Authorities use the Excise Movement Control System (EMCS) to do just that. This excise duty processing in the feeder system is set up for products that are subject to harmonized excise duty types like alcohol, tobacco, and energy products. EMCS is used only in the EU.

7.4.1 Business Process

Figure 7.63 displays the overall business process for EMCS. The figure shows all the parties involved and the sequence in which all transactions take place.

For example, when a manufacturer of tobacco in Belgium wants to send its products to a customer located in Poland, it takes the following steps:

❶ The consignor submits a notification to the customs office of departure in Antwerp, Belgium, which indicates that the goods are relevant for EMCS.

❷ The local customs office of departure replies with a confirmation message if the shipment of the goods is accepted. The customs office also provides the company with an ARC number that has to be printed; this is a unique reference number of the declaration.

❸ After receiving this acceptance, the company can dispatch the excise goods. The goods are physically shipped to the location of the consignee.

❹ The customs authorities send a message to the customs office of destination in Poland. The purpose of this message is to provide the information regarding the EMCS-relevant shipment to the customs office of destination.

5. It is the customs office of destination that forwards this message to the consignee.

6. Next, the goods arrive at the place of destination.

7. The consignee submits a report of receipt.

8. The customs office of destination sends a receipt of the notification to the consignee.

9. The customs office of destination forwards this report of receipt to the customs office of departure.

10. The customs office of departure closes the loop by sending the information back to the consignor. These last two steps run simultaneously.

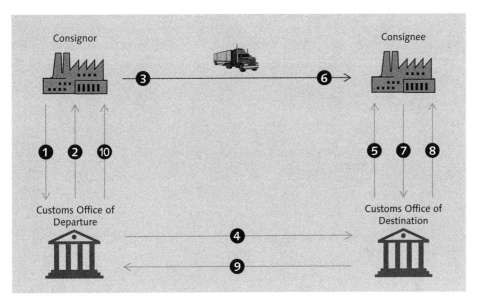

Figure 7.63 Business Process for EMCS

In this way, all concerned parties are informed about the departure and receipt of the excise goods under excise duty suspension.

The section of EMCS process flow relevant for the consignor is illustrated in Figure 7.64.

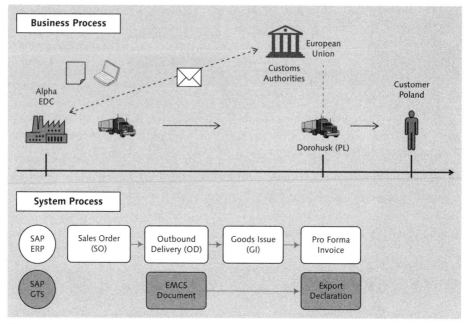

Figure 7.64 EMCS Process Flow

7.4.2 System Process

As with the earlier Customs Management functionality, let's consider the system process of Excise Duty Monitoring.

Inbound Activities

When a supplier sends goods under duty suspension, an electronic incoming message from the local customs authorities appears in SAP GTS. This implies that the process starts in SAP GTS without integration with SAP ERP 6.0.

In this way, your company is informed of the incoming shipment. The message contains the ARC number provided by the customs authorities.

Once the goods arrive, the receiving company can compare the number of goods that are physically delivered to the expected number. The receiving company can accept the shipment if all goods are delivered in the correct quantities. But if there is a discrepancy in quantity or goods delivered, the consignee can accept the goods with restrictions. If the discrepancy is not acceptable, the goods are rejected. You'll need to provide the local customs authorities with this status update.

Once the customs authorities approve the report of receipt filed by the consignee for the concerned shipment, the inbound process is closed. By closing the inbound process, the consignor is released from its responsibilities.

In SAP GTS, an inbound EMCS document from which the communication with the customs authorities can take place is created. From the inbound perspective, there is no link between the feeder system and SAP GTS.

Outbound Activities

A company that wishes to ship excise goods under duty suspension to its customer has to ask permission from the customs authorities before sending these goods. In the outbound process, a transfer of information from the feeder system to SAP GTS is required to create an outbound EMCS document.

The communication with the customs authorities follows the same e-filing process as for the standard export process.

7.4.3 Customizing

Aside from the general customizing activities required to set up Customs Management, there is no need for additional Customizing activities in order to facilitate the EMCS process.

However, it's important to note that the interaction between the feeder system and SAP GTS does not occur via the standard SAP GTS plug-in. You have to set up a customized interface to enable the transfer of information and company-specific triggers to transfer information.

SAP GTS, however, did provide a function module to enable this process (/SAPSLL/API_6800_EMC).

SAP GTS provides a standard interface between EMCS and customs export to communicate the ARC number in the export document. As such, the export confirmation also determines the closing of the EMCS document for the outbound flow.

7.4.4 Master Data

In order to successfully perform e-filing, both the consignor and consignee of the process must have a tax warehouse number maintained in the system. There is no standard interface for this information, meaning that the tax warehouse number must be entered manually in SAP GTS. A customer-specific development is required to automate the transfer.

In order to identify whether a product is EMCS relevant, you must classify the products with excise product codes.

7.5 US Reconciliation Process

Reconciliation is a program that allows an importer to file entry summaries with the applicable government authorities after the actual receipt of the goods. This can be the result of several factors, including the valuation of royalties or assists within particular accounting periods, returned goods provisions, or free trade agreement qualification.

7.5.1 Business and System Processes

The US reconciliation process is managed in SAP GTS and allows you to handle the electronic exchange with the US customs authorities.

The US reconciliation procedure is relevant for the import process. Within the SAP GTS system, the information is kept on the header level in the TRANSPORTA-TION tab. After the creation of the purchase order in the feeder system, the import declaration is created.

You start by creating the purchase order referencing specific data, such as the reason for the reconciliation and the due date. If the reconciliation is based on NAFTA, indicate this in a separate field, as well.

For every import declaration in SAP GTS, you must enter specific reconciliation data. This approach is called *entry-by-entry flagging* because each individual declaration is flagged separately. It is possible to set a default value for the REASON FOR RECONCILIATION SUMMARY. If you use this option, one bill of lading is tied to one customs declaration.

Besides the entry-by-entry approach, another approach is called *blanket reconciliation flagging*, whereby ABI automatically flags all entries of an importer for a given period. In this approach, several bills of lading are tied to one customs declaration.

The reason for reconciliation could be based on three things:

▸ Value (if the customs value is not precisely known due to potential additional costs such as assists, royalties, etc.)

▸ Classification (if the classification is not precisely known and could be modified at a later stage)

▸ Both value and classification

Flagging for reconciliation must be done prior to filing the import declaration to the customs authorities. The reconciliation flag alerts the customs authorities that reconciliation will be done at a later stage.

Then, after the goods have actually been received, the reconciliation summary must be filed with the customs authorities within the pre-defined period of 12 months for NAFTA reconciliation and 21 months for any other reconciliation. In SAP GTS, the reconciliation summary is managed using the SCD functionality via Import • Periodic declaration • Enter Supplementary Customs declaration for a foreign trade organization. There are two ways to do that:

▸ On the entry-by-entry principle, whereby each declaration is reconciled separately.

▸ An aggregate reconciliation, in which several declarations can be reconciled together, and in which case only an absolute increase is taken into consideration. *Absolute increase* refers to changes or adjustments between line items on a given entry that result in an increase to the entry as a whole.

> **Note**
>
> NAFTA- and non-NAFTA–related issues have to be grouped separately.

7.5.2 Customizing

As a prerequisite, the legal regulation for US imports (that is, the US Automated Customs Environment, or ACE) must be configured in standard SAP GTS.

The Customizing steps relevant for the setup of the reconciliation process are the following:

▸ The setup of a document type for SCD, the document type USRECN is delivered in the standard SAP GTS with the correct action provided (US_PD_IM_RECON).

▸ The SCD type for the US reconciliation must be linked to the legal regulation for US import (ACE).

▸ The activity sequences for the customs import declarations should be periodic ('B' relevant for periodic SCD — Confirmed).

▸ The definition of the activity for reconciliation is attached to the import process with a relevant outbound and incoming message as a reply from the customs authorities.

These Customizing activities are additional to the general Customizing required for customs processing. For an overview of the general Customizing activities, refer to Section 7.2.3.

7.6   Electronic Communication

Over the course of this chapter, we have touched upon electronic communication on several occasions. Besides electronic communication with the customs authorities, you can also build an interface that allows you to transfer data to a customs broker. In this case, it is the customs broker who lodges the official declaration with the customs authorities.

Recall that, in order to transfer all required information, SAP GTS uses IDocs. The system provides a standard IDoc with its specific structure; you should use this standard IDoc when a custom-built interface (such as one with a broker) is required.

7.6.1   Standard IDoc

An IDoc consists of two important records: the data record, which contains all the data elements captured from the customs declaration, and status records. Status records are a set of predefined statuses that an IDoc has to go through before it is considered successfully transferred.

Figure 7.65 shows the IDoc details. The box on the left-hand side shows both the data records and status records.

The lower right box contains the SAP GTS field name and actual content that is entered in that specific field.

The upper right box provides more technical information on the message types, basic IDoc type, partner number and type, and port.

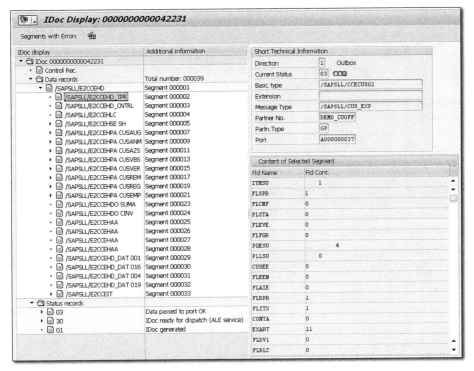

Figure 7.65 Standard IDoc

In order to understand which information an IDoc actually contains, it is useful to look into every data record element of an IDoc. Table 7.10 provides an overview of a few IDoc segments that make it easier to retrieve the information from the IDoc structure.

Data Records Element from IDoc	Description
/SAPSLL/E2CCEHD_TPR	Information from the TRANSPORTATION tab at the header level in a customs declaration.
/SAPSLL/E2CCEHD_CNTRL	Technical information on IDoc.
/SAPSLL/E2CCEHPA_...	Information on partner details that are used in customs declaration.
/SAPSLL/E2CCEHAA	Information on values stored in the LOGISTICS COSTS tab at the header level in a customs declaration.
/SAPSLL/E2CCEHD_DAT	Information related to document dates.
/SAPSLL/E2CCEIT	Information on item details. Each item gets its own separate line with more information at a lower level.

Table 7.10 IDoc Data Records Structure

7.6.2 Electronic Communication Transactions

SAP GTS comes with a few transactions to set up electronic communication and monitor the status of the incoming and outgoing IDocs. These transactions are grouped in the SYSTEM ADMINISTRATION section of SAP GTS, more specifically in SYSTEM COMMUNICATION.

Figure 7.66 shows the transactions within SYSTEM COMMUNICATION. The EDI— COMMUNICATION section is used when setting up the connection with an external party, and EDI MONITORING contains a set of transactions that display the IDocs and is useful for issue solving activities.

Transaction Related to Interface Setup

In EDI PORT DEFINITION, you can add the port that is used during the electronic data interchange. In EDI PARTNER PROFILES you can select which message type (see Figure 7.29) can be sent out and received back per profile.

In order to set up electronic communications with either the customs authorities or a customs broker, it is crucial to add all the required partner profiles here. Figure 7.67 displays the EDI PARTNER PROFILES screen.

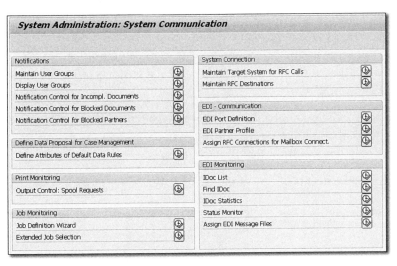

Figure 7.66 System Communication Transactions

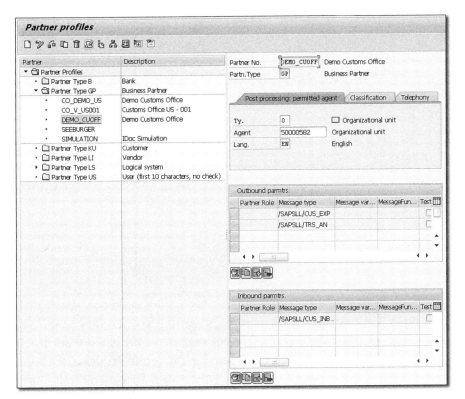

Figure 7.67 Partner Profiles

To set up a partner profile, first choose the partner type GP for business partner and give this business partner the name of the customs office of departure. You need to set up this same partner in the master data as a customs office, as well. In the customs declaration, it must state that this particular customs office is the customs office of departure.

Once the partner profile is created, add all the message types from the Customizing to either the outbound parameters for outbound messages (M-messages) or the inbound parameters for incoming messages (I-messages).

Figure 7.68 shows the details of one of the message types.

Figure 7.68 Details of Message Type from Oubound Parameters

When adding these message types, it is crucial to indicate that they need to be triggered immediately. When you select this option, all IDocs are immediately transferred one by one. If you select Trigger by background program, the IDocs are transferred to the customs authorities only once a background job is performed.

Transactions Related to IDoc Monitoring

The IDoc LIST transaction allows you to search for all IDocs created within a specific time slot. However, it is also possible to search for one particular IDoc using the IDoc number in the selection screen. The results of the query are grouped in outbound and inbound IDocs, as displayed in Figure 7.69. In case of multiple message types, the system also takes this parameter into account to further structure the IDocs.

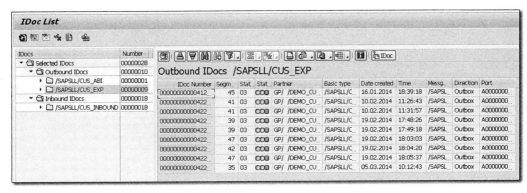

Figure 7.69 IDoc List

By selecting just a single IDoc, you can see the data records and status records, as indicated in Figure 7.65.

While the IDoc List transaction gives a structured overview of the IDocs, FIND IDocs shows an unstructured, flat list of the selected IDocs. The layout of this list is similar to the monitoring option for customs declarations.

IDOC STATISTICS gives a structured overview of all the IDocs with an error message. The output of the list is similar to the output displayed in Figure 7.69. Again, by selecting the IDocs, you can see the actual structure and data that is transferred.

At last, in STATUS MONITOR, you can get additional explanations about whether an IDoc is processed correctly, and in case of an error, the detailed reason of the error. Figure 7.70 shows the results of the query.

The system groups the IDocs based on their processing statuses. Especially in case of an error message, you get the most information on the cause of the issue here.

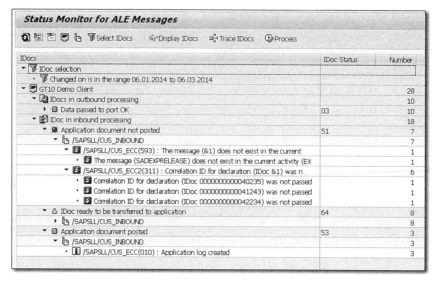

Figure 7.70 IDoc Status Monitoring

7.7 Countries Supported by SAP GTS 10.1

In this last part of this chapter, you will find an overview of all countries that are supported by SAP GTS 10.1 Customs Management.

The import and export processes of countries in Table 7.11 are supported by SAP GTS.

Country	Legal Regulations
Austria	CUSAT
Australia	CUSAU
Belgium	CUSBE
China	CUSCN
Denmark	CUSDK
France	CUSFR
Germany	ATLAS

Table 7.11 Countries Supported by SAP GTS for Import and Export

Country	Legal Regulations
United Kingdom	CUSGB
Netherlands	CUSNL
New Zealand	CUSNZ
Switzerland	CUSCH
United States of America	ACE

Table 7.11 Countries Supported by SAP GTS for Import and Export (Cont.)

Besides the standard import and export processes, SAP GTS also supports the transit functionality for the following countries. Table 7.12 also includes their corresponding legal regulations.

Country	Legal Regulations
Austria	TRSAT
Belgium	TRSBE
France	TRSFR
Germany	TRSDE
United Kingdom	TRSGB
Netherlands	TRSNL
Slovenia	TRSSI
Sweden	TRSSE
Switzerland	TRSCH

Table 7.12 Countries Supported by SAP GTS for Transit

For each of these countries, SAP GTS comes with a standard functioning operative cockpit, including a predefined communication approach, etc.

If the country for which you want to set up the SAP GTS Customs Management capabilities is not in this list, you need to perform the configuration as explained in Section 7.2.3.

7.8   Summary

Throughout the chapter, we have provided an overview of the main concepts and business and system processes of the SAP GTS Customs Management module.

We began the chapter by describing a business case that we used throughout the chapter to provide some hands-on information in the light of actual business needs. For customs documents (Section 7.1), we described all the basic information you need to know before going into depth of the different business processes. If you are not familiar with the functionalities of SAP GTS Customs Management, we highly recommend you start with this section. It focuses on the operative cockpit and monitoring functionalities and guides you through a typical customs declaration. In conclusion, we described all possibilities for communication with the customs authorities.

Section 7.2 provides an in-depth overview of everything there is to say about the standard import and export processes. You found a business description of the process before actually going into the more technical side of the processes. Section 7.2.3 provided all the frequently used and important Customizing settings for Customs Management. The subsection on master data shed some light on the master data elements we hadn't yet described in Chapter 4.

Section 7.3 on special customs procedures provided a high-level overview of the functionalities of the following customs procedures: bonded warehouse (also known as customs warehouse), inward processing relief, outward processing relief, and production under customs control. These procedures are mainly European-oriented, but similar procedures exist all over the world. The legal context of these procedures is often very complex, and during the setup of such procedures, input from someone with deep knowledge of the legal requirements is absolutely vital.

Closely related to these special customs procedures is excise duty monitoring, described in Section 7.4. Again, this entire procedure is European-based. To balance all the European procedures, we included Section 7.5 on the US Reconciliation Process.

If you are interested in how the electronic communication with the customs authorities works or how to monitor your incoming and outgoing IDocs, do not skip Section 7.6. This part described what an IDoc looks like, helped you better understand the structure, and described some transactions that will help you monitor your IDocs closely.

To conclude this Customs Management chapter, we have listed all the countries that are supported by SAP GTS 10.1 Customs Management, with their legal regulations.

Global trade is characterized by financial risks and duties imposed in import and export flows. You can leverage certain business structures and possibilities to help overcome these risks. The SAP GTS Risk Management functionality supports companies in mitigating financial risks when trading globally.

8 Risk Management

The SAP GTS Risk Management module consists of three sections, each covering a specific topic for mitigating risks or gaining advantages in global trade. We'll walk through each of the following in this chapter, which are shown in Figure 8.1:

- Trade Preference Management (Section 8.1) covers the process of requesting vendor declarations, calculating a products preferential eligibility in a free trade agreement, and issuing proof of preferential origin.
- Restitution Management (Section 8.2) handles the process of claiming export refunds under the European Common Agricultural Policy.
- Letter of Credit Processing (Section 8.3) mitigates financial risks by ensuring payment in global transactions.

> **Note**
>
> Unlike Chapter 6 and Chapter 7, this chapter does not open with a section concerning customs documents. These documents are used in Customs Management and Compliance Management to represent feeder system documents such as sales orders, deliveries, and invoices in SAP GTS. However, since Risk Management does not leverage customs documents in its processes, we don't discuss them further here.

Figure 8.1 Risk Management-Relevant Business Processes

We'll discuss the Trade Preference Management functionality in detail throughout the majority of this chapter: it is the most significant functionality within SAP GTS Risk Management. Restitution Management is fading out, and is applicable only in the European Union (EU). The third subchapter covers the supporting functionalities for the letter of credit process, which is less extensive than Trade Preference Management and thus occupies a smaller section.

Throughout this chapter, we'll maintain the same structure as Chapter 6 on Compliance Management and Chapter 7 on Customs Management. We'll elaborate on the business and system processes for these functionalities, providing business cases that illustrate them, and finally discussing the related Customizing and master data specific to each section.

Let's begin with the Risk Management heavyweight, Trade Preference Management.

8.1 Trade Preference Management

The World Trade Organization (WTO) is the international forum that discusses and establishes a legal framework for global trade. It has more than 150 members and has fostered international commerce by reducing import duties, improving market access, and increasing legal certainty.

A basic obligation of WTO member countries is to comply with the *Most Favored Nation* (MFN) principle. This principle establishes that the most favorable treatment of import duties provided from one country to the imports from another must be equally applied to imports from all WTO members without discrimination. However, there is an exemption to the application of this MFN principle: if better treatment is given to one or more countries under the scope of a customs union or preferential trade agreement that provides reduced or zero import duty rates for a wide range of goods, this duty treatment does not necessarily have to be granted to other countries.

In this section, we'll focus on the first sub-functionality of Risk Management: Trade Preference Management, which allows companies to provide their customers with the required proof that the sold goods are eligible for preferential treatment in a specific trade agreement, having already performed the required determination. By leveraging applicable preferential trade agreements, a company and its customers can, in certain scenarios, benefit from preferential duty rates (reduced or zero) in international trade flows, instead of the usually imposed duty rates.

Because the decisions at the WTO require the consensus of all its members, the negotiation rounds to reduce import duties on an MFN basis can be highly complex. For example, the Doha Development Agenda was launched in 2001 to further improve market access for all the WTO members; as of 2014, it has not yet been successfully concluded. Because of the challenge of getting better market access for their own exports, many economies see the implementation of preferential trade agreements (usually referred to as free-trade agreements, or FTAs) as one of the most feasible ways to promote international trade. Currently, more than 230 preferential or FTAs are notified to the WTO—a figure that increases every year.

Furthermore, unilateral preferential treatments are also possible through the Generalized System of Preferences (GSP) program, wherein many developed countries foster manufacturing and exports from less developed countries. The GSP provides a formal system of exemption from the WTO rules like the MFN principle, allowing countries to lower import duties on a non-discriminatory basis for goods originating in developing countries.

Examples of preferential trade can be seen all around the world, with different levels of integration among members. As shown in Figure 8.2, we can identity several regional trade blocks around the globe with different levels of integration. For instance, the EU has achieved a much deeper level of political integration than other regional examples, such as Mercosur.

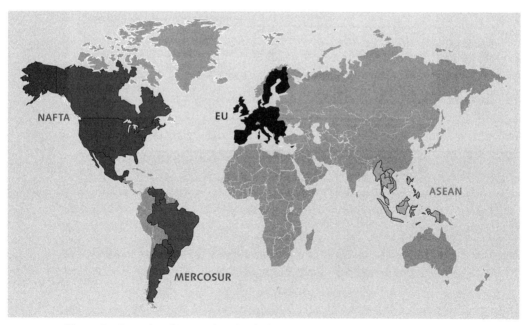

Figure 8.2 Examples of Regional Trade Blocks

Table 8.1 displays the countries included in these trade blocks.

NAFTA	ASEAN	MERCOSUR	EU
▶ Canada	▶ Brunei	▶ Argentina	▶ Austria
▶ Mexico	▶ Cambodia	▶ Brazil	▶ Belgium
▶ United States of America	▶ Indonesia	▶ Paraguay	▶ Bulgaria
	▶ Laos	▶ Uruguay	▶ Cyprus
	▶ Malaysia	▶ Venezuela	▶ Croatia
	▶ Myanmar		▶ Czech Republic
	▶ Philippines		▶ Germany
	▶ Singapore		▶ Denmark
	▶ Thailand		▶ Estonia
	▶ Vietnam		▶ Finland
			▶ France
			▶ Greece
			▶ Hungary
			▶ Ireland
			▶ Italy
			▶ Lithuania
			▶ Luxembourg
			▶ Latvia
			▶ Malta
			▶ Netherlands
			▶ Poland
			▶ Portugal
			▶ Romania
			▶ Spain
			▶ Sweden
			▶ Slovenia
			▶ Slovakia
			▶ United Kingdom

Table 8.1 Member States of Major Regional Trade Blocks

Each country may initiate the process to conclude preferential trade agreements with other countries. For instance, the United States has agreements in place with its neighbor countries through NAFTA, as well as with some additional partners such as South Korea, Panama, Australia, and Israel through other FTAs. Likewise, the EU has an even more extensive list of FTAs in place with third countries all over the world, alongside a comprehensive negotiation agenda for future agreements.

When an agreement's member countries trade with each other and certain conditions are fulfilled, preferential treatment could potentially be applied. Such preferential treatment makes it possible to apply for a reduced or zero import duty rate when importing eligible products. Whether this treatment applies to the specific imported product depends on the preferential status of the concerned good. Instead of the country where the last production step is performed, the preferential country of origin usually takes into account the value added by the manufacturing processes and the source of the used components.

To determine whether a product is considered to have a preferential status in a certain FTA, each FTA incorporates a set of *rules of origin*. These rules specify which conditions a product must fulfill to be eligible for preferential treatment.

The Trade Preference Management module in SAP GTS allows companies to manage, track, and report the trade preference relevancy of their shipped materials. SAP GTS helps determine the preferential status of products being shipped to customers located in a member country of a specific FTA, with the main goal of providing those customers with the required documentation for eligible products in order to allow importation at a reduced or zero import duty rate.

The legal documentation required to avoid duties upon importing goods with preferential origin is issued as a *certificate* or *statement of origin*. In most cases, this proof of origin can be issued only by specifically approved persons or institutions/governmental organizations, but this is established in the applicable rules of the relevant agreement. Issuing the proof of origin requires extensive administration efforts, which you can automate through Trade Preference Management by implementing SAP GTS.

Let's walk through a business case to help demonstrate and understand the often complex concepts, functionalities, and business and system processes of Trade Preference Management.

Gamma's Global Trading Requirements

Gamma manufactures high-end leather shoes for men. In its manufacturing facility in North Carolina, United States, it converts the finest lamb leather into stylish designer shoes.

To manufacture the finishing product, the company reworks and assembles a number of materials procured from vendors all over the world. As shown in Figure 8.3, the shoes' rubber soles are procured in Vietnam, and its shoelaces come from vendors in Peru and Mexico. The fine lamb leather is purchased from a local US vendor, and the wool is sourced from Canada.

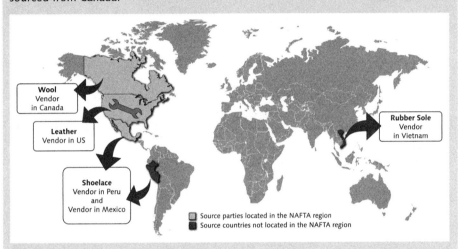

Figure 8.3 Gamma's Source Countries

Because Gamma is located in the United States and some of the components are procured locally in the United States or from Mexico or Canada, Gamma believes it may benefit from the NAFTA agreement.

If Gamma could issue certificates of origin to its customers, stating that their products are of preferential origin in the NAFTA agreement, those customers could avoid paying import duties on the imported goods. This would significantly increase Gamma's attractiveness in the market as a vendor of high-end shoes.

Gamma's main consuming market is Canada, a NAFTA member country, but a minor share of its products is destined for the European market—more specifically, for Germany, as shown in Figure 8.4.

So, in order to manufacture its high-end men's shoes, Gamma procures leather, wool, rubber soles, and shoelaces. In the first manufacturing process, Gamma creates unfinished shoes from the first three components. Next, the second manufacturing process entails adding the shoelace to the unfinished shoe, completing the casual leather shoe.

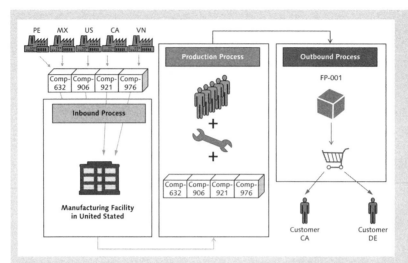

Figure 8.4 Gamma's Inbound, Production, and Outbound Process

Figure 8.5 shows the hierarchy of the final product, its components, and the material prices at which Gamma procures the components sourced from the various vendors. In the case of the finished product, the selling price is indicated.

The figure also shows the HTS tariff code for each component; you use these codes when determining whether the finished product can be shipped as a good with preferential origin.

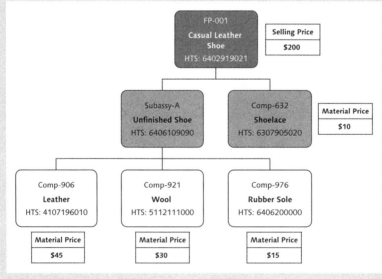

Figure 8.5 Gamma Bill of Material

8.1.1 Business Process

Recall that the purposes of Trade Preference Management are to identify whether products can potentially benefit from a reduced or zero import duty rate and provide customers with the required legal documentation for eligible products.

Prior to determining whether a company can ship goods claiming preferential status, the company needs to acquire the necessary information about the components used in the finished product, as well as the manufacturing process. Figure 8.6 displays the three steps of the trade preference business process.

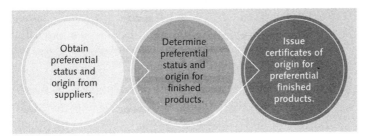

Figure 8.6 Trade Preference Business Process

The first step covers the inbound process of potentially obtaining preferential proof origin for the components used in the manufacturing process. From a vendor's point of view, you may be asked to provide this information to customers who use the products in their own manufacturing process and wish to determine the preferential status of their finished goods. Note, however, that companies may not want to request the origin-related information from all vendors because choosing which vendors to request such proof from is a business decision. Indeed, a company situated in the NAFTA agreement might decide to request such information from only its vendors located in the United States, Canada, and Mexico because it thinks other global vendors will most likely return negative responses.

The preferential-related vendor information is usually provided through specific forms, often called *supplier* or *vendor declarations*. (The applicable FTA provides details on which proof of origin should be provided.) If a company intends to ship the finished product to customers in multiple FTAs, it may need to request a consolidated vendor declaration or multiple vendor declarations from a single vendor.

When dealing regularly with certain vendors, it would be inefficient to request vendor declarations on a transactional basis. As such, vendor declarations in certain FTAs may be issued for a longer term (e.g., one year). *Long-term vendor declarations* (LTVDs) dictate that the vendor's products possess the identical preferential status and origin during the validity period. If the products' preferential status changes, it is the vendor's responsibility to inform its customers of the changes and provide them with updated and accurate data.

Once you've determined the preferential information of the various *components* used in a manufacturing process, the next step is to perform a preference determination on the manufactured *products*. Note that if you can't obtain origin-related information for certain components, you should consider them non-originating from a risk perspective. The preference determination states whether the finished product is eligible for preferential treatment in a certain agreement based on the applicable rule(s) of origin. Again—the requirements that need to be fulfilled to determine whether preference applies are described in the agreement's rule(s) of origin for the finished product in question.

Finally, if the preferential status for the finished good is determined, the company can submit proof of origin to its customers for shipments that include products with preferential status. When applicable, the customer may potentially import the acquired goods duty free or at a reduced-duty tariff. This, in turn, can result in a significant, competitive market advantage for the supplying company.

Figure 8.7 further exemplifies the trade preference business process. In the inbound phase, a company sources components from third countries and requests vendor declarations to obtain the preferential status and origin of the components. In the production phase, the company has to determine whether the product may be exported under preferential treatment.

Finally, the company exports its finished products to third countries, and applicable certificates or invoice statements may be issued when applicable. Depending on existing FTAs and specific rules, the third country customers may benefit from preferential duty rates.

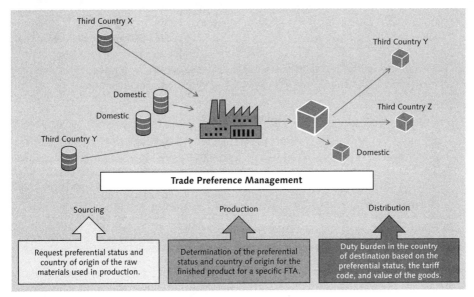

Figure 8.7 Business Processes Relevant for Trade Preference Management

Gamma's Trade Preference Process

To manufacture its casual leather shoe, Gamma procures components locally and from third-country vendors. In order to calculate the preferential status of its finished product, the leather shoe, Gamma requests vendor declarations from the following partners:

▶ The vendor in the United States for the leather component

▶ The vendor in Canada for the wool component

▶ The vendors in Peru and Mexico for the shoelace component

▶ The vendor in Vietnam for the rubber sole component

Recall that it is up to Gamma's management to decide which vendors to request vendor declarations from. They could decide not to request the preferential status of the rubber soles procured in Vietnam because it is very unlikely that this product would ever have a NAFTA preferential status. However, for this business case, Gamma requests vendor declarations from all of its vendors.

In the production phase, Gamma performs the preference calculation for its finished product. To know which requirements the finished product must fulfill to obtain a preferential status, Gamma needs the NAFTA rules of origin applicable to the leather shoe's tariff code. Gamma is then able to use the origin-related information stated in the components' vendor declarations requested from the various vendors to calculate the preferential origin of its finished product.

If the shoes are of NAFTA preferential origin, Gamma can issue certificates of origin to its customers in Canada because they are situated in a NAFTA member country. The Canadian customers can then import the shoes without the burden of paying tariffs. However, because there is currently no FTA in place between the United States and the EU, no certificates of origin can be issued to Gamma's German customers.

The remainder of this section covers key aspects often quoted in Trade Preference Management, including the bill of material (BOM), country of origin, rules of origin, preference comparison methods, and BOM calculation methods.

Transformation of Components into Finished Products

In a manufacturing process, companies process raw materials and intermediate products to create a finished product.

Note

In this chapter, the term *finished product* is used from a business point of view, so it doesn't necessarily imply that the product will not undergo additional manufacturing steps at a later step in the supply chain. The use of the term *finished product* reflects that the product is considered as such for the company selling the product. In the overall supply chain, it might actually be a semi-finished product.

The BOM describes how the finished product is manufactured by stating a hierarchical structure of the raw materials, intermediate products, and associated quantities used in the production process. In Trade Preference Management, the BOM is an important concept because the preference determination looks at all materials and subassemblies used in the BOM to calculate the finished product's preferential status.

BOMs may contain raw materials, components, and subassemblies that are procured externally or produced internally. For each externally procured material, you need to request vendor declarations to know that material's preferential status and origin. On the other hand, in the case of subassemblies produced in-house, you can perform preference determinations before the finished product's preference determination, depending on the calculation method.

Preferential Origin versus Non-Preferential Origin

Whether a product can be exported under preferential treatment depends on whether it can claim preferential origin and status for the preference agreement in place between the exporting and importing countries. The preference determination may be based on the product's various components, where these components are originating from, the amount of processing efforts the finished product has undergone, and the tariff classification of the components and finished product.

Nonetheless, before we can detail the preferential origin determination process, we want to emphasize the difference between the concept of a product's preferential origin and non-preferential origin (also known as *economic origin*). Both concepts have different rules to determine a product's origin and are used for different purposes.

In general, the *non-preferential origin* of a product is the country where the product has undergone the last processing or substantial transformation. You determine the non-preferential origin by applying the exporting country's non-preferential rules; it can be important for anti-dumping policies, trade embargoes, trade quotas, etc. For instance, if company Gamma (situated in the United States) ships goods from the United States to Spain, Gamma needs to look at the non-preferential rules to determine whether it can export goods as US products because no preference agreement is in place between the involved countries.

> **Note**
>
> This concept of non-preferential origin is not relevant under the scope of a preference agreement. A product can have a non-preferential origin and potentially be eligible for claiming a preferential status under a certain preference agreement, but they are not linked.

If a preferential agreement *is* in place between countries, you must look into the agreement's preferential rules of origin related to the exported good's tariff code to determine whether your product can claim preferential origin in that agreement. You can ship the goods to member agreement countries and potentially benefit from a reduced or zero import duty rate only if you can claim preferential origin based on that agreement. We'll cover the concept of rules of origin used to determine a product's preferential eligibility in the following section.

As a result, product labels can't be trusted when determining a product's preferential eligibility. For example, if a company ships a product with a label stating "Made in U.S.A.," as determined by applying non-preferential rules, this does not mean that a Canadian company can assume the product is of US preferential origin according to the NAFTA rules of origin. The US company should determine whether its products have a preferential status by applying the NAFTA rules of origin for that product and informing the Canadian company whether the products are considered preferential in the NAFTA agreement.

Furthermore, assume that a finished product is determined to be of US preferential origin in NAFTA because all of its components originate in Mexico, and it has undergone substantial assembly steps performed in the United States. Because it has a preferential origin within NAFTA, the product may be traded within the NAFTA region under preferential treatment. However, for other agreements, such as the US-CAFTA agreement, the product might not be able to claim preferential origin, because the US-CAFTA preferential rules of origin may deem that the US assembly steps are not sufficient.

Varying FTAs and applicable scenarios can mean that different preference criteria emerge from the preference determination. For instance, NAFTA applies criteria ranging from A through F to indicate that a product is eligible in a specific scenario. The following three scenarios result in the three most common NAFTA preference criteria, all stating the product to be eligible for preferential treatment:

▶ **Preference criterion A**
When a product is wholly obtained or produced in one country, meaning there are no imported components used. As such, the preferential country of origin can be determined as the country where it is obtained or produced. This preferential status is most common to mineral products, animals, and products derived from animals.

▶ **Preference criterion B**
When a product is sufficiently processed to claim preferential status. You determine the latter expression of sufficient processing by applying the product's rules of origin (more on this shortly).

▶ **Preference criterion C**
When a product is fully manufactured using NAFTA originating materials. This might be the case for a US company procuring goods originating in Mexico and

Canada. Because the US company uses these goods only in the manufacturing process, the finished product consists exclusively of NAFTA originating materials.

Please note that the preferential status of a specific product in different FTAs may vary due to unequal rules. For instance, CAFTA rules of origin may state that a product is sufficiently processed to attain the US preferential origin, while the NAFTA rules of origin state that the product does not fulfill the requirements to attain a preferential status.

Rules of Origin

When establishing preference agreements, the concerned contracting parties negotiate the rules.

Contracting parties may leverage these rules as international trade measures by using them to address certain international trade policy issues or attain specific trade purposes. As such, they may stimulate or restrict the trade of specific products by leveraging the rules of origin.

There are two types of rules: base rules and rules specific to the tariff classification of the concerned product. The first type of rule, *agreement base rules* (e.g., tolerance rules, minimal operations, and set of goods) apply to whole agreements and all related products, although exceptions are possible.

For instance, NAFTA applies a general tolerance rule. This is a de minimis rule, stating that if a tariff shift rule is not met, and the value of non-originating, non-tariff shifting materials in the finished product is less than 7%, the finished product can still be considered preferential, independent of its classification code. The general tolerance rule is applied to many agreements and generally varies 7-15%.

Apart from this agreement base rule, the second type of rule is linked to the tariff classification code of the concerned product. The *product-specific rules* encompass various methods to determine a product's preference eligibility, which we'll cover in the following section.

Depending on the specific scenario, one specific rule of origin, a combination of different rules of origin, or even alternative rules of origin may apply.

Preference Determination Methods

As we discussed earlier, if a product is neither wholly obtained/produced nor produced entirely from originating materials, the preference determination looks further into the applicable rules of origin, which is, in turn, specified by the tariff classification code of the finished product, its components, and the legal requirements linked to it.

In general, three types of rules of origin (or a combination thereof) may apply. Although these three types may be worded differently across agreements, they represent similar concepts. In certain agreements, like NAFTA, the three types are generally described as *tariff shift*, *regional value content*, and *manufacturing/processing operations* rules. In other agreements, however, the phrasing generally used is *change of tariff classification*, *value-added*, and *specific* rules.

Tariff Shift/Change of Tariff Classification

To determine whether a finished product has undergone sufficient processing in a particular country to claim preferential status for a preference agreement, the tariff code of the finished product may be compared to those of its components and subassemblies via the tariff shift method.

A rule of origin may require the non-originating components to undergo a *tariff shift*, whereby the HS heading or subheading of the components and finished products should be different. This way, companies prove they have transformed the materials into a new article. The level of detail in required tariff shifts (e.g., heading or sub-heading) depends on the applicable agreement and specific rules.

In most agreements, a de minimis base rule is linked to the tariff shift method. In cases where no tariff shift is obtained, the determination may always fall back on the applicable base rules. If the value of non-originating, non-tariff shifting components accounts for less than the allowed de minimis percentage, preferential origin can still be achieved.

Regional Value Content/Value Added

A second method to determine sufficient processing of the finished good is the regional value content (RVC) or value-added rule. This method states that a minimum of originating content either needs to be present in the finished product or must not exceed a maximum allowance of non-originating materials.

Because there are several methods for calculating the originating content share, the rules of origin specify the permitted calculation methods and what percentage the originating content must attain for the finished product to claim preferential status.

As you consider the various calculation methods, note that the method's descriptions may be worded somewhat differently depending on the applicable agreement:

▶ **Transaction value**

The *transaction value method* considers the finished product's non-originating content and compares that to the transaction value. More specifically, in EU agreements, the non-originating content is compared against the *ex-works* (EXW) *sales price*. For the product to claim preferential origin, the non-originating content may not exceed a given percentage, which depends on the product's tariff classification.

This calculation method is used in the NAFTA agreement, as well, but compares the non-originating content to the *free-on-board* (FOB) *price*.

The comparison against the transaction value includes all the incurred costs of production, marketing, profits, etc.; thus, the required percentage of originating share will be higher for this method than that of the net cost method.

▶ **Net cost**

A second method used in the NAFTA agreement is the *net cost method*. In contrast with the transaction value method, net cost compares the non-originating content against the total cost of the finished product (production and procurement costs).

If the non-originating content does not exceed the allowed percentage stated in the rules of origin, the finished product contains sufficient originating content (direct and indirect costs) and is considered eligible for preferential treatment.

Because the net cost method compares the originating content against the finished product's standard cost, it does not depend on its sales price. Additional costs, such as marketing, shipping, and packing costs are not included in this comparison method. For those reasons, the required RVC percentage will be lower than that of the transaction value method.

▶ **Build-up**

Other agreements, including the ASEAN-Korea (AKFTA) and ASEAN-Austra-lian-New Zealand agreement (AANZFTA), leverage the build-up and build-down methods.

The *build-up method*, which may be referred to as the *direct* method, calculates the originating content as the percentage of the finished product's adjusted value consisting of originating materials.

▶ **Build-down**

As opposed to the build-up method, the *build-down method*, which may be referred to as the *indirect* method, calculates the value added as the percentage of the finished product's adjusted value consisting of non-originating materials.

Manufacturing or Processing Operations/Specific Rules

Other manufacturing or processing rules may be required. These requirements constitute the third method of determining whether a product has been suffi-ciently processed. When applicable, these rules are precisely specified in the rules of origin.

These rules may vary from straightforward to very complex requirements. For instance, in the ASEAN-India agreement (AIFTA), this type of preference determi-nation method is used to confirm that the last production step is performed in the country of export. This is a rather straightforward condition, and most business users are able to evaluate this condition on first sight as being fulfilled or not. For NAFTA, however, these types of rules may be used for complex requirements, mostly specific to the automotive sector (e.g., traced value requirements). These requirements may not be straightforward and may require in-depth knowledge to be validated.

Most rules require components to undergo a tariff shift in the manufacturing pro-cess, the finished product to consist of a certain percentage of originating value, or specific (manufacturing or processing) operations—or a combination of the three types. Eventually, the product's preference determination may result in the following statuses:

▶ Always preferential

▶ To be determined on a transactional basis by comparing the transaction price against a threshold value

▶ Never preferential

In the first scenario, a preferential status is always assigned to the finished product. This may be the case if the product is wholly obtained/produced, produced entirely from originating materials, or always satisfies the applicable rules of origin, independent of the price at which the finished product is sold. This scenario may present itself if a product contains enough originating materials to always pass the net cost method.

The second scenario occurs when a product may be eligible, depending on the finished product's sales price. For instance, this is the case when you apply the transaction value or tariff shift methods. The finished product must exceed a certain value for the originating content share to exceed the required percentage or pass a de minimis rule, if applicable.

The third scenario is when the finished product cannot claim preferential status, no matter what its sale price is. This may be the case, for instance, if the finished product still has the same tariff code as its non-originating components.

In the event that the preference determination does not return a favorable result, a company's management can investigate the causes of the determination result. As such, the company can evaluate its sourcing strategy by selecting alternative vendors who can provide it with originating components, allowing the company's finished product to claim preferential status and origin.

BOM Calculation Methods

You know that the BOM plays a key role in determining the preference eligibility of a manufactured product. A BOM can be a multi-level BOM if intermediate subassemblies are used in the production process. When determining the preferential status of a finished product, you need to apply the rules of origin for the applicable FTA on the components and/or subassemblies.

A finished product's BOM can be exploded according to two distinct logics, resulting in different preference calculation results:

▸ **Top-down method**
You consider the lowest level components of the BOM when performing the preference determination.

▸ **Bottom-up method**
The preference determination starts from the lowest level components of the BOM and works its way up to the finished product. For all subassemblies, a

preference determination is performed on the basis of its subcomponents, and the rule of origin is assigned to the subassembly. Finally, the preferential status of the finished product is determined based on the status and tariff codes of the first level subassemblies.

Depending on FTA, the authorities can either impose companies to use one specific calculation method or, as is most frequently applicable, grant the choice to use both methods, whichever suits the company best.

For example, consider the BOM of Gamma's casual leather shoe, shown in Figure 8.8.

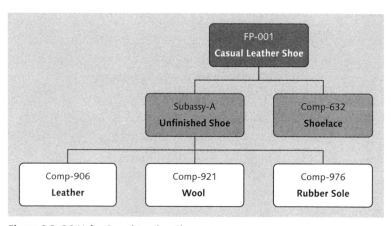

Figure 8.8 BOM for Casual Leather Shoe

When you perform the top-down preference calculation, the lowest level components are taken into consideration. This means that, for each rule related to the originating content, as we discussed earlier, the preferential status of the lowest level components (Comp-906, Comp-921, Comp-976, Comp-632) and their value are considered. For each rule related to tariff codes, the tariff codes of these components are compared to the tariff code of the finished product.

For the bottom-up preference determination, you need to determine the preferential status of each of the subassemblies first. In the example BOM in Figure 8.8, this means performing a preference determination for the unfinished shoe (Subassy-A) according to the applicable rules of origin linked to the subassembly's tariff code. Once you've determined the preferential status of the subassembly, you can then determine the status of the finished product based on the preferential status and tariff codes of the subassembly and shoelace component.

Top-down preference determinations have an advantage in tariff shift compari-son methods because the tariff codes of the lowest level components are then compared to the tariff code of the finished product. When you use the top-down explosion, the tariff shift method neglects all subassemblies, which may come closer to the tariff code of the finished product.

On the other hand, bottom-up explosions are favorable in the case of transac-tional value or net cost comparison methods. The advantage to using bottom-up explosions is an increase in originating value due to subassemblies transforming non-originating components into originating value. The latter is explained in Gamma's comparison of the top-down and bottom-up calculation results.

Gamma's Finished Product Preferential Determination

Consider the scenario for Gamma in which the NAFTA rules of origin for both its finished product and subassembly specify a net cost rule of 55%. This rule means at least 55% of the product's value must be originating. Figure 8.9 shows the BOM and the materials' standard cost used as calculation input.

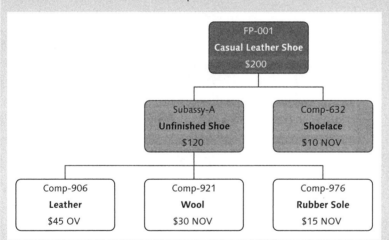

Figure 8.9 BOM for Casual Leather Shoe with Originating Values

Gamma first applies the bottom-up method, so it has to determine the preferential eli-gibility of the unfinished shoe subassembly. Its components consist of the following:

▶ $15 non-originating value (NOV), due to the rubber sole

▶ $75 originating value (OV), due to the leather and wool

▶ $30 originating value, due to manufacturing efforts (the difference between material price and price of its components)

The net cost rule compares the originating value against the subassembly's material price ($120). This results in an originating share of 87.5%, well over the required 55% stated in the net cost rule. As such, the unfinished shoe subassembly is considered to be qualifying for its rules of origin, thus consisting of originating value. In this scenario, a gain of $15 in originating value is realized as a result of the bottom-up method.

In a second step, the preference calculation is performed for the finished product. The finished product is composed of the following:

▶ $10 non-originating value, due to the shoelace
▶ $120 originating value, due to the unfinished shoe
▶ $70 originating value, due to manufacturing efforts

The net cost rule for the finished product now results in an originating share of 95% because $190 of its $200 value is originating. The finished product thus satisfies the rules of origin and is eligible for export under preferential treatment.

If the top-down BOM calculation is applied given the same scenario, the calculation takes the following into account:

▶ $25 non-originating value, due to the rubber sole and shoelace
▶ $75 originating value, due to the leather and wool
▶ $100 originating value, due to manufacturing costs

The finished product is again eligible for preferential treatment because the regional value is set at 87.5%. Note that, although that this calculation results in a lower share of originating value, it makes no difference to the actual preference result.

In today's global environment, BOMs may consist of a multilevel structure with components sourced from various vendors in different countries. Due to the complexity of calculating a BOM's preferential status, it is nearly impossible to perform the preference determinations if they are not properly automated by a supporting system.

Next, we'll elaborate on the system process to describe how SAP GTS supports and automates the described business process.

8.1.2 System Process

Whereas the previous section covered the trade preference business process, this section will extensively cover the different steps of SAP GTS preference management. After a general overview of the various steps, we'll discuss each step in detail from a system point of view and link it to the business case of Gamma, our fictional shoe manufacturer.

Figure 8.10 shows the SAP GTS system process and its different steps. Like in Figure 8.4, you can distinguish among inbound, production, and outbound processes.

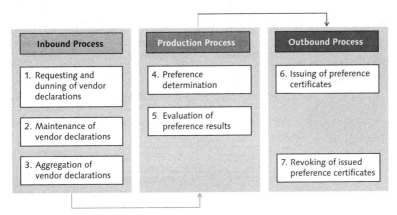

Inbound Process	Production Process	Outbound Process
1. Requesting and dunning of vendor declarations	4. Preference determination	6. Issuing of preference certificates
2. Maintenance of vendor declarations	5. Evaluation of preference results	
3. Aggregation of vendor declarations		7. Revoking of issued preference certificates

Figure 8.10 Trade Preference System Process

The inbound process objective was to obtain vendor declarations for all components procured externally. In SAP GTS, this is performed in three subsequent steps.

❶ The origin of each relevant externally procured component is requested from the applicable vendors. This is the so-called vendor solicitation process for which SAP GTS uses *long-term vendor declarations* (LTVDs). SAP GTS collects the relevant purchase orders and material documents from the feeder system in a worklist, which allows you to easily request LTVDs from the corresponding vendors.

The Trade Preference Management module is built with a worst-case principle for preference determination. Whenever a component has no preferential status maintained, the system assumes that this component has a negative preferential status. As such, if vendors do not respond to the LTVD request, you should send out reminders, also known as LTVD dunning.

❷ Once the vendors respond to the LTVD request, the components' preferential information needs to be captured in the system. A component does not obtain preferential status until it has been expressly marked and entered in the system, which is performed now. Both the preferential status and preferential country of origin are captured from the returning vendor declaration and entered in the system for each vendor-component combination.

❸ Components may be multi-sourced, meaning that they are procured from multiple vendors. As such, the origin-related information concerning a specific component from these vendors is aggregated in this step, the last of the inbound process. Because only one aggregated status can be used during preference calculations, SAP GTS aggregates the preferential status of that component obtained by different vendors. Again, the system aggregation is done according to a worst-case principle because one vendor with a negative status affects all other vendors with a positive status. The aggregated preferential status is then stamped on the product's material master data.

❹ Once you've received and maintained the preferential information for the sourced components, as well as classified the components and finished product with an HS code, you can perform the preference determination for the finished product in the fourth system process step. Once you maintain the preferential status and tariff classification codes of the components and subassemblies, you can perform the preference determination for the finished product. The result of this preference determination is stored on the material master in SAP GTS.

❺ The results from the preference determination are evaluated on a transactional basis whether the transaction is eligible for preferential treatment. When creating a sales order or billing document, you can flag a checkbox to indicate whether the order is eligible.

Furthermore, standard SAP GTS provides a standard report for capturing all preference determination results. As such, a company's management can look further into finished products with non-favorable preference results, possibly to evaluate the causes and possibilities to change the result of the preference determination. You might do this by maintaining missing components' preferential information or replacing non-originating components with originating components from a different vendor. As such, these finished products may also be eligible for preferential treatment.

❻ This step of the trade preference system process is issuing the proof of origin to the company's customers, based in member FTA countries. Certificate of origin documents are issued on a transactional basis or for a certain period.

When issued on a transactional basis, you can print the certificate documents via the Customs Management module of SAP GTS (please refer to Chapter 7), which usually operates on a transactional basis for printing documents.

Depending on the applicable FTA, the proof of origin may be issued with a validity date. In NAFTA, the certificate's validity, the so-called blanket period, may be used to cover multiple shipments of identical goods imported within the validity period. Blanket certificates (see Figure 8.16 for an example) may be issued via the SAP GTS Risk Management module. The latter process is referred to in SAP GTS as the *vendor declarations for customer's purpose*.

Note that agreements often limit the use of these blanket certificates. NAFTA allows both the use of blanket certificates and issuing certificates of origin on a transactional basis, but for ASEAN agreements, certificates can only be issued on a transactional basis. In such cases, the preferential documents are printed from the SAP GTS Customs Management module.

❼ As displayed in Figure 8.10, one additional step might occur. If a finished product's preferential status changes or is lost during the blanket certificate's validity period, the relevant certificates need to be revoked. This may occur due to a different sourcing strategy, component pricing changes, or changes to the finished product's selling price. In this case, SAP GTS automatically creates entries to re-issue the proof of origin with the updated information.

Figure 8.11 displays the SAP GTS selection screen where Trade Preference Management-related transactions are found. From the SAP GTS area menu, you can access the Trade Preference Management selection screen via RISK MANAGEMENT • PREFERENCE PROCESSING. The selection screen provides three expandable tabs that correspond to the inbound, outbound, and production processes, respectively, as discussed in Section 8.1.1.

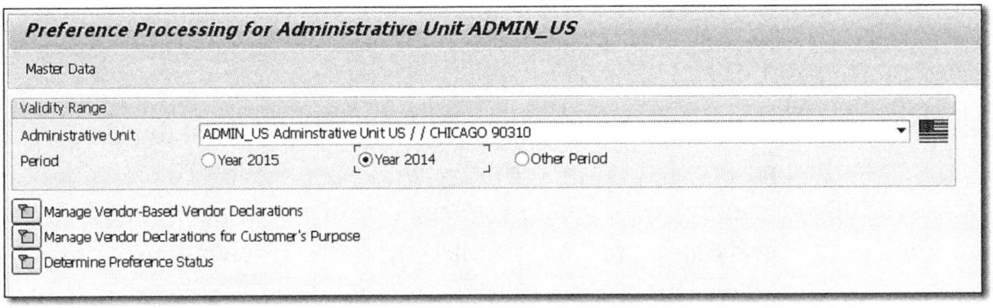

Figure 8.11 Preference Selection Screen

In the SAP GTS Trade Preference Management module, all preference-related flows are based on administrative units. An *administrative unit* (AU) is not a physical representation of a company, but it represents a plant or plant group (multiple plants) as a single point of contact for all the administration related to Trade Preference Management. We'll discuss the concept and setup of AUs further in Section 8.1.3.

Before you can perform any trade preference steps, you need to select an AU. Furthermore, because the preference administration needs to be performed at least once a year, it is also important to select the relevant period. In light of the Gamma business case, a US AU is selected, for which NAFTA is set up as an active agreement.

Now that we've gotten a brief glimpse of the seven system process steps in SAP GTS, let's examine each one closer using the Gamma business case.

Requesting and Dunning of Vendor Declarations

In SAP GTS Trade Preference Management, there are two distinct ways of managing the vendor solicitation process to obtain the required origin-related information for externally procured components and subassemblies. First, there is a form-based process in which you perform the vendor solicitation using forms. You can print these forms in SAP GTS to be sent to the relevant vendors. The vendors can then enter the preferential information of their sold products on these forms and return the information, via either postal mail or email.

Note that the standard NAFTA form for vendor solicitation is the official certificate of origin document, identical to the document that will be finally sent out to a company's customers in the NAFTA region. This is not equal in all agreements, however; for instance, the European vendor soliciting documents differ from the actual certificate of origin.

Apart from forms, the second option is to configure a web portal to manage the vendor solicitation process. Configuring a web portal allows companies to request LTVDs by sending their vendors an email with a link, where vendors can enter the vendor declaration information directly, without relying on forms.

Upon creation of purchase orders and goods receipts or material documents in the feeder system, an entry in a worklist for requesting LTVDs is triggered. Note that this entry is generated only if the document's vendor is relevant for requesting vendor declarations. You can manually change the relevance of vendors in SAP GTS; system setup is discussed further in Section 8.1.3.

You can configure which documents trigger the vendor solicitation process. For example, if you set purchase orders as the trigger to request an LTVD, then entries in the worklist are created at an earlier stage in the inbound process. On the other hand, because LTVDs cannot be deleted from the system, an LTVD request based on a purchase order that is later canceled cannot be removed from the system and can potentially have a negative impact on the preference determination of a finished product.

The advantage of leveraging goods receipts or material documents as triggers for creating entries in the worklist is the certainty that the components are actually delivered at your warehouse. Consequently, LTVDs are not requested or maintained for components that were included in the purchase order but not actually delivered to the relevant plant. The disadvantage here is that LTVDs are requested and maintained at a later stage in the inbound process. Note that you can choose to set both document types as trigger documents.

For the activated document types, an entry is created in the worklist for requesting vendor declarations if the following prerequisites apply:

▶ The relevant plant in the transactional document is assigned to the specific AU in SAP GTS.

▶ The purchased product and vendor are considered relevant for requesting vendor declarations.

▶ No LTVDs already exist for this product-vendor combination for the current period. If an LTVD already exists, there is no need to request a new declaration unless it reaches the end of its validity period.

Figure 8.12 shows the SAP GTS menu screen, focusing on the tab for managing vendor-based vendor declarations. This tab contains all transactions required for the inbound trade preference process. The subsequent tabs cover the outbound and production processes, respectively.

The worklist for requesting LTVDs is shown on the left side of Figure 8.12. As discussed, all triggering documents (purchasing and material documents) create entries in this worklist. From the worklist, LTVDs are either printed as a form or sent via email to the relevant vendor to request the preferential status of the components procured from the corresponding vendor.

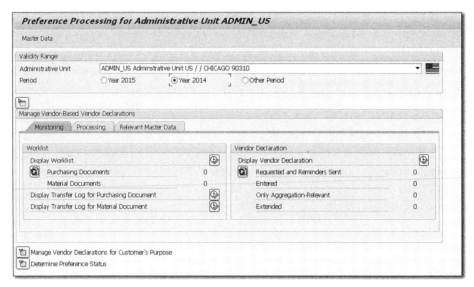

Figure 8.12 Vendor-Based Vendor Declarations Menu

Once requested, the entry is removed from the worklist and transferred to the REQUESTED AND REMINDERS SENT worklist on the right side of Figure 8.12, where all requested and maintained LTVDs can be monitored.

Note that, besides creating a worklist for requesting LTVDs based on purchase orders and material documents, you can also send requests manually in GTS before starting the actual purchasing flow. This can be useful for companies making a sourcing decision between different vendors to see which of them can provide originating materials advantageous for the preference determination. Based on that information, you can make an informed decision about trading with a specific vendor.

If no statements of origin are received from the vendor, you can send a dunning letter at designated intervals (e.g., when no information is received from a certain vendor for a specific component after 30 days). The SAP GTS Trade Preference Management module allows you to track the issue date of the LTVD request and automatically generate dunning letters in case of a delayed response.

Besides the dunning functionality, SAP GTS can also create a transition period between subsequent years. Because LTVDs are normally valid for a period of only one year, you need to request and maintain the vendor declarations each year. To facilitate this process and divide the work over a period of time, you can configure a transition period in which vendor-component combinations maintained for the current year automatically create an entry in the worklist for LTVD requests for the following year.

Gamma's Vendor Solicitation Process

To manufacture its casual leather shoe, the finished product that will eventually be shipped to its customers, Gamma needs to procure certain components from various vendors.

Gamma does not request vendor declarations prior to the purchasing process, but does request the LTVDs that are generated in the worklist triggered by the purchase and material documents.

Gamma places purchase orders for the following:

▶ Comp-921 (wool): 2,500 pieces from a vendor in Canada
▶ Comp-906 (leather): 1,000 pieces from a vendor in the United States
▶ Comp-976 (rubber sole): 1,750 pieces from a vendor in Vietnam
▶ Comp-632 (shoelaces): 2,490 pieces from a vendor in Mexico
▶ Comp-632 (shoelaces): 120 pieces from a vendor in Peru

Let's say that three purchase orders and two goods receipt documents serve as the trigger for creating entries in the worklist to request the LTVDs. You can see the result of creating the purchase and material documents in the WORKLIST section of Figure 8.13, where the worklist now contains three purchase and two material documents.

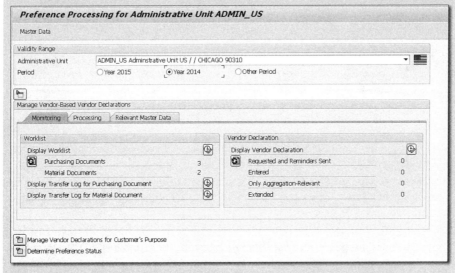

Figure 8.13 Vendor-Based Vendor Declarations after Triggering Documents

Figure 8.14 displays Gamma's worklist to request the LTVDs. It gives an overview per vendor of all the components for which you need to request the origin-related information. For convenience, SAP GTS mentions the vendors with the external business partner ID or the vendor number used in the feeder system.

The FOLLOW-ON FUNCTION icon in Figure 8.14 allows Gamma's users to trigger an LTVD request directly from this list. In one LTVD, you can request the preferential status of multiple components, on the condition that they are supplied by the same vendor.

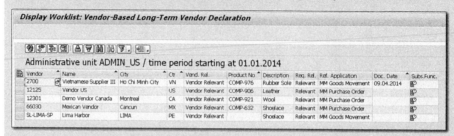

Display Worklist: Vendor-Based Long-Term Vendor Declaration

Administrative unit ADMIN_US / time period starting at 01.01.2014

Vendor	Name	City	Ctr	Vend. Rel.	Product No	Description	Req. Rel.	Ref. Application	Doc. Date	Subs.Func.
2700	Vietnamese Supplier III	Ho Chi Minh City	VN	Vendor Relevant	COMP-976	Rubber Sole	Relevant	MM Goods Movement	09.04.2014	
12125	Vendor US		US	Vendor Relevant	COMP-906	Leather	Relevant	MM Purchase Order		
12301	Demo Vendor Canada	Montreal	CA	Vendor Relevant	COMP-921	Wool	Relevant	MM Purchase Order		
66030	Mexican Vendor	Cancun	MX	Vendor Relevant	COMP-632	Shoelace	Relevant	MM Purchase Order		
SL-LIMA-SP	Lima Harbor	LIMA	PE	Vendor Relevant		Shoelace	Relevant	MM Goods Movement		

Figure 8.14 Worklist for Requesting LTVDs

Gamma's users execute the follow-on function for each business partner. Because the company works with the printed form-based method, each LTVD request triggers a selection screen to specify how the form is to be printed.

Once the printing criteria are specified, the summarization screen displayed on Figure 8.15 is given, specifying all products for which a request for origin-related information to one specific vendor is sent.

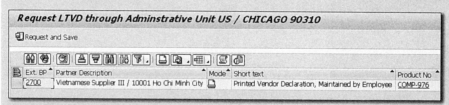

Request LTVD through Adminstrative Unit US / CHICAGO 90310

Request and Save

Ext. BP	Partner Description	Mode	Short text	Product No
2700	Vietnamese Supplier III / 10001 Ho Chi Minh City		Printed Vendor Declaration, Maintained by Employee	COMP-976

Figure 8.15 LTVD Request to the Vietnamese Vendor

Once requested and saved, the vendor declaration is printed as an empty NAFTA certificate of origin form, as displayed in Figure 8.16, which Gamma sends to the corresponding vendor to complete.

Furthermore, standard SAP GTS allows Gamma to attach a cover letter with a formal request to the vendor, as well as a list of products for which it requires origin-related information from that vendor.

Once all LTVD requests are sent out, the entries are removed from the first worklist and moved to the subsequent worklist, where requested and maintained LTVDs are listed, as you can see in Figure 8.17. The three purchasing documents and two material documents are now found in the REQUESTED AND REMINDERS SENT section.

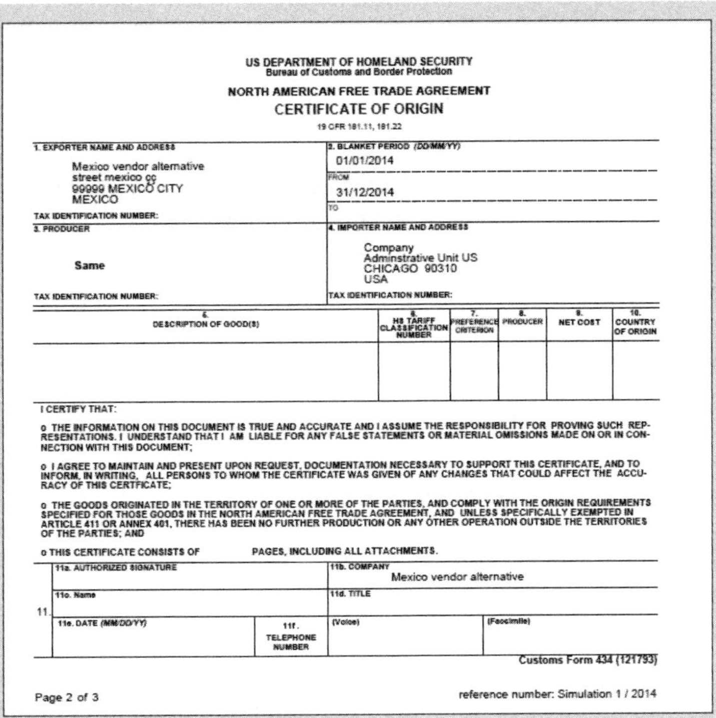

US DEPARTMENT OF HOMELAND SECURITY
Bureau of Customs and Border Protection

NORTH AMERICAN FREE TRADE AGREEMENT
CERTIFICATE OF ORIGIN
19 CFR 181.11, 181.22

1. EXPORTER NAME AND ADDRESS
Mexico vendor alternative
street mexico cc
99999 MEXICO CITY
MEXICO
TAX IDENTIFICATION NUMBER:

2. BLANKET PERIOD (DD/MM/YY)
FROM 01/01/2014
TO 31/12/2014

3. PRODUCER
Same
TAX IDENTIFICATION NUMBER:

4. IMPORTER NAME AND ADDRESS
Company
Adminstrative Unit US
CHICAGO 90310
USA
TAX IDENTIFICATION NUMBER:

5. DESCRIPTION OF GOOD(S)	6. HS TARIFF CLASSIFICATION NUMBER	7. PREFERENCE CRITERION	8. PRODUCER	9. NET COST	10. COUNTRY OF ORIGIN

I CERTIFY THAT:

o THE INFORMATION ON THIS DOCUMENT IS TRUE AND ACCURATE AND I ASSUME THE RESPONSIBILITY FOR PROVING SUCH REPRESENTATIONS. I UNDERSTAND THAT I AM LIABLE FOR ANY FALSE STATEMENTS OR MATERIAL OMISSIONS MADE ON OR IN CONNECTION WITH THIS DOCUMENT;

o I AGREE TO MAINTAIN AND PRESENT UPON REQUEST, DOCUMENTATION NECESSARY TO SUPPORT THIS CERTIFICATE, AND TO INFORM, IN WRITING, ALL PERSONS TO WHOM THE CERTIFICATE WAS GIVEN OF ANY CHANGES THAT COULD AFFECT THE ACCURACY OF THIS CERTFICATE;

o THE GOODS ORIGINATED IN THE TERRITORY OF ONE OR MORE OF THE PARTIES, AND COMPLY WITH THE ORIGIN REQUIREMENTS SPECIFIED FOR THOSE GOODS IN THE NORTH AMERICAN FREE TRADE AGREEMENT, AND UNLESS SPECIFICALLY EXEMPTED IN ARTICLE 411 OR ANNEX 401, THERE HAS BEEN NO FURTHER PRODUCTION OR ANY OTHER OPERATION OUTSIDE THE TERRITORIES OF THE PARTIES; AND

o THIS CERTIFICATE CONSISTS OF PAGES, INCLUDING ALL ATTACHMENTS.

11.
11a. AUTHORIZED SIGNATURE
11b. COMPANY Mexico vendor alternative
11c. Name
11d. TITLE
11e. DATE (MM/DD/YY)
11f. TELEPHONE NUMBER (Voice) (Facsimile)

Customs Form 434 (121793)

Page 2 of 3
reference number: Simulation 1 / 2014

Figure 8.16 NAFTA Certificate of Origin

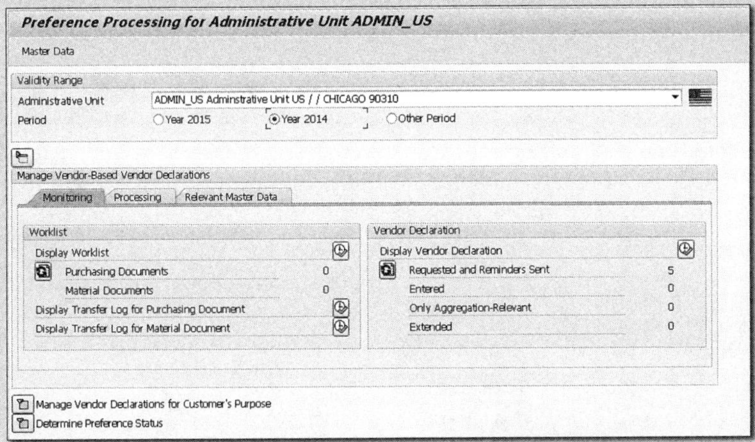

Figure 8.17 Vendor-Based Vendor Declarations Menu after Requesting LTVDs

The next step for Gamma is to maintain the information it receives from the various vendors.

Maintaining Vendor Declarations

The origin-related information for each component must be stored in SAP GTS to allow an accurate preference determination. Note that, when no origin is recorded, SAP GTS considers the product to have a non-preferential status.

If the vendor receives the LTVD on the paper form, he needs to return the completed document to the issuing company. Then, you need to manually enter the content of the document in SAP GTS. If the vendor is requested to enter the LTVD via a web portal, the preferential status and origin can be entered there. These entries must then be validated by the requesting company before they are loaded from the portal into SAP GTS.

For each product, you can enter the preference indicator and, if applicable, the preferential country of origin. As with the preference criteria in Section 8.1.1, the possible NAFTA preference indicators range from the following:

▶ A: Wholly obtained/produced

▶ B: Goods satisfying the specific rules of origin

▶ C: Produced entirely from originating materials

▶ N/E: Not eligible

If one of the first three criteria is applicable, you can maintain the preferential country, as well, assuming the country is Canada, the United States, or Mexico in the case of a NAFTA scenario.

Gamma Receives Preferential Information from its Vendors

A few weeks after Gamma sent out the paper LTVD requests, it received responses from all vendors, complete with the required preferential information. This means that there's no need for Gamma to send out dunning forms.

The following information is found on the completed NAFTA LTVDs, stating whether the component is preferential and, in the case of preferential origin, the preferential country of origin:

▶ Comp-921 (wool): goods wholly obtained, Canada

▶ Comp-906 (leather): goods wholly obtained, United States

▶ Comp-976 (rubber sole): not preferential

▶ Comp-632 (shoelaces): goods wholly produced, Mexico

▶ Comp-632 (shoelaces): not preferential

The Canadian, US, and Mexican vendors confirmed the preferential status of their components for the NAFTA agreement. However, the vendors from Vietnam and Peru replied that their components do not meet the agreement's requirements.

Because this information has been obtained through paper forms, Gamma users need to enter the information manually in GTS. Figure 8.18 displays the screen where the preferential information is maintained. Note that, for a specific product, SAP GTS creates an entry for each agreement active in the selected AU. Consequently, a component's preferential information for the NAFTA agreement may differ from that for other agreements.

Figure 8.18 Worklist with Requested and Maintained LTVDs

Gamma's users enter the information received from the various vendors for the requested LTVDs, as seen in Figure 8.19. Since NAFTA is the only active agreement for Gamma's AU, you can maintain each product only with NAFTA-specific preferential information. When selected, each save triggers an aggregation logic, which we'll discuss in the following system step.

Figure 8.19 Maintain LTVD Preference Data

Aggregating Vendor Declarations

In the contemporary business environment, multi-sourcing is more the rule than the exception. When it comes to multi-sourcing, the aggregation of LTVDs is required to consolidate the preferential information received by different vendors into one preferential status for each component for a certain agreement. For example, one vendor can provide a preferential LTVD for a component, while another vendor selling the same component may not. The logic applied by SAP GTS is the "worst-case scenario," meaning that, if one vendor cannot provide preferential origin or the preferential status for a component is not maintained, then SAP GTS considers the specific component to lack preferential origin status across all vendors.

Gamma's Aggregated Preference Data

In the previous step, Gamma received the completed LTVDs from its vendors. This information was maintained in the SAP GTS system, which performs an aggregation on the components sourced from multiple vendors.

The shoelaces (Comp-632) used in the production process of the finished product are multi-sourced from vendors in Mexico and Peru.

The Mexican vendor confirmed his components to be wholly obtained, with Mexico as the preferential country of origin. But the vendor in Peru replied that his components are non-preferential. SAP GTS consolidates this information and, according to the worst-case principle, visualized in Figure 8.20, concludes that the multi-sourced component is not of preferential origin.

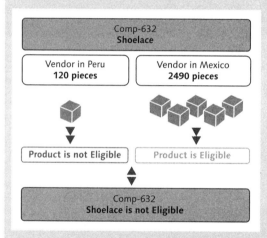

Figure 8.20 Preferential Status Aggregation Logic

Looking back at the finished product's BOM, shown in Figure 8.21, the following information is now obtained to use as input in the preference determination:

- Comp-632 (shoelaces): Non-originating value ($10)
- Comp-906 (leather): Originating value ($45)
- Comp-921 (wool): Originating value ($30)
- Comp-976 (rubber sole): Non-originating value ($15)

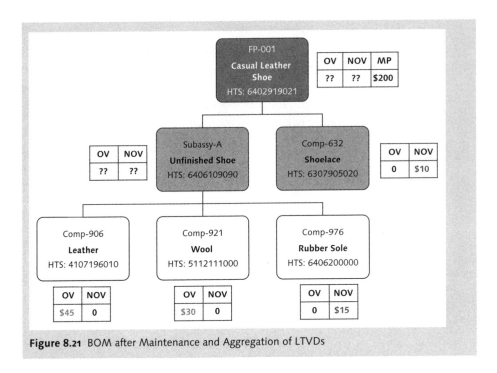

Figure 8.21 BOM after Maintenance and Aggregation of LTVDs

As we discussed earlier, the result of maintaining the LTVD information is stamped on the product master in GTS in the TEXT OF PREFERENCE column of the PREFERENCE tab. Figure 8.22 shows this for the shoelace component.

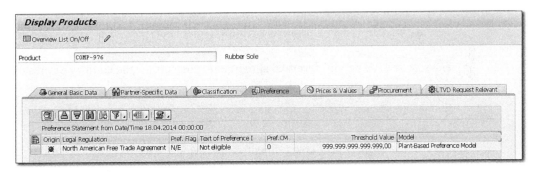

Figure 8.22 Preference Data on the Material Product Master

SAP GTS uses the preference data on the product master in the next step to perform the preference determination for the finished product and possibly subassemblies, depending on the applicable BOM-explosion method.

Preference Determination

When completing the inbound process of requesting (and potentially dunning), maintaining, and aggregating LTVDs, you can perform the preference determination for the finished product. This is the starting point of the second stage of the three-stage business process, and it has its own dedicated PREFERENCE DETERMINATION tab, shown in Figure 8.23.

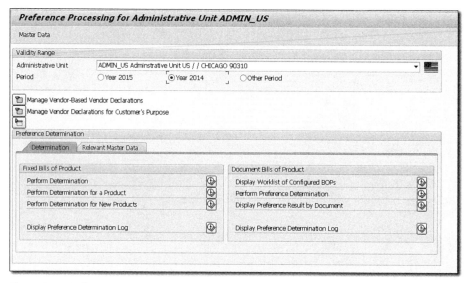

Figure 8.23 Preference Determination Menu

The preference determination of finished goods in SAP GTS is based on the following factors:

▸ The selected AU and preferential agreements relevant for the country of the AU

▸ The preference model—that is, a one-on-one mapping between plant and AU (plant-based) or a many-to-one mapping, assigning multiple plants to one AU (cross-plant)

▸ The finished product and its classification code (based on the classification code and agreement, the applicable rules of origin are selected).

▸ The components used to produce the finished product based on the BOM

▸ The preferential status of the components based on the received LTVDs

- The classification codes of the components as they will be used to determine the outcome of a tariff shift rule
- The cost of the components, which is needed to calculate the regional content value
- The BOM calculation model (top-down or bottom-up explosion)

When running the preference determination, the BOM transferred from the feeder system to SAP GTS is exploded, and the preferential status is determined for each active agreement in the appropriate AU.

The classification of the finished good and components are taken into account, and the applicable preference rules are applied. Note that you can display the preference rules of a specific FTA at any time in RISK MANAGEMENT • PREFERENCE PROCESSING—MASTER DATA • DISPLAY RULES OF AN AGREEMENT, as long as the rules have been uploaded or entered manually in SAP GTS.

In light of the Gamma business case, Figure 8.24 displays the applicable rules for Gamma's casual leather shoe. The screen's header shows which free trade agreement is applicable and whether it is active.

Display Preference Rules for Agreement _DNAF

Preference Agreement	_DNAF	North American Free Trade Agreement
Status of Agreement	▣	Active
Rule Set of Agreement	_DNAFTA_US	North American Free Trade Agreement - US
Related Numbering System	US_HTS1	Harmonized Tariff Schedule of the United States

Preference Zones: Number 3

Country Group	Description
_DCA	Canada
_DMX	Mexico
_DUS	United States

Preference Rules - Base Rules: Number 1

Rule Type	Description	Rule	Start date	End Date
4	General Tolerance Rule	RPDEMIN	01.01.1995	01.01.4000

Preference Rules - Item-Related Rules: Number 1

Tariff Number	Standard Rule	Alternative Rule	Start date	End Date	Additional Condition
6402	RR6401		01.01.1995	01.01.4000	

Figure 8.24 Preference Rules for Gamma's Casual Leather Shoe

Let's briefly refer back to Section 8.1.1, which elaborated on the rules of origin. SAP GTS distinguishes between base rules and item-related rules. The base rules apply to the whole agreement and all included products. Tariff code-specific rules can include a standard rule, alternative rule, and possibly additional conditions.

Recall that there are several ways for a product to claim preferential status. When a product is not wholly obtained/produced or produced entirely from originating materials, it can still claim a preferential status and origin if it has been sufficiently processed. This sufficient processing can be determined by applying three methods: tariff shift, regional value content, and manufacturing or processing operations.

The methods and rules of origin that can be automated in SAP GTS are translated into one of six SAP GTS preference comparison methods:

▶ External preference document (0)

▶ Transaction value (1)

▶ Net cost (2)

▶ Tariff shift (3)

▶ Build-up (4)

▶ Build-down (5)

The first comparison method (0) is applied when the preferential status and origin is manually maintained on the finished product's master data.

The tariff shift method rules are translated in the third SAP GTS comparison method (3), while the various methods used to calculate the originating content value are translated as comparison methods (1, 2, 4, and 5).

However, the manufacturing or processing operations cannot be translated into the rules of origin used by SAP GTS. These requirements are present in SAP GTS as additional conditions, which are text descriptions of the imposed requirement. If such additional conditions apply, manual intervention is required to confirm that the conditions for that product are met. You must then flag the product in SAP GTS as fulfilling that condition. You can do this via RISK MANAGEMENT • PREFERENCE PROCESSING — MASTER DATA • ASSIGN CONDITIONS TO A PRODUCT.

Take a look at Figure 8.24. The rules that apply to the leather shoe are one NAFTA base rule and an item-related standard rule. When you display a specific rule, you'll see a log like the one in Figure 8.25, which displays the NAFTA base rule, applicable to all classification codes in the NAFTA agreement.

As we discussed earlier, the NAFTA base rule is a general tolerance rule—more specifically, a de minimis calculation with a threshold of 7%. This means that if a tariff shift rule applies, but not all non-originating components fulfill the tariff shift requirements, and if the value of non-originating products not undergoing a tariff shift in the finished product's BOM is less than or equal to 7% of the finished product value, then the finished product can still claim a preferential status.

Detailed Information	
🔲 ⑫ 🔍 Technical Information 🖺 🖨 🖺 🖺 ⑩0 ✎0 △0 🖺4 ℹ️ Help	
Base Rule	Nu...
▾ 🖺 4 - General Tolerance Rule (01.01.1995 - 01.01.4000)	4
▾ 🖺 RPDEMIN	3
▾ 🖺 De Minimis	2
▸ 🖺 7,00 (LE -Smaller than or equal to)	1

Figure 8.25 NAFTA General Tolerance Rule

Whereas the base rule applies to all products, the item-related rules shown in Figure 8.26 relate only to products with the corresponding tariff code. In this scenario, the rule is rather straightforward to interpret because no alternative rule or conditions apply.

Detailed Information	
🔲 ⑫ 🔍 Technical Information 🖺 🖨 🖺 🖺 ⑩0 ✎0 △0 🖺14 ℹ️ Help	
Rules for Tariff Number 6402	Nu...
▾ 🖺 Standard Rule (01.01.1995 - 01.01.4000)	14
▾ 🖺 RR6401 ("And" Operation)	13
▾ 🖺 RPHE640610	3
▾ 🖺 HS Check	2
▸ 🖺 640610 (E -Interval Selection Excluded)	1
▾ 🖺 RPRVC_N55	3
▾ 🖺 Regional Value Content	2
▸ 🖺 55,00 (GE -Greater than or equal to) - Net Cost Method	1
▾ 🖺 RPTS4	3
▾ 🖺 Tariff Shift	2
▸ 🖺 (4-Place Heading)	1
▾ 🖺 RRHE6401	3
▾ 🖺 HS Check	2
▸ 🖺 6401 - 6405 (E -Interval Selection Excluded)	1

Figure 8.26 NAFTA Item-Related Rules for Gamma's Leather Shoe

The standard rule is an AND operation, signifying that the requirements below are all needed to satisfy the standard rule. Note that for other rules, an OR operations may apply. For instance, such a rule may state that if either a transaction value *or* a net cost method is fulfilled, the rule is satisfied.

For the standard rule in Figure 8.26 to be satisfied, the following requirements all need to be met:

▶ HS check: The finished product may not include non-originating components classified with HTS code 640610.

▶ Regional value content: The net cost method is applied, stating that at least 55% of the finished product's value must be NAFTA-originating.

▶ Tariff shift: All non-originating components must undergo a header tariff shift.

▶ HS check: The finished product may not include non-originating components with classification code 6401-6405.

Thus, the standard rule falls under the net cost method, for which a few additional tariff requirements apply.

The rules of origin can be either uploaded from a file provided by a content provider or manually configured in the system. In both cases, the rule needs to consist of one of the comparison methods discussed in Section 8.1.1. If a rule consists of a more complex rule or requirement that cannot be automated, you need to implement it as an additional condition.

As a result of the preference determination based on the rules of origin, SAP GTS calculates one of three possible statuses, each with a specific SAP GTS symbol and threshold value. Note that these results correspond to the preference determination results discussed with the trade preference business process in Section 8.1.1.

▶ Preferential status

▶ Preferential status depending on a threshold value

▶ Non-preferential status

If you can assign a preferential status to a finished product, the result is visualized as a green square symbol and assigned a threshold value of *minus infinite*, meaning that the product is preferential regardless of the selling price because the price will always be above the minus infinite threshold.

A second scenario may occur when a finished product is eligible for preferential treatment depending on the product's sales price. In this scenario, the result of the finished product is visualized as a yellow triangle symbol. The assigned threshold value is the value at which the non-originating value of a product's components occupies an acceptable share in the finished product, as determined in the preference rules. If the product is sold at a price lower than the threshold value, the non-originating components occupy a larger share in the total value than acceptable by the preference rules, and the product can no longer claim preferential status.

If no preferential status is applicable for the finished product, the result is visualized as a red circle symbol and assigned a threshold value of *plus infinite*. This signifies that, no matter how high the selling price is set, the product can never be eligible for preferential treatment in the given agreement because the selling price can never exceed the plus infinite threshold.

The system performs the calculations for all applicable rules in parallel. Afterwards, the most advantageous outcome is taken as the outcome for the entire preference determination. In contrast to other functionalities within the Trade Preference Management module, the worst-case principle is *not* applied.

Preferential Eligibility of Gamma's Finished Products

In the previous actions, Gamma obtained the preferential status for all of its components, so it is now ready to perform the preferential calculation.

Because the NAFTA allows performing both top-down and bottom-up BOM explosions, Gamma performs both calculations. Based on the calculation results, Gamma will determine which BOM explosion method is most favorable to apply.

Figure 8.27 shows the BOM considered in the top-down calculation. SAP GTS neglects the subassembly and takes into account only the lowest level components. Recall that this technique is more favorable in tariff shift comparison methods because the lowest level components are more likely to undergo tariff shifts than the subassemblies.

Based on the four components, the system applies the preferential rules and determines the origin for the finished product.

You can see the result of the top-down preference calculation in the calculation log of Figure 8.28, from which Gamma observes that its finished product is eligible for preferential treatment.

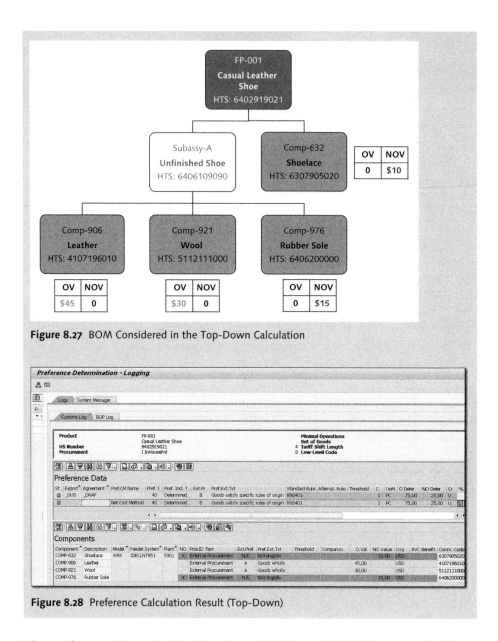

Figure 8.27 BOM Considered in the Top-Down Calculation

Figure 8.28 Preference Calculation Result (Top-Down)

The preference determination log shown in Figure 8.28 is the most significant screen in the SAP GTS Trade Preference Management flow, from a systems point of view. To better grasp the logic and structure attained in the screen, let's break it down into different sections.

The screen is divided into a header, finished product, and components section. The header contains basic information concerning the finished product, including product name and number, HTS classification code, and procurement indicator (procured externally, produced in-house, or a mix of the two).

Figure 8.29 shows the most significant information found in the component section that SAP GTS uses as input for performing the preference calculation.

Components

Component	Description	NO	ProInd	Ext.Pref.	Pref.Ext.Txt	Threshold Val.	Comparis. Pri...	O.Val.	NO V...	RVC Bene...	Currency
COMP-632	Shoelace	X	E	N/E	Not eligible				10,00		USD
COMP-906	Leather		E	A	Goods wholly...			45,00			USD
COMP-921	Wool		E	A	Goods wholly...			30,00			USD
COMP-976	Rubber Sole	X	E	N/E	Not eligible				15,00		USD

Figure 8.29 Components Log in the Preference Determination (Top-Down)

As you can see in Figure 8.27, only the lowest level components are taken into consideration, while the calculation ignores the subassembly. The system retrieves the following information to correctly perform the preferential calculation, corresponding with the columns in Figure 8.29:

▶ Component product number.

▶ Component product description.

▶ Flag depicting a non-originating component (if flagged, the entry for that component is marked red).

▶ Procurement indicator transferred from the feeder system.

▶ External preference indicator provided by the vendor of the specific component in the vendor solicitation process.

▶ SAP GTS description of the component's preference indicator.

▶ Threshold value at which the component is considered originating. This column applies when you're dealing with subassemblies as a component in the preference calculation, and we'll discuss it in the bottom-up calculation method.

▶ Like the previous value, the comparison price column applies to subassemblies, and we'll discuss it in the bottom-up calculation method.

▶ The following two columns specify the amount of originating or non-originating value. SAP GTS considers the component's material price and checks the non-originating flag to determine whether the product consists of originating or non-originating value.

▶ The last column specifies the regional value content benefit that is gained by applying the specific calculation method. This also applies to the bottom-up method, and we'll discuss it later.

Apart from this information, other data available at the component level includes the component classification codes, component quantity used in the finished product, preference model, plant, and feeder system.

The actual result of the finished product preference calculation is shown in detail on Figure 8.30.

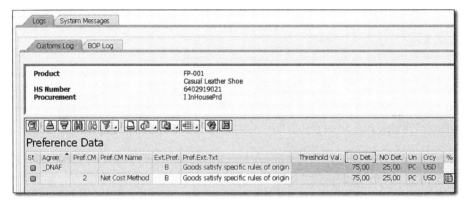

Figure 8.30 Header and Finished Product Log in the Preference Determination (Top-Down)

SAP GTS calculates the applicable rules for each agreement relevant to the corresponding AU. As we explained for Figure 8.26, the net cost method is the sole comparison method included in the preferential rules for Gamma's finished product (although it is combined with tariff shift requirements).

The first column in the calculation log depicts the originating status. This value is aggregated on a "best-case" principle, meaning that if the rules of origin for a product contains multiple comparison methods, satisfying any one is sufficient for the finished product to claim originating status.

The top entry for each agreement is a summary copy of the entry with the most favorable result. For Gamma, the finished product preference determination results in a favorable preference status with external preference indicator B, signifying that the finished good satisfies the specific rules of origin. As we discussed earlier, the applied net cost method results in either a positive or negative calculation result, thus leaving the THRESHOLD VALUE column empty.

However, for other comparison methods (e.g., transactional value), the preferential eligibility can depend on the eventual sales price of the finished product. In such situations, SAP GTS calculates the threshold value at which the finished good is preferential.

Furthermore, the amount of originating and non-originating value in the finished product's BOM is specified. These values, together with the manufacturing efforts, are used to determine the originating content share. The button found in the far right column of the net cost method entry shows the detailed originating content calculation of Figure 8.31. As previously determined, the various components consist of $75 originating and $25 non-originating value. On top of that, the system derives an additional $100 in production efforts; the finished product's material price is $200. Combined, the originating share accounts for 87.5%, equal to the value calculated in the analogous business process calculation.

Label	Origin. Value	Non-Origin. Value	Total	% Share of Total Costs
Components	75,00	25,00	100,00	50,000
Production Costs	100,00		100,00	50,000
Net Costs	175,00	25,00	200,00	
Non-Originating Share in %		12,500		
Originating Share (RVC) in %	87,500			
Currency	USD			

Figure 8.31 Regional Value Content Share (Top-Down)

The result of the preference determination is updated in the finished good's product master in SAP GTS.

Running a Bottom-Up Calculation on Gamma's Finished Product

Following the top-down calculation, Gamma performed a bottom-up calculation. The BOM calculation now starts at the bottom and works its way up.

The system first determines the preferential status for the subassembly, and then combines that information with the shoelace component to determine the finished product's preferential eligibility.

For the subassembly's preference determination, the system takes into account the BOM, as you can see in Figure 8.32, followed by a preference determination taking into account the BOM, as displayed in Figure 8.34. Finally, the result is shown in Figure 8.35.

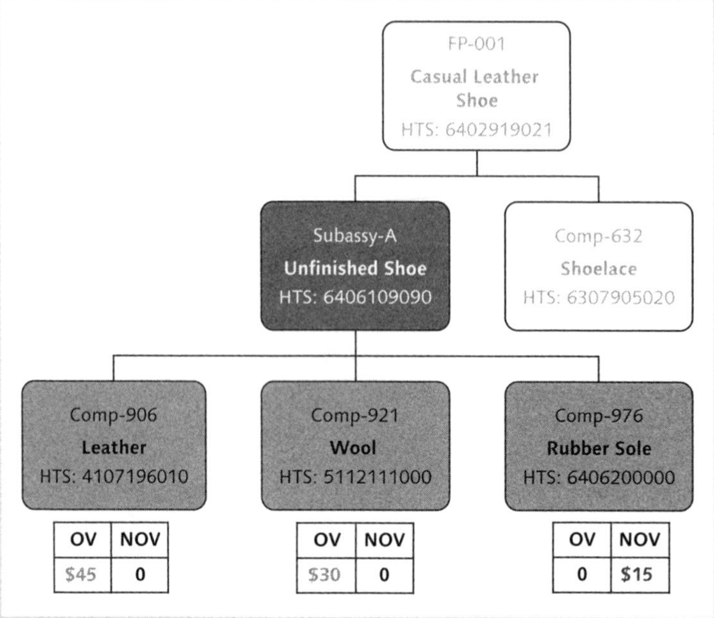

Figure 8.32 BOM Considered in the Bottom-Up Subassembly Determination

Apart from the CUSTOMS LOG tab at the top of Figure 8.30, which reveals the actual determination relevant to the finished product, the BOP LOG tab gives insight into the determination of each subassembly in the finished product's BOM.

Figure 8.33 shows this BOP tab for the bottom-up determination. As seen in the ASSEMBLIES section, two preference determinations were performed: first on the subassembly and second on the finished product. The rules of origin for the subassembly's tariff code also entail a net cost method of 55%. Because only $15 of the subassembly's total value ($120) is of non-originating value, the subassembly is eligible for preferential treatment. Thus, the whole subassembly is considered to be originating, including the previously non-originating $15 component.

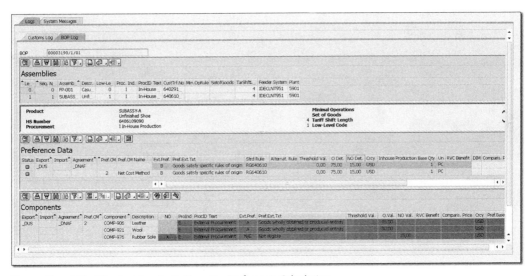

Figure 8.33 Bill of Product Log in Bottom-Up Preference Calculation

After determining the subassembly's eligibility, the system takes into account the BOM, as shown in Figure 8.34.

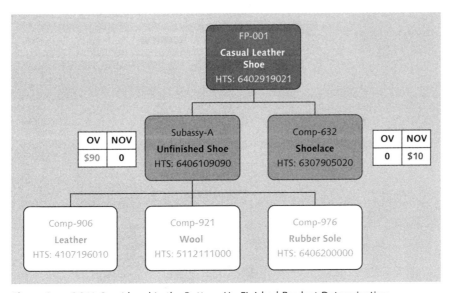

Figure 8.34 BOM Considered in the Bottom-Up Finished Product Determination

The result of the preference determination is displayed in Figure 8.35. Note that, as opposed to the result of Figure 8.28, which included all four components, only two products are considered in the preference determination: the subassembly and the shoelace component.

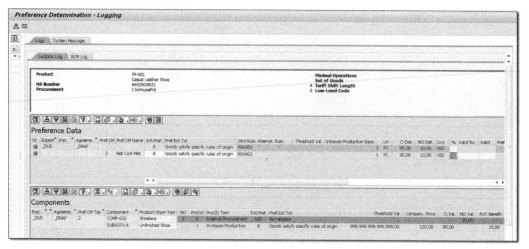

Figure 8.35 Preference Calculation Result (Bottom-Up)

The subassembly is used in the finished product's preference determination as consisting of $90 worth of originating components, as displayed in Figure 8.36, which is an enlarged image of the component section of Figure 8.35. By leveraging the bottom-up calculation method, you include the non-originating rubber sole component as originating value, resulting in a $15 regional value content (RVC) benefit.

Component	Product Short Text	NO	ProInd	Ext.Pref.	Pref.Ext.Txt	Threshold Val.	Comparis	O.Val.	NO Val.	RVC Benefit	Crcy
COMP-632	Shoelace	X	E	N/E	Not eligible				10,00		USD
SUBASSY-A	Unfinished Shoe		I	B	Goods satisfy spe	999.999.999.999.999,00-	120,00	90,00		15,00	USD

Figure 8.36 Components Log in the Preference Determination (Bottom-Up)

Finally, Figure 8.37 shows the originating share calculation for the finished product's net cost method. In total, 95% of the finished product's value is originating, well satisfying the net cost requirements.

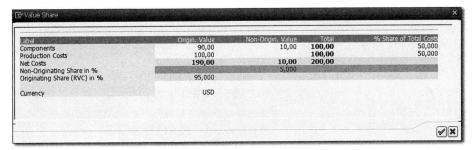

Figure 8.37 Regional Value Content Share (Bottom-Up)

Gamma Opts to Perform the Bottom-Up Determination

After Gamma investigated both the top-down and bottom-up calculations, it was apparent that either method resulted in a favorable preference eligibility. When Gamma runs the determination, the preference result is transferred to the SAP GTS product master shown in Figure 8.38.

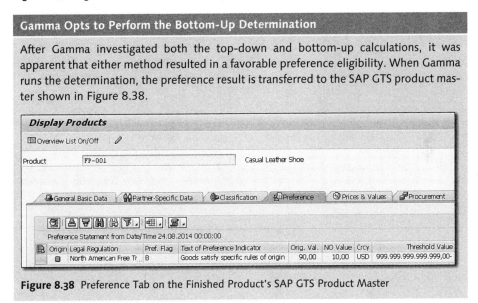

Figure 8.38 Preference Tab on the Finished Product's SAP GTS Product Master

Evaluating Preference Results

In the fifth step of the trade preference system process, the results from the preference determination are used in sales documents to determine the finished product's eligibility for preferential treatment.

Whenever a sales or billing document in the feeder system is created or changed, the system crosschecks the transaction price in the sales order or billing document with the preference threshold value set in SAP GTS. Note that, depending on the preference agreement, this might be the ex-works, FOB, or another price.

If the product is sold at a net price that exceeds the threshold value set in SAP GTS, the finished product is of preferential origin and eligible for preferential treatment.

SAP GTS provides management personnel with a standard transaction for evaluating the preference data from the company's products. You access this transaction through RISK MANAGEMENT • PREFERENCE PROCESSING — MASTER DATA • DISPLAY PREFERENCE DATA FOR PRODUCTS, and it is displayed in Figure 8.39.

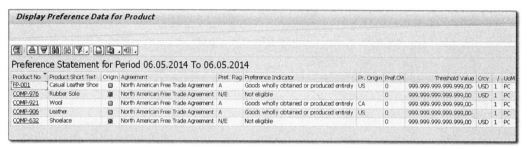

Figure 8.39 Evaluating a Product's Preference Results

Gamma Evaluates the Preference Data of its Products

Gamma's management decides to take a look into the preference results of its product, as displayed in Figure 8.39.

For Gamma's finished product, the product is of preferential origin in the NAFTA agreement, visualized with the green symbol and preferential indicator B. Note that SAP GTS sets the preferential country of origin for the finished product as the country of the AU performing the preference determination.

Furthermore, because the preferential origin is independent of the sales price, the threshold value is set at minus infinite: no matter how low the sales price of the finished product in the sales order or billing document goes, the product is always eligible for preferential treatment when shipping to NAFTA customers.

The next step for Gamma is to issue proof of origin to its customers when applicable, allowing the company to enjoy the benefits of the NAFTA free trade agreement.

Issuing Vendor Declarations

In addition to determining whether a product meets the rules of origin for a given FTA, the key component of claiming the preferential status upon importing the product into the country of destination is the actual proof of origin. This proof can vary depending on the agreement and country of destination. As such, proof of origin can be issued as a certificate of origin (official document) or statement of origin (e.g., on the supporting invoice).

These certificates or statements must be printed when the goods are sold from the country of departure. In SAP GTS, the process starts when an export declaration is generated in the Customs Management module as a result of the creation of a billing document in the feeder system. At that time, you determine the preferential origin of the product by comparing the transaction sales price (ex-works or FOB) against the preferential threshold value.

Because of the integration between the SAP GTS Risk Management and Customs Management modules, the certificates of origin can be printed alongside other export documentation. Note that the printing process may also be performed in the feeder system.

Figure 8.40 shows the PREFERENCE tab on the item level in the customs export declaration, which compares the transaction sales price (EXW or FOB) from the feeder system's billing document against the SAP GTS preference threshold value. Note that you need to configure the PREFERENCE tab on customs declarations in SAP GTS. When an authorized preference status is assigned, a certificate of origin can be printed and issued to the specific customer.

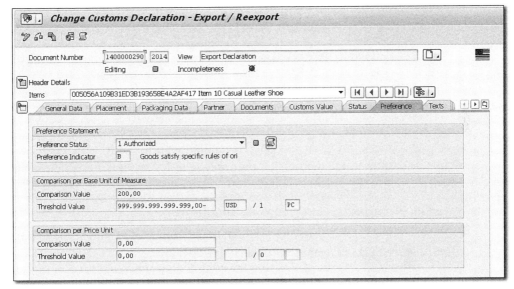

Figure 8.40 Preference Tab on the Export Declaration in the Customs Management Module

If proof of origin is issued as a blanket certificate (e.g., as done with NAFTA) and, thus, not on a transactional basis, you can issue the proof as an LTVD for the customer's purposes in the SAP GTS Risk Management module. The main advantage of issuing proof of origin via the Risk Management module is the capability to monitor all issued LTVDs. As such, if a blanket period expires or a BOM's preferential status changes after a newly performed calculation, the system detects which LTVDs are to be revoked or re-issued.

The administration steps for issuing, monitoring, and revoking LTVDs for the customer's purposes is done in MANAGE VENDOR DECLARATIONS FOR CUSTOMER'S PURPOSE pane of the preference processing menu, displayed in Figure 8.41.

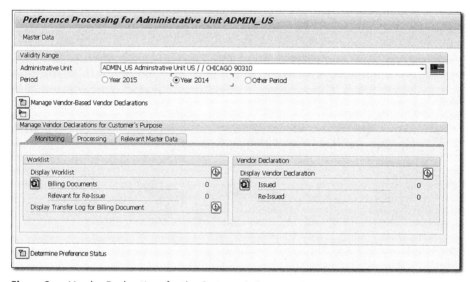

Figure 8.41 Vendor Declarations for the Customer's Purposes Menu

In the left worklist of Figure 8.41, all relevant billing documents from the feeder system are captured for monitoring purposes. The following criteria determine whether a billing document is relevant:

▶ The supplying plant is assigned to the specific AU.

▶ The customer is located in one of the member countries of one of the preferential agreements relevant to the specific AU.

▶ The customer is relevant to issuing vendor declarations. Like requesting vendor declarations, customers can be manually flagged in SAP GTS as not relevant for issuing certificates of origin.

If these conditions are met, the creation of a billing document in the feeder system generates an entry in the worklist.

Whenever a company wants to issue LTVDs to its customers, you can check the worklist. For all entries proposed in the worklist, customers can be issued an LTVD, either claiming preferential status or reporting non-preferential status. Because LTVDs cannot be effectively sent out from the worklist, you need to perform a different transaction accessed via RISK MANAGEMENT • PREFERENCE PROCESSING • MANAGE VENDOR DECLARATIONS FOR CUSTOMER'S PURPOSE • PROCESSING • ISSUE VENDOR DECLARATION.

If a finished product qualifies only when the sales price exceeds a calculated threshold value, the system presumes a worst-case scenario. At the moment of issuing, all billing documents for that vendor-product combination are compared to the threshold value calculated in the preference determination. If all prices exceed the threshold, a positive LTVD is issued. If one of the billing documents reports a price below the threshold, a negative LTVD is issued.

Gamma Issues Blanket Certificates to Its Customers

After performing the preference determination for its finished product, Gamma received a number of sales orders from its customers in Canada and Germany. As suspected, only the Canadian importers are able to benefit from the NAFTA agreement.

Figure 8.42 displays the worklist for issuing LTVDs for customer purposes and contains three entries for different Canadian customers.

Display Worklist: Long-Term Vendor Declaration for Customer's Purpose

Administrative unit ADMIN_US / time period starting at 01.01.2014

Ext. BP	Partner Description	Name of Pa	Product No	Product Short Text	Ref. No.	Item	Ref. Date
485	Customer Canada / Vancouve	Ship-to Party	FP-001	Casual Leather Shoe	90038401	10	29.04.2014
490	Demo Customer Canada / Montreal				90038402	10	
14444	Company Canada / Vancouver B0C 0A9				90038403	10	

Figure 8.42 Worklist Containing LTVDs for the Customer's Purposes

To effectively send out the LTVDs, Gamma needs to access the Issue Vendor Declaration transaction, which automatically detects the LTVDs that are relevant to be sent out. This results in the screen displayed in Figure 8.43. Upon saving, the LTVDs are printed, ready to be sent to the customers. Because the LTVDs specify that Gamma's finished product is eligible for preferential treatment, Gamma's objective of allowing its customers to benefit from the NAFTA agreement has been achieved, which may significantly increase Gamma's market attractiveness as a vendor of high-end leather shoes.

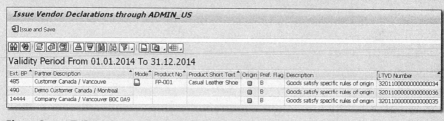

Figure 8.43 LTVDs to Be Sent to the Relevant Customers

Revoking and Re-Issuing Vendor Declarations

If a finished product's preferential status changes during an issued LTVD's blanket period, the issued LTVD becomes invalid. As such, you need to inform customers that the finished product is no longer eligible for preferential treatment. SAP GTS is able to revoke inaccurate vendor declarations and re-issue them with the updated information.

You need to perform the preference determination on finished products on a periodic basis (e.g., once a year), as well as whenever the finished product undergoes significant changes (e.g., changes in the BOM's structure or components with a changing preferential status).

As such, it is possible that a finished product for which an LTVD has been sent out with a preferential (or non-preferential) status is later assigned a different status due to a new result in the preference determination. Such a scenario might be the result of the following events:

- Changes in the finished product's BOM
- Changes in component material prices

▶ A different sourcing strategy, resulting in non-originating sourced components

▶ Creation of a billing document that reports a price below the threshold value calculated by the finished product's preference determination

If such a situation occurs, SAP GTS automatically creates an entry in the LTVD for the customer's purposes worklist and flags the LTVDs sent out to customers for that finished product as relevant for re-issuing.

As with printing the LTVDs for the customer's purposes, you need to access a different transaction to re-issue the LTVDs because this cannot be performed directly from the worklist. The transaction to re-issue LTVDs is accessed via RISK MANAGEMENT • PREFERENCE PROCESSING • MANAGE VENDOR DECLARATIONS FOR CUSTOMER'S PURPOSE • PROCESSING • RE-ISSUE VENDOR DECLARATION.

Loss of Preferential Status for Gamma Vendor

After Gamma performed the preference determination for its finished product and issued positive LTVDs to its customers, it received new LTVDs from its vendors in Canada and the United States stating that their wool and leather products were no longer of preferential origin.

Gamma updates the origin-related information in the worklist containing the maintained LTVDs and performs the preference determination again. As such, Figure 8.44 displays the BOM used in the new preference determination.

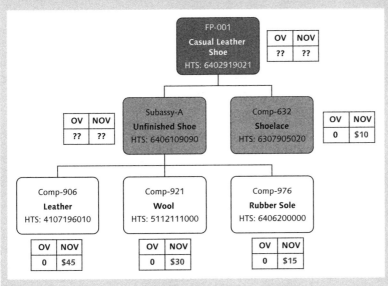

Figure 8.44 Finished Product's BOM after New Vendor LTVDs

Neither the top-down nor bottom-up explosion results in a favorable preference result. Because the finished product contains $100 worth of non-originating components and $100 worth of originating manufacturing costs, the RVC is set at 50%—below the required 55% stated in the rules of origin.

As such, Gamma needs to revoke the LTVDs that were sent out to their customers to inform them that the finished product is no longer eligible for preferential treatment. By refreshing the worklist displayed in Figure 8.45, Gamma notices that some of their issued LTVDs must be reissued.

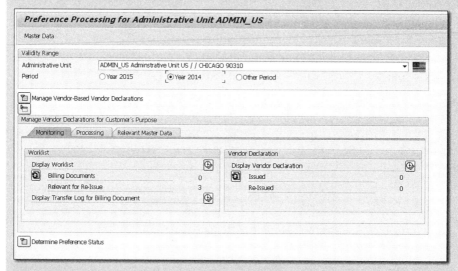

Figure 8.45 Worklist for Managing Vendor Declarations for the Customer's Purposes

By accessing the dedicated transaction to re-issue the LTVDs, SAP GTS detects the three LTVDs that were previously sent out with a positive preferential status, displayed in Figure 8.46. The ISSUE AND SAVE button triggers the LTVDs to be revoked and new LTVDs to be printed with updated information, alongside a cover letter explaining to Gamma's customers the change in its finished product's preferential status.

Status	Ext.	Partner Description	Product	Product Short Text	Orig. (Old)	Description	LTVD Number	Year	Origin	Description
	485	Customer Canada / Vancouve	FP-001	Casual Leather Shoe		Checked: OK	32011000000000000037	2014		Checked: Not OK
	490	Demo Customer Canada / Montreal				Checked: OK	32011000000000000039			Checked: Not OK
	14444	Company Canada / Vancouver BOC 0				Checked: OK	32011000000000000038			Checked: Not OK

Re-Issue Vendor Declarations Through ADMIN_US

Issue and Save

Key Date 18.04.2014

Figure 8.46 Re-Issuing Vendor Declarations

8.1.3   Customizing

Let's take a look at the Customizing steps necessary for leveraging SAP GTS to automate a company's Trade Preference Management, including the following topics:

- Organizational structure
- Legal regulations
- Rules of origin
- Feeder system plug-in

The Customizing activities for configuring trade preference functionalities follows the SAP GTS logic, whereby general activities (e.g., defining legal regulations) are grouped in the GLOBAL TRADE SERVICES • GENERAL SETTINGS menu while others are addressed in the specific section under GLOBAL TRADE SERVICES • RISK MANAGEMENT • PREFERENCE PROCESSING.

Organizational Structure

Recall from Chapter 3 and the start of Section 8.1.2 that additional organizational structure elements are needed in the SAP GTS Trade Preference Management functionality—more specifically, *administrative units*. An AU is not a physical representation of a company; it simply represents a plant or a group of plants as a single point of contact for all the administration related to Trade Preference Management.

Like the settings for FTOs and LUs (refer to Chapter 3), a plant group can be assigned to one AU. Such a setup is known as a cross-plant preference model. The advantage of such a preference model is that the preference administration of multiple plants can be grouped. Concretely, this means that, if several plants procure a specific component from the same vendor, an LTVD needs to be requested and maintained only once for all plants assigned to the plant group. For products produced in multiple plants of the plant group, a preference determination needs to be run only once. This calculation is valid for all plants in which the good is manufactured. Finally, if a customer sources the same finished product from multiple plants, a certificate of origin needs to be issued only once if these plants are grouped in the same plant group. The downside of this preference model is that sourcing non-originating components in one plant affects the other parts of the plant group.

As opposed to the cross-plant preference model, a plant-based preference model entails only a single plant being linked to an AU. For such a preference model, you need to perform the vendor solicitation, preference determination, and issuing of certificates for each plant individually.

The latter preference model may require significantly more administration efforts from the company's users but offers a higher degree of flexibility and accuracy in the preference determination because the various steps are performed for each plant individually.

Before defining AUs, you have to define the BOM evaluation method for the relevant plants. If you apply a plant-based model, thus creating a one-to-one relationship between plant and AU, you need to define the feeder system's plants for which this preference model is applied in GLOBAL TRADE SERVICES • GENERAL SETTINGS • ORGANIZATIONAL STRUCTURE • DEFINE PLANT-BASED BOM EVALUATION.

The plants that are to be grouped in a plant group to apply a cross-plant based BOM evaluation method are defined in GLOBAL TRADE SERVICES • GENERAL SETTINGS • ORGANIZATIONAL STRUCTURE • DEFINE CROSS-PLANT BOM EVALUATION.

The AUs are created via either GLOBAL TRADE SERVICES • RISK MANAGEMENT • PREFERENCE PROCESSING • ORGANIZATIONAL STRUCTURE • DEFINE ADMINISTRATIVE UNITS FOR VENDOR DECLARATIONS or the standard business partner transaction. AUs are created as business partners with the specific business partner role SLLMGR. The country of the AU determines which FTAs are relevant to the assigned plant or plant group.

Once created, AU characteristics must be assigned. You access this via GLOBAL TRADE SERVICES • RISK MANAGEMENT • PREFERENCE PROCESSING • ORGANIZATIONAL STRUCTURE • DEFINE ADMINISTRATIVE UNITS ATTRIBUTES. For each AU, you need to assign either a plant or plant group, determining the preference model that is applied, as displayed in Figure 8.47.

Next, you need to assign a currency and exchange rate type. The currency you specify is used in all preference calculations. If a BOM contains elements expressed in a different currency, the conversion is performed based on the specified exchange rate type.

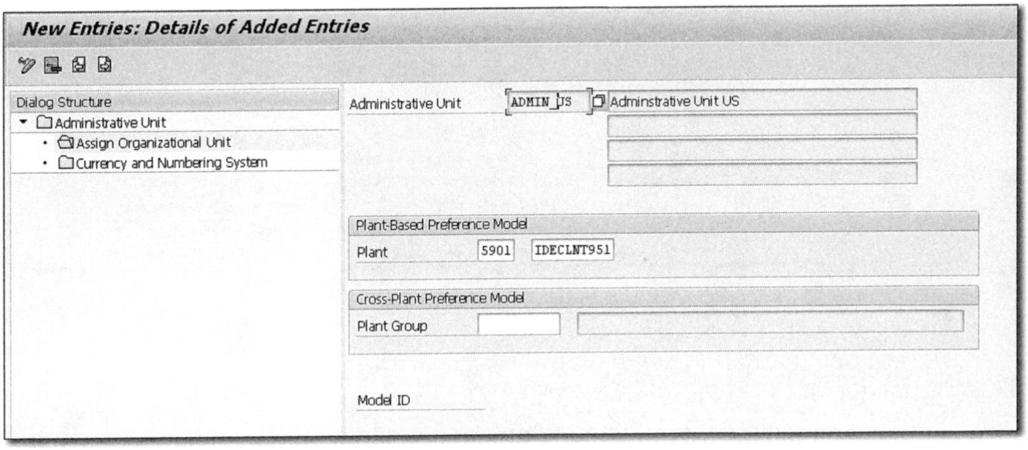

Figure 8.47 Administrative Unit Characteristics

Finally, assign a numbering scheme to the AU that will be used in all preference determinations performed for that AU. You can also choose to configure the numbering scheme based on the preference agreement. By choosing the latter, you can use multiple numbering schemes for the preference determination within one AU.

Legal Regulations

Preference agreements are created as legal regulations under the general settings menu, which includes all regulations for the three SAP GTS modules, accessed via GLOBAL TRADE SERVICES • GENERAL SETTINGS • LEGAL REGULATIONS • DEFINE LEGAL REGULATION. The preference agreements are assigned a specific PREFERENCE LAW legal regulation code, as displayed for the NAFTA and PANEG agreements in Figure 8.48.

As with the Compliance and Customs Management-related legal regulations, you need to activate trade preference-related regulations at the country-group level in both the general settings menu and the Risk Management-specific menu.

Rules of Origin

Rules of origin, or preference rules, are a quintessential aspect of preference agreements. They describe the terms according to which goods can be determined as eligible for preferential treatment.

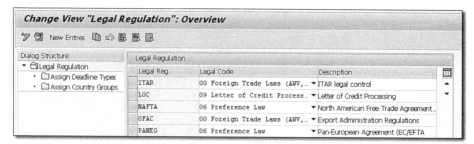

Figure 8.48 Define Preference Agreements as Legal Regulations

You can upload these preference rules either via XML files or by manually maintaining them via Customizing. The XML files consist of all the rules of origin and can be purchased from certain content providers, which is the recommended approach for loading rules of origin in SAP GTS. The transaction to upload such an XML file is accessed via RISK MANAGEMENT • PREFERENCE PROCESSING—MASTER DATA • AGREEMENT RELATED DATA • UPLOAD RULES FROM XML FILES.

In the manual process, you need to enter preference rules via several Customizing steps. Depending on the number and complexity of rules, this can be a very time-consuming process. This procedure is not recommended because the risk of errors in setting up the different rules may impact the trade preference determination results and eventually result in non-compliance.

The following sections describe at a high level the various steps you need to consider when manually setting up preference rules.

Rule Set

A *rule set* is the grouping of all preference rules assigned to a preferential agreement, and it is linked to a numbering scheme based on the configuration of the AU or the preferential agreement itself. You can set up the rule set definition via GLOBAL TRADE SERVICES • RISK MANAGEMENT • PREFERENCE PROCESSING • DEFINE RULE SET.

If you upload rules of origin via XML files, the rule set is added to the system automatically. In the subsequent Customizing step, the preference legal regulations are to be assigned to a specific rules set via GLOBAL TRADE SERVICES • RISK MANAGEMENT • PREFERENCE PROCESSING • ASSIGN PREFERENCE AGREEMENT TO RULE SET.

Procedures

In the first versions of SAP GTS, all calculation or comparison methods in the system were based on the rules of origin applicable to the EU and NAFTA agreement. As of SAP GTS 10.1, two new comparison methods were introduced: the build-up and build-down methods discussed in Section 8.1.1. These comparison methods were necessary to automate calculations for, among others, the ASEAN and CAFTA agreements.

From a system perspective, SAP GTS preference determinations are based on the rules of origin applicable to the EU and United States. Nonetheless, the system provides the required Customizing and framework capabilities to cover other preferential trade agreements.

There are six preference rule procedures within the EU-based concept:

▶ Third country
▶ 50:50 check
▶ Heading change
▶ No heading change
▶ HS heading
▶ Conditions

The first two procedures are based on a percentage of non-preferential components, the next three are based on the component's specific classification codes, and the last one is based on operations and conditions expressed as a text description. NAFTA-based procedures follow a similar approach, but with their own specific procedures.

You can define the procedures via the Customizing path GLOBAL TRADE SERVICES • RISK MANAGEMENT • PREFERENCE PROCESSING • DEFINE PROCEDURE FOR RULE SETS WITH EU/NAFTA-BASED CONCEPT.

Define Preference Rules—Group Together Procedures

In the next step, you maintain the rules themselves via GLOBAL TRADE SERVICES • RISK MANAGEMENT • PREFERENCE PROCESSING • DEFINE PREFERENCE RULES—GROUP TOGETHER PROCEDURES. When you are manually entering the rules of origin applicable to Gamma's finished product (see Figure 8.26), you need to enter one procedure group to represent the standard rule. The group consists of four procedures, combined via an AND statement.

You can create additional conditions via GLOBAL TRADE SERVICES • RISK MANAGEMENT • PREFERENCE PROCESSING • DEFINE CONDITIONS. You can then add these text conditions to a procedure to represent a certain condition a finished product must meet to be eligible for preferential treatment.

Furthermore, to capture the hierarchical structure of preference rules, procedure groups can be contained in rule groups. This means that, for instance, you can allow two OR procedures to be captured within a higher level AND procedure. Linking procedures to rule groups is performed via GLOBAL TRADE SERVICES • RISK MANAGEMENT • PREFERENCE PROCESSING • DEFINE PREFERENCE RULES—LINK RULE GROUPS.

Assign Rules to Agreement and Classification

Finally, the procedure and rule groups are assigned to a specific classification code as primary or alternative rules. Agreement base rules and classification code-specific rules are to be assigned, respectively, in GLOBAL TRADE SERVICES • RISK MANAGEMENT • PREFERENCE PROCESSING • ASSIGN BASE RULES TO AN AGREEMENT and ASSIGN RULES TO AGREEMENT AND CLASSIFICATION.

Feeder System Plug-In

As prerequisite for applying Trade Preference Management, you need to flag the required document types as relevant for Risk Management in the feeder system plug-in. This entails purchasing and material document types to trigger the worklist for requesting LTVDs and billing documents to trigger the issuing of LTVDs.

Furthermore, in the feeder system's plug-in, use a specific transaction to set up the BOM transfer to SAP GTS via SAP GLOBAL TRADE SERVICES—PLUG-IN • CONTROL DATA FOR TRANSFER TO SAP GLOBAL TRADE SERVICES • CONTROL TRANSFER OF BILLS OF PRODUCT FOR PREFERENCE AND RE-EXPORT. The BOM transfer settings can be defined on three hierarchical levels: global, country, and plant.

You can split the settings for BOM transfers initially between those concerning static BOMs and those concerning configurable BOMs. For a specific BOM application, you can configure a preference model (plant-based or cross-plant model) and BOM explosion type (top-down or bottom-up), as shown in Figure 8.49.

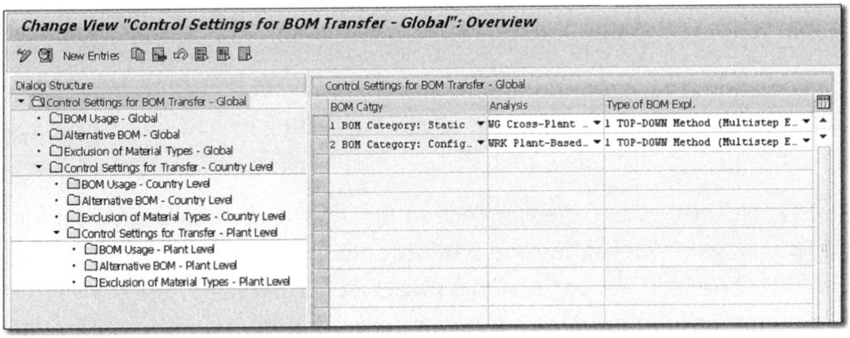

Figure 8.49 BOM Control Settings at the Country Level

8.1.4 Master Data

This section describes the master data elements required for Trade Preference Management, including master data related to the following:

- Materials
- Organizational structure elements
- Vendors/customers

Next, we'll elaborate further on each of the required master data elements.

Materials

Evidently, master data concerning materials needs to be transferred from the feeder system to SAP GTS. This includes transferring the following:

- Materials
- Procurement indicators
- Bills of material (BOMs)
- Standard cost of materials

Initially, all finished products, components, and BOMs used in the trade preference process must be transferred from the feeder system to SAP GTS.

In order for SAP GTS to either request an LTVD or perform a preference determination for a certain material, it must transfer the material's procurement indicators. This means that SAP GTS requests LTVDs only for components that are externally procured.

As first described in Section 8.1.1, the BOM is part of performing the preference determination, so you need to transfer the BOM structures for all subassemblies produced in house, as well as finished products. Finally, you need to transfer the materials standard costs to SAP GTS for use as originating or non-originating values in the preference determination.

As we discussed in the final step of Section 8.1.2, you need to run preference determinations again when a finished product undergoes changes due to a changing BOM structure, component material prices, or something else. To keep this information accurate, you can sync BOMs, material prices, and other master data between the feeder system and SAP GTS via change pointers. To ensure compliance, put a process in place to ensure that the preference determination results are always up to date and accurate.

You transfer this master data in the SAP GTS user menu within the feeder system under the tab INITIAL TRANSFER OF MASTER DATA • SAP RISK MANAGEMENT • TRANSFER MATERIAL MASTERS/TRANSFER BOMS/DETERMINE PROCUREMENT INDICATORS AND INITIAL TRANSFER/DETERMINE MATERIAL PRICES AND INITIAL TRANSFER.

You must classify all products managed in the preference module according to the applicable classification schemes (Combined Nomenclature/TARIC in Europe, HTS) because the rules of origin are defined for and linked to these classification schemes.

Vendors/Customers

For the trade preference inbound process, purchase orders and material documents are captured in the worklist for requesting LTVDs. Entries in the applicable worklist entail vendor-product combinations for which you can initiate the vendor solicitation process.

As with the worklist for requesting LTVDs, a similar worklist for issuing LTVDs for the customer's purposes is available. This worklist captures all outbound billing documents for the relevant products and countries, including customer-product combinations stating which LTVDs are relevant to be issued, as discussed in Section 8.1.2.

For these processes to function, you must transfer both vendors and customers from the feeder system.

Note that it is possible to flag vendors and customers as irrelevant for requesting or issuing LTVDs. The outcome is that these vendors and customers are not captured in the respective worklists.

You access the transaction to mark vendors as irrelevant for LTVD requests via Risk Management • Manage Vendor-Based Vendor Declarations • Relevant Master Data • Assign Vendor, and it is displayed in Figure 8.50. A similar transaction is available in Manage Vendor Declarations for Customer's Purpose, to set customers as irrelevant for issuing LTVDs.

Assign Vendors to Administrative Unit

For. Trade Org.:	Administrative Unit	ADMIN_US		Administrative Unit US			
Administrative Unit	Vendor	External Vendor Number	Vendor Name	Rele...	Relevance of Partner for LTVDs	Cor...	Mode of Long-Term Vendor D...
ADMIN_US	311	2410	Vendor Ivory Coast	◼◯◯ X		☐	
ADMIN_US	312	2420	Vendor Indonesia	◯◯◼		☐	
ADMIN_US	313	2430	Vendor Brazil	◯◯◼		☐	
ADMIN_US	314	2440	Vendor New Zealand	◼◯◯ X		☐	
ADMIN_US	315	2450	Vendor France	◯◯◼		☐	
ADMIN_US	316	2460	Vendor Turkey	◼◯◯ X		☐	
ADMIN_US	317	2470	Vendor China	◯◯◼		☐	

Figure 8.50 Marking Vendors as Irrelevant for LTVD Requests

The first subchapter of the SAP GTS Risk Management module covered the Trade Preference Management functionality that serves the objective of issuing proof of origin to customers stating that the sold product may be imported under the preferential treatment of a free trade agreement.

By proving the preferential origin of the sold products according to the FTA's rules of origin, customers may import the goods with a reduced or zero duty rate. Being able to issue proof of origin to customers may significantly increase a company's market competitiveness.

SAP GTS supports the Trade Preference Management functionality with seven system process steps, extensively discussed and exemplified by means of a business case.

In the following subchapters, we'll turn our attention to the Restitution Management and Letter of Credit Processing functionalities in SAP GTS.

8.2   Restitution Management

While the previous subchapter reviewed the reduction of imposed import tariffs for a company's customers by leveraging preference agreements, Restitution Management deals with claiming export funds. More specifically, Restitution Management covers the EU-specific topic of recovering export subsidies a company might be entitled to when exporting agricultural products.

The European Union introduced the Common Agricultural Policy (CAP) after World War II as a program to ensure stable and secure food supplies in Europe at reasonable prices for consumers, as well as an acceptable standard of living for European farmers by securing their income.

Over the years, the CAP implemented a range of supporting policies for the agricultural industry. To stimulate agricultural productivity, Europe provided subsidies for the amount of output produced, but this ultimately resulted in huge surpluses that had to be sold on third-country markets, where prices were lower than in the European market.

To support the export of agricultural products with the objective of closing the gap between EU prices and production costs with third-country prices, export refunds were provided. These refunds are called *restitutions*, and they are the focus of this SAP GTS subchapter.

The CAP's restitution policy has been heavily debated because the restitutions gained from exporting agricultural products cause disturbances in global markets. Because developing countries often rely on their agricultural industry, they are harmed by European companies who may claim restitutions when exporting to developing countries.

Although the system is still in place, support for restitutions has been reduced to zero over the years as a result of international pressure. Nonetheless, the policy might be leveraged again by increasing the restitution rates when the agricultural industry is in need of financial support.

Restitution Management is a process that requires correct and timely documentation and can be tedious if not automated or supported by a system. Furthermore, if companies are not fully compliant with the predetermined requirements, they risk fines. Because the agriculture industry is a high-volume business, the sum of many smaller restitution amounts may result in a significant total refund amount.

SAP GTS supports the various steps required for claiming export restitutions. Using the same structure as the last subsection on Trade Preference Management, this Risk Management subchapter will employ a business case to discuss the business and system process and elaborate on the relevant master data and Customizing steps.

In this business case, we'll make the assumption that it is possible to claim restitutions for exported products, although the restitution rates are currently reduced to zero.

Delta's Global Trade Requirements

Delta is an agricultural company in Belgium. Its main activities consist of producing and shipping all sorts of pasta products. The products it uses in the production process are all procured from domestic vendors.

Although Europe is Delta's main consumer market, it frequently has surplus stock that it exports to non-EU countries, such as Russia, as displayed in Figure 8.51.

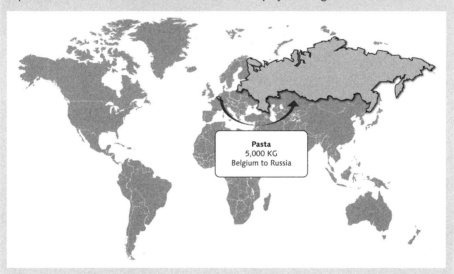

Pasta
5,000 KG
Belgium to Russia

Figure 8.51 Delta's Export to Russia

Under the CAP, Delta recognizes that its pasta products contain basic products eligible for export refunds and investigates which requirements and procedures it must address in order to claim restitutions.

8.2.1 Business Process

In order to complete the process of claiming export refunds, a company may need to fulfill certain prerequisites before shipping and meet multiple requirements during shipping.

Figure 8.52 displays the Restitution Management business process, which has three steps. First, the company needs to communicate with the customs authorities to obtain the required licenses for the agricultural products the company is exporting.

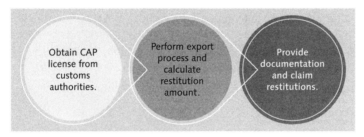

Figure 8.52 Restitution Management Business Process

Once the company has obtained the licenses, the actual export process takes place: products are sold and shipped to a non-EU customer. Depending on the requirements of the specific customs authorities, the restitution may be claimed either when the exported goods leave the customs territory or when the shipment has arrived in the country of destination.

If the latter requirement is fulfilled, the actual export refunds may be claimed, which is the last step of the business process. The appropriate documentation, such as proof of export, valid licenses, and so on, is to be sent to the customs authorities, and then the calculated restitutions may be claimed. In this respect, the T5 customs form is a significant document because it provides proof that the goods left the EU.

In some cases, such as exporting low volumes of agricultural goods consisting of a low total weight or exporting for humanitarian reasons, a company might claim export refunds without needing an export license. However, because the agricultural industry is typified by high-volume shipments, European companies wanting to claim export refunds for agricultural products usually require a CAP license.

The granting of a CAP license from the applicable national customs authorities depends on several aspects, such as the product type, weight, value, country of destination, and a minimum quantity that needs to be shipped in a given timeframe. Further requirements for restitution eligibility are determined based on the required documentation and imposed time limits to submit that documentation. For this reason, claiming refunds when shipping to a particular country might require documented proof that the exported goods have *left* the customs territory, while a different country of destination may require proof that the goods have actually *arrived* in that country.

When you request a CAP license, you negotiate an agreement with the customs authorities either to export a limited quantity of a CAP product or set a maximum refund quantity that may be claimed by exporting products eligible for restitutions. CAP licenses are issued with a limited timeframe, implying that the quantity or value on the license should be fully written off by the end of the license validity period. To ensure that companies are compliant with what has been determined in the CAP license, the requesting party is required to set up a security to cover the CAP license.

Whenever you export restitution-relevant goods, you need to assign a valid CAP license to the shipment. The CAP license is then depreciated with the value or quantity of the exported goods, and part of the security is released at the moment the goods exit the EU (or in certain cases, when they arrive at the country of destination). If, however, a company is not compliant with the predetermined rules or does not export the required quantity in the license's validity period, a part of or the entire security may be forfeited to the authorities.

Furthermore, an exception of the standard business process as displayed in Figure 8.52 may be made by allowing advance refunds. Because exporting products to third countries at a market price lower than that in the EU significantly affects a company's cash flow, the CAP policy allows advance payment of the refunds in certain scenarios. In such cases, companies may claim restitutions before the goods have left the customs territory.

Advance payment of restitutions requires the exporting party to set up a security for the amount of 110% of the advanced export refunds. If the shipment does not fulfill the predetermined requirements, customs authorities may claim part of or the entire security amount. This may be the case, for instance, if not all materials arrive in the country of destination. Another possible cause is that the materials have been damaged during the shipment and are no longer of a fair and marketable quality.

For restitution purposes, we distinguish between two types of agricultural goods: basic (or Annex I) products and processed (or non-Annex I) products.

▶ **Annex I products**
Annex I products are all *basic products* originating from the agricultural sector. This includes meat, sugar, cereals, eggs, rice, fruits, vegetables, and dairy products.

Annex I products are usually directly given a specific restitution rate defined per basic product. The restitution amount equals the total weight of the Annex I product multiplied by the restitution rate, in Euros, per 100 kg.

However, in some cases, Annex I products may contain components not eligible for restitutions. In such cases, the Annex I product may be assigned a recipe to determine the amount of eligible components in the Annex I product.

▶ **Non-Annex I products**
Non-Annex I products, or *processed agricultural products* (PAPs), are products resulting from processing Annex-I products. PAPs cover a wide range of processed goods, including processed dairy products, beverages, prepared foods and sauces, and many more.

There is no single rate for Non-Annex I products to calculate the restitution amount. The basis for the calculation is the recipe linked to the final product. The restitution amount can be calculated based on the recipe that stipulates the various basic products contained in the processed good.

Although the CAP applies to only Annex I products, many exported processed goods contain significant quantities of agricultural basic products. So, you can claim export refunds for Non-Annex I goods, as well, by receiving the restitution amount of all basic products contained in the finished product.

To know which exported products are eligible for restitution purposes, classify products using a 12-digit code (the eight-digit combined nomenclature and a four-digit CAP restitution code).

When you request a license for exporting Annex I goods, providing the appropriate CAP classification code is sufficient. However, when you export processed Non-Annex I goods, customs authorities require the recipe of that product, which details the basic products eligible for export refunds that are contained in the finished product. For that given recipe, customs authorities may provide a recipe code to be used on export documents, which they can then refer to when calculating the restitution amount, to facilitate the process.

The process of maintaining CAP licenses and securities with their remaining value, quantities, and validity dates; tracking shipments; and filing the required documentation on time can be a daunting task when it is not automated or properly supported by an appropriate system. We'll discuss the SAP GTS system process to support restitution processes in the next section.

Delta's Restitution Process

Because Delta exports Non-Annex I goods to a non-EU country, it was informed that it should request a CAP license to claim export refunds for the basic agricultural products used to produce the finished product.

Figure 8.53 displays Delta's restitution business process. First, it needs to contact the local Belgian customs authorities. It will request an export CAP license to export its finished product and claim export refunds for the basic agricultural products contained in the finished product.

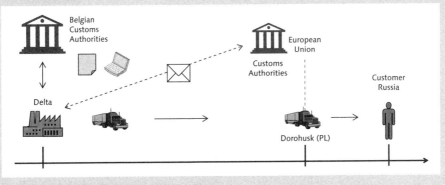

Figure 8.53 Delta's Restitution Business Process

To receive the export license, Delta must provide the customs authorities with the recipe showing the basic products contained in the finished product and their corresponding CAP classification codes.

Figure 8.54 displays the recipe Delta provides to the local customs authorities. It states that 100 kg of pasta contains 80 kg of flour and 15 kg of eggs; both are Annex I products originating in EU territory, so they are eligible for restitutions. Other products used to produce the pasta, such as water, salt, and herbs, are not included in the recipe because they are not eligible for restitutions.

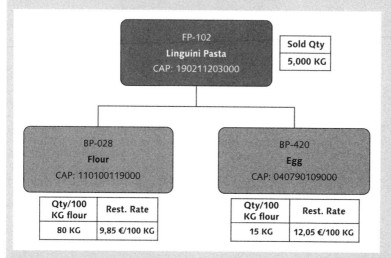

Figure 8.54 Recipe of Delta's Finished Product

At this stage, the customs authorities may provide Delta with a recipe code that can be used on their export declarations to facilitate the process of claiming restitution amounts.

With this information, customs authorities issue a CAP license to Delta, which sets up a security with its local bank to cover the amount stated on the license.

The customs authorities determine that documented proof of the goods leaving the customs territory (the T5 customs form) is sufficient for Delta to claim the export refunds. Thus, when Delta exports its pasta product, it receives a confirmation from the customs office in Dorohusk, Poland when the goods have left the European territory. At that point, Delta can provide the required documentation to the local customs authorities to claim the export refunds.

Figure 8.54 also displays the restitution rates applicable at the time of the refund claim. In total, almost €485 of restitutions can be claimed for that particular export. Because the agricultural industry is a high-volume sector, the sum of modest restitution amounts can result in a significant gain for company Delta. With the restitution claim granted, the shipped quantity is depreciated from the license.

8.2.2 System Process

You know that applying for restitutions entails several requirements before and during the export process. Let's look at the different system process steps in SAP GTS to support this business process. Figure 8.55 displays the link between the system and business process.

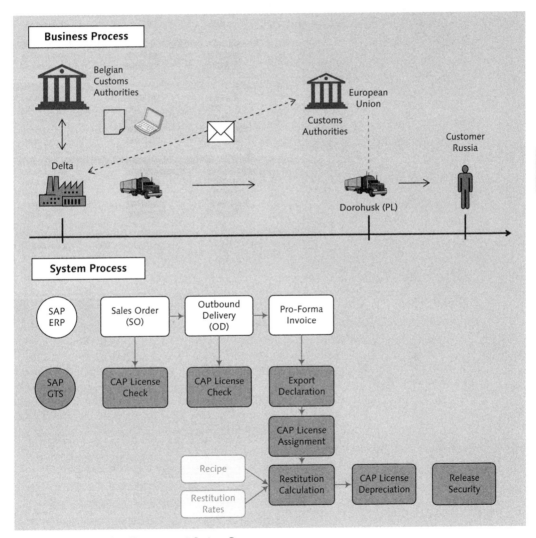

Figure 8.55 Restitution Management System Process

Besides restitution SAP GTS prerequisites such as BOM recipes and CAP licenses, which we'll discuss later in this section, the Restitution Management system process starts when a sales order is created in the feeder system. The sales order already contains information required for the restitution process, such as the specific product quantities and net weight of the items.

When transferred, a subsequent customs document is created in SAP GTS, and the items included in the document are screened for Restitution Management relevancy. A product or material inside a product's BOM can be eligible for restitution, given that it is assigned a valid CAP classification code, and a restitution rate exists for that CAP number and country of destination.

For each restitution-relevant product, the system checks whether a CAP license is required. These licenses are maintained as master data in SAP GTS, and we'll discuss them further in Section 8.2.4. If a license is required, you can assign it manually to the relevant product or configure the system so that SAP GTS automatically assigns the license to the customs document.

As far as licenses go, the SAP GTS Restitution Management module works similarly to Compliance Management, both in the way they are set up and how they are selected by means of a license determination strategy. If SAP GTS finds an adequate CAP license (or multiple, if allowed), then the values or quantities found in the customs document are written off the license.

If no license is assigned or SAP GTS does not find adequate licenses to cover the document, the document can either be blocked for further processing or generate a warning message without blocking users from further processing the document.

In the next step of creating the outbound delivery, you can repeat the license determination procedure or copy over the license from the sales order, depending on Customizing settings.

As discussed in Section 8.2.1, the following product categories can be eligible for restitution management:

▸ **Annex I basic products**
The basic, or Annex I, products are derived directly from the agricultural sector, including, among other things, sugar, meat, and eggs. For our business case, these are the flour and egg products.

SAP GTS determines the restitution amount for Annex I products by multiplying the weight retrieved in the SAP GTS customs document by the product's restitution rate. Note that SAP GTS always uses the net weight in calculating the restitution amount.

The applicable restitution rate is retrieved based on the following information:

▶ CAP classification code

▶ Country or country group of destination

▶ Date of export

Furthermore, in certain cases, Annex I products may consist of a recipe, meaning that they contain components not eligible for restitutions. As with processed products, the eligible components determine the restitution amount.

▶ **Non-Annex I processed products**

Processed, or Non-Annex I, products are goods that are obtained by processing the aforementioned basic products. For our business case, the pasta is a Non-Annex I product.

This category includes products such as sauces, food preparations, and beverages. For this category, you need to maintain recipes in SAP GTS and assign them to the finished product in order to determine which of the ingredients are relevant for restitution calculation. For more information regarding recipes, please refer to Section 8.2.4.

SAP GTS checks the finished product's assigned recipe, determines the restitution rate for each intermediate and basic product contained in the recipe, and calculates the restitution value for each component. The full restitution amount is then the sum of the calculated sub-values.

If the shipment's sales and delivery order are not blocked for further processing, you can create a pro-forma invoice in the feeder system. This pro-forma invoice (or any billing document activated for Restitution Service) is the most significant document in Restitution Management because it triggers the creation of an export declaration in SAP GTS, triggering the full restitution process. For more information on export declaration documents, please refer to Chapter 7 on Customs Management.

Once SAP GTS finds valid CAP licenses to cover the items in the customs declaration document, a restitution calculation takes place. This calculation is a crucial step in the restitution process because it is the basis for the amount of export refunds the company claims from the customs authorities.

The restitution calculation takes into account the item's net weight, relevant restitution rate, and, when applicable, the product's recipe. Finally, the CAP license is depreciated with the calculated restitution amount or item quantity, depending on which type of license applies.

SAP GTS also offers options for simulating the restitution calculation. Knowing the restitution amount up front may help companies accurately forecast the cash flows resulting from export refunds. The main difference with the actual calculation is that the calculated restitution amount cannot be saved and is, thus, not written to the database.

You have a choice between two types of restitution calculation simulations:

► **Restitution calculation simulation by product**
In this simulation type, you can create an export scenario by specifying the exported product, quantity, country of destination, and date. The system simulates what restitution amount could be claimed if such an export process takes place.

► **Restitution calculation simulation by customs document**
Once an SAP GTS shipment document is available, you can perform a simulation of the restitution calculation on it to have a clear view of the entitled export refunds.

The restitution process can be integrated with the export process in SAP GTS Customs Management. This way, you can use the export declaration for filing the required restitution documents with the customs authorities, as well.

When the export refunds have been claimed, the amount that was provided for the applicable CAP license may be released from the security. You access the transaction to release securities via the SAP GTS area menu RISK MANAGEMENT • RESTITUTION • RELEASE SECURITIES.

Supporting and Automating Delta's Export Restitution Process

Delta has been communicating with the Belgian customs authorities to find out what information is required for the CAP export license to ship its pasta products to Russia.

Because Delta is using SAP GTS to support its restitution process, it starts by maintaining the restitution rates published by European entities. Because it currently exports only the pasta products, the restitution rates for flour and egg are entered as shown in Figure 8.56.

Figure 8.56 Maintaining Flour and Egg Restitution Rates

The next step is for Delta to create the applicable recipes and assign them to the finished product. Figure 8.57 displays the recipe for Delta's pasta product, which is the system translation of Figure 8.54. The recipe specifies that 100 kg of the finished product contains 80 kg of product BP-028 (flour) and 15 kg of product BP-420 (egg), the products eligible for restitutions contained in the finished product.

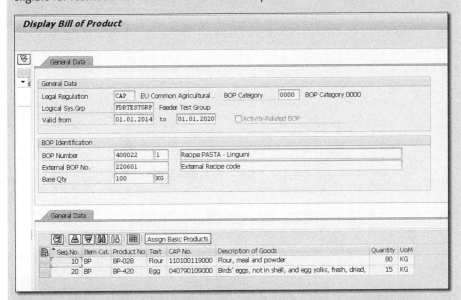

Figure 8.57 BOM Recipe for Delta's Pasta Product

Eventually, Delta receives the confirmation and external license number for a Non-Annex I license, specifying a restitution amount of €85,000, which it can eventually claim by exporting sufficient products.

Delta creates the license in SAP GTS, along with a security to cover the restitution amount specified on the license. Upon creation of the sales order in the feeder system, SAP GTS performs a license check and assigns the new CAP license. Because Delta can claim the export refunds only once the goods have left the customs territory, it runs a simulation on the sales order to calculate the eventual restitution amount to incorporate into its cash flow estimates.

Figure 8.58 displays the log of the restitution calculation. For the exported Non-Annex I product, it recognizes the BOM recipe assigned to the product, containing two products eligible for claiming export refunds.

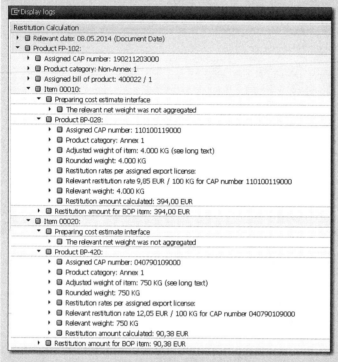

Figure 8.58 Simulation of Restitution Calculation

SAP GTS looks at the recipe, which states that 100 kg of the finished product contains 80 kg of product BP-028. As such, the total exported weight of the latter product is 4,000 kg. By multiplying the weight (4,000 kg) by the applicable restitution rate (€9.85/ 100 kg), you find that the calculated restitution amount that can be claimed is €394.

Like the previous calculation, the calculated restitution amount for product BP-420 is €90.38. Combined, Delta could claim export refunds in the amount of €484.38.

When the customs declaration is available in SAP GTS Customs Management, the Restitution tab on the item level states the amount of export refunds that may be claimed for the corresponding item, as displayed in Figure 8.59.

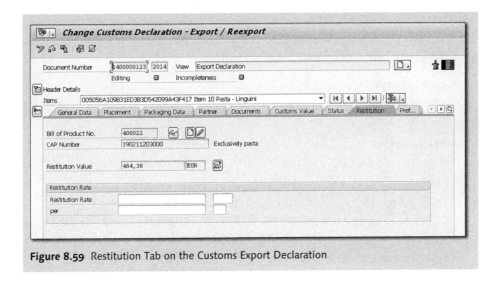

Figure 8.59 Restitution Tab on the Customs Export Declaration

8.2.3 Customizing

This section will provide a high-level overview of the Customizing steps necessary to set up the Restitution Management process in SAP GTS. As with Trade Preference Management, we assume the relevant document types have already been flagged for Risk Management in the feeder plug-in.

Define Numbering Scheme of CAP Numbers

You must assign CAP numbers to products that are eligible for restitution and consist of an eight-digit *combined nomenclature* (CN) code and an additional four-digit restitution code. Before maintaining the CAP numbers, you must define a numbering scheme within SAP GTS with a hierarchy structure that is compliant with customs requirements. The standard numbering scheme defined by SAP GTS for the CAP numbers is EU_CAP. Once you've configured the numbering scheme, you can either create the necessary CAP numbers manually or upload them into SAP GTS via XML files. The next step is to classify all restitution-relevant products.

Activate Restitution Service

To seamlessly integrate Restitution Management with the standard business export process, you'll need to activate a few things:

▶ **Document types**
You must activate the applicable sales, delivery, and billing document types for restitution processing.

▶ **Item categories**
You must activate the applicable item categories linked to the previously defined document types for restitution processing.

▶ **Legal regulations**
SAP GTS provides Common Agricultural Policy Restitution as a standard legal regulation relevant for restitution processing. This legal regulation must be activated for the relevant countries to enable the Restitution Management process.

Define Automatic Determination Procedure for Export License Types

A variety of determination procedures have been pre-defined in the standard SAP GTS solution. A determination procedure defines the system's logic for identifying applicable license types. This determination procedure is defined not only for Restitution Management processes, but also for license control purposes within Compliance Management.

Define Type of Recipe

SAP GTS applies recipes to identify the ingredients of a finished product eligible for restitution management. Recipes are maintained as BOPs in SAP GTS. When you're defining a type of recipe, one of two proportion types is available: the proportional value of eligible components in a recipe is specified as either a percentage portion or a quantity-based portion of the finished product.

Define Item Category of Recipe

Besides the recipes types, it is important to define recipe item categories to accurately map the item data in BOPs. The item data are the individual ingredients within the finished product. The following item categories have been pre-defined in the standard SAP GTS solution:

- Basic product (BP)
- Finished product (FP)
- Intermediate product (IP)
- Scrap (RJ)
- Text item (TX)

Define Aggregation Rules for Document Items

The expected restitution amount is calculated in advance. The calculation of the total restitution amount for an export customs document is based on restitution rates that the customs authorities issue and the aggregated amount of the items. Aggregation rules are applied to aggregate document items according to specific criteria. You identify which fields in the documents must be identical for either basic or final products. The system can then aggregate all the basic or final product items in the document with the same value in the same fields.

Restitution calculation can be based on the following options:

- BOP
- License
- CAP number
- Combined aggregation (a combination of the above items)

Control Settings for Restitution

The control settings determine, for example, which products are subject to Legal Control. They also control the granularity and sequence of determination procedures used for CAP licenses.

The settings specified for the restitution legal regulation include the following:

- **Allowed Status**
  Various statuses for the CAP license can be defined here. Entries can range from "license created" and "license active" to "license expired," indicating the applicable status of the CAP license.
- **Assign Time Zone to Deadline Type**
  The validity date for the CAP licenses or export dates needs to be defined at that level.

▶ **Rounding Rules**
The system applies rounding rules for export refund calculation. The following types of rounding rules can be defined:

- ▶ One common rounding rule
- ▶ Product category-specific rounding rule

Define Types of Securities for Restitution

Similar to configuring CAP licenses, security types need to be defined in SAP GTS. The type of security defines which objects to check, how to update the security, and which attributes to maintain in the security. The applicable attributes include customs offices, FTOs, legal units, and excluded countries.

Define Types of Common Agricultural Policy Licenses

CAP license types to be used for restitution management are also to be defined in SAP GTS. This includes the objects to be checked for each document item to determine an applicable CAP license. Furthermore, the possible attributes to be maintained in a license are to be specified, as well. Note that this logic is similar to licenses for Compliance Management purposes.

Moreover, if a security is considered mandatory for this license type, set the SECU-RITY REQUIRED flag for the specific license type.

Define/Assign Export Refund

This last section defines the types of customs duty that are relevant for restitution in export processes and specifies the framework the system uses to calculate the restitution amounts. The framework represents the customs duty types for a legal regulation.

8.2.4 Master Data

A few master data elements are required in order to enable Restitution Management in SAP GTS; we'll cover them next.

CAP Licenses

Recall from the system process section that two license types can be maintained for Restitution purposes:

▸ **Annex I licenses**
These licenses are set up for exporting basic products. Annex I licenses specify a quantity of specific CAP products that should be exported in the given time-frame.

▸ **Non-Annex I licenses**
Whereas Annex I licenses cover basic products, the Non-Annex I licenses cover processed or finished goods. This license type is different because it is gener-ally product independent and specifies a cap on the restitution amount, as opposed to a product quantity, that can be received.

Restitution Securities

In order to guarantee that the applicant complies with the prerequisites for apply-ing for a CAP license, you have to provide a security amount. That security can be released or retained based on whether the prerequisites are ultimately satisfied. The following security types can be maintained in SAP GTS:

▸ Cash payments

▸ Guarantors

▸ Mortgages

▸ Sureties

The restitution service automatically determines a valid security for the export license.

Restitution Rates

Restitution rates are part of the restitution master data you need to manually maintain in SAP GTS, as shown in Figure 8.56. Because restitution rates are valid for a given timeframe, companies are required to update these rates with the most accurate information.

The following need to be maintained for every restitution rate:

- Legal regulation
- Type of restitution
- Country/country group of destination
- Validity period for the restitution rate
- CAP number

Based on the CAP license attributes, SAP GTS determines the applicable restitution rate and applies it in the restitution calculation.

Recipes

You need to manually maintain recipes in SAP GTS in order to reflect the details of all ingredients relevant for the finished product. This information is relevant for the system in order to retrieve the necessary details for items that are restitution relevant. Recipes are maintained in SAP GTS in a similar way as the BOP (or BOM). Figure 8.60 displays the hierarchical level that structures how a finished product may be set up by assigning a recipe.

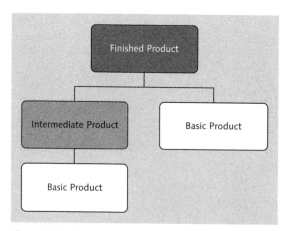

Figure 8.60 Restitution Management Recipe Structure

This second subchapter of the SAP GTS Risk Management module covered the Restitution Management process, in which you may claim export refunds when exporting agricultural products from an EU country to a non-EU country.

However, over the years, the restitution rates have dropped and have now mostly been reduced to zero. Because this functionality has all but disappeared, Restitution Management is a less significant part of SAP GTS Risk Management than Letter of Credit Processing and mainly Trade Preference Management.

In the subsequent and final subchapter of SAP GTS Risk Management, we'll discuss Letter of Credit Processing, a payment mechanism used to mitigate certain risks of global trade.

8.3 Letter of Credit Processing

For companies active in global trade, the assurance of payment as exporter and also the guaranteed delivery of goods under the negotiated terms as buyer are desirable and greatly facilitate the global trade process.

Letter of Credit Processing is the third and final piece of the SAP GTS Risk Management module, covering the letter of credit payment mechanism that supports both exporting and importing parties in mitigating certain risks of international trade.

Because of the significant physical distance between business partners and potential underlying legal or political conditions, increased risks arise for both exporting and importing parties in global trade transactions. On one hand, a seller or exporting party faces the financial risk of not receiving payment for the shipment because it is often difficult to determine the reliability and creditworthiness of business partners. As a result, sellers are reluctant to ship goods without a payment in advance or guarantee of payment. On the other hand, a buyer or importing party faces the risk of receiving the shipment later than the promised delivery date or varying from the terms agreed upon in the initial sales contract (e.g., different product quality levels than was negotiated). Because of these risks, buyers are reluctant to pay up front for a shipment that yet has much uncertainty.

To help overcome or reduce these risks, the intermediate role of financial institutions and payment methods such as letters of credit are used to address the inherent uncertainties.

A *letter of credit* (L/C), also referred to as a *documentary credit*, guarantees an exporter's payment and ensures that the shipment occurs to the terms negotiated by the two parties. It is a legally binding document issued by a financial institution (called the *issuing bank*) at the request of its client (the *buyer*). The document is a written commitment that the issuing bank will pay the seller's bank (called the *advising bank*) as long as the seller complies with the shipment's terms and conditions as written in the L/C.

The L/C thus acts as a seller's guarantee of payment. Even if the buyer ultimately fails to pay or even goes bankrupt, the payment is guaranteed by the issuing bank. The financial risk of a buyer's inability to pay is thus transferred from the seller to the issuing bank.

Aside from the aforementioned benefit for the exporting party, L/Cs as payment instruments may be advantageous to importing parties, as well. From the buyer's point of view, the L/C reduces the risk of having to pay for the shipment in advance, not knowing whether the shipped goods fully match the product descriptions or requirements as negotiated. The buyer must pay only if all terms and conditions of the L/C have been met by the vendor, which can, for instance, include the ultimate shipment date and required documents.

Required documents generally include transportation documents such as a bill of lading, but by specifying the need for additional aspects, such as inspection certificates, the importer may be guaranteed that the seller will meet the agreed upon quantities and quality of the goods. Furthermore, because the L/C guarantees the exporter's payment, the buyer may often negotiate more favorable trade terms.

Using L/Cs as payment instrument differs from standard transactions in that it imposes a process of payment against documents rather than payments against goods. For exporters, the monetary transaction takes place only after the L/C and required documentation are submitted to the advising bank. For importers, the payment is made only when receiving the L/C and documentation from the issuing bank. This flow of documentation and payments is further explained in Section 8.3.1.

As with Trade Preference Management and Restitution Management, we'll look into the business and system processes for Letter of Credit Processing, consider a business case, and discuss the relevant Customizing steps and master data.

Iota's Global Trading Requirements

Iota, a manufacturing company situated in the United States, ships to various customers in third countries. One of its customers is situated in Beijing, China, as displayed in Figure 8.61.

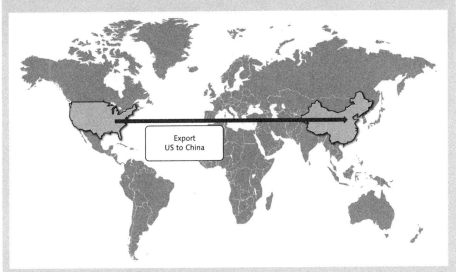

Figure 8.61 Business Case: Iota's Export to China

Iota and the Chinese customer have agreed to facilitate the payment via an L/C because they find it advantageous to both parties. Iota's bank and its Chinese customer's bank will serve as advising and issuing bank, respectively.

8.3.1 Business Process

The L/C process involves a number of parties, displayed in Figure 8.62. The figure with the corresponding explanations below provides an overview of the relevant actors and factors involved during a transaction with an L/C as a payment instrument.

Let's walk through the L/C business process:

❶ The business process starts when a buyer and seller enter into a sales contract. The buyer places a purchase order at the selling party, who sends an order confirmation. These documents generally contain the terms for the sale, such as the agreed upon pricing, delivery date, and incoterms.

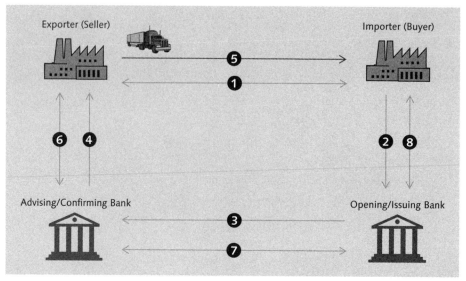

Figure 8.62 Letter of Credit Business Process

❷ In order to pay for the ordered goods or services, the buying party reaches out to its bank to request an L/C with the exporter as the beneficiary, which is the second step of Figure 8.62. The buyer specifies all the details that should be contained in the L/C, such as the transaction price, delivery date, and incoterms as negotiated with the selling party, as well as required documentation. The financial institution issuing the L/C is named the opening or issuing bank.

❸ After approving the request for the L/C, the issuing bank sends it to an advising bank in accordance with the buyer's instructions. The advising bank is generally located in the country where the exporter performs the transaction and may or may not be the company's bank.

❹ The advising bank initially verifies the content of the L/C for its authenticity and subsequently informs the seller of the incoming L/C. Note that both the issuing and advising bank may charge a certain fee for their services.

At the moment the exporter receives the L/C from the advising bank, the exporting party needs to examine the L/C to ensure that it corresponds to all terms and conditions as negotiated in the sales agreement. The exporter should also confirm that the requirements and required documentation stated in the L/C can be fulfilled or produced.

When the exporting party ships the goods and submits the required documentation, the advising bank examines whether all requirements are met. If there are any discrepancies, payment is no longer guaranteed for the seller. If the exporting company examines and finds faults or discrepancies in the L/C or notices required documents that it cannot produce, then an amendment is made. Only when all parties agree to the amendments are they incorporated into the L/C.

During the sales negotiations, the exporter may request a financial institution to add its confirmation to the L/C. The advising bank or a different bank is then requested to confirm the L/C, and by doing so, that bank assumes the same responsibilities as the issuing bank to guarantee the seller's payment as long as requirements of the L/C are met.

Sometimes, a seller may want to confirm an L/C when it has concerns about the credibility of the issuing bank in regards to its ability to fulfill the payment. This often occurs when the issuing bank is situated in a politically or economically unstable country. Confirmation from the advising bank, often the exporter's bank, further increases the guarantee of payment because the exporter has the promise of payment from two banks if it meets all the L/C's requirements.

❺ In the fifth step of the business process, the exporter arranges the shipment of the goods and prepares to obtain the required documents specified in the L/C. For ocean shipments, for instance, the bill of lading obtained from the carrier when goods are transferred onto the vessel may be a required document in the L/C.

❻ After the exporter ships the order, he may demand payment by presenting the L/C, together with all required documents, in the stipulated timeframe to the advising bank, or in the case of a confirmed L/C, the confirming bank. Note that, in Figure 8.62, the advising bank is also acting as the confirming bank. The bank checks the L/C's requirements, reviews in detail whether all documents and requirements are met and accurate, and notifies the exporter of any discrepancies.

If the L/C has been confirmed, the confirming second bank has guaranteed the exporter's payment, and the exporter may be paid immediately, depending on the negotiated conditions.

❼ Once the confirming bank has examined the documents and agreed on their accuracy, the L/C and various documents are forwarded to the issuing bank in return for payment. The opening bank also examines the documents to ensure compliance with the L/C's terms and requirements. If it is agreed that the requirements have been met, the payment is made to the advising/confirming bank. Note that, if the L/C is *not* confirmed, the payment to the exporter can take place only after the issuing bank has transferred the payments to the advising bank.

❽ In the eighth and final step, the opening bank delivers the stipulated documents (such as the shipment's bill of lading) to the importer to allow it to take possession of the goods. Once the payment from the importer to the issuing bank is made, the L/C cycle is complete.

Iota Receives a Letter of Credit to Cover its Export to China

When negotiating a sales order for a total worth of $100,000, the Chinese customer contacts its bank in Beijing to open an L/C with the US company Iota as the beneficiary. The Beijing bank uses the existing line of credit with its Chinese client to cover the L/C's amount.

The Beijing bank sends the L/C, containing all negotiated terms such as pricing and incoterms, to company Iota's bank in Washington. The Washington bank examines the L/C for authenticity and notifies Iota of the L/C's arrival.

Once Iota confirms that all terms and conditions in the L/C are accurate and can produce the required documentation, Iota prepares to ship the goods. Note that, in this business case, Iota does not request a confirming bank because it has determined the Beijing bank's reputation to be reputable and trustworthy, and so does not feel the need to involve a confirming bank.

Iota dispatches the goods to China in accordance with the predetermined conditions and hands the shipment over to a carrier when loading the goods onto a vessel, for which it receives a bill of lading document.

With the shipment underway, Iota obtains and presents the advising Washington bank with the valid L/C, including the bill of lading, a customer invoice, and other documentation proving that the L/C's terms and conditions are met.

The Washington bank examines the submitted documents in detail and transfers them to the issuing Beijing bank after approval. Once the issuing bank has examined and approved the documents, as well, it transfers the payment of $100,000 to the Washington bank, who transfers the payment to Iota.

The Beijing bank delivers the documents to the Chinese importer in return for payment. The bill of lading allows the Chinese customer to take possession of the goods from the shipment's carrier, which concludes the global transaction between the two parties.

8.3.2 System Process

The SAP GTS system process to support L/C payment processes is displayed in Figure 8.63. Note that Figure 8.63 and the subsequent explanation follow the export scenario, which is similar in most aspects to the import process. However, in the export scenario, additional steps are taken to obtain the required documents for the L/C.

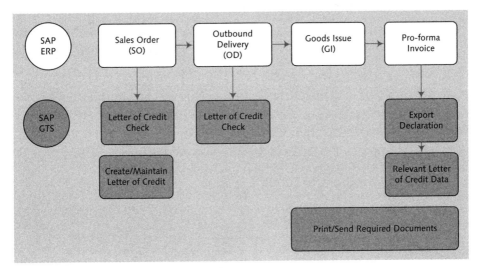

Figure 8.63 Letter of Credit Export System Process

The SAP GTS Letter of Credit Processing flow works, in many aspects, in a similar manner as the Compliance Management outbound process. Upon creation of a sales order in the feeder system, the generated customs document in SAP GTS is checked for an applicable L/C legal regulation, and the document's business partners are checked for Letter of Credit Processing relevancy. This is similar to documents checked if relevant for a certain export legal regulation.

Again similar to the Legal Control functionality, Letter of Credit Processing leverages a determination strategy that may be set up to let the system automatically assign an applicable L/C to the sales order.

If SAP GTS cannot find an existing L/C to cover the document, the sales order is blocked for Letter of Credit Processing. Once an issuing bank has issued an L/C on the importer's behalf, the exporter may manually create an L/C in SAP GTS, accessed via RISK MANAGEMENT • LETTER OF CREDIT PROCESSING • MASTER DATA • MAINTAIN LETTER OF CREDIT.

The L/C document in SAP GTS may be created with all the attributes and requirements as the physical document received from the advising bank. This process is analogous to setting up licenses in SAP GTS for import or export Legal Control. Furthermore, attachments may be added to the SAP GTS L/C, such as a scan of the official document received from the issuing or advising bank.

Once maintained in the SAP GTS, the L/C is to be assigned to the blocked sales order via RISK MANAGEMENT • LETTER OF CREDIT PROCESSING • EXPORT • PROCESS MANUAL ASSIGNMENT.

After you create an outbound delivery in the feeder system, the L/C check is performed once more. Once the subsequent pro-forma invoice generates a customs export declaration, the relevant L/C information is assigned to the export declaration on a dedicated LETTER OF CREDIT tab, as displayed in Figure 8.64.

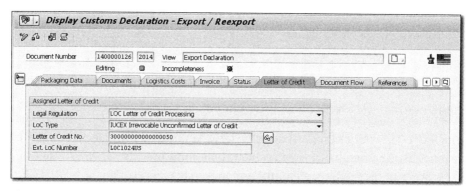

Figure 8.64 Letter of Credit Tab on the Customs Export Declaration

Once shipped, the necessary documents may be printed from SAP GTS and submitted to the bank for validation and subsequent payment. Figure 8.65 displays the SAP GTS representation of the L/C, and is noticeably similar to a Compliance Management Legal Control license.

As Legal Control licenses, an L/C contains a number of attributes, including the involved banks, documents to be presented to the bank, incoterms, terms of payment, and so on. Figure 8.65 displays the COMMUNICATION attribute, which allows documents to be printed directly from the SAP GTS Letter of Credit Processing or forwarded electronically to the bank.

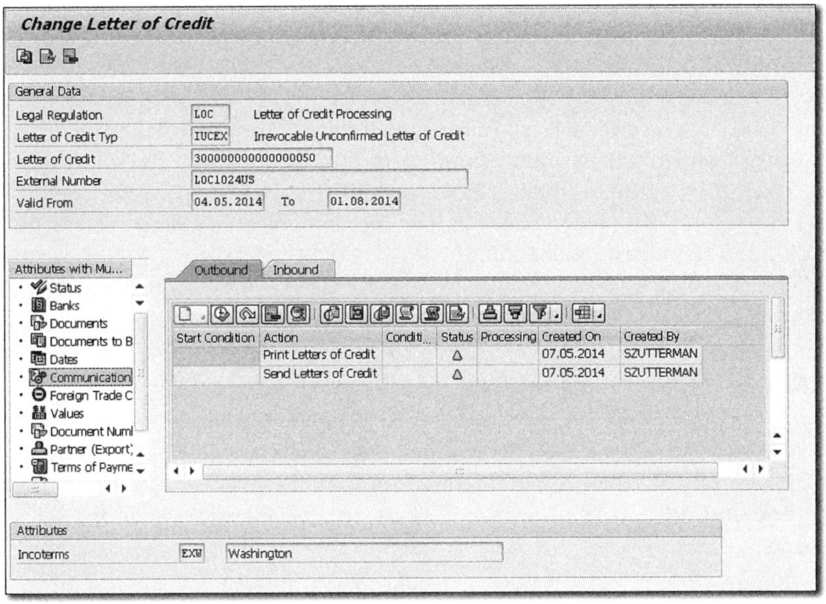

Figure 8.65 Printing and Electronic Sending of Letter of Credit

However, note that, for electronic communication with banks, you need to implement and configure a connection and communication for L/Cs; this may require additional technical developments.

Similarly, when receiving an L/C from the advising bank, this may happen electronically, automatically loading the L/C in SAP GTS; it might also require equal technical developments.

Once the L/C and required documents are submitted at the advising or confirming bank and payment has been received, the process is complete. SAP GTS provides archiving transactions to retrieve all customs export declarations and the assigned L/Cs.

Maintaining and Facilitating Iota's Letters of Credit with SAP GTS

As Iota performs business with its Chinese customer through Letter of Credit Processing, the Chinese business partner in SAP GTS is indicated as relevant for the Letter of Credit Processing functionality.

After the sale has been negotiated with the Chinese customer, Iota's feeder system employees can generate a sales order, which is transferred to SAP GTS. SAP GTS first checks whether the document is considered relevant for Letter of Credit Processing.

When it is deemed relevant, SAP GTS checks the various objects in the customs document to look for an applicable L/C. Since no L/C has yet been entered, SAP GTS blocks the sales order in the feeder system.

A few days later, Iota receives the L/C from the Washington bank, which acts as Iota's advising bank. Payment administrators examine the L/C information, and when they deem all information accurate, create a corresponding L/C in SAP GTS with identical attributes, such as the Washington bank business partner number, required documents, transaction value, terms of payment, etc.

After the L/C is created, Iota's employees manually assign the L/C to the sales order so they can further process the shipment. With the goods ready to be shipped to Beijing, an outbound delivery is created, which is again transferred to SAP GTS and checked for an L/C, found by the system, and automatically assigned.

Subsequently, Iota employees create the pro-forma invoice generating a customs export declaration in SAP GTS. Via the SAP GTS Customs Management module, Iota employees perform all necessary activities to file the shipment with the customs authorities. The next and final step for Iota is to obtain all necessary documents to fulfill the L/C's requirements.

From the L/C in SAP GTS, Iota can view which documents are required and mark them as complete once they have been obtained, as displayed in Figure 8.66. Once all documents are obtained, they are submitted to the advising bank, and the payment is received, ending the L/C process.

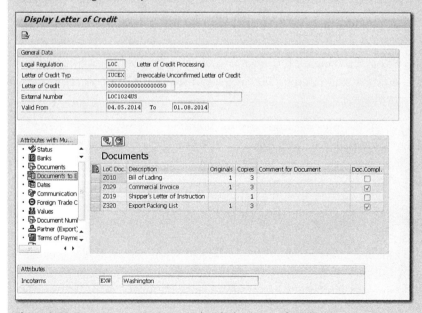

Figure 8.66 Documents to Be Presented with the Letter of Credit

8.3.3   Customizing

The Customizing settings discussed in this section provide a high-level overview of the necessary Customizing to leverage the SAP GTS Letter of Credit Processing functionality. Here, we assume that the required document types have been flagged as relevant for Risk Management in the feeder system plug-in for SAP GTS.

The Customizing settings under GENERAL SETTINGS within SAP Risk Management include settings for the printing and electronic sending of messages, as mentioned in the L/C system process. However, they are not elaborated on further due to the additional technical requirements of electronic messaging.

Generic Customizing settings for Letter of Credit Processing similar to those of the SAP GTS Compliance Management and Customs Management functionalities include the following:

▶ Activating legal regulation

▶ Assigning determination procedure for active legal regulations

▶ Defining procedure for automatic determination of letter of credit types

Define Partner Groups Relevant to Letters of Credit

In this Customizing activity, partner groups relevant for Letter of Credit Processing are defined. In the master data section, customers and vendors need to be assigned to such a partner group for SAP GTS to check the transactional documents for an applicable L/C.

Control Settings for Letter of Credit Processing

For an L/C legal regulation, the following control settings may be applied:

▶ PARTNER GROUP LOC DETERMINATION COUNTRY OF DEPARTURE/DESTINATION
Determines which partner function is used to determine the departure/destination country, where the departure country is used for the import scenario and the destination country used for the export scenario.

Relevant partner functions are defined in the partner group. These relevant partner functions are checked on a transactional basis to determine the destination/departure country.

▶ DETERMINATION PROCEDURE
For each L/C legal regulation, the relevant determination procedure must be selected and assigned. This procedure is necessary to allow the system to identify the relevant L/C types.

▶ SEQUENTIAL DETERMINATION
If this flag is set, the system determines the license types hierarchically.

▶ SENDING OF MAIL
If you check this flag, the system automatically sends an email if the customs document is blocked due to a missing or invalid L/C. When activating this setting, take corresponding actions in the system communications and workflow settings to define which user group should be notified when a document block is set.

▶ MULTIPLE COUNTRY GROUPS
If this flag is set, the system checks for appropriate L/C types at all country group levels in which the country of destination in the customs document item is assigned to the current relevant legal regulation.

Define Letter of Credit Types

The various L/C types that may be defined, created, and managed in SAP GTS include the following:

▶ **Revocable L/C**
A revocable L/C can be modified or cancelled at any time by the issuing bank without notifying the beneficiary. In reality, this type is generally not used as a payment mechanism because it offers very little security to the exporter.

▶ **Irrevocable, unconfirmed L/C**
Irrevocable L/Cs may not be canceled or amended without the confirmation of the issuing bank, advising bank, and beneficiary.

As discussed in Section 8.3.1, an unconfirmed L/C implies no presence of a confirming bank. As such, the exporter's bank assumes an advising role, and the promise of payment is guaranteed by only the issuing bank.

The advising bank notifies the beneficiary of the L/C, but it is not obligated to honor the payment.

▶ **Irrevocable, confirmed L/C**
To increase the guarantee of payment for the exporter, a bank may be

requested to confirm the L/C. By doing so, the confirming bank also has an obligation to guarantee the payment if the exporter meets the L/C's requirements.

Furthermore, the characteristics of each L/C type need to be specified, as displayed in Figure 8.67.

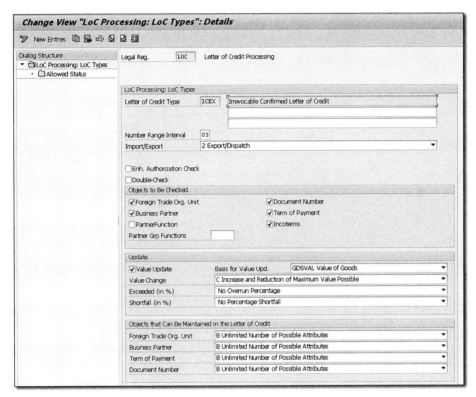

Figure 8.67 Letter of Credit Type Attributes

Let's walk through some of these characteristics:

▶ **Objects to be checked**
Similar to the Compliance Management license determination, the document objects that need be checked to search for an applicable L/C may be specified. For the settings of Figure 8.67, SAP GTS would check a document for FTO, document number, terms of payment, incoterms, and the business partner number to find an applicable L/C.

▶ **Communication**
The communication works in a similar manner as SAP GTS Customs Management by defining the communication characteristics through an action profile. The specified action profile enables external communications, for instance, for printing documents and dispatching electronic messages. Furthermore, email messages may be sent to inform personnel of blocked L/C documents.

▶ **External identification**
If the responsible bank uses a name for the L/C type that differs from the name maintained in the system, you can maintain this name as the external identification.

Note

Additional L/C types than the three previously mentioned types may be configured in SAP GTS. Different L/C types may then be assigned a different set of attributes depending on specific requirements (e.g., when shipping to or from certain countries).

8.3.4 Master Data

This section will describe the few master data elements required in order to enable the SAP GTS Letter of Credit Processing functionality.

Maintain Business Partners

SAP GTS needs to know whether the customer or vendor used in the transaction is relevant for Letter of Credit Processing. For this reason, the applicable business partners must be assigned to a partner group relevant for Letter of Credit Processing. This is a manual task accessed via RISK MANAGEMENT • LETTER OF CREDIT PROCESSING • MASTER DATA • MAINTAIN BUSINESS PARTNERS.

These partner groups are defined via the Customizing setting DEFINE PARTNER GROUPS RELEVANT TO LETTERS OF CREDIT.

Maintain Letters of Credit

Each L/C must be separately created as master data. L/C maintenance is similar to the process of license management. For each L/C, a number of attributes, depending on the Customizing settings, may be maintained, as shown earlier in Figure

8.65 and Figure 8.66. These attributes include the L/C's status, issuing or advising/confirming bank (depending on import or export process), required documents, dates, values, partners, text, terms of payment, and others. Additional information, such as scanned documents, may be attached to the SAP GTS L/C, as well.

Maintain Determination Strategy

Similar to License Control (see Chapter 6), SAP GTS requires an L/C determination strategy for each L/C legal regulation. This step determines, based on the set criteria in Customizing, which factors should be considered to determine an applicable L/C.

This subchapter discussed Letter of Credit Processing, the third and final functionality of SAP GTS Risk Management. L/Cs are used as payment instruments to guarantee payment to the exporter and to guarantee to the importer that the goods are shipped as negotiated in stipulated terms and conditions.

SAP GTS supports L/C payments by allowing the creation and maintenance of L/Cs in SAP GTS with its corresponding attributes. Using SAP GTS, companies can follow up on delivery dates and required documents and access archiving reports to retrieve all previously performed L/C transactions.

8.4   Summary

This chapter tackled the three SAP GTS Risk Management functionalities that mitigate risks or support certain processes in global trade

As we discussed, the first and main Risk Management functionality, Trade Preference Management, covers the requirements and processes that need to be performed to reach the end goal of issuing proof of origin to customers situated in preferential agreements. This way, products may be exported under preferential treatment, implying a reduced or zero duty rate for the importing party. Being able to issue proof of origin may significantly increase a company's market competitiveness by allowing customers to import products without having to pay import duties.

Determining a product's preferential eligibility and ensuring that accurate proof of origin is provided is a daunting task that can be supported and automated by using SAP GTS.

The inbound aspect of requesting and aggregating preferential information, the production process of determining a finished product's preferential origin in a specific agreement, and the outbound process of issuing proof of origin are covered in seven subsequent process steps.

The second functionality, Restitution Management, covered the process of claiming export refunds for agricultural exports from the EU to non-EU countries. However, the use of this functionality has diminished over the years because of reducing restitution rates. Because the restitution rates have recently dropped to zero, restitution amounts can no longer be claimed.

SAP GTS supports Restitution Management by providing capabilities for the creation, maintenance, and tracking of restitution licenses and securities. Furthermore, transactions are provided for the simulation and calculation of restitution amounts.

The third and final functionality, Letter of Credit Processing, covered the process of leveraging the L/C as a payment mechanism and the supporting capabilities of SAP GTS. Through L/Cs, both exporting and importing parties can protect themselves against the risks of trading in a global environment.

The SAP GTS Letter of Credit Processing capabilities include the creation, maintenance, and assignment of L/Cs in SAP GTS. Through Letter of Credit Processing, companies may monitor the validity dates and required documentation and submit L/Cs to the bank via printing or electronic messaging.

In the next chapter, we'll take a look at the standard SAP GTS reports over the three main modules. In addition to the reporting capabilities provided by SAP GTS, we'll address interaction with SAP Business Warehouse (BW), which can be leveraged to develop customized reports to support global trade processes.

Customs authorities require companies to record and keep transactional documentation relating to customs activities. To satisfy these regulatory requirements, they need an automated and comprehensive reporting system. Furthermore, they can use reports internally for operational and analysis purposes. This chapter covers the SAP GTS and SAP BW capabilities for dealing with these requirements.

9 SAP GTS and SAP BW Reporting

Companies are subject to customs regulations to track and trace shipments, monitor the status of goods, and maintain involved parties and trade restrictions or measures. Additionally, certain customs authorities may require periodic reports to demonstrate an audit trail of merchandise-related data.

With SAP GTS, you can create the necessary reports in order to comply with these regulations. You can enhance the standard reports as necessary to suit the specific business requirements, or you may need to create additional reports.

This chapter is divided into two sections. The first covers the SAP GTS reporting capabilities, which are standard reports that are readily available when installing the SAP GTS instance. The second section addresses SAP Business Warehouse (BW) reporting. By leveraging SAP BW, you can tailor and customize reports to address specific needs and business requirements in order to analyze large sets of data that enable you to draw valid conclusions and make sound business decisions.

9.1 SAP GTS Reporting

SAP GTS is built to support various business trade processes and can generate various reports throughout its different modules. You can access two main types of reports through SAP GTS:

▶ *Standard or descriptive reports* collect data from the system retrospectively; for example, you may use them to display an audit trail for business partners screened against the sanctioned party lists.

▶ *Transactional or operational reports* are reports on which you can perform further actions (e.g., displaying a list of blocked documents and providing capabilities to release them, if needed).

SAP GTS reports are listed in the SAP Advanced List Viewer (ALV), meaning that they are provided in an SAP-standard list format and user interface. ALV reports offer a set of standard functions that help analyze a report's output or help tailor the existing reports to specific requirements.

Figure 9.1 shows the most significant functions this reporting format offers. Using these functions, you can sort, filter, and download the report (e.g., to an Excel or HTML file).

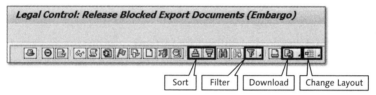

Figure 9.1 ALV Report Functions

In addition, you can change the report layout to better suit your business requirements or reflect the needs of a specific user. Figure 9.2 shows the screen for changing a report's layout. You can hide, add, or reorder certain columns of a standard report. Besides the displayed columns, you can specify a sort order or add filters. After customizing the report's layout, you can save it for later use or make it the default.

The main advantage of this functionality is that you can tailor the customized layout of the standard report to certain scenarios or personnel. In practical terms, this means that companies can default a specific layout for a standard report to better suit and support their personnel's needs by disabling unnecessary or adding wanted columns. Furthermore, you can create different layouts of the same report for different users. As such, certain users with less authorization and requiring less information could be assigned a standard report layout containing fewer columns than their colleagues are.

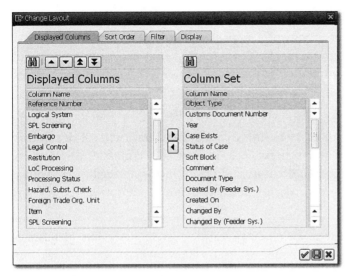

Figure 9.2 Change ALV Report Layout

The section on SAP GTS reporting is structured in the three main GTS functional areas: Compliance Management, Customs Management, and Risk Management.

Note that the menu path specified in each table found in this chapter has its roots in the SAP GTS area menu. Furthermore, all reports can be found in Appendix A, listed with the corresponding transaction codes.

9.1.1 Compliance Management Reporting

Reports available in the Compliance Management module provide both operational and descriptive reports. The former are used in daily operations: reviewing blocked documents, analyzing these reports, and taking action accordingly to process the business flows. On the other hand, descriptive reports serve as audit trails for topics such as the screening history of business partners and the import/export control information of documents, payments, and licenses.

The focus of this first reporting section lies on those reports within the three Compliance Management sub-functional areas (SPL, Embargo, and Legal Control), followed by reports related to master data. For each of these topics, the reports are grouped in domains that follow the same logic. For each domain, we will elaborate one report that serves a significant business purpose.

Sanctioned Party List

In the current global environment, companies are obligated to comply with all applicable regulatory requirements. Consequently, they may not perform any trade with any parties named on government agency or country-specific denied party lists.

To prevent trading with sanctioned parties, SAP GTS allows you to perform sanctioned party list screenings on business partners and transactional documents. Besides the actual screening process, SAP GTS provides a number of reports to support business decisions and ensure full compliance with regulatory requirements (e.g., audits). SPL reporting can be divided into monitoring, audit trail, and master data areas.

The *monitoring area* covers all reports regarding screening results of business partners, documents, and payments, while also allowing practitioners to take further actions based on these screening results. If, for instance, a sales order is generated in the feeder system and the system identifies the customer as an entry on a sanctioned party list, then an SAP GTS block is enforced. You could then investigate the customer and reason for the SPL block in the monitoring area. After investigating the reason for the SPL block, you can make decisions such as whether to release the document or customer (e.g., due to a false positive SPL check).

Table 9.1 contains the SPL reports found in the monitoring area. Whereas blocked business partners may be released directly from the Display Blocked Business Partner report, documents and payments may be released by consulting dedicated Release Blocked Documents/Payments reports. Note that the latter reports are duplicate reports of Display Blocked Documents/Payments apart from the addition of a CANCEL SPL BLOCK button. From a business perspective, this enables separation of authority, allowing some users to analyze the screening blocks, while giving only a select few the ability to release business partners from SPL blocks.

Report Name	Menu Path
SPL—Display Blocked Business Partners	SANCTIONED PARTY LIST SCREENING • TAB LOGISTICS • DISPLAY BLOCKED BUSINESS PARTNERS
SPL—Display Blocked Documents	SANCTIONED PARTY LIST SCREENING • TAB LOGISTICS • DISPLAY BLOCKED DOCUMENTS

Table 9.1 Transactional Sanctioned Party List Screening Reports

Report Name	Menu Path
SPL—Display Blocked Payments	SANCTIONED PARTY LIST SCREENING • TAB FINANCIAL ACCOUNTING • DISPLAY BLOCKED PAYMENTS
SPL—Release Blocked Documents	SANCTIONED PARTY LIST SCREENING • TAB LOGISTICS • MANUALLY RELEASE BLOCKED DOCUMENTS
SPL—Release Blocked Payments	SANCTIONED PARTY LIST SCREENING • TAB FINANCIAL ACCOUNTING • MANUALLY RELEASE BLOCKED PAYMENTS

Table 9.1 Transactional Sanctioned Party List Screening Reports (Cont.)

The Display Blocked Business Partners report provides a highly detailed view of all blocked customers, vendors, etc., in SAP GTS. From a business perspective, users can analyze their business partners in this report and decide whether to clear (e.g., due to a false positive) or confirm the imposed block.

Figure 9.3 shows the selection screen for the Display Blocked Business Partners report.

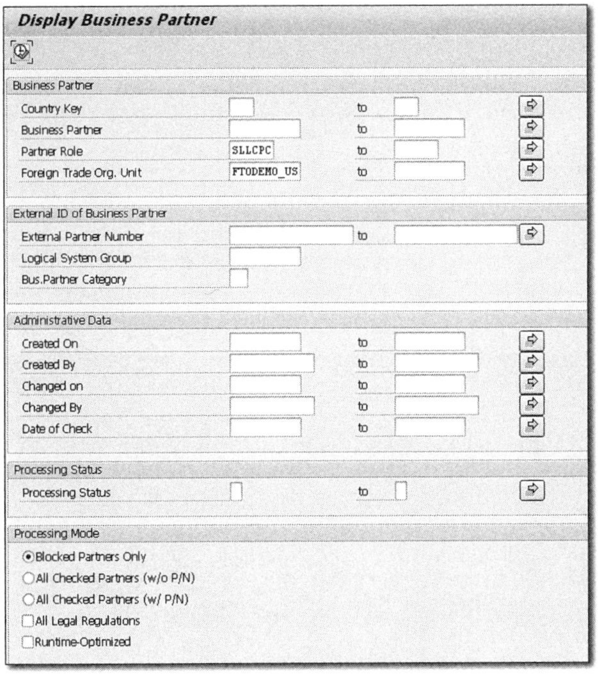

Figure 9.3 Display Blocked Business Partners Selection Screen

To enable an analysis of the companies' business partners, specify the FOREIGN TRADE ORGANIZATION UNIT and PARTNER ROLE (e.g., customer, vendor, bank, etc.) fields. Furthermore, you can choose to display only blocked business partners or all checked partners, whether blocked or not.

The report shown in Figure 9.4 is the result of this selection screen. It lists all blocked business partners (customers) by external and internal BP number. It also shows information specific to the SPL screening, such as the legal regulation against which the block occurs, data used for the screening process, and validity term of the block. All partners, whether they are blocked by the system or not, may be manually released, put on a negative or positive list, or manually blocked within this report. For further information regarding this topic, please consult Chapter 6 on Compliance Management.

Display Business Partner

Sanctioned Party List Screening | Release Partner | Positive List | Negative List | Confirm Block | On Hold

Blocked Business Partners

Status	LS Group	B	External Partner Number	Business Partner	C	Case S	Legal Reg.	C	P	AddressNo.	Date of SPL Screening	Sanct. Block
	FDRTESTG	0	90001	961			SPLUS			18333	29.11.2013 16:21:43	☑
	FDRTESTG	0	11005	1003			SPLUS			18424	02.12.2013 10:57:03	☑
	FDRTESTG	0	11005	1003			SPLUS			18481	02.12.2013 10:57:03	☑
	FDRTESTG	0	11112	1005			SPLUS			18482	02.12.2013 10:57:03	☑
	FDRTESTG	0	55004	625			SPLUS			12122	26.11.2013 14:24:28	☑
	FDRTESTG	0	55513	934			SPLUS			12418	18.06.2013 21:32:56	☑
	FDRTESTG	0	3906	671			SPLUS			12171	26.11.2013 14:26:31	☑
	FDRTESTG	0	9001	685			SPLUS			12183	18.11.2013 11:37:03	☑
	FDRTESTG	0	2005	827			SPLUS			12318	18.11.2013 16:19:02	☑

Figure 9.4 Display Blocked Business Partners Report

Table 9.2 lists reports that cover actions taken on business partners or transactional documents.

Report Name	Menu Path
SPL—Display Business Partners on the Negative List	SANCTIONED PARTY LIST SCREENING • TAB LOGISTICS • DISPLAY NEGATIVE LIST BUSINESS PARTNERS
SPL—Display Business Partners on the Positive List	SANCTIONED PARTY LIST SCREENING • TAB LOGISTICS • DISPLAY POSITIVE LIST BUSINESS PARTNERS
SPL—Display Analyze Reasons for Release	SANCTIONED PARTY LIST SCREENING • TAB CROSS-AREA MONITORING • ANALYZE REASONS FOR RELEASE

Table 9.2 Reports Listing Actions Taken Related to SPL Screening

From a legal and compliance perspective, releasing business partners for which the system imposes an SPL block is an action that requires careful consideration. Therefore, the ability for companies to review employees' past actions (and motivations for those actions) is important. You can access legacy information on those actions in the Analyze Reasons for Release report.

Figure 9.5 shows the selection screen of the Analyze Reasons for Release report. The most relevant fields to conduct the report are to search on a certain legal regulation and specify the reason object, determining whether the report displays a list of released documents or a list of released business partners.

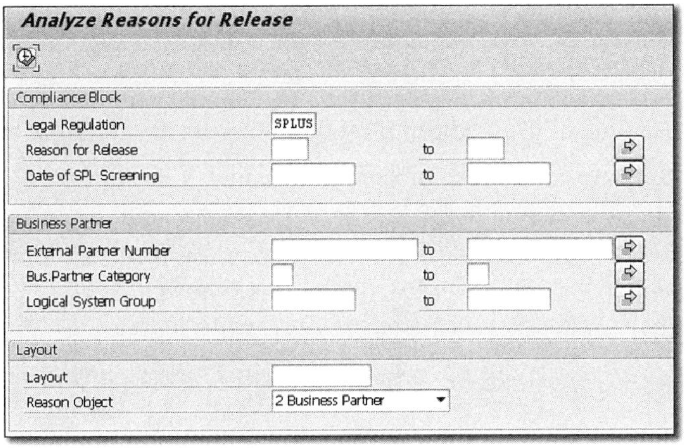

Figure 9.5 Analyze Reasons for Release Report Selection Screen

Figure 9.6 gives an example of the report itself. The report was executed with "Business Partner" as the reason object, so it displays all previously blocked business partners that have been released with a specified reason. For the example report shown, business partners have been manually released for either a false positive match on the business partner's location or a false positive match on the business partner's name. The report outlines release description and business partner information, as well as the time and responsible party of release.

The *audit trails* are the second area covered by the SPL reporting. Companies need to log and keep all SPL screening results regarding business partners, documents, and payments available for audit purposes. SAP GTS stores all information related to the screening activities (e.g., SPL screening, manual releases, and manual blocks) that have been performed in the system, rendering the required documentation accessible in case of eventual audits.

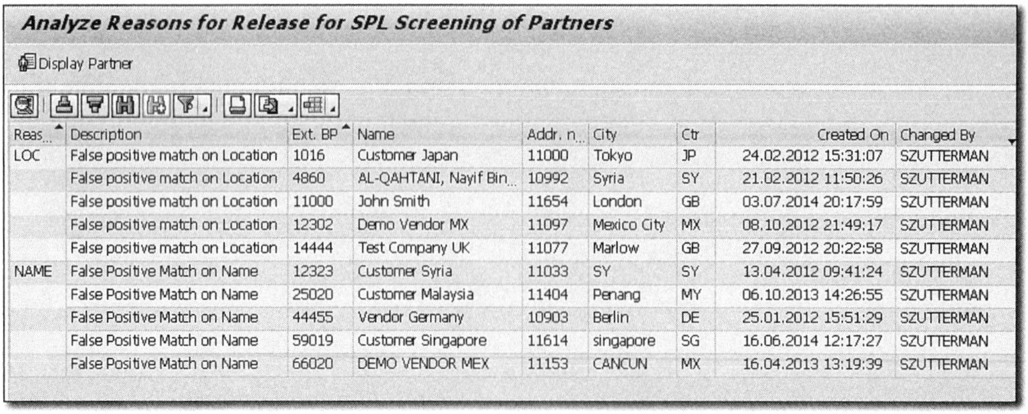

Analyze Reasons for Release for SPL Screening of Partners

Display Partner

Reas...	Description	Ext. BP	Name	Addr. n...	City	Ctr	Created On	Changed By
LOC	False positive match on Location	1016	Customer Japan	11000	Tokyo	JP	24.02.2012 15:31:07	SZUTTERMAN
	False positive match on Location	4860	AL-QAHTANI, Nayif Bin...	10992	Syria	SY	21.02.2012 11:50:26	SZUTTERMAN
	False positive match on Location	11000	John Smith	11654	London	GB	03.07.2014 20:17:59	SZUTTERMAN
	False positive match on Location	12302	Demo Vendor MX	11097	Mexico City	MX	08.10.2012 21:49:17	SZUTTERMAN
	False positive match on Location	14444	Test Company UK	11077	Marlow	GB	27.09.2012 20:22:58	SZUTTERMAN
NAME	False Positive Match on Name	12323	Customer Syria	11033	SY	SY	13.04.2012 09:41:24	SZUTTERMAN
	False Positive Match on Name	25020	Customer Malaysia	11404	Penang	MY	06.10.2013 14:26:55	SZUTTERMAN
	False Positive Match on Name	44455	Vendor Germany	10903	Berlin	DE	25.01.2012 15:51:29	SZUTTERMAN
	False Positive Match on Name	59019	Customer Singapore	11614	singapore	SG	16.06.2014 12:17:27	SZUTTERMAN
	False Positive Match on Name	66020	DEMO VENDOR MEX	11153	CANCUN	MX	16.04.2013 13:19:39	SZUTTERMAN

Figure 9.6 Analyze Reasons for Release for SPL Screening of Business Partners Report

Table 9.3 gives an overview of all SPL audit trail reports. Reports are available to trace activities related to business partners, documents, and payments.

Report Name	Transaction
Display Audit Trail of Address Check for Business Partner	Sanctioned Party List Screening • Tab Logistics • Display Audit Trail for Business Partners
Display Audit Trail of Documents Address Check	Sanctioned Party List Screening • Tab Logistics • Display Audit Trail for Documents
Display Audit Trail of Address Check for Payment Documents	Sanctioned Party List Screening • Tab Financial Accounting • Display Audit Trail for Payments
SPL Audit Trail for External Auditor—Business Partner	Sanctioned Party List Screening • Tab Cross-Area Monitoring • Display Audit Trails for Partner
SPL Audit Trail for External Auditor—Documents	Sanctioned Party List Screening • Tab Cross-Area Monitoring • Display Audit Trails for Documents

Table 9.3 SPL Audit Trail Reports

Two extended audit reports—one for partners and one for documents—are available specifically for external auditors as a starting point for their audit activities, but the reports can also be consulted for internal purposes.

Figure 9.7 shows the selection screen for the extended report Display Audit Trails for External Auditor—Partner. In this report, you give an audit trail on a certain business partner (or multiple partners) by entering the external partner number.

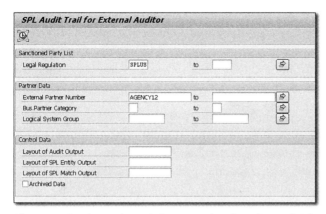

Figure 9.7 Display Audit Trails for External Auditor (Partner) Selection Screen

Figure 9.8 displays the outcome of executing the report with the given parameters in the selection screen.

Figure 9.8 Audit Trail Report for a Business Partner

The audit report stipulates that, for the initial SPL check, the business partner passed the SPL screening, represented by the two green checkmarks at the bottom line of the audit trail. For the consecutive system checks, the business partner failed on the system check (signified by the red symbols). However, in the top line, the audit trail reveals that the business partner has been manually released, with a specified reason FALSE POSITIVE HIT.

Finally, the SPL master data reports in Table 9.4 contain information related to the lists of sanctioned party entries against which the system performs the SPL checks. As the actual lists containing sanctioned parties are usually uploaded in an XML format acquired from a content provider, the information in these lists is more informative and legacy in nature, compared to previously discussed reports, which serve a greater operational importance.

Report Name	Menu Path
Display Sanctioned Party Lists	SANCTIONED PARTY LIST SCREENING • TAB MASTER DATA • DISPLAY OVERVIEW LIST
Display Structured View of Sanctioned Party Lists	SANCTIONED PARTY LIST SCREENING • TAB MASTER DATA • DISPLAY STRUCTURED LIST
Display Expiring Sanctioned Party List Entries	SANCTIONED PARTY LIST SCREENING • TAB MASTER DATA • DISPLAY EXPIRING SANCTIONED PARTY LISTS
Display Change History of Sanction Lists	SANCTIONED PARTY LIST SCREENING • TAB MASTER DATA • DISPLAY CHANGE HISTORY

Table 9.4 SPL Master Data Reports

Embargo

Similar to restrictions on trading with sanctioned parties, trading restrictions are imposed for dealing with parties in embargoed countries. For a more detailed overview on embargoes, refer to the Compliance Management chapter.

The SAP GTS embargo reporting capabilities are more restricted than those found in SPL reporting, but do roughly follow the same logic. Since embargo-related data is rather concise, all data extracted from SAP GTS is linked to the embargo status of a business partner, document, or payment.

Each embargo-related report is twofold:

▶ One report describes the import situation of the embargo, including purchasing processes, incoming payments, and the import situation of business partners.

▶ The other report specifies the export situation of the embargo, entailing the sales processes, outgoing payments, and export situation of business partners.

Table 9.5 (import) and Table 9.6 (export) give an overview of the embargo reports. As with the SPL reports, two reports are provided to display the blocked documents and payments. From a business perspective, these reports provide the capability to filter on the documents that require further attention. Additionally, two reports allow the manual release of those documents and payments. Note that, apart from an added CANCEL EMBARGO BLOCK flag, the additional reports to release the documents/payments are the equivalent of the display reports.

Report Name	Menu Path
Display Blocked Import Documents	LEGAL CONTROL—IMPORT • DISPLAY BLOCKED DOCUMENTS
Display Blocked Payment Receipt Documents	LEGAL CONTROL—IMPORT • DISPLAY BLOCKED PAYMENTS
Release Blocked Import Documents (Embargo)	LEGAL CONTROL—IMPORT • RELEASE BLOCKED DOCUMENTS
Release Blocked Payment Receipt Documents (Embargo)	LEGAL CONTROL—IMPORT • RELEASE BLOCKED PAYMENTS

Table 9.5 Transactional Embargo Reports (Import)

Report Name	Menu Path
Display Blocked Export Documents	LEGAL CONTROL—EXPORT • DISPLAY BLOCKED DOCUMENTS
Display Blocked Outgoing Payment Documents	LEGAL CONTROL—EXPORT • DISPLAY BLOCKED PAYMENTS

Table 9.6 Transactional Embargo Reports (Export)

Report Name	Menu Path
Release Blocked Export Documents (Embargo)	LEGAL CONTROL—EXPORT • RELEASE BLOCKED DOCUMENTS
Release Blocked Outgoing Payment Documents (Embargo)	LEGAL CONTROL—EXPORT • RELEASE BLOCKED PAYMENTS

Table 9.6 Transactional Embargo Reports (Export) (Cont.)

Figure 9.9 shows the selection screen from the Release Blocked Export Documents (Embargo) report. If you leave all fields blank, the results list all transactional export documents (e.g., sales orders and deliveries) on which the system has imposed an embargo block. To focus the list to a specific search criterion, input information into the LEGAL REGULATION, FOREIGN TRADE ORGANIZATION, and REFERENCE NUMBER fields.

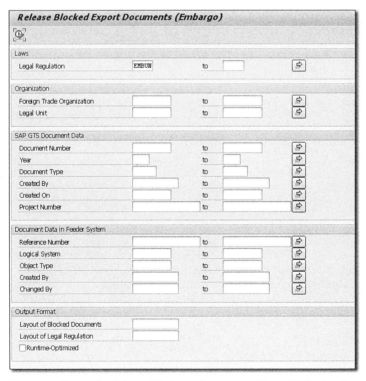

Figure 9.9 Report for Released Embargo Documents (Export) Selection Screen

Figure 9.10 shows the result of running the report, providing a rundown of export documents that have an imposed embargo block. In contrast to the Display Blocked Export Documents report, there is the addition of the green checkmark button and the ability to release the document with a reason (and possible comments) for release, which you can consult later for audit purposes.

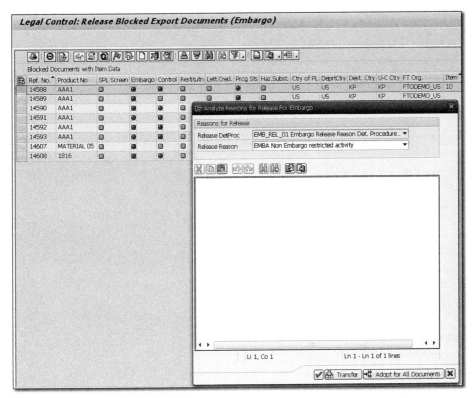

Figure 9.10 Report of Embargo Blocked Documents (Export) with the Option to Release

Table 9.7 (import) and Table 9.8 (export) provide further information relating to embargo actions taken on documents and payments. The first two reports in these tables list all documents and payments released for embargo, containing the technical and release data, including the time of release and person responsible. A separate report allows analyzing the reason as to why it was released (e.g., the documents consisted of a non-embargo–restricted activity).

Report Name	Menu Path
Display Released Import Embargo Documents	LEGAL CONTROL—IMPORT • DISPLAY RELEASED DOCUMENTS
Display Released Embargo Payment Receipts	LEGAL CONTROL—IMPORT • DISPLAY RELEASED PAYMENTS
Analyze Reasons for Release for Import Embargo	LEGAL CONTROL—IMPORT • ANALYZE REASONS FOR RELEASE
Display Business Partners with Embargo Situation—Import	LEGAL CONTROL—IMPORT • BUSINESS PARTNERS WITH EMBARGO SITUATION

Table 9.7 Descriptive Reports Related to Embargo (Import)

Report Name	Menu Path
Display Released Export Embargo Documents	LEGAL CONTROL—EXPORT • DISPLAY RELEASED DOCUMENTS
Display Released Embargo Outgoing Payments	LEGAL CONTROL—EXPORT • DISPLAY RELEASED PAYMENTS
Analyze Reasons for Release for Export Embargo	LEGAL CONTROL—EXPORT • ANALYZE REASONS FOR RELEASE
Display Business Partners with Embargo Situation—Export	LEGAL CONTROL—EXPORT • BUSINESS PARTNERS WITH EMBARGO SITUATION

Table 9.8 Descriptive Reports Related to Embargo (Export)

The Display Business Partners with Embargo Situation (Export) report allows a company to analyze its business partners in embargoed situations, providing a clear view of which operations they may not perform with certain business partners, including in what timeframe to consider these restrictions.

Figure 9.11 shows the selection screen for this report. You must simulate the list of embargoed business partners based on a certain legal regulation and key date. The KEY DATE field is required because each embargo has a set validity period and, thus, affects the outcome of the report. You can further narrow the search by specifying a country of departure and the category of business partners (e.g., customers or vendors).

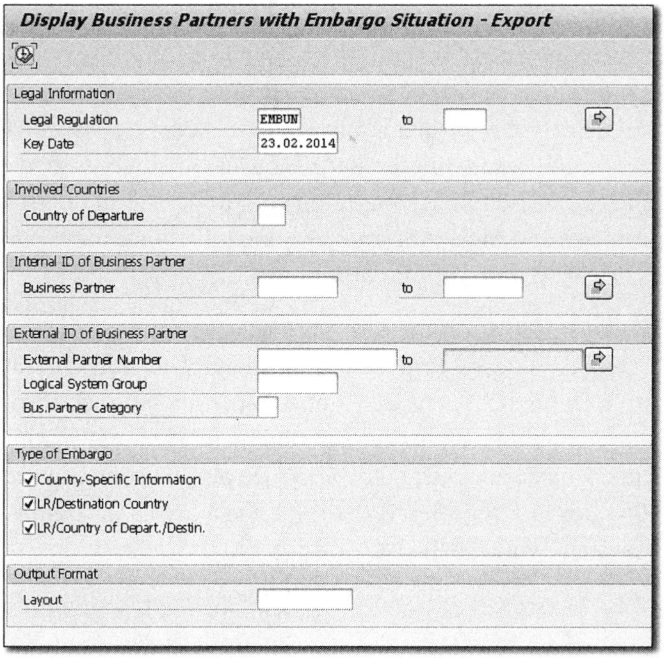

Figure 9.11 Analyzing Business Partners in Embargo Situation (Export) Report Selection Screen

Figure 9.12 shows the result of executing this report. It shows which business partners are residing in an embargoed situation, for how long, and for which country of departure.

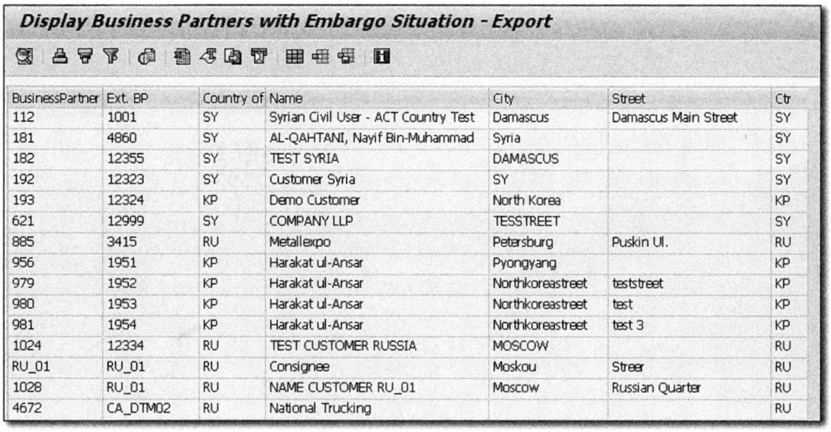

Display Business Partners with Embargo Situation - Export

BusinessPartner	Ext. BP	Country of	Name	City	Street	Ctr
112	1001	SY	Syrian Civil User - ACT Country Test	Damascus	Damascus Main Street	SY
181	4860	SY	AL-QAHTANI, Nayif Bin-Muhammad	Syria		SY
182	12355	SY	TEST SYRIA	DAMASCUS		SY
192	12323	SY	Customer Syria	SY		SY
193	12324	KP	Demo Customer	North Korea		KP
621	12999	SY	COMPANY LLP	TESSTREET		SY
885	3415	RU	Metallexpo	Petersburg	Puskin Ul.	RU
956	1951	KP	Harakat ul-Ansar	Pyongyang		KP
979	1952	KP	Harakat ul-Ansar	Northkoreastreet	teststreet	KP
980	1953	KP	Harakat ul-Ansar	Northkoreastreet	test	KP
981	1954	KP	Harakat ul-Ansar	Northkoreastreet	test 3	KP
1024	12334	RU	TEST CUSTOMER RUSSIA	MOSCOW		RU
RU_01	RU_01	RU	Consignee	Moskou	Streer	RU
1028	RU_01	RU	NAME CUSTOMER RU_01	Moscow	Russian Quarter	RU
4672	CA_DTM02	RU	National Trucking			RU

Figure 9.12 Report of Business Partners in an Embargo Situation (Export)

Legal Control

Legal control reports provide information about the legal checks and blocks performed on documents and which licenses are assigned, or are to be used, to resolve these blocks. The reports can be divided in three sections: transactional documents, license management, and master data reports. Analogous to the embargo reporting, each report is twofold: one report for import legal control, including purchasing processes and incoming payments, and the other for export legal control, entailing sales processes and outgoing payments.

Table 9.9 (import) and Table 9.10 (export) provide the reports related to transactional documents. The Display Blocked Import/Export Documents and Display Blocked Payment Receipts/Outgoing Payments reports are the same as those mentioned in the embargo reporting section: you can obtain detailed information about the reason of the imposed legal control block. The Display Existing Import/Export Documents reports act as a repository where you can access all transactional documents in the system, whether blocked or not.

Report Name	Menu Path
Display Blocked Import Documents	LEGAL CONTROL—IMPORT • DISPLAY BLOCKED DOCUMENTS
Display Blocked Payment Receipts	LEGAL CONTROL—IMPORT • DISPLAY BLOCKED PAYMENTS
Display Existing Import Documents	LEGAL CONTROL—IMPORT • DISPLAY EXISTING DOCUMENTS
Display Existing Payments Receipts	LEGAL CONTROL—IMPORT • DISPLAY AVAILABLE PAYMENTS

Table 9.9 Transactional Reports Related to Legal Control (Import)

Report Name	Menu Path
Display Blocked Export Documents	LEGAL CONTROL—EXPORT • DISPLAY BLOCKED DOCUMENTS
Display Blocked Outgoing Payments	LEGAL CONTROL—EXPORT • DISPLAY BLOCKED PAYMENTS

Table 9.10 Transactional Reports Related to Legal Control (Export)

Report Name	Menu Path
Display Existing Export Documents	LEGAL CONTROL—EXPORT • DISPLAY EXISTING DOCUMENTS
Display Existing Outgoing Payments	LEGAL CONTROL—EXPORT • DISPLAY AVAILABLE PAYMENTS

Table 9.10 Transactional Reports Related to Legal Control (Export) (Cont.)

As part of resolving legal control blocks, you can assign licenses to the documents that involve materials requiring import or export licenses. SAP GTS provides a number of reports to keep track of these licenses and to which documents they have been assigned.

Table 9.11 (import) and Table 9.12 (export) list these reports. For more detailed information on license management, consult the Compliance Management chapter.

Report Name	Menu Path
Display Existing Import Licenses	LEGAL CONTROL—IMPORT • DISPLAY EXISTING IMPORT LICENSES
Display Assigned Documents to Licenses	LEGAL CONTROL—IMPORT • DISPLAY ASSIGNED DOCUMENTS
Display Determination Strategy (Import)	LEGAL CONTROL—IMPORT • DISPLAY DETERMINATION STRATEGY
Tracking of ITAR Control-Relevant Products (Import)	LEGAL CONTROL—IMPORT • TRACK CONTROL-RELEVANT PRODUCTS

Table 9.11 Reports Related to Legal Control License Management (Import)

Report Name	Menu Path
Display Existing Export Licenses	LEGAL CONTROL—EXPORT • DISPLAY EXISTING EXPORT LICENSES
Display Existing Agreements	LEGAL CONTROL—EXPORT • DISPLAY EXISTING AGREEMENTS

Table 9.12 Reports Related to Legal Control License Management (Export)

Report Name	Menu Path
Display Assigned Documents to Licenses	LEGAL CONTROL—EXPORT • DISPLAY ASSIGNED DOCUMENTS
Display Assigned Licenses to Agreements	LEGAL CONTROL—EXPORT • ASSIGNED DOCUMENTS/EXPORT LICENSES
Display Determination Strategy (Export)	LEGAL CONTROL—EXPORT • DISPLAY DETERMINATION STRATEGY
Tracking of ITAR Control-Relevant Products (Export)	LEGAL CONTROL—EXPORT • TRACK CONTROL-RELEVANT PRODUCTS

Table 9.12 Reports Related to Legal Control License Management (Export) (Cont.)

Within the Legal Control functionality of SAP GTS, the Display Existing Export Licenses and Display Assigned Documents to Licenses transactions are useful for maintaining an overview of all licenses present in the system, including validity dates, remaining quantity, and more. To keep an eye on license renewal, a business may run the first mentioned report to retrieve a list of licenses with an almost-expiring validity date, near-zero quantity, etc. The second mentioned report provides detailed information about which documents are assigned to a certain license, with data such as item information, weight, decrementing quantity, etc.

The Display Existing Export Licenses report gives the company an overview of the export licenses maintained in SAP GTS. You'll have to specify a legal regulation for which the report displays the applicable licenses as shown in Figure 9.13. You can use other selection criteria (e.g., license type, status, validity date, product number, etc.) to enable a more detailed search.

Figure 9.14 shows the result of running the report for EAR licenses. The existing EAR licenses are grouped by license type and display information, such as the corresponding external license number, quantity and value data, validity period, and so on.

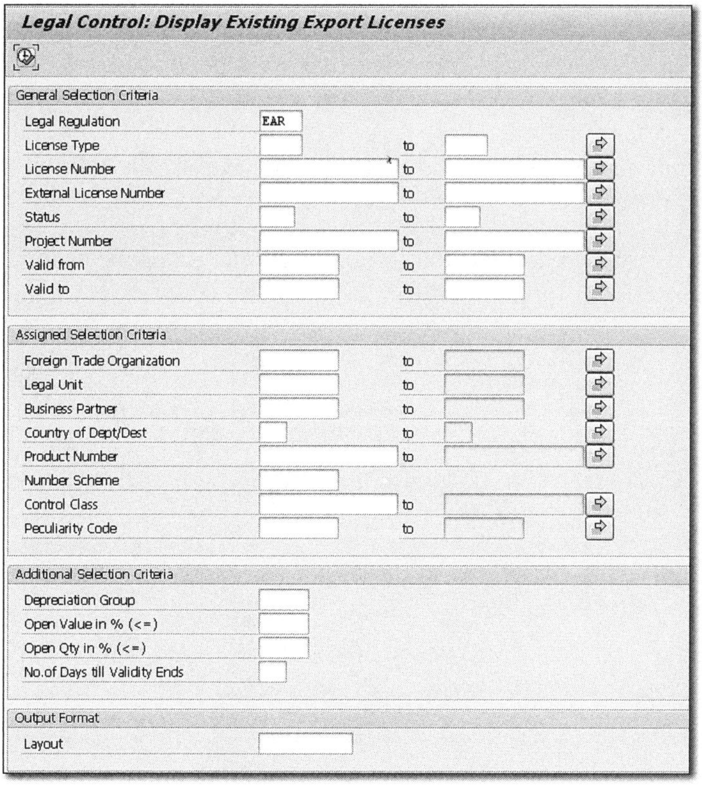

Legal Control: Display Existing Export Licenses

General Selection Criteria

Legal Regulation	EAR		
License Type		to	
License Number		to	
External License Number		to	
Status		to	
Project Number		to	
Valid from		to	
Valid to		to	

Assigned Selection Criteria

Foreign Trade Organization		to	
Legal Unit		to	
Business Partner		to	
Country of Dept/Dest		to	
Product Number		to	
Number Scheme			
Control Class		to	
Peculiarity Code		to	

Additional Selection Criteria

Depreciation Group	
Open Value in % (<=)	
Open Qty in % (<=)	
No.of Days till Validity Ends	

Output Format

Layout	

Figure 9.13 Display Export Licenses Selection Screen

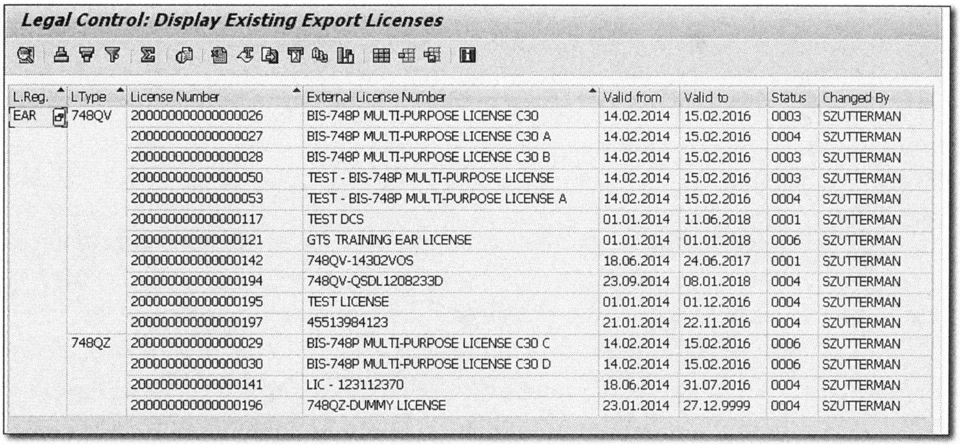

Legal Control: Display Existing Export Licenses

L.Reg.	LType	License Number	External License Number	Valid from	Valid to	Status	Changed By
EAR	748QV	20000000000000026	BIS-748P MULTI-PURPOSE LICENSE C30	14.02.2014	15.02.2016	0003	SZUTTERMAN
		20000000000000027	BIS-748P MULTI-PURPOSE LICENSE C30 A	14.02.2014	15.02.2016	0004	SZUTTERMAN
		20000000000000028	BIS-748P MULTI-PURPOSE LICENSE C30 B	14.02.2014	15.02.2016	0003	SZUTTERMAN
		20000000000000050	TEST - BIS-748P MULTI-PURPOSE LICENSE	14.02.2014	15.02.2016	0003	SZUTTERMAN
		20000000000000053	TEST - BIS-748P MULTI-PURPOSE LICENSE A	14.02.2014	15.02.2016	0004	SZUTTERMAN
		20000000000000117	TEST DCS	01.01.2014	11.06.2018	0001	SZUTTERMAN
		20000000000000121	GTS TRAINING EAR LICENSE	01.01.2014	01.01.2018	0006	SZUTTERMAN
		20000000000000142	748QV-14302VOS	18.06.2014	24.06.2017	0001	SZUTTERMAN
		20000000000000194	748QV-QSDL1208233D	23.09.2014	08.01.2018	0004	SZUTTERMAN
		20000000000000195	TEST LICENSE	01.01.2014	01.12.2016	0004	SZUTTERMAN
		20000000000000197	45513984123	21.01.2014	22.11.2016	0004	SZUTTERMAN
	748QZ	20000000000000029	BIS-748P MULTI-PURPOSE LICENSE C30 C	14.02.2014	15.02.2016	0006	SZUTTERMAN
		20000000000000030	BIS-748P MULTI-PURPOSE LICENSE C30 D	14.02.2014	15.02.2016	0006	SZUTTERMAN
		20000000000000141	LIC - 123112370	18.06.2014	31.07.2016	0004	SZUTTERMAN
		20000000000000196	748QZ-DUMMY LICENSE	23.01.2014	27.12.9999	0004	SZUTTERMAN

Figure 9.14 Report of Existing Export Licenses

413

Master Data

We can divide the reports located in the Compliance Management master data section into reports concerning product classification, product re-export, or country information. Note that, although reports related to SPL lists and existing licenses are considered master data reports as well, they have already been covered in the previous sections.

Table 9.13 gives an overview of all classification master data reports. For more information regarding classification, please consult Chapter 5 about classification.

Report Name	Menu Path
Classify via Worklist (Import)	CLASSIFICATION/MASTER DATA • IMPORT VIEW • CLASSIFY VIA WORKLIST
Classify via Worklist (Export)	CLASSIFICATION/MASTER DATA • EXPORT VIEW • CLASSIFY VIA WORKLIST
Maintain Import Control Classification Numbers	CLASSIFICATION/MASTER DATA • MAINTAIN IMPORT CONTROL CLASSIF. NUMBERS
Maintain Export Control Classification Numbers	CLASSIFICATION/MASTER DATA • MAINTAIN EXPORT CONTROL CLASSIF. NUMBERS
Display Analyzed Classifications	CLASSIFICATION/MASTER DATA • ANALYZE PRODUCT CLASSIFICATION

Table 9.13 Classification Master Data Reports

For companies that handle large numbers of materials, manually classifying one product at a time can be a tedious task. SAP GTS provides reports to display a selection of materials that have not yet been classified and allows you to make mass changes on the selected materials. As such, a classification effort can take place in a shorter timeframe by mass classifying similar products.

Figure 9.15 depicts the selection screen to run the list of yet-to-be-classified materials via a worklist. Mandatory fields include the KEY DATE and LEGAL REGULATION fields, as well as the choice to classify for import/arrival or export/dispatch. The latter choice has an impact only if the Customizing setup of a legal regulation is different for import and export. If, however, that legal regulation applies in both directions (e.g., ITAR active for both import and export), the classification applies for both, as well. Furthermore, you can choose to run the report for all unclassified materials with a certain product status (e.g., new, changed in feeder system, entered in SAP GTS, etc.).

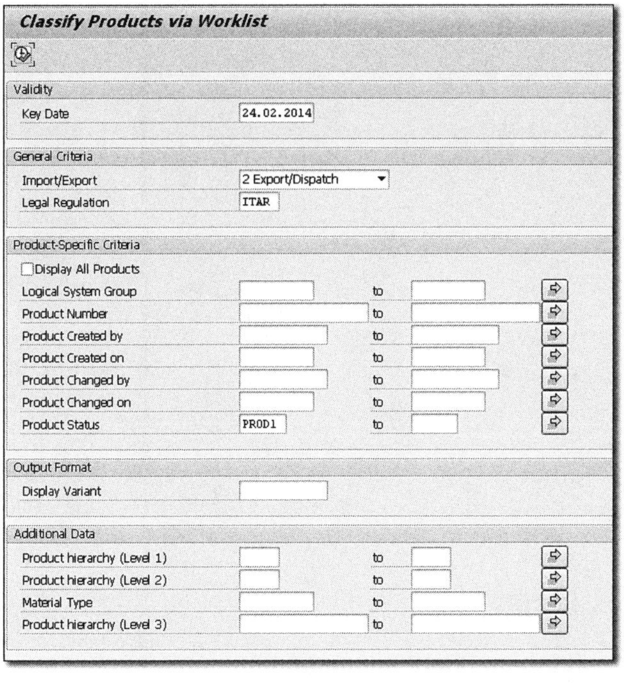

Figure 9.15 Report to Classify Products via Worklist Selection Screen

Figure 9.16 shows the output of the report: a rundown list of all products that have not yet been assigned an ECCN for the numbering scheme of the given legal regulation. The products with a red status in the EXPORT column will result in a legal control block on the corresponding documents, because the product has not been classified for that legal regulation. In addition, products with a green export status have no specific ECCN code assigned, but are classified with an active No CONTROL flag. Thus, the system clears these products in the control check for the applicable legal regulation.

You can use the Display Analyzed Classifications report in a number of ways. It allows compliance personnel to view and analyze the classification of its products over various legal regulations or search products that are similarly classified. Note that this transaction covers the analysis of compliance classification codes (ICCN and ECCN) but not customs classification codes.

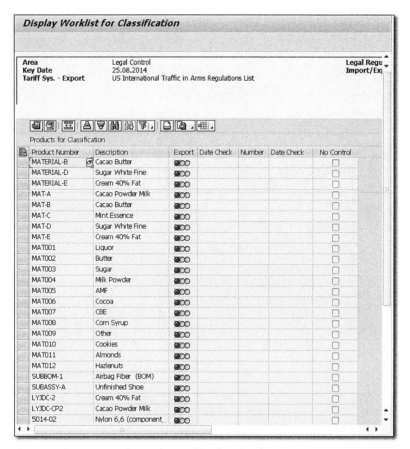

Figure 9.16 Report Displaying the Worklist for Classification

The selection screen, of which the logical system group is the only mandatory field, is shown in Figure 9.17. By entering a certain product (or range of), you can analyze the classification over the various legal regulations. In the example in Figure 9.17, a user searches all existing products that have been classified as an ITAR product with ECCN code VIII(h).

Figure 9.18 shows the output of the report. All products classified as an ITAR product with ECCN code VIII(h) are listed alongside corresponding data, such as validity date, grouping, peculiarity code, and No Control flag. Thus, this is an effective report for users or companies wanting to group all products linked to a certain ECCN.

Table 9.14 lists reports related to compliance master data.

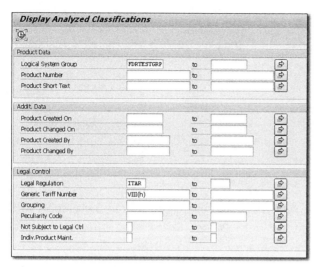

Figure 9.17 Analyze Product Classifications Selection Screen

Display Classified Products

L.Reg.	Scheme	LS Group	Product Number	Product Master Short Text	Number	No Contr...
EAR	USECC	FDRTESTGRP	AAA1	Stud A	7E001	
			BRAKE SYSTEM	Finished Product 1734	9A002	
			COMP-01	Nylon 6,6 (component 1)	9A002	
			COMP-02	Solution-died Nylon 6 (component 2)	9A002	
			COMP-0833	Component 1 - Alcohol		X
			COMP-1929	Component 3 - Chemicals		X
			COMP-4230	Component 2 - Sugar		X
			COMP-9910	Component 4 - API Zofran		X
			COMPONENT 1	Stud A	7E001	
			COMPONENT 2		7E001	
			CP_14	Component 4 (FP_01)		X
			CP-01	Zofran - Component 1		X
			CP-02	Zofran - Component 2		X
			DEMO-TP-BOM	Airbag Fiber (BOM)		X
			DEMO-TP-COMP-1	Nylon 6,6 (component 1)		X
			DEMO-TP-COMP-2	Solution-died Nylon 6 (component 2)		X
			DUMMY_MATERIAL	dummy material master	1A001	
			EKH-013	R&D equipment	3A233	X
			EKH-014	R&D equipment 014	1C350.b.24	X
			EKH-015	R&D equipment 015		X
			EKH-057	21" Flat Screen Monitor	8A018	X
			FP_10	Stud A		X
			FP-001	Casual Leather Shoe		X
			FP-002			X
			FP-01	ZOFRAN 2MG/ML 4MLX5 AMP INJ BK		X
			FP-2000	Bars and Kisses		X
			FP-343178	Caramel Delight		X
			FP-5014-02			X
			FP-569235	Almond Chocolate Bar		X
			FP-801	Finished Product - Rotor		X
			FP-BNK	Bars and Kisses		X
			FP-CAR	Caramel Delight		X

Figure 9.18 Report to Analyze Product Classifications

Report Name	Menu Path
Display Multilevel Bill of Material Structure	CLASSIFICATION/MASTER DATA • DISPLAY BOMS FOR PRODUCT
Display Determination Log of Re-Export Shares	CLASSIFICATION/MASTER DATA • DISPLAY CALCULATION LOG
Display Re-Export Data for Product	CLASSIFICATION/MASTER DATA • DISPLAY RE-EXPORT DATA FOR PRODUCT

Table 9.14 Compliance-Related Product Master Data Reports

The Display Multilevel Bill of Material report allows you to generate a report with the bill of material (BOM) information assigned to a certain product or several products.

The selection screen for this report, shown in Figure 9.19, requires you to specify a logical system and product number (or range of product numbers); alternative BOM and BOM usage are optional specifications.

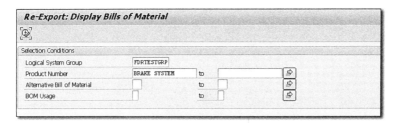

Figure 9.19 Display Product BOMs Selection Screen

The result, shown in Figure 9.20, displays the specified product's BOM; a hierarchical structure of its subcomponents; and additional information, such as the plant, required quantity in the BOM, amount, and currency. Note that the AMOUNT column specifies the value used for that component in a de minimis calculation for re-export purposes.

In SAP GTS, you can assign countries to country groups via Customizing in order to manage legal regulations, duty rates, and so on at a country group level. The result can be a more efficient process and more holistic overview. The report in Table 9.15 provides an overview of the Customizing settings regarding country/country groups. Note that because this data is maintained via Customizing, the report serves only descriptive purposes.

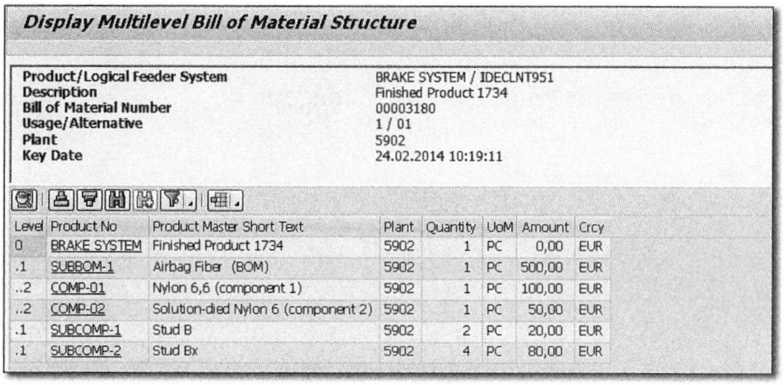
Display Multilevel Bill of Material Structure

Product/Logical Feeder System	BRAKE SYSTEM / IDECLNT951
Description	Finished Product 1734
Bill of Material Number	00003180
Usage/Alternative	1 / 01
Plant	5902
Key Date	24.02.2014 10:19:11

Level	Product No	Product Master Short Text	Plant	Quantity	UoM	Amount	Crcy
0	BRAKE SYSTEM	Finished Product 1734	5902	1	PC	0,00	EUR
.1	SUBBOM-1	Airbag Fiber (BOM)	5902	1	PC	500,00	EUR
..2	COMP-01	Nylon 6,6 (component 1)	5902	1	PC	100,00	EUR
..2	COMP-02	Solution-died Nylon 6 (component 2)	5902	1	PC	50,00	EUR
.1	SUBCOMP-1	Stud B	5902	2	PC	20,00	EUR
.1	SUBCOMP-2	Stud Bx	5902	4	PC	80,00	EUR

Figure 9.20 Multilevel Bill of Material Structure Report

Report Name	Menu Path
Display Country Assignment to Country Group	Classification/Master Data • Display Country Assignment to Ctry Grp

Table 9.15 Country Assignment Master Data Report

Entering a country of departure/destination in the selection screen (as shown in Figure 9.21) produces a list of country groups to which the specified country has been assigned (Figure 9.22). When you enter a country group rather than a country of departure, the report lists all countries that are part of that country group.

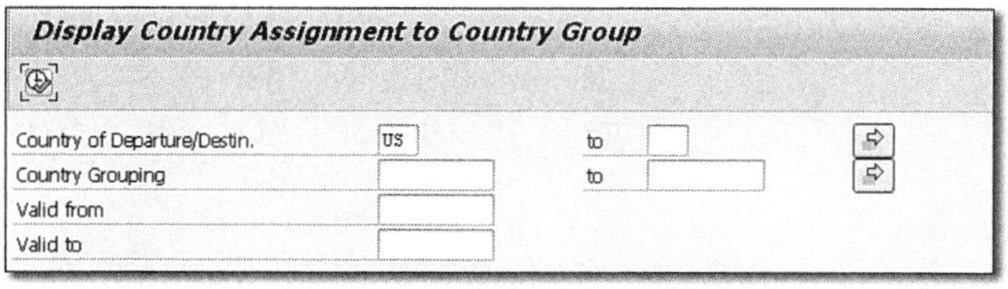
Display Country Assignment to Country Group

Country of Departure/Destin. US to
Country Grouping to
Valid from
Valid to

Figure 9.21 Country/Country Groups Assignment Selection Screen

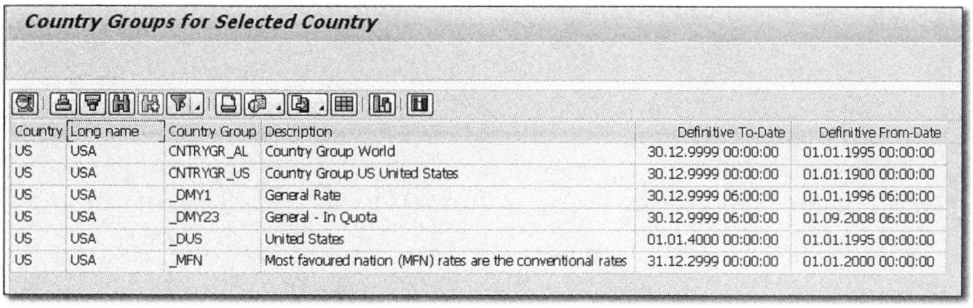
Country Groups for Selected Country

Country	Long name	Country Group	Description	Definitive To-Date	Definitive From-Date
US	USA	CNTRYGR_AL	Country Group World	30.12.9999 00:00:00	01.01.1995 00:00:00
US	USA	CNTRYGR_US	Country Group US United States	30.12.9999 00:00:00	01.01.1900 00:00:00
US	USA	_DMY1	General Rate	30.12.9999 06:00:00	01.01.1996 06:00:00
US	USA	_DMY23	General - In Quota	30.12.9999 06:00:00	01.09.2008 06:00:00
US	USA	_DUS	United States	01.01.4000 00:00:00	01.01.1995 00:00:00
US	USA	_MFN	Most favoured nation (MFN) rates are the conventional rates	31.12.2999 00:00:00	01.01.2000 00:00:00

Figure 9.22 Report Listing the Assignment Country/Country Groups

Having focused on reporting for Compliance Management—and, more specifically, the reporting aspects of SPL Screening, Embargo, and Legal Control—we now turn our attention to the reports on Customs Management.

9.1.2 Customs Management Reporting

In an international trade environment where goods are crossing borders, information regarding these goods, the applicable duties and taxes, and safety and security data are essential. Similar to Compliance Management reporting, SAP GTS provides reports to support the customs processes discussed in detail in the Customs Management chapter.

Within SAP GTS Customs Management reporting, three subcategories are to be listed:

- Customs documents providing data on the general import and export functionalities
- Reports related to special customs procedures, where the focus of the reports lies mostly on inventory levels
- Reports concerning customs master data

Let's look at each one in turn.

Customs Documents

The reports for customs documents provide information on the general inbound and outbound declarations in SAP GTS. Table 9.16 (import) and Table 9.17 (export) list these reports.

Report Name	Menu Path
Activities in the Customs Processing Area (Import)	IMPORT • TAB IMPORT • DISPLAY INBOUND ACTIVITIES
Display Available Customs Import Declarations	IMPORT • TAB IMPORT • DISPLAY CUSTOMS DECLARATIONS
Worklist for Customs Declaration Prior to Goods Receipt	IMPORT • TAB IMPORT • ENTER DECLARATION PRIOR TO GOODS RECEIPT

Table 9.16 General Customs Reports (Import)

Report Name	Menu Path
Worklist for Customs Declaration After Goods Receipt	IMPORT • TAB IMPORT • WORKLIST: CUSTOMS DECL. AFTER GOODS RECEIPT
Display Unassigned Customs Bill of Lading	IMPORT • TAB IMPORT • DISPLAY UNASSIGNED CUSTOMS BILL OF LADING

Table 9.16 General Customs Reports (Import) (Cont.)

Report Name	Menu Path
Activities in the Customs Processing Area (Export)	EXPORT • TAB EXPORT • DISPLAY OUTBOUND ACTIVITIES
Display Available Customs Export Declarations	EXPORT • TAB EXPORT • DISPLAY CUSTOMS DECLARATIONS
Monitor Export Confirmation for Customs Declaration	EXPORT • TAB EXPORT • EXPORT CONFIRMATION MONITORING
Display Export Document Flow	EXPORT • TAB EXPORT • DISPLAY EXPORT DOCUMENT FLOW

Table 9.17 General Customs Reports (Export)

As extensively discussed in the Customs Management chapter, SAP GTS is equipped with an operative cockpit from which you can access in a report all documents that require further attention, grouped into activities. This is the most consulted report in the operational customs process. Because the documents in this report are divided into different worklists, it is easy for companies with a large trade customs team to split the workload of the people based on these processes.

Figure 9.23 shows the selection screen that runs the report for all inbound activities still requiring attention. If you run the report but leave all data fields blank, you'll get a list of all inbound flows across the different FTOs that have not yet been completed.

To narrow the search, you can enter a specific FTO, resulting in the report shown in Figure 9.24. The report shows the different steps in that FTO's import process, with the number of documents present in each activity. From the report, you can access and further process customs declarations.

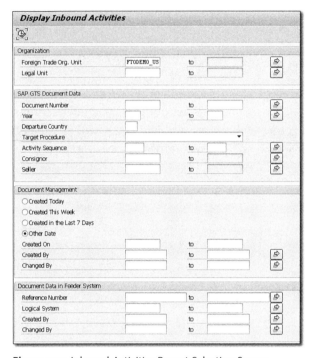

Figure 9.23 Inbound Activities Report Selection Screen

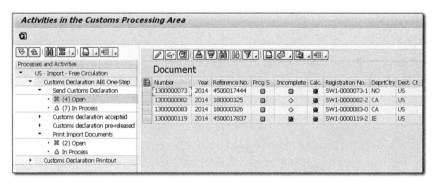

Figure 9.24 Report of Import Activities in Customs Processing Area

Aside from the general import process, similar reports exist for the inbound activities related to transit, presentation to customs authorities, and pre-declaration. Because these reports follow a similar approach, we won't discuss them here.

Table 9.17 lists the export equivalent of the previously discussed reports. Again, the operational cockpit report containing the outbound activities to further process is the most significant and follows the same logic as the import report.

Besides the operative cockpit, the customs monitoring functionality in SAP GTS provides an alternative way of displaying an overview of the customs declarations.

The Display Available Customs Export Declarations report lists all customs declarations, independent of the activity they are in. Besides these open declarations, the report also enables you to track fully processed and completed documents and cancelled documents, serving as an audit rather than an operational report.

Figure 9.25 shows the selection screen for the existing export declarations report.

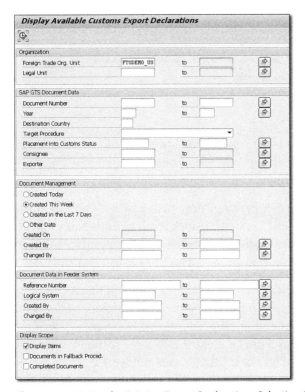

Figure 9.25 Listing the Existing Export Declarations Selection Screen

It is generally the same selection screen as that for the operative cockpit, with the addition of a few extra selection options. For example, you can run the report to show only reports residing in a fallback procedure (e.g., for a single person authorized to handle these documents) or only the completed declarations (e.g., for audit purposes).

Figure 9.26 displays the result of executing the report, which lists all existing export declarations for the specified FTO, with corresponding data such as processing status, item information, etc.

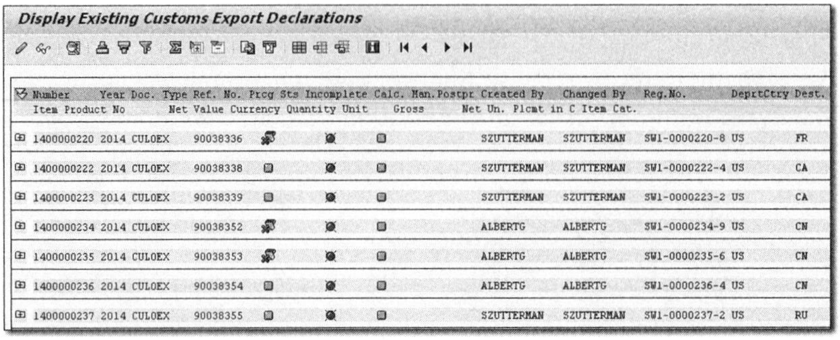

Figure 9.26 Report of Existing Export Declarations

Special Customs Procedures

Special procedure reports provide information on specific customs procedures, including bonded warehouse (BWH), inward processing relief (IPR), outward processing relief (OPR), and processing under customs control (PUCC).

Because these processes distinguish between duty-paid and duty-unpaid stock, most related reports give you a full overview of stock levels and stock movements of products related to these special customs procedures. For more information on special customs procedures, please consult the Customs Management chapter.

For declaring to customs authorities, it's important to maintain the overview of duty-unpaid stock levels. To support this overview, SAP GTS provides reports for each of the previously mentioned customs procedures that list an overview of the stock movements. Stock list reports can be divided into three sections: Overview of Individual Stock Items, Stock Overview, and Receipt and Issues.

The Overview of Individual Stock Items shows the receipt and issue postings that have an economic impact on the special procedure products. Because SAP GTS processes the special procedure products on a first-in, first-out basis, the system links each receipt posting with the corresponding issue postings. This relation between receipt and issue postings is also included in those reports. Furthermore, because declaring duty-unpaid stock levels on a periodic basis in the customs warehouse is mandatory in most regions, an additional report is available. This Display Stock List with Starting and Ending Stocks report provides the duty-unpaid start- and end-stock levels for a specific customs product in the requested timeframe; you can then declare these to the customs authorities.

The Stock Overview reports list the customs warehouse stock present for the special procedure products for each respective category (duty-paid/unpaid, reserved/not reserved).

Finally, the Receipt and Issues reports show all receipt and issue postings in chronological order for a certain product, which allows analyzing the goods movements and related stock changes of a certain special procedure product.

Table 9.18 lists the reports concerning individual stock items for the four SAP GTS-supported special procedures.

Report Name	Menu Path
Display Duty-Unpaid Individual Stock Item (BWH)	MONITORING FOR INVENTORY-MANAGED CUSTOMS PROCEDURES • TAB CUSTOMS WAREHOUSE • DISPLAY DUTY-UNPAID INDIVIDUAL STOCK ITEMS
Display Stock List with Starting and Ending Stock (BWH)	MONITORING FOR INVENTORY-MANAGED CUSTOMS PROCEDURES • TAB CUSTOMS WAREHOUSE • DISPLAY OPENING/CLOSING STOCK
Display Individual Stock Item (IPR)	MONITORING FOR INVENTORY-MANAGED CUSTOMS PROCEDURES • TAB INWARD PROCESSING • DISPLAY INDIVIDUAL STOCK ITEMS
Display Individual Stock Item (OPR)	MONITORING FOR INVENTORY-MANAGED CUSTOMS PROCEDURES • TAB OUTWARD PROCESSING • DISPLAY INDIVIDUAL STOCK ITEMS
Display Individual Stock Item (PUCC)	MONITORING FOR INVENTORY-MANAGED CUSTOMS PROCEDURES • TAB PUCC • DISPLAY INDIVIDUAL STOCK ITEMS

Table 9.18 Special Customs Procedures Individual Stock Items Reports

Figure 9.27 shows the selection screen for the BWH individual stock item report. Note that this selection screen is identical to those of the other special customs procedures. For a given customs warehouse ID, you can access the receipt and issue postings with an economic impact for up to five special procedure products (customs products). Additionally, you need to enter a stock posting period in which the receipt and issues took place.

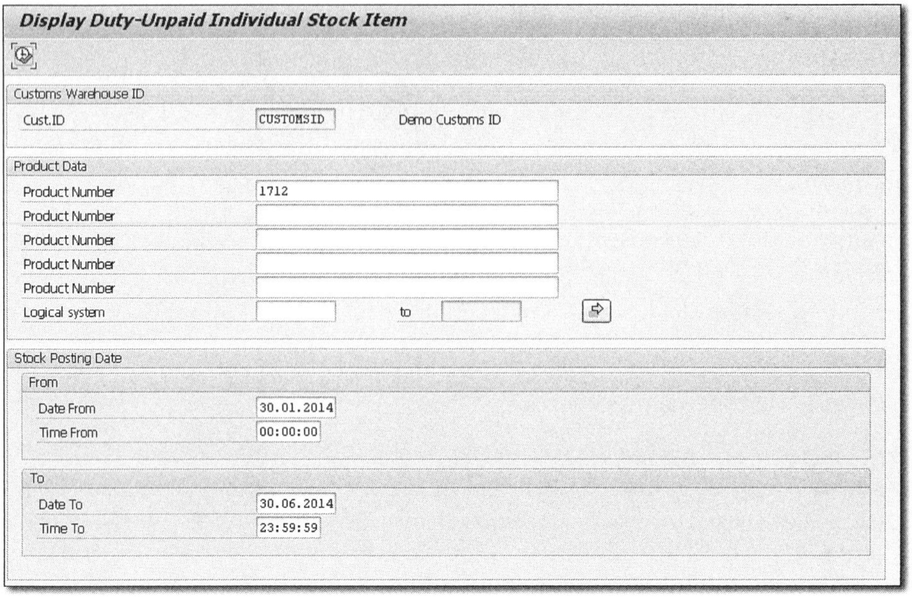

Figure 9.27 Selection Screen to Display BWH Duty-Unpaid Individual Stock Items

Figure 9.28 shows the result of the individual stock item report for BWH. Each line represents either a receipt (green plus sign) or issue (red minus sign) posting. Every product issue that has an economic impact (e.g., bringing duty-unpaid goods into free circulation) is linked to a receipt. From the report, you can access the bespoke products, receipt documents, and issue documents immediately.

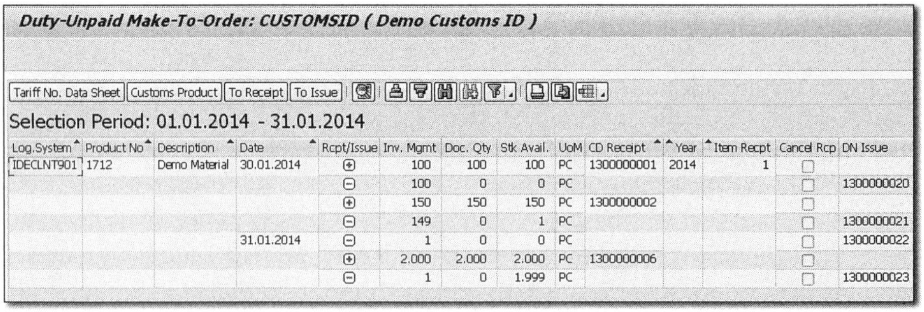

Log.System	Product No	Description	Date	Rcpt/Issue	Inv. Mgmt	Doc. Qty	Stk Avail.	UoM	CD Receipt	Year	Item Recpt	Cancel Rcp	DN Issue
IDECLNT901	1712	Demo Material	30.01.2014	⊕	100	100	100	PC	1300000001	2014	1	☐	
				⊖	100	0	0	PC				☐	1300000020
				⊕	150	150	150	PC	1300000002			☐	
				⊖	149	0	1	PC				☐	1300000021
			31.01.2014	⊖	1	0	0	PC				☐	1300000022
				⊕	2.000	2.000	2.000	PC	1300000006			☐	
				⊖	1	0	1.999	PC				☐	1300000023

Figure 9.28 Report of BWH Duty-Unpaid Individual Stock Items

Note that the way to declare duty-paid and duty-unpaid stock levels is dependent on the region and applicable customs regulations.

Table 9.19 lists the reports that provide an overview of the stock levels for each category (duty paid/unpaid, reserved/not reserved). The selection screen is identical to Figure 9.27, with the exclusion of a stock postings timeframe.

Report Name	Menu Path
Display Stock Overview (BWH)	MONITORING FOR INVENTORY-MANAGED CUSTOMS PROCEDURES • TAB CUSTOMS WAREHOUSE • DISPLAY STOCK OVERVIEW
Display Stock Overview (IPR)	MONITORING FOR INVENTORY-MANAGED CUSTOMS PROCEDURES • TAB INWARD PROCESSING • DISPLAY STOCK OVERVIEW
Display Stock Overview (OPR)	MONITORING FOR INVENTORY-MANAGED CUSTOMS PROCEDURES • TAB OUTWARD PROCESSING • DISPLAY STOCK OVERVIEW
Display Stock Overview (PUCC)	MONITORING FOR INVENTORY-MANAGED CUSTOMS PROCEDURES • TAB PUCC • DISPLAY STOCK OVERVIEW

Table 9.19 Special Customs Procedures Stock Overview Reports

As the stock overview reports show the total stock of customs products at a given time, independent of stock postings period. Figure 9.29 shows the output of the report, providing the actual levels of the four stock categories for a certain customs product. From this report, you can directly access the customs product and a receipt/issue or first-in, first-out list for the product over a period of up to 12 months. Additionally, via this report, you can move duty-paid or duty-unpaid stock directly into free circulation or place it in the respective reserved stock for scrapping.

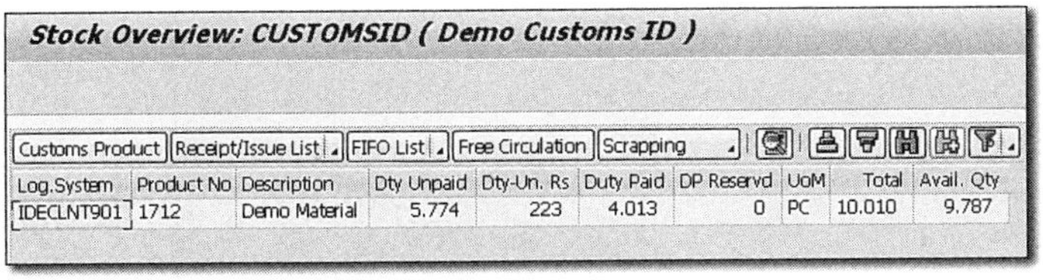

Figure 9.29 BWH Stock Overview Report

Table 9.20 gives an overview of the receipt/issue list reports, which provide an overview of all incoming and outgoing flows related to the customs products. Unlike the individual stock item reports, these reports list all flows, regardless of category (duty paid/unpaid, reserved/not reserved), in chronological order, giving an overview of the exact movements of the specific customs products.

Report Name	Menu Path
Display Receipt/Issue List (BWH)	Monitoring for Inventory-Managed Customs Procedures • Tab Customs Warehouse • Display Receipts and Issues
Display Receipt/Issue List (IPR)	Monitoring for Inventory-Managed Customs Procedures • Tab Inward Processing • Display Receipts and Issues
Display Receipt/Issue List (OPR)	Monitoring for Inventory-Managed Customs Procedures • Tab Outward Processing • Display Receipts and Issues
Display Receipt/Issue List (PUCC)	Monitoring for Inventory-Managed Customs Procedures • Tab PUCC • Display Receipts and Issues

Table 9.20 Special Customs Procedures Receipt and Issue Reports

The same selection screen as in Figure 9.27 applies, resulting in the receipt/issue postings in a certain customs warehouse for no more than five customs products over a specified timeframe.

Figure 9.30 displays the outcome of the report. Each line represents either a receipt or an issue posting, with the corresponding stock category, and provides direct access to each receipt or issue document.

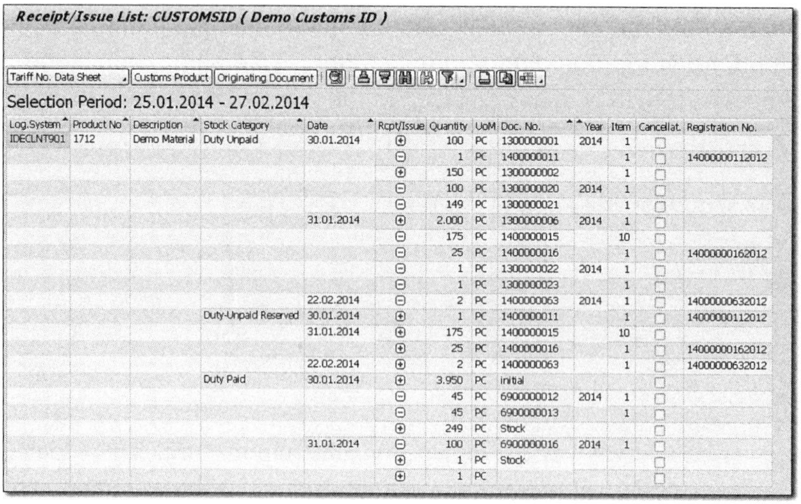

Receipt/Issue List: CUSTOMSID (Demo Customs ID)

Tariff No. Data Sheet | Customs Product | Originating Document

Selection Period: 25.01.2014 - 27.02.2014

Log.System	Product No	Description	Stock Category	Date	Rcpt/Issue	Quantity	UoM	Doc. No.	Year	Item	Cancellat.	Registration No.
IDECLNT901	1712	Demo Material	Duty Unpaid	30.01.2014	+	100	PC	1300000001	2014	1	☐	
					−	1	PC	1400000011		1	☐	14000000112012
					+	150	PC	1300000002		1	☐	
					−	100	PC	1300000020	2014	1	☐	
					−	149	PC	1300000021		1	☐	
				31.01.2014	+	2.000	PC	1300000006	2014	1	☐	
					−	175	PC	1400000015		10	☐	
					−	25	PC	1400000016		1	☐	14000000162012
					−	1	PC	1300000022	2014	1	☐	
					−	1	PC	1300000023		1	☐	
				22.02.2014	−	2	PC	1400000063	2014	1	☐	14000000632012
			Duty-Unpaid Reserved	30.01.2014	+	1	PC	1400000011		1	☐	14000000112012
				31.01.2014	+	175	PC	1400000015		10	☐	
					+	25	PC	1400000016		1	☐	14000000162012
				22.02.2014	+	2	PC	1400000063		1	☐	14000000632012
			Duty Paid	30.01.2014	+	3.950	PC	initial			☐	
					−	45	PC	6900000012	2014	1	☐	
					−	45	PC	6900000013		1	☐	
					+	249	PC	Stock			☐	
				31.01.2014	−	100	PC	6900000016	2014	1	☐	
					+	1	PC	Stock			☐	
					+	1	PC				☐	

Figure 9.30 Report with the Receipt and Issue Postings in the Specified Timeframe

Master Data

The last section of Customs Management reporting concerns reports related to master data.

In certain customs procedures, you may need appropriate authorizations from the customs authorities. The customs authorities grant these authorizations to companies that have proven reliable in these procedures and allow them to handle certain customs-relevant processes or apply simplified procedures in the import/export process. These authorizations can range from granting a company permission to use a customs warehouse, participate in inward/outward processing control, process under customs control, or apply a simplified customs procedure to its import/export or transit process.

You can enter authorizations (and specifications such as the status, FTO, customs offices, texts, etc.) granted by the authorities as master data in SAP GTS.

Aside from authorizations, certain countries require companies to deposit securities when importing goods. This procedure helps customs authorities ensure that companies pay the amount of duties they owe. You can enter securities as master data in SAP GTS in the same way as authorizations or licenses. The specific type and attributes of the securities depend on Customizing settings and regulations received from or communicated by the customs authorities.

Table 9.21 lists the master data reports in SAP GTS related to previously discussed authorizations and securities.

Report Name	Menu Path
Display Existing Import Processing Securities	MASTER DATA • TAB AUTHORIZATIONS/SECURITIES • MONITOR SECURITIES FOR CUSTOMS PROCESSING
Display Existing Dispatch Securities	MASTER DATA • TAB AUTHORIZATIONS/SECURITIES • MONITOR TRANSIT SECURITIES
Display Existing Import/ Export Authorizations	MASTER DATA • TAB AUTHORIZATIONS/SECURITIES • MONITOR AUTHORITIES FOR CUSTOMS PROCESSING
Display Dispatch/Presentation Authorizations	MASTER DATA • TAB AUTHORIZATIONS/SECURITIES • MONITOR TRANSIT AUTHORIZATIONS

Table 9.21 Customs Reports Related to Authorizations and Securities

Figure 9.31 shows the selection screen for displaying the existing authorizations. According to the specified screen, you run a report for the Belgian customs regulation (CUSBE), searching for authorizations that possess an active status (0002) and are applicable to the Belgian FTO.

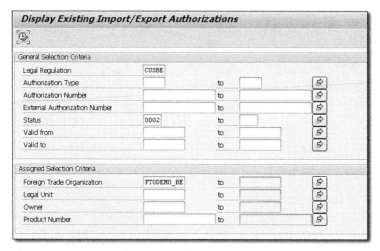

Figure 9.31 Existing Authorizations Selection Screen

Figure 9.32 shows that the Belgian FTO is authorized by the customs authorities to apply simplified import and export procedures and leverage a BWH.

L.Reg.	LTy	License Number	External License Number	Valid from	Valid to	Im/Ex	Status
CUSBE	VVEX	120000000000000005	SIMPLIFIED EXPORT	02.02.2014	31.12.2099	2	0002
	VVIM	120000000000000004	SIMPLIFIED IMPORT	01.01.2014	31.12.2099	1	0002
	VVZL	130000000000000013	BONDED WAREHOUSE	02.02.2014	31.12.2099	3	0002

Figure 9.32 Report of Existing Authorizations

Furthermore, you can distinguish master data reports relating to the customs product classification. Table 9.22 gives an overview of all master data reports related to customs product classification. Note that these reports consider customs classification (e.g., tariff and commodity codes), not the legal control classification.

Report Name	Menu Path
Classify Products via Worklist	CLASSIFICATION • TAB CLASSIFICATION • CLASSIFY VIA WORKLIST
Display Product Catalog	CLASSIFICATION • TAB CLASSIFICATION • DISPLAY PRODUCT CATALOG
Display Monitoring for Customs Products	MASTER DATA • TAB CUSTOMS PRODUCTS • DISPLAY PRODUCT MONITOR

Table 9.22 Master Data Reports Related to Customs Classification

The Display Product Catalog report serves the same purpose as the Analyze Product Classification report discussed in Figure 9.18. You can apply it to search all products and analyze their classifications or search all products that have been classified using a specific code. Note that this report allows you to analyze both compliance codes (e.g., ICCN and ECCN) and customs classification codes (e.g., HTS tariff codes and Schedule B commodity codes).

Figure 9.33 shows the selection screen of the Display Product Catalog report. In the type of numbering scheme, you can choose between the various import and export numbering schemes that have been set up in the system. Furthermore, you can enter a customs classification code (or range of classification codes) to get a more detailed report.

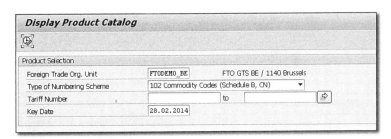

Figure 9.33 Displaying the Product Catalog Selection Screen

In this example, we ran the report without entering a specific classification code and specified only the Schedule B commodity codes numbering scheme. The output of this selection screen results in the report shown in Figure 9.34: a list of all products with a customs classification code, with corresponding data such as unit of measure, numbering scheme, and classification validity period.

Prod. Catalog for Demo FTO BE / 1210 Brussels

Commodity Codes (Schedule B, CN) Key Date: 25.08.2014

Tariff Number	Numbering Scheme Name	Product Number	Product Master Short Text	Log. Sys. Group	BUn
30041000	Commodity Codes - EU	FP-ZOFRAN	ZOFRAN 2MG/ML 4MLX5	FDRTESTGRP	PC
73181550		1712	Electric Motor 128761-11	FDRTESTGRP	
		1719	R&D equipment 2	FDRTESTGRP	
		MATERIAL TTT	Pinacolyl Alcohol Tricolore	FDRTESTGRP	
		1752	Demo Material BWH	FDRTESTGRP	
73181559		1705	Stud A	FDRTESTGRP	
		1720	Stud B tp	FDRTESTGRP	
		1788	Encryption Mat - Restricted	FDRTESTGRP	
85250001		1749	COMPONENT 2_TRADE PREF	FDRTESTGRP	
		1748	COMPONENT 1_TRADE PREF	FDRTESTGRP	
		1732	Stud B trade	FDRTESTGRP	
		FP_1	Finished Product 1	FDRTESTGRP	
		FP_01	Stud A	FDRTESTGRP	
		1756	120 mm MORTAR AMMUNITION	FDRTESTGRP	
		1717	Stud B FG	FDRTESTGRP	
		1704	Unilever Test Material	FDRTESTGRP	
85255000		CP_12	Component 2 (FP_01)	FDRTESTGRP	
85362010		1750	Controlled Item - Demo	FDRTESTGRP	
		1740	Component 1 (1739)	FDRTESTGRP	
		CP_13	Component 3 (FP_01)	FDRTESTGRP	
		CP_11	Component 1 (FP_01)	FDRTESTGRP	
85423101		MAT_DEMO_BONDED	21" Flat Screen Monitor	FDRTESTGRP	EA
		FP_10	Stud A	FDRTESTGRP	PC
		CP_01	Component 1 (FP_01)	FDRTESTGRP	
		1729	Stud B trade	FDRTESTGRP	
		1739	Finished product GTS TP event	FDRTESTGRP	
		1718	Stud B trade	FDRTESTGRP	
85423201		1707	Stud A	FDRTESTGRP	
		1708	Stud A	FDRTESTGRP	
		1716	Stud B tp	FDRTESTGRP	

Figure 9.34 Report Displaying the Product Catalog

Having considered the reporting aspects for SAP GTS Customs Management, specifically customs documents and special customs procedures, let's move on to reports from the final module of SAP GTS, Risk Management.

9.1.3 Risk Management Reporting

As with Compliance Management and Customs Management reporting, let's look at the subdivisions of Risk Management: Trade Preference Management, Restitution Management, and Letter of Credit Processing.

Trade Preference Management

The Trade Preference Management module in SAP GTS Risk Management allows companies to manage, track, and report the trade preference status in order to determine the trade preference relevancy of the concerned products. You can logically group the relevant reports for trade preference processing in reports concerning vendor-based vendor declarations, vendor declarations for the customer's purposes, and product preference determination.

Note that all these reports depend on the specified administrative unit (AU), which you must enter before running any of the following reports. The AU determines which free trade agreements and specific characteristics to apply. For a more detailed overview of this topic, please consult the Risk Management chapter.

Table 9.23 gives an overview of the lists concerning vendor-based vendor declaration reports. These reports support the process of requesting, dunning, and aggregating long-term vendor declarations (LTVDs) from vendors.

Report Name	Menu Path
Display Worklist for Vendor-Based Long-Term Vendor Declaration	PREFERENCE PROCESSING • MANAGE VENDOR-BASED VENDOR DECLARATIONS • TAB MONITORING • DISPLAY WORKLIST
Monitoring of Vendor-Based Long-Term Vendor Declaration	PREFERENCE PROCESSING • MANAGE VENDOR-BASED VENDOR DECLARATIONS • TAB MONITORING • DISPLAY VENDOR DECLARATION
Aggregate Long-Term Vendor Declarations	PREFERENCE PROCESSING • MANAGE VENDOR-BASED VENDOR DECLARATIONS • TAB PROCESSING • AGGREGATE VENDOR DECLARATION
Assign Vendors to Administrative Unit	PREFERENCE PROCESSING • MANAGE VENDOR-BASED VENDOR DECLARATIONS • TAB RELEVANT MASTER DATA • ASSIGN VENDOR

Table 9.23 Vendor-Based Vendor Declaration Reports

Figure 9.35 shows the selection screen for displaying the worklist of vendor-based vendor declarations. In order to run the report, you must enter an AU. Optionally, you can filter the report for a certain vendor or product (or range of products).

Figure 9.36 displays the worklist report. It shows the product-vendor combinations eligible for requesting LTVDs. From this report, you can initiate the actual requesting process. Once the vendor declaration is requested, that product-vendor combination is moved from the worklist report to the Monitoring of Long-Term Vendor Declarations report.

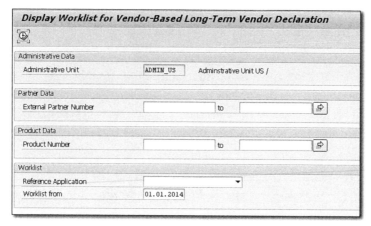

Figure 9.35 Vendor-Based Vendor Declaration Worklist Selection Screen

Display Worklist for Vendor-Based Long-Term Vendor Declaration

ADMIN_US Adminstrative Unit US /

Vendor	Name	City	Ctr	Vend. Rel.	Product No	Product Master Short Text	Req. Rel.	Ref. Application
7400	Norplant AS	Oslo	NO	Vendor Relevant	AA11	Cell phone base station	Relevant	MM Goods Movement
12122	Vendor MX		MX	Vendor Relevant	DEMO-TP-01	Component 2 - Trade Pref	Relevant	MM Purchase Order
				Vendor Relevant	DEMO-TP-02	Component 2 - Trade Pref	Relevant	MM Purchase Order
				Vendor Relevant	DEMO-TP-03	Component 2 - Trade Pref	Relevant	MM Purchase Order
				Vendor Relevant	EMT-2	Component 2 - Trade Pref	Relevant	MM Purchase Order
				Vendor Relevant	EMT-3	Component 2 - Trade Pref	Relevant	MM Purchase Order
				Vendor Relevant	EMT-4	Component 2 - Trade Pref	Relevant	MM Purchase Order

Figure 9.36 Worklist for Vendor-Based Vendor Declarations

Whereas Table 9.23 elaborated on the reports concerning requesting LTVDs from vendors, Table 9.24 lists the reports that support the process of issuing LTVDs to customers.

Report Name	Menu Path
Display Worklist Long-Term Vendor Declaration for Customer's Purposes	PREFERENCE PROCESSING • MANAGE VENDOR DECLARATIONS FOR CUSTOMER'S PURPOSE • TAB MONITORING • DISPLAY WORKLIST

Table 9.24 Reports Concerning Vendor Declarations for Customer Purposes

Report Name	Menu Path
Monitoring of Long-Term Vendor Declaration for Customer's Purposes	PREFERENCE PROCESSING • MANAGE VENDOR DECLARATIONS FOR CUSTOMER'S PURPOSE • TAB MONITORING • DISPLAY VENDOR DECLARATION
Assign Customer to Administrative Unit	PREFERENCE PROCESSING • MANAGE VENDOR DECLARATIONS FOR CUSTOMER'S PURPOSE • TAB RELEVANT MASTER DATA • ASSIGN CUSTOMER

Table 9.24 Reports Concerning Vendor Declarations for Customer Purposes (Cont.)

In the previous report example (Figure 9.36), we elaborated on the worklist to request LTVDs. An analogous report is available for issuing LTVDs for the customer's purposes. As stated, when preference declarations are processed, you can review them in the monitoring report. Figure 9.37 shows the selection screen for the Monitoring of LTVDs for Customer's Purposes report.

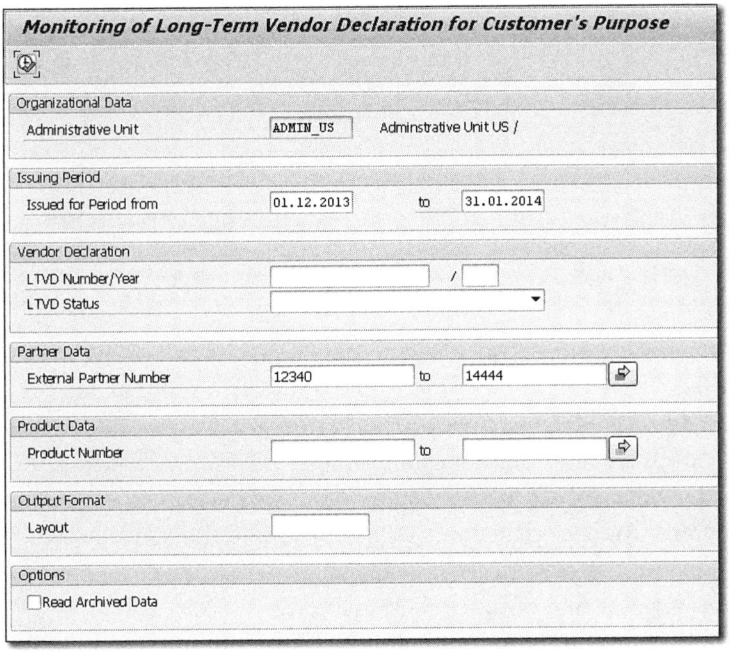

Figure 9.37 Monitoring Issued Vendor Declarations to Customers Selection Screen

By executing the report for a certain issuing period and using two business partners as selection criteria, you can produce the report shown in Figure 9.38. The report lists the LTVDs issued to the requested business partners, with corresponding data such as the preferential status, validity period, tariff numbers, etc.

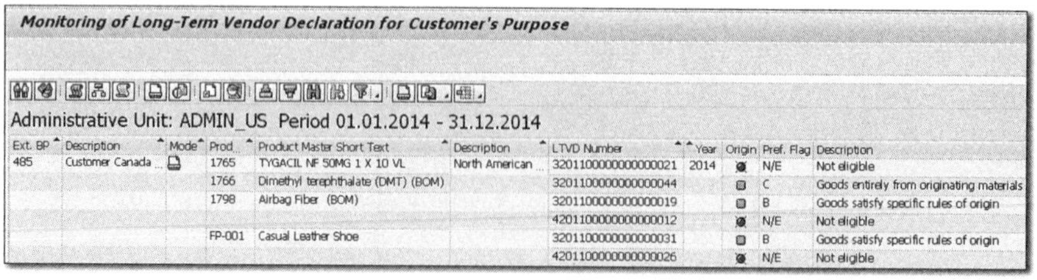

Figure 9.38 Report of Issued Vendor Declarations for Customer's Purpose

Finally, Table 9.25 lists the reports that support the process of calculating the preferential status of a company's products.

Report Name	Menu Path
Display Preference Determination Log	PREFERENCE PROCESSING • PREFERENCE DETERMINATION • TAB DETERMINATION • DISPLAY PREFERENCE DETERMINATION LOG
Display Worklist of Configured BOMs	PREFERENCE PROCESSING • PREFERENCE DETERMINATION • TAB DETERMINATION • DISPLAY WORKLIST OF CONFIGURED BOPs
Display Preference Result by Document	PREFERENCE PROCESSING • PREFERENCE DETERMINATION • TAB DETERMINATION • DISPLAY PREFERENCE RESULT BY DOCUMENT

Table 9.25 Reports Concerning Preference Determination

SAP GTS logs and archives all preference determination results, providing a complete overview of the preference characteristics of a company's goods at all times. You can print this information via the Display Preference Determination Log report to be used for analysis or audit reasons. Figure 9.39 shows the selection screen for this report that archives the detailed preference calculation results. You must select a timeframe for the calculations to take place and the plant for which the determination will be performed. Optionally, you can filter the report on specific products or by the outcome of the preferential status.

Figure 9.40 shows output of the report; for each product preference calculation, it retrieved all details of that calculation, providing the outcome of the different calculation methods.

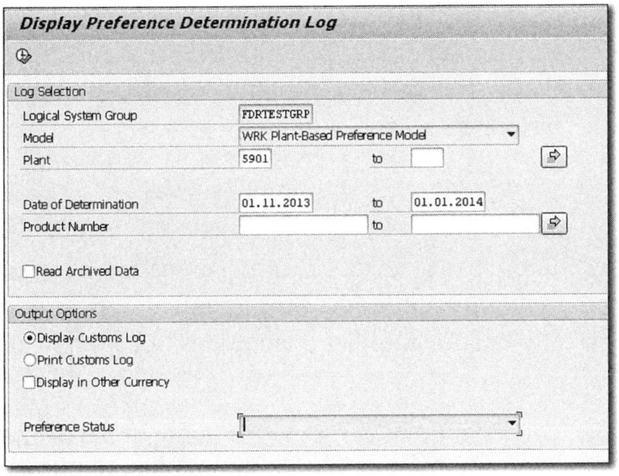

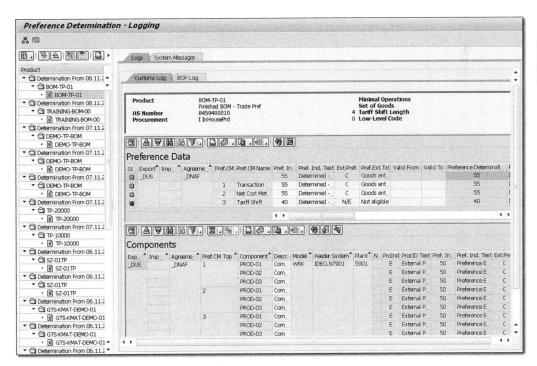

Figure 9.39 Preference Determination Log Selection Screen

Figure 9.40 Preference Determination Log Report

This section covered SAP GTS reports supporting companies during all three stages of the trade preference process. First, we covered reports supporting the requesting, dunning, and aggregating of LTVDs from their vendors. Second, we discussed SAP GTS-provided reports for analyzing BOM preference calculations for analysis and audit reasons. Finally, we walked through issuing and monitoring vendor declarations for the customer's purposes.

Restitution Management

Recall from Chapter 8 that Restitution Management concerns companies active in food and agriculture industries in Europe. Under the EU's Common Agricultural Policy (CAP), it is possible to receive export subsidies (restitutions) for set agricultural products.

In the SAP GTS restitution flow, you enter CAP licenses, securities (granted by the customs authorities), and restitution rates in SAP GTS, ensuring that all aspects for requesting and receiving export restitutions are fulfilled. You can check each document transferred to SAP GTS for restitution relevancy; if relevant, the system checks whether the products require an export license. The SAP GTS check calculates the restitution rates to be recovered and depreciates the value from the appropriate CAP license.

You can group reports that support this restitution process into document reports, restitution calculation reports, and master data reports.

Table 9.26 lists the reports related to restitution documents. Because each transactional document can be checked for restitution, SAP GTS can impose a block on these documents if the correct restitution licenses are lacking or inadequate.

Report Name	Menu Path
Display Blocked Restitution Documents	RESTITUTION • DISPLAY BLOCKED RESTITUTION DOCUMENTS
Display Existing Advance Notices	RESTITUTION • EXISTING ADVANCE NOTICES
Display Assigned Restitution Documents	RESTITUTION • DISPLAY ASSIGNED RESTITUTION DOCUMENTS

Table 9.26 Reports Concerning Restitution Documents

Similar to the legal control process, reports are foreseen for displaying lists of blocked documents. Figure 9.41 shows the selection screen for documents blocked for a restitution check. You can filter the list by FTO; reference number; or reason for the block, such as missing restitution license, missing product master information, and so on.

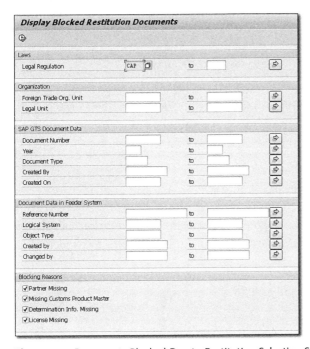

Figure 9.41 Documents Blocked Due to Restitution Selection Screen

Figure 9.42 displays the report output, which is similar to the compliance report of displaying blocked documents. From this report, you can access a log giving detailed information into the nature of the block.

Restitution: Display Blocked Documents

Blocked Documents with Item Data

Ref. No.	Item	Product No	DeprtCtry	Dest. Ctry	Log.System	SPL Screen	Embargo	Control	Restitutn	Lett.Cred.	Prcg Sts	Haz.Subst.	FT Org.
14653	10	BP-028	BE	RU	IDECLNT901				●		●		FTODEMO_BE
14654		FP-102	BE	RU					●		●		FTODEMO_BE
14655		FP-102	BE	RU					●		●		FTODEMO_BE
14656		BP-420	BE	RU					●		●		FTODEMO_BE
14659		FP-102	BE	CN					●		●		FTODEMO_BE

Figure 9.42 Report Listing All Documents with a Restitution Block

In a restitution flow, a calculation takes place that multiplies the product's restitution rates by the exported quantity to determine the expected restitution amount. Table 9.27 contains the SAP GTS reports related to this restitution calculation.

Report Name	Menu Path
Simulate Restitution Calculation	RESTITUTION • SIMULATE CALCULATION
Simulate Restitution Calculation per Document	RESTITUTION • SIMULATE CALCULATION PER DOCUMENT
Calculate Restitution per Customs Declaration	RESTITUTION • CALCULATE RESTITUTION PER CUSTOMS DECL.

Table 9.27 Reports Concerning Restitution Calculations

Figure 9.43 presents the selection screen of the Simulate Restitution Calculation report, which you can use to simulate what restitution amount to expect when exporting certain goods.

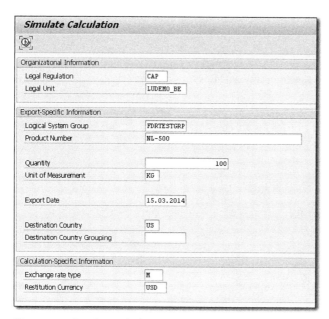

Figure 9.43 Simulate Calculation Selection Screen

As an example, the report simulates an export from Belgium to the United States and involves the export of 100 kg of product NL-500.

Figure 9.44 shows the result of the restitution calculation. Product NL-500 (let's say that it represents yogurt) is maintained in SAP GTS as a BOM consisting of two components (milk and fruit, or items 00010 and 00020). The report shows the entire calculation of the two components, including the respective restitution rates, relevant weight in the BOM, calculated restitution amount, and converted amount to the requested currency.

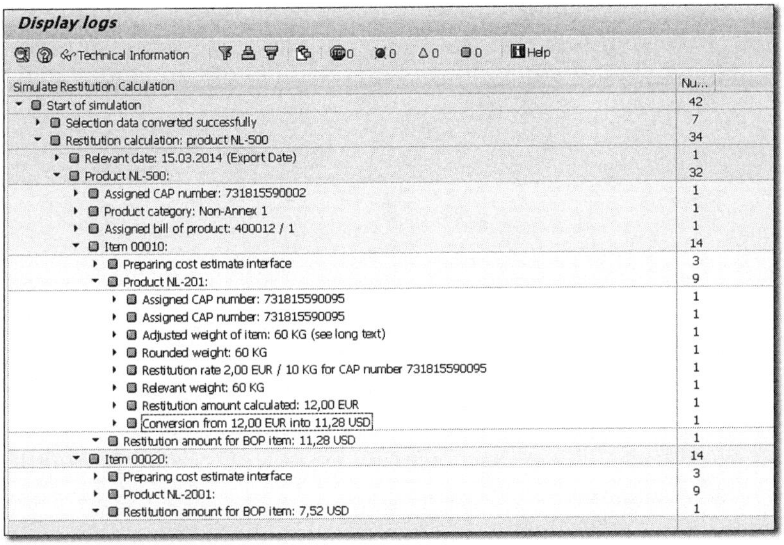

Figure 9.44 Report Displaying the Simulated Restitution Calculation

Finally, you enter licenses, securities, and restitution rates in SAP GTS as master data supporting the restitution management process. Table 9.28 lists the reports related to this master data.

Report Name	Menu Path
Display Produced CAP Licenses	RESTITUTION • DISPLAY PRODUCED CAP LICENSES
Display Provided Securities	RESTITUTION • DISPLAY PROVIDED SECURITIES
Maintain Restitution Rates	RESTITUTION • MASTER DATA • MAINTAIN RESTITUTION RATES

Table 9.28 Reports Concerning Restitution Master Data

To process the calculations, you first need to maintain restitution rates in the system. Figure 9.45 displays the selection screen for displaying/maintaining the restitution rates. For the legal regulation and type of restitution, the restitution rates are displayed for a specified country of destination and validity interval. Optionally, you can also enter a specific CAP number (or range of CAP numbers) to analyze only those restitution rates.

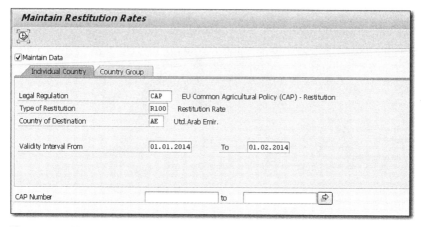

Figure 9.45 Maintaining Restitution Rates Selection Screen

Figure 9.46 shows the output of the report: the restitution rate linked to the corresponding CAP number. The rate specifies the restitution amount that can be expected per sold weight unit.

Maintenance: Restitution Rates for Restitution Rate

Legal Regulation: CAP   EU Common Agricultural Policy (CAP) - Restitution   Number   4

Country of Destination: AE Utd.Arab Emir., Period 01.01.2014 - 01.02.2

CAP Number	Description	Res	De	Valid from	Valid to	C	Amou	Curre	/	U	Code	Cal	Tare
731815590091	CAP COMPONENT 2	R100	AE	01.11.2012	31.12.2999	1	0,50	EUR	1	KG			0,00
731815590092	CAP COMPONENT	R100	AE	26.10.2012	31.12.2999	1	0,20	EUR	1	KG			0,00
731815590095	CAP COMPONENT NA1, ...	R100	AE	01.11.2012	31.12.2999	1	0,30	EUR	1	KG			0,00
731815590096	CAP COMPONENT 2, NA ...	R100	AE	01.11.2012	31.12.2999	1	0,70	EUR	1	KG			0,00

Figure 9.46 Report Listing the Restitution Rates

SAP GTS restitution reports support the process of retrieving restitution amounts as a result of the European export of products eligible for agricultural subsidies.

The next section handles the Letter of Credit Processing reports, which enable companies to help mitigate the financial risks common to international trade processes.

Letter of Credit Processing

To help overcome the credit risk linked to international transactions, the intermediate role of financial institutions and payment methods such as the letter of credit (L/C) are used. By using an L/C, an importer does not need to pay in advance for the requested goods or services, reducing his risk of paying for something that does not fully meet the described goods or services. On the other hand, using an L/C is advantageous for the exporter because it guarantees that he will be paid. For more details on the L/C process, please consult Chapter 8.

Table 9.29 lists the SAP GTS reports supporting the L/C process.

Report Name	Menu Path
Display Blocked Letter of Credit Documents (Import)	Letter of Credit Processing • Tab Import • Display Blocked Letter of Credit Documents
Display Assigned Letter of Credit Documents (Import)	Letter of Credit Processing • Tab Import • Display Assigned Letter of Credit Documents
Display Blocked Letter of Credit Documents (Export)	Letter of Credit Processing • Tab Export • Display Blocked Letter of Credit Documents
Display Assigned Letter of Credit Documents (Export)	Letter of Credit Processing • Tab Export • Display Assigned Letter of Credit Documents
Display Existing Letters of Credit	Letter of Credit Processing • Tab Master Data • Display Existing Letters of Credit

Table 9.29 Letter of Credit-Related Reports

Because the Display Blocked Letter of Credit Documents reports (analogous to the Blocked Restitution Documents report shown in Figure 9.42) and Display Assigned Letter of Credit Documents reports assume the same logic as those discussed in previous sections, we won't discuss them further here.

Section 9.1 covered the reports available to support the three main SAP GTS functional areas: Compliance Management (SPL Screening, Embargo, and Legal Control), Customs Management (customs documents and special customs procedures), and Risk Management (Trade Preference Management, Restitution Management, and Letter of Credit Processing). Note that the SAP GTS reports discussed here are found in Appendix A1, along with their respective transaction codes.

Let's turn our attention to SAP Business Warehouse reporting, through which more extensive and company-tailored reports may be customized. By installing SAP BW, you can use customized reports to get more extensive analysis capabilities than those offered by the previously discussed standard SAP GTS reports.

9.2 SAP BW Reporting

SAP Business Warehouse (BW) serves as analytical, reporting, and data warehousing system. SAP BW brings significant capabilities and benefits to enhance standard SAP GTS reporting.

SAP BW stores both SAP and non-SAP data and allows fast and dynamic reporting based on the stored data. This information is stored in SAP BW's data warehouse in the following structures:

▶ *InfoObjects* are the smallest information units in SAP BW and are divided into characteristics/dimensions (which typically answer questions such as what, where, and who) and key figures/measures (which typically address questions such as how many).

▶ An *InfoCube* describes a self-contained dataset of relational tables arranged according to the star schema: a large fact table in the middle surrounded by several dimension tables.

▶ A *DataStore object* (DSO) combines key fields (e.g., document number, document item) with data fields (e.g., document status, item property).

Simply stated, all of these are *InfoProviders*: objects or views relevant for reporting and for which queries can be created, and thus, extracted for analyzing and reporting purposes.

Assuming that a few prerequisites are met, the integration between SAP GTS and SAP BW is standard. First, you have to set up an RFC connection between SAP BW and SAP GTS. Then, you have to enable the data transfer from SAP GTS to

SAP BW via Customizing by activating the data transfer to SAP BW on FTO, document type, and item category level.

Figure 9.47 shows the integration between SAP GTS and SAP BW. As previously mentioned, SAP BW extracts data from both SAP and non-SAP systems. For the purposes of this book, the extraction from the SAP GTS source system and SAP ERP 6.0 source system are required.

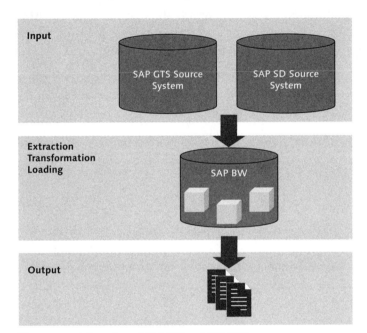

Figure 9.47 Integration of SAP BW and SAP GTS

The programs that determine what information is transferred and stored in SAP BW are called *data extractors*. In the extraction, transformation, and loading (ETL) phase of the SAP GTS-SAP BW integration, data extractors fetch the changed (delta) information on a regular basis and combine data from multiple SAP GTS tables to transform them into a specific format.

Once ETL is finalized, master data and transactional data is accessible in SAP BW and allows for multidimensional analyses from various business perspectives. For example, you can access consolidated data from different modules (SAP GTS, SAP ERP 6.0, etc.) via a single report.

9.2.1 SAP GTS Extractors

When you are setting up SAP BW for integration with SAP GTS, three standard *InfoSources* with corresponding extractors are provided. One InfoSource covers the customs documents data (which also includes Risk Management data); the second covers customs documents legal control, and the third is applied for customs procedures with economic impact (e.g., BWH).

All the data that can be extracted within the areas of these InfoSources are listed in Appendix B. Note that, in addition to the standard extractors, you can use custom extraction tools to extract specific data from various data sources.

InfoSources contain a number of *key figures*. These key figures are numeric values or quantities (e.g., net price or quantity) used in the output reports as objects for analysis.

Each of the three standard InfoSources also comes with a number of standard queries. Queries relate to actual reports and specify which data is leveraged.

Customs Documents Data

The first InfoSource (0SLL_CD_1) relates to customs documents. It consists of data from customs documents created in SAP GTS. *Customs documents* should be interpreted here in a broad sense, including import and export business transactions such as customs processing, transit procedure, trade preference processing, and restitution.

The standard reports run for this functional area relate to certain key figures. The customs documents InfoSource key figures include the following:

- Calculated duties (e.g., antidumping and third country)
- Customs value
- Total duties
- Net price
- Net weight
- Number of items
- Quantity
- Statistical value

In this customs area, three sorts of standard queries are available:

▶ Customs import/export analysis

▶ Customs import/export per product

▶ Customs import/export per country

The first query runs an analysis of the total number of imported/exported items (by customs value, net price, etc.) per FTO, legal unit, customs procedure, or tariff code. The second query results in the same report per product number, while the third query provides the report per departure/destination country.

Customs Documents — Legal Control

The second InfoSource (0SLL_CD_02) relates to the Legal Control aspects of the import and export flows. It consists of Legal Control data concerning the import and export documents created in SAP GTS.

The Legal Control InfoSource key figures include the following:

▶ Net value

▶ Net weight

▶ Gross weight

▶ Number of items

▶ Quantity

Similarly to the customs document InfoSource, import/export queries exist for Legal Control purposes.

Analogous to standard SAP GTS reporting, queries launch a selection screen that you can use as a filtering tool. Figure 9.48 shows the selection screen for running the Export Analysis per Country query.

Note that, for this example, we used the BEx Analyzer to visualize the report. The BEx Analyzer is an analysis and reporting tool of SAP Business Explorer (BEx), which is embedded in Microsoft Excel.

Figure 9.49 shows the output of running the query. The report lists the export analysis per COUNTRY OF DEPARTURE. You can analyze key figures such as the net price and gross weight and net weight per country of departure, per consignee, and so on.

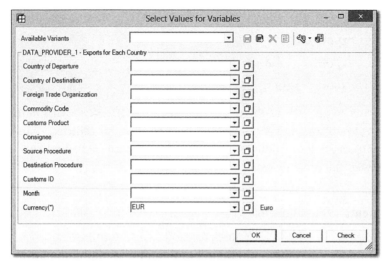

Figure 9.48 Selection Screen for Legal Control Export per Country

Exports for Each Country

Author SAP   Status of Data 22/11/2013 13:12:25

| Chart | Filter | Information |

Table

Country of Departure	Country of Destination	Consignee	Net Price	Gross Weight	Net Weight
BE	AE	622	86,03 EUR	21 KG	18 KG
	CN	102	91 044,00 EUR	658 KG	336 KG
		131	1 650,00 EUR	29 KG	18 KG
		183	900,00 EUR	10 KG	8 KG
	IR	155	100,00 EUR	1 KG	1 KG
	MX	962	10 000,00 EUR	4 KG	3 KG
	Result		103 780,03 EUR	723 KG	383 KG
US	CA	102	0,00 EUR	0 TON	0 TON
		534	7 244,09 EUR	0 TON	0 TON
		541	4 842,52 EUR	0 TON	0 TON
		612	52 047,24 EUR	0 TON	0 TON
		Not assigned	0,00 EUR	0	0
	CN	102	5 186,61 EUR	MIXED CURRENCY/UNIT	MIXED CURRENCY/UNIT
	DE	180	2 362,20 EUR	0 TON	0 TON
	GT	579	0,00 EUR	0 TON	0 TON
	PR	1016	118,11 EUR	0 TON	0 TON
	SE	564	7 231,97 EUR	4 TON	3 TON
		573	43 640,73 EUR	1 TON	0 TON
	Result		122 673,49 EUR	MIXED CURRENCY/UNIT	MIXED CURRENCY/UNIT
#	#	586	0,00 EUR	0 KG	0 KG
		Not assigned	0,00 EUR	53 KG	27 KG
	Result		0,00 EUR	53 KG	27 KG
Overall Result			226 453,52 EUR	MIXED CURRENCY/UNIT	MIXED CURRENCY/UNIT

Figure 9.49 Legal Control—Exports per Country

The strength of the SAP BW reports lies in its customizable and versatile nature. Analysts can continuously change the report by adding or removing variables, inserting KPI metrics, and so on to help analyze large numbers of data transactions in order to make valid conclusions and support business decisions.

You can apply SAP BW content in three ways:

▶ Without modifications: This option covers the basic reporting requirements.

▶ With modifications: You change delivered BI content by modifying the installed objects.

▶ Using BI content as the template to further build customized reporting: This is the approach taken in most cases.

Customs Procedures with Economic Impact

The third InfoSource (0SLL_CD_3) relates to information concerning closing portions for the processing of customs procedures with economic impact (e.g., BWH). We won't elaborate here because the same logic as the previously discussed InfoSources applies.

9.2.2 Advantages and Usage

The following are core advantages of using SAP BW for reporting:

▶ Customized reporting can be continuously adapted by adding and removing variables, inserting filters, and so on. As such, valuable data may be filtered and extracted from large sets of transactional data.

▶ Data visualization through various frontend reporting tools (such as SAP BEx Analyzer, SAP BusinessObjects tools, etc.) can, for example help companies create insightful dashboards presenting significant KPI metrics tailored to different users.

▶ SAP BW content contains a range of objects that simplify the implementation of an SAP BW system and speed up the construction of an effective reporting system

▶ Because you use SAP BW, you can combine data from various systems (SAP or non-SAP) into a single report. For example, this makes data extraction from multiple systems to a spreadsheet for further analysis redundant, since data from SAP and non-SAP systems may be imported in SAP BW.

9.3 Summary

In the beginning of this chapter, we distinguished between standard SAP GTS reporting and SAP BW reporting. SAP GTS reporting covers all reports available in SAP GTS to support the different business processes. These reports can be either descriptive (for analysis and audit trail reasons) or operational (allowing practitioners to take further actions on the shown reports). SAP GTS reporting capabilities are available for each of the three functional areas: Customs Management, Compliance Management, and Risk Management.

In contrast, SAP BW offers you a dynamic reporting platform that is highly customizable, allowing very specific and detailed reports for analysis purposes. This ensures companies can extract the most valuable details from large amounts of data to optimize their business intelligence strategy.

In the next chapter, we will elaborate on the technical objects related to SAP GTS. Our coverage of technical objects (though not strictly related to this chapter) includes topics such as user exits and business add-ins in both the SAP ERP 6.0 plug-in and in SAP GTS. You can use these technical objects to enhance SAP GTS or modify it to suit a company's business requirements.

When routine Customizing settings aren't enough to address your business requirements, turn to technical objects.

10 Technical Objects in SAP GTS

The Customizing settings covered in previous chapters reflect organization-specific business requirements. In some cases, however, requirements may be so specific that no Customizing arrangement offers a way of setting them up. In those cases, it may be necessary to use one or more SAP technical objects.

This chapter is divided into two parts to cover the technical objects within the SAP ERP 6.0 plug-in and those within SAP GTS.

10.1 Technical Objects in the SAP ERP 6.0 Plug-In

Our objective here is to approach the technical objects from a process point of view. Within the SAP ERP 6.0 plug-in, various business add-ins (BAdIs) and user exits influence both master data and transactional data. The two main functionalities of those objects are controlling the transfer of data and enriching that data for SAP GTS.

10.1.1 Master Data

Recall from Chapter 4 that non-transactional data exists in SAP GTS and is transferred from the feeder system on a transactional basis. Upon transfer, this master data passes through the SAP ERP 6.0 plug-in allowing system enhancement. This enhancement permits you to control the transfer and enrich the master data transmitted. This allows the implementation of common business requirements.

A typical requirement for controlling the transfer of master data is related to legal requirements. For example, in some cases, employees are set up in the system as customers. However, in certain countries, it is illegal to screen employees against a sanctioned party list. An implementation disabling the transfer of such business partners allows the use of SAP GTS to screen business partners except for employees, without any manual interaction.

Enrichments of master data between SAP ERP 6.0 and SAP GTS are usually implemented to comply with the customs authorities. Sometimes, the commercial descriptions of materials in SAP ERP 6.0 are not sufficient for customs purposes; during the transfer, you can enrich this data with a more detailed description.

Table 10.1 lists the user exits that enable business requirements by controlling and enriching master data; you can access them in the Customizing settings via Transaction SPRO • SALES AND DISTRIBUTION • FOREIGN TRADE/CUSTOMS • SAP GLOBAL TRADE SERVICES—PLUG-IN • USER EXITS FOR SAP GLOBAL TRADE SERVICES.

Enhancement	User Exit	Functionality	Master Data
SLLLEG02	EXIT_SAPLSLL_LEG_BOMR3_002	Control	BOM
SLLLEG02	EXIT_SAPLSLL_LEG_BOMR3_003	Enrichment	BOM
SLLLEG04	EXIT_SAPLSLL_LEG_PRR3_002	Control	Material
SLLLEG04	EXIT_SAPLSLL_LEG_PRR3_004	Enrichment	Material
SLLLEG05	EXIT_SAPLSLL_LEG_PARR3_001	Control and enrichment	Business partner (customer)
SLLLEG05	EXIT_SAPLSLL_LEG_PARR3_003	Control and enrichment	Business partner (vendor)

Table 10.1 Common User Exits for Control and Enrichment of Master Data

Note

Additional user exits are available for the enhancements mentioned in Table 10.1, including functionalities for modifying table key fields between SAP ERP 6.0 and SAP GTS.; you can access them in the Customizing settings via Transaction SPRO • SALES AND DISTRIBUTION • FOREIGN TRADE/CUSTOMS • SAP GLOBAL TRADE SERVICES—PLUG-IN • USER EXITS FOR SAP GLOBAL TRADE SERVICES.

10.1.2 Transactional Data

Different SAP ERP 6.0 processes are passed on to SAP GTS via the SAP ERP 6.0 plug-in for the activated services. Various technical objects exist to control the transfer and enrich the transmitted data. For transactional data, both user exits and BAdI definitions are available with the same functionality: the data sequentially passes through the user exit, followed by the BAdI implementation.

A widely used application for the transfer control is the implementation of *filters*. In some cases, the requirement may be to exclude documents linked to a specific company code, sales organization, plant, or other information available in the document in SAP ERP 6.0. Such filters allow you to enable SAP GTS based on organizational structure and geographic characteristics in order to enable global rollouts. All settings are process driven and specific to the chosen service, such as Compliance Management, Customs Management, and Risk Management.

Enrichments of transactional data between SAP ERP 6.0 and SAP GTS are usually implemented to comply with legal requirements and to enrich SAP GTS with custom SAP ERP 6.0 enhancements—for example, to include additional shipment/transportation data set up in the system or enrich and map the different SAP ERP 6.0 pricing conditions toward SAP GTS using custom objects. The standard interface and purpose of the statistical value in SAP ERP 6.0 are usually not in line with the specific customs requirements.

Table 10.2 lists the user exits that enable these business requirements via the control and enrichment of transactional data; you can access them in the Customizing settings via Transaction SPRO • SALES AND DISTRIBUTION • FOREIGN TRADE/CUSTOMS • SAP GLOBAL TRADE SERVICES—PLUG-IN • USER EXITS FOR SAP GLOBAL TRADE SERVICES.

Enhancement	Function Exit	Functionality
SLLLEG01	EXIT_SAPLSLL_LEG_CDPIR3_001	Control
SLLLEG01	EXIT_SAPLSLL_LEG_CDPIR3_002	Enrichment

Table 10.2 User Exits for Control and Enrichment of Transactional Data

Table 10.3 lists the BAdIs that enable the control and enrichment of transactional data; you can access them in the Customizing settings via Transaction SPRO • SALES AND DISTRIBUTION • FOREIGN TRADE/CUSTOMS • SAP GLOBAL TRADE SERVICES— PLUG-IN • BUSINESS ADD-INS FOR SAP GLOBAL TRADE SERVICES • EDIT CONTROL OF DOCUMENT TRANSFER/CHANGE AND SUPPLEMENT DOCUMENT DATA FOR TRANSFER.

BAdI Definition	Functionality	Scope
/SAPSLL/CTRL_MM0A_R3	Control	Purchasing documents
/SAPSLL/CTRL_MM0B_R3	Control	Inbound delivery
/SAPSLL/CTRL_MM0C_R3	Control	Material document
/SAPSLL/CTRL_SD0A_R3	Control	Sales documents
/SAPSLL/CTRL_SD0B_R3	Control	Outbound delivery
/SAPSLL/CTRL_SD0C_R3	Control	Billing document
/SAPSLL/IFEX_MM0A_R3	Enrichment	Purchasing documents
/SAPSLL/IFEX_MM0B_R3	Enrichment	Inbound delivery
/SAPSLL/IFEX_MM0C_R3	Enrichment	Material document
/SAPSLL/IFEX_SD0A_R3	Enrichment	Sales documents
/SAPSLL/IFEX_SD0B_R3	Enrichment	Outbound delivery
/SAPSLL/IFEX_SD0C_R3	Enrichment	Billing document

Table 10.3 BAdIs for Control and Enrichment of Transactional Data

Note

Additional function exits and BAdIs are available in the SAP ERP 6.0 plug-in and influence the transactional data based on their specific processes. These include specific functionalities for technical setup, trade preferences, and customs warehousing.

10.2 Technical Objects in SAP GTS

Let's consider the most used technical objects from a process point of view, with regard to the services they enhance. Within SAP GTS, numerous BAdIs are available to adapt and enrich the standard functionality. We'll explain the added value of a technical object by offering examples of commonly used business practices for each service.

10.2.1 Compliance Management

The BAdIs that enable modifications related to compliance services can be found in Table 10.4. Let's look at common business requirements:

▶ **Determination strategies**
You can further enhance the determination of the legal regulation by taking into account additional business partners that describe the actual, legal end user of the product, instead of merely basing the determination on the departing or destination country or country group.

Another application for modifying the legal regulation occurs when the transport route crosses several countries. For example, for the de minimis calculation, you can retrieve the most critical country and select the corresponding legal regulation, optimizing the process.

You can modify the determination of licenses, taking into account legal requirements, by using transactional data. License determination can, for example, take into account the statistical value of a product and compare it to a threshold before assigning an applicable license.

▶ **Defaulting data**
Compliance defaulting data comes into play particularly when you are creating licenses for which global requirements are applicable. The global management team can predefine the setup of the licenses. Another application is defaulting the text fields to print on customs forms, which later can be picked up from the licences.

▶ **Processing options upon release of blocked documents**
A commonly used BAdI within the compliance section allows SAP GTS to interact with SAP ERP 6.0 upon the release of a blocked document. Business requirements include automatic mailing functionality, printing forms, and updating documents upon release.

BAdI Definition	Description
/SAPSLL/LCLIC_PROP	Default data when entering and editing licenses.
/SAPSLL/LCC_DOCUMENT	Check within Legal Control. Determination strategies.
/SAPSLL/CUHD_RELEASE -	Release blocked documents.

Table 10.4 Common BAdIs for Compliance Management

You can access a complete list of available BAdIs for compliance services in the Customizing settings via Transaction SPRO • GLOBAL TRADE SERVICES • COMPLIANCE MANAGEMENT • BUSINESS ADD-INS FOR COMPLIANCE MANAGEMENT.

10.2.2 Customs Management

The BAdIs that enable modifications related to customs services can be found in Table 10.5. Let's look at common business requirements:

▶ **Process determination**
Within the same legal regulation, it can occur that a different activity in the process needs to be determined—for example, to differentiate processes that need further processing with a broker via a paper-based instruction sheet or electronic communication with the customs authority. The further processing method can be made based on the destination country or type of products to be exported.

▶ **Valuation of duties in the duty framework**
In the duty framework, you can specify additional duty types and populate them from SAP ERP 6.0. However, you're required to perform additional calculations for other duty types that are mentioned on instruction sheets for the broker. This BAdI enables the modification of the standard duty types, as well as the calculation of new values.

▶ **Modification of EDI messages**
The adaption of EDI messages is particularly useful when it comes to communicating with a broker. Enriching the available messages allows you to specify data elements the broker needs. Another option is to enhance those messages before SAP GTS is supported for the country. This lets you meet the legal requirements with the standard available interface.

BAdI Definition	Description
/SAPSLL/CUS_PROC_DET_GR	Process determination upon goods receipt
/SAPSLL/CUS_PROC_DET_INV	Process determination for billing document
/SAPSLL/DUTY_CALC_EV	Customs duty calculation: valuation of duties
/SAPSLL/ECC_INBOUND	EDI inbound processing
/SAPSLL/CUS_ECC	EDI outbound processing and incompleteness checks

Table 10.5 Common BAdIs for Customs Management

You can access a complete list of available BAdIs for customs services in the Customizing settings via Transaction SPRO • GLOBAL TRADE SERVICES • CUSTOMS MANAGEMENT • BUSINESS ADD-INS FOR CUSTOMS MANAGEMENT

10.2.3 Risk Management

The most common business requirement within Risk Management is the creation of an overall dashboard. SAP GTS provides different logs for trade preferences; these logs consist of the relevant data. However, the creation of a dashboard would provide insights into the general product qualification and overview of the LTVD request during a specific time frame. This technical object consists of the aggregation of different standard SAP GTS transactions.

You can access available process-specific BAdIs for risk services in the Customizing settings via Transaction SPRO • GLOBAL TRADE SERVICES • RISK MANAGEMENT • BUSINESS ADD-INS FOR RISK MANAGEMENT.

10.2.4 Other Technical Objects

In SAP GTS, another important technical object is the Adobe Interactive Form. Many legally required paper forms are available within SAP GTS, but they need to be enhanced with data mapping and minor layout changes. A BAdI for enhancing the form mapping across all forms is available, enabling you to make changes on the paper-based form without altering the actual transactional or master data of the customs declaration. The modified data is then passed to the interface of the specific form.

Many other BAdIs for enhancing the different services for specific business and legal requirements are also made available. These are listed in the appendices.

You can access an extensive list of available BAdIs for overall purposes in the Customizing settings via Transaction SPRO • GLOBAL TRADE SERVICES • GENERAL SETTINGS • BUSINESS ADD-INS FOR GLOBAL TRADE SERVICES, and a specific list of available BAdIs for electronic compliance reporting via Transaction SPRO • GLOBAL TRADE SERVICES • ELECTRONIC COMPLIANCE REPORTING • BUSINESS ADD-INS FOR ELECTRONIC COMPLIANCE REPORTING.

10.3 Summary

The requirements for implementing a global trade services solution are very specific to the business process, relevant countries, and specific legal and tax requirements. Therefore, many technical objects are available to extend and enhance the standard functionality to comply with those specific requirements.

For the technical objects within the SAP ERP 6.0 plug-in, there's an important distinction between user exits, control, and enrichment BAdIs. We've discussed how master data and transactional data can be transferred from the feeder system to SAP GTS and how it can be filtered or enhanced. And then, when it came to the technical objects within SAP GTS, we gave an overview of the most used BAdIs with a business requirement.

In the next chapter, we'll give a future outlook for SAP GTS. This will comprise some global trade trends and planned released functionalities.

In conclusion, let's take a look at the direction SAP GTS is headed in terms of future enhancements.

11   The Future Direction of SAP GTS

Generally speaking, the development of the SAP GTS solution[1] has followed two major principles. Although they may sometimes seem to conflict with each other, they have tremendously helped—and continue to help—the solution to be first-class and top-ranking for more than a decade. These are *continuous improvement* and *strategic innovation*.

A few additional factors influence these principles and merit mentioning:

▸ Introduction of and changes to local, regional, and global legal regulations and procedures

▸ Market demand, requirements, and needs of GTS users

▸ General strategies and changes in IT and, in particular, within SAP

---

1   The information in this chapter is confidential and proprietary to SAP and may not be disclosed without the permission of SAP. This chapter is not subject to your license agreement or any other service or subscription agreement with SAP. SAP has no obligation to pursue any course of business outlined in this document or any related presentation, or to develop or release any functionality mentioned therein. This chapter, or any related presentation, and SAP's strategy and possible future developments, products, and/or platforms directions and functionality are all subject to change and may be changed by SAP at any time, for any reason, without notice. The information in this chapter is not a commitment, promise, or legal obligation to deliver any material, code, or functionality. This chapter is provided without a warranty of any kind, either express or implied, including but not limited to the implied warranties of merchantability, fitness for a particular purpose, or non-infringement. This chapter is for informational purposes and may not be incorporated into a contract. SAP assumes no responsibility for errors or omissions in this chapter, except if such damages were caused by SAP's willful misconduct or gross negligence.

All forward-looking statements are subject to various risks and uncertainties that could cause actual results to differ materially from expectations. Readers are cautioned not to place undue reliance on these forward-looking statements, which speak only as of their dates, and they should not be relied upon in making purchasing decisions.

The dynamism of legal regulations and procedures is a constant. Similarly, changing market and user needs challenge SAP GTS Product and Solution Management team to openly listen to the market, deeply delve into the business needs of various organizations in different industries, and collaborate with SAP GTS customers on potential solution approaches. Finally, changes to IT tactics are predetermined by global invention and evolution in the industry, in which SAP is playing a leading role. Nevertheless, such inventions and evolutions could have quite a strong influence on existing solutions like SAP GTS and might require not only re-thinking, but even redesigning, existing and future functionality.

As a matter of fact, the inventors of SAP GTS have already had the right vision and strategy of thinking ahead: design, develop, and deliver a modular, exceptionally flexible solution based on a platform idea, deeply integrated into SAP ERP and capable of being integrated in non-SAP environments to meet the high expectations of all stakeholders in foreign trade. Today, this approach still forms the basis of the success of future releases, invention of new functions and modules, development of enriched functionalities, and path of transformation.

11.1 Planned Innovations for SAP GTS

At SAP, all product and solution management teams follow clear and well-defined rules to ensure prime quality and the best reliability on any solution delivered to the market. This applies not only when developing new releases, but also to the entire lifecycle of any solution in mainstream maintenance.

The SAP GTS Product and Solution Management team follows these rules strictly to ensure the highest quality and least disruptive operation of the SAP GTS solution for customers. Following these rules includes the proper scheduling of release cycles, which normally last 18-24 months, depending on influencing factors, which are sometimes foreseeable, but can also be unforeseeable.

11.1.1 The Next Release

After the official release of the current version SAP GTS 10.1 in the first quarter of 2013, the next one is scheduled for release 24 months later, in the first quarter of 2015. This first delivery of a new release is called *release to customer* (RTC), also known by the more common term *ramp-up*.

A dedicated number of SAP GTS customers will be invited to join the ramp-up phase, which is important to prove the marketability of a new release. The ramp-up phase typically lasts for approximately six months and is followed by the *general availability* (GA) of the solution to the entire market.

11.1.2 Upcoming Releases

The SAP GTS Product and Solution Management team aims to provide innovation across the three solution areas: Customs Management, Compliance Management, and Risk Management. However, the influencing factors could impact the development to focus more on one specific area but would still include the deployment of the other areas to keep pace with innovation.

Foreign Trade Zone

Functionality that supports the operation of Foreign Trade Zones (FTZs) (Figure 11.1) in the United States will considerably enhance the SAP GTS support of US customer operations.

Related solution enhancements could include the following:

▶ Automatic tracking of inventories held in FTZs

▶ Accurate consumption of inventories related to manufacturing within an FTZ

▶ Interfaces with US Customs to report goods movements in and out of an FTZ

▶ Support processes related to import and export within zones

This functionality would offer a few key benefits:

▶ Enabling reduced duty costs associated with the import of goods and components

▶ Reducing expenses associated with operating in an FTZ due to manually tracking and reporting inventory, manufacture, and movements

▶ Improving data accuracy through full integration with backend systems of record

▶ Faster processing through certified interfaces with US Customs

▶ Enabling high-volume processing through FTZs by leveraging in-memory technology

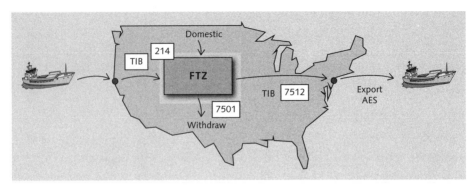

Figure 11.1 FTZ Process Scenarios

In-Memory Optimization

In-memory technology provided by SAP—that is, SAP HANA—will considerably improve performance for SAP GTS users and help them to benefit from comprehensive reporting and analytic capabilities. For example, Figure 11.2 shows a customs export analysis on a number of declaration items by country of destination and year of the declaration.

Related enhancements to SAP GTS include the following:

▸ Key processes in Customs Management, Compliance Management, and Trade Preference Management enhanced to leverage the SAP HANA database for improved response time and performance

▸ Robust search capabilities to improve data-intensive processes, such as classification

▸ Broader availability of operational trade data for use in analytics based on SAP HANA (SAP HANA Live offerings)

This functionality would offer a few key benefits:

▸ Enhanced operational performance in global trade processes

▸ Dramatic improvement in global trade reporting response times

▸ Analytics spans across applications of SAP Business Suite applications (integrated analytics)

▸ Full ability to leverage in-memory database investments across the enterprise, including global trade management

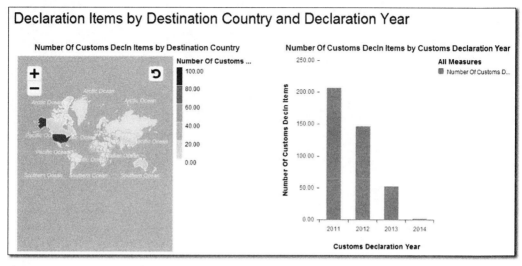

Figure 11.2 SAP HANA Live for SAP GTS

Enhanced User Experience

The use of SAP Fiori apps and the SAP Smart Business Cockpit will not only improve the user experience, but also enable a smooth, non-disruptive upgrade path.

Related enhancements to SAP GTS would include the following:

▶ The most important metrics for global trade services presented in an easy-to-understand form

▶ Customization of information from key performance indicators (KPI) to match business needs and user roles

▶ The ability to drill down and take action where needed

This functionality would offer a few key benefits:

▶ Keeping important information up front via customizable KPI tiles, as shown in Figure 11.3

▶ Leveraging launch pad in SAP Fiori apps to organize a user's areas to monitor

▶ Making insight actionable by integrating with transactional SAP Fiori apps

463

Figure 11.3 SAP Fiori Trade Compliance Manager Cockpit

Simplified Communication

Localizations occur when a solution is enabled in a country to directly and electronically file customs entries (that is, e-filing) for import, export, and special customs procedures with the local authorities, such as the AES/ABI system in the United States, the PLDA system in Belgium, or the ATLAS system in Germany.

The standard SAP GTS solution already provides a considerable number of localizations. With the official release of the new country localizations for China, Sweden, and Spain recently, the footprint of SAP GTS has again been extended substantially.

In order to support customers in countries that have not yet been localized and assist them with an indirect customs communication (for example, via brokers), a standardized broker interface will help to leverage broker relationships via automated communication.

Related enhancements to SAP GTS would include the following:

▶ Using certified customs interfaces to reduce costs and improve processing times when self-filing is a business strategy

▶ Using a standardized broker interface to automate the exchange of trade data with brokers when self-filing is not deemed feasible

- Employing a class-based framework for country localization
- Using interface documentation based on the World Customs Organization (WCO) customs authority

This functionality would offer a few key benefits:

- Enabling global trade cost reductions by supporting self-filing in countries and regions such as Europe, the Middle East, and Africa, where such practices are common
- Simplifying the exchange of trade data with brokers through a standard interface (single window), minimizing interface customization efforts and costs
- Leveraging SAP GTS in additional countries and regions where localization is delivered through company relationships with customs brokers
- Leveraging a partner ecosystem for additional country localization

High-Volume Partner Screening

The new solution, built on the in-memory technology, will enable effective business partner screening in high-volume environments and considerably enhance screening performance, flexibility, and scope.

Related enhancements to SAP GTS would include the following:

- Supporting high-volume business processes, such as web-based stores, with business partner compliance by screening names and addresses
- Utilizing greater business rule flexibility to tailor the degree of screening required based on critical business factors
- Simplifying the use of virtually any type or size of government or organizational list containing denied or suspect parties for screening activities
- Enabling the use of business partner screening processes by a broader range of industries

This functionality would offer a few key benefits:

- Improving compliance by extending partner screening to web-based business processes
- Reducing compliance efforts by assuring that the focus is on critical business processes

- Ensuring that partner compliance processes can flexibly support current and future governmental requirements
- Enabling the use of a standard, proven partner-screening solution across multiple industries to minimize customization and costs

Simplified Classification

In order to simplify the time-consuming but inevitable business process of classifying products, the existing capabilities for guided classification will be improved considerably. Furthermore, user interface enhancements should provide noticeable improvements in user experience and productivity.

Related enhancements to SAP GTS would include the following:

- Robust search capabilities utilizing SAP HANA to improve data-intensive classification activities
- Support for mass classification with guided proposals based on classification data and existing classified products
- Improved UI for simplification

This functionality would offer a few key benefits:

- Improving efficiency and speed for classifying products and reducing reliance on printed materials and institutional knowledge
- Increasing information for decision making
- Reducing dependency on third-party tools
- Improving the user experience

Legal Changes and Continuous Improvement

All ongoing activities are aimed at improving existing capabilities, enhancing compliance, and supporting new and changing business processes and legal requirements related to global trade operations.

Related enhancements to SAP GTS would include the following:

- Legal changes for all supported, localized countries
- In the United States, a transition from automated commercial system (ACS) to transition to automated commercial environment (ACE)

- WCO data model-based customs system, like in New Zealand and the Netherlands

- Excise Movement and Control System (EMCS) for Germany, Belgium, the Netherlands, and the United Kingdom

- Leveraging customer input via the Customer Connection program, including topics such as customs management

- Monitoring and capitalizing on trends across global trade, such as the single window concept and single authorization/simplified procedures (SASP)

This functionality would offer a few key benefits:

- Ongoing compliance with global trade regulations

- A single platform supporting trade requirements globally

- Standard support in SAP software for processes to implement legal changes to global trade processes

- Improved user productivity through dramatic increases in speed and usability

- Assurance of continued benefits from customer investments in SAP GTS

- Rapid time to value

- Lower, fixed implementation time and cost

11.2 The Future Direction of SAP GTS

Of course, generally speaking, plans are subject to change and nobody is in the position to predict the future. With that in mind, let's get a preview of the future direction for the SAP GTS solution beyond the coming release.

The following areas are being considered for the future direction of SAP GTS development:

- Cloud-based SAP GTS
  - Continued expansion of global trade functions as cloud-based services
  - Including public and private cloud-based offerings
- Next-generation business partner screening
  - Reduced operational delays by assuring real-time, high-performance partner-screening processes

- ▶ Using proven, standard functions to support all industries and minimize requirements for high-cost, niche solutions
- ▶ Utilizing a single solution to meet all screening requirements, regardless of related business processes (sales, procurement, HR, finance, and so on)
- ▶ Single global trade platform
  - ▶ Support for single-window concepts as they are formalized by countries and regions around the world
  - ▶ Leveraging functions within SAP GTS and its global ecosystem to meet compliance and customs requirements around the world
- ▶ Global data optimization
  - ▶ Leveraging in-memory virtual data models to support cross-application data gathering and analysis for enhanced global trade and supply chain visibility
  - ▶ Processing high volumes of data and multiple decision criteria to focus on not only minimizing costs, but also increasing profitability on global trade and supply chain operations
- ▶ High-volume origin optimization management
  - ▶ Simplification of high-volume, certificate-of-origin management
  - ▶ Simulation functions to understand the impact of sourcing decisions
  - ▶ Added visibility and tracking of product origin to support regulatory reporting, such as conflict minerals

Again, the three solution areas—Customs Management, Compliance Management, and Risk Management—are on the agenda for the future direction of SAP GTS, and the SAP GTS Product and Solution Management team will put all efforts into reaching a future direction with new innovation and leveraging the new technologies.

Appendices

A   Standard Reporting

This appendix offers additional information on standard reporting available in SAP GTS. The different standard reporting functionalities are divided into reporting in the Compliance Management, Customs Management, and Risk Management modules.

A.1   Compliance Management

This section outlines the different standard reporting functionalities in Compliance Management.

A.1.1   Master Data Reporting

Table A.1 lists the different standard master data reports in Compliance Management.

Report Name	Transaction
Master Data—Classify via Worklist (Import)	/SAPSLL/PR_CLWB_001
Master Data—Classify via Worklist (Export)	/SAPSLL/PR_CLWB_002
Master Data—Display Bill of Materials for Product	/SAPSLL/REXCALCBOM
Master Data—Display Country Assignment to Country Group	/SAPSLL/CTYGRP_DISP
Master Data—Display Analyzed Product Classification	/SAPSLL/PR_DISPPRCON
Master Data—Maintain Import Control Classification Numbers	/SAPSLL/LLNS_001
Master Data—Maintain Export Control Classification Numbers	/SAPSLL/LLNS_002

Table A.1 Master Data Reporting in Compliance Management

A.1.2   SPL Reporting

Table A.2 lists the different standard reports that are available for SPL in Compliance Management.

Report Name	Transaction
SPL—Analyze Reasons For Release	/SAPSLL/CS_SPL
SPL—Display Structured List	/SAPSLL/SPL_AR01
SPL—Display Expiring Sanctioned Party Lists	/SAPSLL/SPL_AR02
SPL—Display Change History	/SAPSLL/SPL_AR03
SPL—Display Overview List	/SAPSLL/SPL_AR04
SPL—Display Audit Trails For Partner	/SAPSLL/SPL_AT_BP
SPL—Display Audit Trails For Documents	/SAPSLL/SPL_AT_DOC
SPL—Display Audit Trails For Payments	/SAPSLL/SPL_AT_DOCFA
SPL—Display Audit Trail for External Auditor—Documents	/SAPSLL/SPL_AT_EXT_D
SPL—Display Audit Trail for External Auditor—Partner	/SAPSLL/SPL_AT_EXT_P
SPL—Display Blocked Business Partners	/SAPSLL/SPL_BLBPLO
SPL—Display Blocked Documents	/SAPSLL/SPL_BLCD
SPL—Display Blocked Payments	/SAPSLL/SPL_BLCD_FI
SPL—Display Negative List Business Partner	/SAPSLL/SPL_NEGBPLO
SPL—Display Positive List Business Partner	/SAPSLL/SPL_POSBPLO
SPL—Display Audit Trail for External Auditor—Documents	/SAPSLL/SPL_AT_EXT_D

Table A.2 SPL Reporting in Compliance Management

A.1.3 Embargo Reporting

Table A.3 lists the different standard reports that are available for embargos in Compliance Management.

Report Name	Transaction
Embargo—Display Released Embargo Documents (Import)	/SAPSLL/REL_DOC_EMBI
Embargo—Display Released Payments (Import)	/SAPSLL/REL_FI_EMBI
Embargo—Analysis (Import)	/SAPSLL/CS_EMBIMP

Table A.3 Embargo Reporting in Compliance Management

Report Name	Transaction
Embargo—Business Partners With Embargo Situation (Import)	/SAPSLL/EMB_BP_IMP
Embargo—Display Released Embargo Documents (Export)	/SAPSLL/REL_DOC_EMBE
Embargo—Display Released Payments (Export)	/SAPSLL/REL_FI_EMBE
Embargo—Analysis (Export)	/SAPSLL/CS_EMBEXP
Embargo—Business Partners with Embargo Situation (Export)	/SAPSLL/EMB_BP_EXP

Table A.3 Embargo Reporting in Compliance Management (Cont.)

A.1.4 Legal Control Reporting

Table A.4 lists the different standard reports for Legal Control in Compliance Management.

Report Name	Transaction
Legal Control—Display Blocked Export Customs Documents	/SAPSLL/BL_DOCS_EXP
Legal Control—Display Blocked Import Documents	/SAPSLL/BL_DOCS_IMP
Legal Control—Display Blocked Outgoing Payments	/SAPSLL/BL_FI_EXP
Legal Control—Display Blocked Payment Receipts	/SAPSLL/BL_FI_IMP
Legal Control—Display Existing Licenses	/SAPSLL/LCLIC04
Legal Control—Display Existing Agreements	/SAPSLL/LCLIC04_AGR
Legal Control—Display Existing Export Licenses	/SAPSLL/LCLIC04_EXP
Legal Control—Display Existing Import Licenses	/SAPSLL/LCLIC04_IMP
Legal Control—Display Assigned Documents to Licenses	/SAPSLL/LCLIC05
Legal Control—Display Assigned Documents to Agreements	/SAPSLL/LCLIC05_AGR
Legal Control—Display Assigned Export Documents	/SAPSLL/LCLIC05_EXP
Legal Control—Display Assigned Import Documents	/SAPSLL/LCLIC05_IMP
Legal Control—Display All Existing Documents	/SAPSLL/CUOR04

Table A.4 Legal Control Reporting in Compliance Management

Report Name	Transaction
Legal Control—Display All Existing Export Documents	/SAPSLL/CUOR04_EXP
Legal Control—Display All Existing Import Documents	/SAPSLL/CUOR04_IMP
Legal Control—Display All Existing Payments	/SAPSLL/CUHD_FI
Legal Control—Display All Existing Outgoing Payments	/SAPSLL/CUHD_FI_EXP
Legal Control—Display All Existing Payment Receipts	/SAPSLL/CUHD_FI_IMP
Legal Control—Tracking of ITAR Control-Relevant Products	/SAPSLL/ITAR_TRACE
Legal Control—Display Determination Strategy	/SAPSLL/CD_DISPLAY

Table A.4 Legal Control Reporting in Compliance Management (Cont.)

A.2   Customs Management

This section lists the standard reporting functionalities of Customs Management.

A.2.1   Master Data Reporting

Table A.5 lists the different master data reports in Customs Management.

Report Name	Transaction
Classify Products via Worklist (Tariff Codes)	/SAPSLL/PR_CLWB_101
Classify Products via Worklist (Commodity Codes)	/SAPSLL/PR_CLWB_102
Display Product Catalog	/SAPSLL/PR_CAT_DISPL
Display Business Partners' Trade Identification Numbers	/SAPSLL/BP_MAIN_CUS
Display Own Organization's Trade Identification Numbers	/SAPSLL/BP_MAIN_COMP
Display Business Identification Number (BIN)	/SAPSLL/BP_MAIN_BIN
Display Monitoring for Customs Products	/SAPSLL/MD_PR_MON
Display Customs Office Numbers	/SAPSLL/BP_MAIN_DNR

Table A.5 Master Data Reporting in Customs Management

Report Name	Transaction
Maintain Tariff Code Numbers	/SAPSLL/LLNS_101
Maintain Numbering Scheme	/SAPSLL/LLNS_102

Table A.5 Master Data Reporting in Customs Management (Cont.)

A.2.2 Import and Export Reporting

Table A.6 lists the different import and export standard reports in Customs Management.

Report Name	Transaction
Display Available Customs Export Declarations	/SAPSLL/CULO_CUS_EXP
Display Export Document Flow	/SAPSLL/CORFEX_DISP
Display Available Customs Import Declarations	/SAPSLL/CULO_CUS_IMP
Worklist Customs Declaration before Goods Receipt	/SAPSLL/CIBD_01
Monitor Securities	/SAPSLL/LCLICI04
Display Documents Assigned to Securities	/SAPSLL/LCLICS05_IMP
Monitor Authorizations	/SAPSLL/LCLICCDF04
Display Complete Stock Overview (Background Job)	/SAPSLL/IVM_VIEWALL
Display Duty-Unpaid Individual Stock (Background Job)	/SAPSLL/IVM_FIFOALL
Duty-Unpaid Individual Stock Item—Extended View (Background Job)	/SAPSLL/IVM_FIFOEXT
Display Duty-Unpaid Make-to-Order Stock	/SAPSLL/IVM_FIFO
Display Individual Stock Item for Inward Processing	/SAPSLL/IVMC_FIFO_IP
Display Individual Stock Item for Outward Processing	/SAPSLL/IVMP_FIFO
Display Individual Stock Item for Processing under Customs Control	/SAPSLL/IVMC_FIFO_PU
Display Stock Overview for Customs Warehouse	/SAPSLL/IVM_VIEW
Display Stock Overview for Inward Processing	/SAPSLL/IVMC_VIEW_IP

Table A.6 Import and Export Reporting in Customs Management

Report Name	Transaction
Display Stock Overview for Outward Processing	/SAPSLL/IVMP_VIEW
Display Stock Overview for Processing under Customs Control	/SAPSLL/IVMC_VIEW_PU
Display Receipts and Issues for Customs Warehouse	/SAPSLL/IVM_INOUT
Display Receipts and Issues for Inward Processing	/SAPSLL/IVMC_INOU_IP
Display Receipts and Issues for Outward Processing	/SAPSLL/IVMP_INOUT
Display Receipts and Issues for Processing under Customs Control	/SAPSLL/IVMC_INOU_PU

Table A.6 Import and Export Reporting in Customs Management (Cont.)

A.3 Risk Management

Finally, we now list standard reports in Risk Management.

A.3.1 Trade Preference Management Reporting

Table A.7 lists the different standard reports for Trade Preference Management in Risk Management.

Report Name	Transaction
Display Worklist for Vendor-Based Long-Term Vendor Declaration	/SAPSLL/PRE_WLI_001
Monitoring Vendor-Based Long-Term Vendor Declaration	/SAPSLL/PRE_VDI_210
Aggregate Long-Term Vendor Declarations	/SAPSLL/PRE_VDI_301
Assign Vendor to Administrative Unit	/SAPSLL/PARMA_MA_CPS
Display Worklist: Long-Term Vendor Declaration for Customer's Purposes	/SAPSLL/PRE_WLO_001
Monitoring of Long-Term Vendor Declaration for Customer's Purposes	/SAPSLL/PRE_VDO_710

Table A.7 Trade Preference Management Reporting in Risk Management

Report Name	Transaction
Display Calculation Log	/SAPSLL/PRE_CAL_404
Display Worklist of Configured BOMs	/SAPSLL/PRE_KMT_410
Display Preference Result by Document	/SAPSLL/PRE_KMT_412

Table A.7 Trade Preference Management Reporting in Risk Management (Cont.)

A.3.2 Letter of Credit Processing Reporting

Table A.8 lists the standard reports for Letter of Credit Processing in Risk Management.

Report Name	Transaction
Display Blocked Letter of Credit Documents (Export)	/SAPSLL/LOC_BLCD_EXP
Display Assigned Letter of Credit Documents (Export)	/SAPSLL/LC_LOC_EXP
Display Blocked Letter of Credit Documents (Import)	/SAPSLL/LOC_BLCD_IMP
Display Assigned Letter of Credit Documents (Import)	/SAPSLL/LC_LOC_IMP
Display Existing Letters of Credit	/SAPSLL/LCLIC04_LOC

Table A.8 Letter of Credit Processing Reporting in Risk Management

B   Standard Extractors

This appendix gives additional information on standard extractors between SAP GTS and SAP BW.

Table B.1 shows detailed information on standard InfoProviders.

Data Type	Specification	Description
InfoCube	0SLL_C01	Customs Document
	0SLL_C02	Customs Document—Legal Control
	0SLL_C03	Termination of Customs Procedure with Economic Significance
DataStore objects	0SLL_DS01	Customs Document
	0SLL_DS02	Customs Document—Legal Control
	0SLL_DS03	Termination of Customs Procedure with Economic Significance
	0SLL_DS1B	Supplementary Customs Declaration Bonded Warehouse to Free Circulation

Table B.1 Standard InfoProviders

Recall from Chapter 9 that several extractors can be differentiated in SAP GTS:

▶ Extractors for customs document
▶ Extractors for legal control
▶ Extractors for bonded warehousing (BWH), including the supplementary customs declaration (SCD).

We'll offer the InfoCubes and DataStore objects (DSOs) for each type of extractor.

B.1   Customs Documents

The customs document InfoCube contains transactional data from customs documents created in SAP GTS, such as customs declarations and customs shipments that were created in following services:

- ▶ Customs processing
- ▶ Transit procedure
- ▶ Preference processing
- ▶ Restitution handling

Table B.2 lists the different InfoCubes for customs documents.

Name	Technical Name
Base Unit of Measure	0BASE_UOM
Calendar Year/Month	0CALMONTH
Calendar Year/Quarter	0CALQUARTER
Calendar Year	0CALYEAR
Change Run ID	0CHNGID
Incoterms Part 1	0INCOTERMS
Record Type	0RECORDTP
Request ID	0REQUID
Antidumping Duty	0SLL_ADUDU
Authorization Number	0SLL_AUTNO
Customs Bill of Product Number	0SLL_BOPNO
Requested Concession	0SLL_CCAFA
Status of Customs Document	0SLL_CDSTA
Customer Number of Consignee (Export)	0SLL_CRECP
Customs Status of Goods	0SLL_CSSTA
Country of Destination	0SLL_CTYAR
Country of Departure	0SLL_CTYDP
Country of Origin	0SLL_CUCOO
Type of Customs Document	0SLL_CUITA
Placement into a Customs Status (Procedure)	0SLL_CUPRO

Table B.2 InfoCubes in Customs Documents

Name	Technical Name
Customs Currency	0SLL_CURCU
Preference Currency	0SLL_CURPR
Restitution Currency	0SLL_CURRE
Customs Value	0SLL_CUSVA
Type of Declaration	0SLL_DCTYP
Customs ID for Customs Procedure with Economic Significance	0SLL_ECPID
Customs Business Transaction Type	0SLL_EXART
Indicator: Customs Doc. or Transit Doc.	0SLL_FCOTD
Indicator: Relevance to Preference Processing	0SLL_FRELP
Indicator: Relevance to Restitution	0SLL_FRELR
Foreign Trade Organizational Unit	0SLL_FTORG
Indicator: Import/Export	0SLL_INDEI
Legal Unit	0SLL_LEGUN
Legal Regulation for Customs Processing/Transit Processing	0SLL_LREGC
Legal Regulation for Preference Processing	0SLL_LREGP
Legal Regulation for Restitution	0SLL_LREGR
Mode of Transport at Border	0SLL_MTBRC
Inland Mode of Transport	0SLL_MTRDO
Net Price/Invoice Value	0SLL_NETVA
Numbering Scheme for Commodity Code	0SLL_NSCCC
Numbering Scheme for Common Agricultural Policy No.	0SLL_NSCRC
Numbering Scheme for Tariff Code No.	0SLL_NSCTC
Country for Commodity Code	0SLL_NUCCC
Country for Tariff Code Number	0SLL_NUCTC
Commodity Code	0SLL_NUMCC

Table B.2 InfoCubes in Customs Documents (Cont.)

Name	Technical Name
Number of Items	0SLL_NUMIT
Common Agricultural Policy Number	0SLL_NUMRC
Tariff Code Number	0SLL_NUMTC
Declarant	0SLL_PDECL
Representative of Declarant	0SLL_PDECS
Duty for Pharmaceutical Products	0SLL_PHPDU
Office of Departure	0SLL_PODEP
Office of Destination	0SLL_PODES
Office of Entry	0SLL_POENT
Office of Exit	0SLL_POEXI
Destination Procedure	0SLL_PRDES
Consignee	0SLL_PRECP
Preferential Customs Duty	0SLL_PREDU
Indicator: Preference Eligibility	0SLL_PREFL
Indicator: Preference Is Price-Dependent	0SLL_PREPD
Customs Product	0SLL_PROD
Comparison Value for Preference	0SLL_PRRVA
Source Procedure	0SLL_PRSRC
Threshold Value for Preference	0SLL_PRTVA
Consignor	0SLL_PSEND
Payment Method	0SLL_PYTYP
Quantity in Base Unit of Measure	0SLL_QUANB
Quantity in Document Unit of Measure	0SLL_QUAND
Export Refund	0SLL_RESVA
Number of Security for Customs Processing/Transit Procedure	0SLL_SECNC

Table B.2 InfoCubes in Customs Documents (Cont.)

Name	Technical Name
Number of Security for Restitution	0SLL_SECNR
Statistical Value	0SLL_STAVA
Customs Total	0SLL_SUMDU
Suspension of Duty	0SLL_SUSDU
Third-Country Duty	0SLL_TCODU
Vendor Number of Consignor (Import)	0SLL_VSEND
Gross Weight	0SLL_WEIGR
Net Weight	0SLL_WEINE
Unit of Measure	0UNIT
Weight Unit	0UNIT_OF_WT

Table B.2 InfoCubes in Customs Documents (Cont.)

Table B.3 lists the different DSOs in customs documents.

Object Type	Name	Technical Name
Characteristic	Customs Document Item Number	0SLL_CDITN
Characteristic	Customs Doc. No.	0SLL_CDNUM
Characteristic	Customs Doc. Year	0SLL_CDYEA
Unit of measurement	Base Unit of Measure	0BASE_UOM
Characteristic	Incoterms (Part 1)	0INCOTERMS
Data packet characteristic	BW Delta Process: Update Mode	0RECORDMODE
Characteristic	Additional Data 1	0SLL_ADDD1
Characteristic	Additional Data 2	0SLL_ADDD2
Characteristic	Additional Data 3	0SLL_ADDD3
Key figure	Antidumping Duty	0SLL_ADUDU
Characteristic	Authorization Number	0SLL_AUTNO

Table B.3 DataStore Objects in Customs Documents

Object Type	Name	Technical Name
Characteristic	Customs Bill of Product Number	0SLL_BOPNO
Characteristic	Requested Concession	0SLL_CCAFA
Characteristic	Customs Doc. Date	0SLL_CDDAT
Characteristic	Status of Customs Document	0SLL_CDSTA
Characteristic	Creation Date	0SLL_CRDAT
Characteristic	Customer Number of Consignee (Export)	0SLL_CRECP
Characteristic	Customs Status of Goods	0SLL_CSSTA
Characteristic	Country of Destination	0SLL_CTYAR
Characteristic	Country of Departure	0SLL_CTYDP
Characteristic	Country of Origin	0SLL_CUCOO
Characteristic	Type of Customs Document	0SLL_CUHDA
Characteristic	Item Category in Customs Document	0SLL_CUITA
Characteristic	Placement into a Customs Status (Procedure)	0SLL_CUPRO
Unit of measurement	Customs Currency	0SLL_CURCU
Unit of measurement	Preference Currency	0SLL_CURPR
Unit of measurement	Restitution Currency	0SLL_CURRE
Key figure	Customs Value	0SLL_CUSVA
Characteristic	Type of Declaration	0SLL_DCTYP
Characteristic	Customs ID for Customs Procedure with Economic Significance	0SLL_ECPID
Characteristic	Customs Business Transaction Type	0SLL_EXART
Characteristic	Export Date	0SLL_EXDAT
Characteristic	Indicator: Customs Doc. or Transit Doc.	0SLL_FCOTD
Characteristic	Indicator: Relevance to Preference Processing	0SLL_FRELP

Table B.3 DataStore Objects in Customs Documents (Cont.)

Object Type	Name	Technical Name
Characteristic	Indicator: Relevance to Restitution	0SLL_FRELR
Characteristic	Foreign Trade Organizational Unit	0SLL_FTORG
Characteristic	Incoterms (Part 2)	0SLL_INCOL
Characteristic	Indicator: Import/Export	0SLL_INDEI
Characteristic	Legal Unit	0SLL_LEGUN
Characteristic	Legal Regulation for Customs Processing/ Transit Processing	0SLL_LREGC
Characteristic	Legal Regulation for Preference Processing	0SLL_LREGP
Characteristic	Legal Regulation for Restitution	0SLL_LREGR
Characteristic	Mode of Transport at Border	0SLL_MTBRC
Characteristic	Inland Mode of Transport	0SLL_MTRDO
Key figure	Net Price/Invoice Value	0SLL_NETVA
Characteristic	Numbering Scheme for Commodity Code	0SLL_NSCCC
Characteristic	Numbering Scheme for Common Agricultural Policy No.	0SLL_NSCRC
Characteristic	Numbering Scheme for Tariff Code No.	0SLL_NSCTC
Characteristic	Country for Commodity Code	0SLL_NUCCC
Characteristic	Country for Tariff Code Number	0SLL_NUCTC
Characteristic	Commodity Code	0SLL_NUMCC
Key figure	Number of Items	0SLL_NUMIT
Characteristic	Common Agricultural Policy Number	0SLL_NUMRC
Characteristic	Tariff Code Number	0SLL_NUMTC
Characteristic	Declarant	0SLL_PDECL
Characteristic	Representative of Declarant	0SLL_PDECS
Key figure	Duty for Pharmaceutical Products	0SLL_PHPDU
Characteristic	Office of Departure	0SLL_PODEP

Table B.3 DataStore Objects in Customs Documents (Cont.)

Object Type	Name	Technical Name
Characteristic	Office of Destination	0SLL_PODES
Characteristic	Office of Entry	0SLL_POENT
Characteristic	Office of Exit	0SLL_POEXI
Characteristic	Destination Procedure	0SLL_PRDES
Characteristic	Consignee	0SLL_PRECP
Key figure	Preferential Customs Duty	0SLL_PREDU
Characteristic	Indicator: Preference Eligibility	0SLL_PREFL
Characteristic	Indicator: Preference Is Price-Dependent	0SLL_PREPD
Characteristic	Customs Product	0SLL_PROD
Key figure	Comparison Value for Preference	0SLL_PRRVA
Characteristic	Source Procedure	0SLL_PRSRC
Key figure	Threshold Value for Preference	0SLL_PHPDU
Characteristic	Consignor	0SLL_PSEND
Characteristic	Payment Method	0SLL_PYTYP
Key figure	Quantity in Base Unit of Measurement	0SLL_QUANB
Key figure	Quantity in Document Unit of Measure	0SLL_QUAND
Key figure	Export Refund	0SLL_RESVA
Characteristic	Number of Security for Customs Processing/Transit Procedure	0SLL_SECNC
Characteristic	Number of Security for Restitution	0SLL_SECNR
Key figure	Statistical Value	0SLL_STAVA
Key figure	Customs Total	0SLL_SUMDU
Key figure	Suspension of Duty	0SLL_SUSDU
Key figure	Third-Country Duty	0SLL_TCODU
Characteristic	Vendor Number of Consignor (Import)	0SLL_VSEND
Key figure	Gross Weight	0SLL_WEIGR

Table B.3 DataStore Objects in Customs Documents (Cont.)

Object Type	Name	Technical Name
Key figure	Net Weight	0SLL_WEINE
Unit of measurement	Unit of Measure	0UNIT
Unit of measurement	Weight Unit	0UNIT_OF_WT

Table B.3 DataStore Objects in Customs Documents (Cont.)

B.2 Legal Control

The customs document (Legal Control) InfoCube contains data from replicated customs documents that were created in the following services in SAP GTS:

- Legal Control—import
- Legal Control—export

The InfoCube contains, among other information, data from customs documents such as legal regulations for legal controls, item categories, depreciation groups for import and export license depreciation, and the quantities of goods for import or export.

Table B.4 lists the different InfoCubes for Legal Control.

Name	Technical Name
Base Unit of Measure	0BASE_UOM
Calendar Year/Month	0CALMONTH
Calendar Year/Quarter	0CALQUARTER
Calendar Year	0CALYEAR
Change Run ID	0CHNGID
Record Type	0RECORDTP
Request ID	0REQUID
Customer Number of Bill-To Party (Export)	0SLL_CBITP
Customer Number of Payer (Export)	0SLL_CPAYE

Table B.4 Overview of InfoCubes for Legal Control

Name	Technical Name
Customer Number of Ship-To Party (Export)	0SLL_CSHTP
Customer Number of Sold-To Party (Export)	0SLL_CSOTP
Country of Destination	0SLL_CTYAR
Country of Departure	0SLL_CTYDP
Billing Country	0SLL_CTYIV
Country—Physical Location	0SLL_CTYPL
Type of Customs Document	0SLL_CUHDA
Item Category in Customs Document	0SLL_CUITA
Customer Number of Ultimate Consignee (Export)	0SLL_CULCO
Depreciation Group	0SLL_DPRGR
Foreign Trade Organizational Unit	0SLL_FTORG
Indicator: Import/Export	0SLL_INDEI
Legal Unit	0SLL_LEGUN
Legal Regulation for Legal Control	0SLL_LREGL
Numbering Scheme for Import/Export Control Classif. Number	0SLL_NSCLC
Currency for Net Value	0SLL_NTCUR
Net Value	0SLL_NTVAL
Number of Items	0SLL_NUMIT
Import Control Classif. No./Export Control Classif. No.	0SLL_NUMLC
Bill-to Party	0SLL_PBITP
Forwarding Agent	0SLL_PFWDA
Goods Supplier	0SLL_PGSUP
Payer	0SLL_PPAYE
Customs Product	0SLL_PROD
Ship-to Party	0SLL_PSHTP
Sold-to Party	0SLL_PSOTP

Table B.4 Overview of InfoCubes for Legal Control (Cont.)

Name	Technical Name
Ultimate Consignee	0SLL_PULCO
Vendor	0SLL_PVEND
Quantity in Base Unit of Measure	0SLL_QUANB
Quantity in Document Unit of Measure	0SLL_QUAND
Vendor Number of Forwarding Agent (Export)	0SLL_VFWDA
Vendor Number of Goods Supplier (Import)	0SLL_VGSUP
Vendor Number of Vendor (Import)	0SLL_VVEND
Gross Weight	0SLL_WEIGR
Net Weight	0SLL_WEINE
Unit of Measure	0UNIT
Weight unit	0UNIT_OF_WT

Table B.4 Overview of InfoCubes for Legal Control (Cont.)

B.3 Bonded Warehouse and Supplementary Customs Declaration

The InfoCube for discharging customs procedures with economic impact contains data from customs declarations from the SAP Customs Management area of SAP GTS. Among other things, the InfoCube contains product data and data for the subsequent customs procedure with links to the respective declarations in the customs procedure with economic impact.

Table B.5 lists the different InfoCubes in BWH.

Name	Technical Name
Calendar Year/Month	0CALMONTH
Calendar Year/Quarter	0CALYEAR
Unit of Measure	0UNIT

Table B.5 InfoCubes for BWH

Name	Technical Name
Weight Unit	0UNIT_OF_WT
Change Run ID	0CHNGID
Record Type	0RECORDTP
Request ID	0REQUID
Antidumping Duty	0SLL_ADUDU
Stock Quantity	0SLL_CQUAN
Country of Destination	0SLL_CTYAR
Country of Departure	0SLL_CTYDP
Country of Origin	0SLL_CUCOO
Customs Currency	0SLL_CURCU
Customs Value	0SLL_CUSVA
Customs ID for Customs Procedure with Economic Significance	0SLL_ECPID
Foreign Trade Organizational Unit	0SLL_FTORG
Numbering Scheme for Tariff Code No.	0SLL_NSCTC
Country for Tariff Code Number	0SLL_NUCTC
Tariff Code Number	0SLL_NUMTC
Duty for Pharmaceutical Products	0SLL_PHPDU
Destination Procedure	0SLL_PRDES
Preferential Customs Duty	0SLL_PREDU
Customs Product	0SLL_PROD
Source Procedure	0SLL_PRSRC
Unit of Measure for Stock Quantity	0SLL_STUNI
Customs Total	0SLL_SUMDU
Suspension of Duty	0SLL_SUSDU
Third-Country Duty	0SLL_TCODU

Table B.5 InfoCubes for BWH (Cont.)

C   The Authors

Yannick Jacques is a partner in Deloitte's SAP practice. He is based in Brussels and leads the SAP GTS practice globally. Yannick has over 18 years of experience in SAP ERP implementations with a particular focus in the implementation of SAP GTS by applying leading practice methodologies.

Yannick has worked with clients around the world including the US, Asia, and Europe. His experience includes managing multi-disciplinary teams and delivering large-scale global projects that are localized to meet the business needs and regulatory requirements of the territories in which his clients operate.

Yannick is a civil engineer and holds a master's degree in mechanics. Yannick is fluent in French, Dutch, and English.

Nick Moris is a partner in Deloitte's Customs & Global Trade practice in Brussels. He leads the customs and global trade automation team, which provides companies and public bodies with support and advice on a worldwide basis with respect to technology solutions for tax and accounting.

In particular, Nick focuses on global trade solutions and has accumulated a lot of expertise regarding SAP (including SAP GTS, SAP FT, SAP EH&S, SAP IS-OIL, and SAP Beverage). Nick and his team supported multiple multinationals in setting up international trade processes in SAP ERP.

Deloitte Tax LLP director **Chris Halloran** is one of the leads with Deloitte Tax's Customs and Global Trade practice, where he heads the U.S. trade automation service offering. With a focus on designing and architecting export and import requirements using SAP GTS, Chris has extensive experience deploying trade software solutions and transforming related process, data, and supply chain management.

Chris also advises clients on a wide range of international trade matters, including compliance reviews and audit support; export controls and related requirements for EAR, ITAR, OFAC, and other country-specific requirements; implementing compliance programs and management systems; performing strategic assessments; and maximizing operational efficiencies via business process improvements and automated trade software implementations. Chris is also a licensed US Customs Broker.

Pablo Lecour is the director of Deloitte Customs and Global Trade. He has significant global experience in trade compliance with a particular focus in advising companies on selecting and implementing global trade management software solutions and designing international trade compliance programs by applying leading practice methodologies. Pablo has advised companies in multiple industry sectors on export controls, customs compliance, and trade automation. Pablo also leads the SAP GTS implementation offering in the UK and has supported numerous implementations across industry sectors. Pablo frequently speaks at international trade conferences on building effective internal compliance programs and implementing trade management software solutions.

Prior to joining Deloitte, Pablo worked at The Boeing Company in a number of different roles including global trade controls and corporate audit functions.

Pablo holds a bachelor of arts in international relations and economics from Claremont McKenna College and a Kellogg-WHU Executive MBA from the Kellogg School of Management and WHU Otto Beisheim School of Management. Pablo is fluent in Spanish, French, and English.

Contributor

Kai Seela is a Senior Director in SAP GTS Solution Management. He is based at the SAP headquarters in Walldorf, Germany, and has responsibility for the SAP GTS solution and roadmap. Kai works closely with the SAP GTS product and development team to ensure the solution meets the requirements of the customers, covers and adopts legal requirements and changes, and fully supports the SAP strategies and visions. He has more than 19 years of experience in IT, working in project management, business development and solution management positions with a particular focus on foreign trade and economics.

Kai has worked with clients around the world including North and Latin America, EMEA, MENA and Asia-Pacific. His experience includes management of multinational implementation projects, business development for new regions and markets, and development and localization of standardized software solutions to meet industry-specific and regulatory requirements.

Kai is a functional executive of one of the biggest SAP GTS User Groups and a valued speaker on various events. He holds a bachelor's degree of business administration in foreign trade and economy.

Index

■ Effectively implement and configure the entire GRC 10.0 suite

■ Proactively manage regulatory change, meet business needs, and direct corporate compliance

■ Quickly identify and manage risk with a single unified view of your entire GRC process

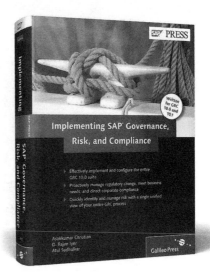

Asokkumar Christian, D. Rajen Iyer, Atul Sudhalkar

Implementing SAP Governance, Risk, and Compliance

Unsure how to navigate the wild waters and changing tides of corporate compliance and governance? With this comprehensive guide to SAP's Governance, Risk, and Compliance (GRC) module, plot your GRC course with confidence. Written for today's busy GRC consultants, project managers, and analysts, this book will explore the core components of the GRC module— Access Control, Process Control, and Risk Management and their implementation. Learn how to configure and implement the necessary dimensions, master data, and rules setup for all three core components of GRC. Build a strong GRC foundation that is both adaptive and reactive to regulatory pressures, corporate policies, and unanticipated risk.

712 pp., 2014, 79,95 Euro / US$ 79.95
ISBN 978-1-59229-881-5

www.sap-press.com

■ Plan and optimize: Improve service, maximize use, and reduce costs

■ Manage: Process orders, schedule bookings, and tender shipments

■ Integrate: Utilize the full potential of SAP ERP, EWM, Event Management, and GTS

■ Based on TM 9.0 and 9.1

Bernd Lauterbach, Dominik Metzger, Stefan Sauer, Jens Kappauf, Jens Gottlieb, Christopher Sürie

Transportation Management with SAP TM

Get your products from point A to point B as efficiently as possible. Whether you are a consultant or logistics provider, learn how to make your transportation management processes transparent, accessible, and adaptable with this comprehensive guide to Transportation Management functionality and configuration. Keep your business on the road to success!

1079 pp., 2014, 79,95 Euro / US$ 79.95
ISBN 978-1-59229-904-1

www.sap-press.com

Interested in reading more?

Please visit our website for all new
book and e-book releases from SAP PRESS.

www.sap-press.com